The Fundamentals of Swedish Law

A Guide for Foreign Lawyers and Students

LAURA CARLSON

 Studentlitteratur

Art. No 33565
ISBN 978-91-44-07872-4
Edition 2:2

© Laura Carlson and Studentlitteratur 2012
www.studentlitteratur.se
Studentlitteratur AB, Lund

Cover design by Francisco Ortega
Cover photo: Martine Castoriano

Printed by Holmbergs i Malmö AB, Sweden 2013

To my beloved daughter Lovisa,

We are all slaves to the law,
so that we might be free.

Cicero

SUMMARY OF CONTENTS

CONTENT

TABLES AND DIAGRAMS

ACKNOWLEDGMENTS

For this second edition, I am indebted a great extent to the same circle of readers with a few new faces, Elisabeth Ahlinder, Mohammed Ali, Annika Blekemo, Viola Boström, Jonas Ekfeldt, Ronnie Eklund, Claes Granmar, Moa Kindström Dahlin, William McKechnie, Jori Munukka, Erik Persson, Jane Reichel, Caroline Saf, Gustaf Sjöberg, Jessika van der Sluijs, Sanna Wolk and Mauro Zamboni. Thanks also go to my new course administrator for Swedish Law in Context, Paulina Rehbinder, for her excellent administration of the course. Next, I have to mention my eternal gratitude to Agita Akule Larsson, without whom this second edition and basically anything I achieve would not be possible. Thanks are insufficient for everything Agita does. Last, I would like to thank Bengt Dotevall, Magnus Holmberg and Claes Ringqvist at Stockholm's Internationella Handelsskola for their unfailing support this past decade. A chapter on Intellectual Property Rights and Unfair Trade Practices has been added to this second edition. Other changes have been motivated by the rather significant changes recently in Swedish law, particularly with respect to the constitutional act, the Instrument of Government, and within European Union law in light of the Lisbon Treaty.

In the continuing endeavor to include the current state of the law in so many areas, I would be grateful to any readers wishing to point out any mistakes or suggest any improvements. I can most easily be reached at amsvensk@telia.com.

Last, I want to once again thank my family, my husband, Fredrik Gustafsson, for his tireless proofreading and excellent comments, a small price in the larger scheme of things, and my daughter Lovisa for her patience in once again going through this process.

Laura, 2012, Knivsta

ABBREVIATIONS

AD	*Arbetsdomstolens domar,* case reporter for the Labor Court
CISG	The United Nations Convention for the International Sale of Goods, also known as the Vienna Convention
EC	European Communities
EEA	European Economic Area
EEC	European Economic Communities
EU	European Union
HFD	*Högsta förvaltningsdomstolens årsbok,* case reporter for the Supreme Administrative Court
JK	*Justitiekanslern* ("JK"), Chancellor of Justice
JO	*Justitieombudsmännen* ("JO") or *Riksdagens ombudsmän,* the Parliamentary Ombudsmen
JP	Code of Judicial Procedure
LC	Land Code
NJA	*Nytt juridiskt arkiv,* case reporter for the Supreme Court
PC	Penal Code
RÅ	*Regeringsrättens Årsbok,* case reporter for the Supreme Administrative Court prior to 2010
SEK	Swedish crowns (currency)
SFS	*Svensk författningssamling,* legislative reporter
SOU	*Statens Offentliga Utredningar,* Parliamentary Inquiry
TEU	Treaty on the European Union (formerly the Maastricht Treaty)
TFEU	Treaty on the Functioning of the European Union (originally the Treaty of Rome and the Treaty Establishing the European Community)

The Institutions and Systems

This book serves as an introduction to the Swedish legal system and laws for a foreign reader. Divided into three parts, this first one addresses broader institutional subjects such as constitutional law, European Union law and procedural law. The second part addresses the basics: beginning with family law, and then going on to agency, contracts, debtor and creditor law, followed by property law and ending with tort law. More specific topics of contract and commercial law are taken up in part three: business organizations, sales, intellectual property rights and unfair trade practices, labor and employment law, ending with land leases and landlord/tenant law. These presentations are not meant to be exhaustive but rather are intended to give the reader a sufficient understanding of the Swedish legal system and law to be somewhat orientated when faced with a legal question. As such, the first chapter discusses the Swedish political and legal systems generally.

The Institutions and Legal System

Capturing the essence of a legal system, the sum of a people, history and culture, in simply a few pages is a daunting, if not impossible task. At the same time, the new Europe of cross-border legal education and transactions renders it a necessity. Swedish national law can be traced back to the mid-fourteenth century, while the provincial laws are several hundred years older. The focus of this book, however, is on today's legal system and law, perched as it is on the cusp of this new era.

This first chapter concerns the modern institutional structures, both political and legal, delineating the Swedish legal system as set out in the constitutional acts. Section one below describes the national institutions, section two local government, and section three the judiciary, legal system and lawyers. Another parameter defining the Swedish legal system is European Union law, a result of Sweden's membership in the European Communities as of 1995. This is addressed separately in Chapter Three, which is devoted to EU Law. The limits of state power as exercised against the individual, the other major component of constitutional law, is discussed in the next chapter.

The Swedish Constitution comprises four separate constitutional acts as enumerated in Article 3 of the first chapter of the Instrument of Government (*Regeringsform* 1974:152): The Instrument of Government itself; The Freedom of the Press Act (*Tryckfrihetsförordning* 1949:105); The Fundamental Law on the Freedom of Expression (*Yttrandefrihetsgrundlag* 1991:1469); and the Act on Succession (*Successionsordning* 1810:926).[1] Constitutional acts are not designated as such explicitly by title, but rather by the legislative process through which they are enacted. This procedure, established by tradition

---

1   These constitutional acts are also referred to as fundamental laws. For English translations of these constitutional acts, *see* the Parliament's website at riksdagen.se.

dating back to the Parliament of 1766, is now set out in Article 14 of the eighth chapter of the Instrument of Government. A proposed constitutional act must be approved by two separate sessions of Parliament at least nine months apart, with a national election held between the sessions. The standing parliamentary Constitutional Committee (*konstitutionsutskottet*) can grant exceptions to these requirements with a five-sixths majority. This procedure is seen as giving a guarantee that a constitutional proposal is not adopted simply on a political whim. If the majority of citizens does not approve of the measure after the first parliamentary vote, they then have the option of electing different parliamentary representatives for the second vote and subsequently can effect a different outcome. The Instrument of Government is divided into fifteen chapters:

Chapter 1 – The Basic Principles of the Form of Government;
Chapter 2 – Fundamental Rights and Freedoms;
Chapter 3 – The Parliament;
Chapter 4 – The Work of the Parliament;
Chapter 5 – The Head of State;
Chapter 6 – The Government;
Chapter 7 – The Work of the Government;
Chapter 8 – Acts of Law and Other Provisions;
Chapter 9 – National Finances;
Chapter 10 – International relations;
Chapter 11 – Administration of Justice;
Chapter 12 – Administration of Government;
Chapter 13 – Parliamentary Review;
Chapter 14 – Local Government; and
Chapter 15 – War and Threat of War.

Due to space constraints, the focus in the following discussion is mainly on the allocation of political power and the courts.

The form of government is set out in Article 1 of the first chapter of the Instrument of Government: "All public power in Sweden emanates from the people."[2] Swedish democracy is to be founded "on the free formation of

---

2   *All offentlig makt i Sverige utgår från folket.*

opinion and on universal and equal suffrage. It is to be realized through a representative and parliamentary polity and through local self-government." Public power is to be exercised under the law; in other words, Sweden is to adhere to the rule of law.

1.1 The National Institutions

Sweden is a parliamentary democracy with a constitutional monarchy.[3] The monarch is the head of state, but today has mostly titular and representative duties.[4] However, the King is the chair of the Advisory Council on Foreign Affairs (*utrikesnämnden*) and can decide to hold their meetings behind closed doors. As of 1999, the Lutheran Church of Sweden no longer is the state church and no longer has an automatic power to tax. The Lutheran Church can request that the State help collect membership dues as a part of the tax collection system, a right that other religious congregations now also have.[5]

The distribution of political power in Sweden as espoused in the 1974 Instrument of Government is one of a separation of function, not separation of power. The Swedish Parliament[6] is to be the ultimate source of political

---

3 The king originally was elected and the monarchy did not become hereditary until 1544 with King Gustav Vasa's family. It became a constitutional monarchy in 1809. The king held legislative power officially until 1974 when the present Instrument of Government was adopted, formalizing the shift in legislative power that had been occurring successively from the king to the Parliament since the loss of Norway in 1905. One of the last vestiges of the rights of the nobility (*adel*) in general was dismantled as late as 2003, when the legislative status of the regulations governing the House of Nobility (*Riddarhusordning* 1866:37 p. 1) was amended. The House of Nobility (*Riddarhuset*) is now a private organization. For information on this organization in English, *see* its website at riddarhuset.se.

4 The Act on Succession (*Successionsordning* 1810:926) prescribes the order of accession to the crown. It was amended in 1979 to allow the oldest child, regardless of sex, to receive the crown.

5 The Lutheran Church of Sweden became the official state church under King Gustav Vasa in the 1530's. Every person born in Sweden automatically became a member of the Church until 1999 when the Church officially separated from the state. Only the monarch is now required to be a member of the Swedish Lutheran Church. For more information on the Swedish Lutheran Church in English, *see* its website at svenskakyrkan.se.

6 For more information on the Swedish Parliament in English, *see* its website at riksdagen.se.

power as seen by Article 4 of the first chapter, stating that "[t]he Parliament is the foremost representative of the People." The Parliament in its turn votes on the Prime Minister, who appoints the Government.

1.1.1 THE PARLIAMENT

The Parliament as an assembly arguably dates back to a meeting at Arboga in 1435. Consisting of four chambers under King Gustav Vasa – the clergy, nobility, merchants and farmers – the Parliament became bicameral in 1866 and unicameral in 1971. Today it has 349 representatives who are elected every four years. In contrast, European Union elections are held every five years.

The Parliament passes national laws, as well as sets the national taxes and budget. The work of Parliament is regulated by chapters three and four of the Instrument of Government and by the Riksdag Act of 1974 (*Riksdagsordning* 1974:153).[7] The Riksdag Act is not a constitutional act, but still has heightened requirements as to amendment: Two parliamentary votes with an election in between, or a qualified majority of at least three-fourths of the votes cast with at least one-half of the parliamentary members voting.

There are presently sixteen standing parliamentary committees (*utskott*) covering the topics of the labor market (*arbetsmarknadsutskottet*), state finances (*finansutskottet*), civil affairs (*civilutskottet*), defense (*försvarsutskottet*), justice (*justitieutskottet*), constitutional issues (*konstitutionsutskottet*), cultural affairs (*kulturutskottet*), environment and agriculture (*miljö- och jordbruksutskottet*), industry and trade (*näringsutskottet*), taxation (*skatteutskottet*), social insurance (*socialförsäkringsutskottet*), health and welfare (*socialutskottet*), transportation and communication (*trafikutskottet*), education (*utbildningsutskottet*), foreign affairs (*utrikesutskottet*) and the Committee on European Union Affairs (*EU-nämnden*). There are also parliamentary working groups, including the Swedish delegation to the Parliamentary Assembly of the Council of Europe (*Europarådets svenska delegation*), Swedish Inter-Parliamentary Group (*IPU-delegation*), War Delegation (*krigsdelegation*), Swedish Delegation to the Nordic Council

---

7   An English translation of the Riksdag Act is available at the website of the Parliament at riksdagen.se. The Riksdag Act was a constitutional act until 1974 and the adoption of the new Instrument of Government.

(*Nordiska rådets svenska delegation*), Swedish Delegation to the Organization for Security and Co-operation in Europe (*OSSE-delgation*), Advisory Council on Foreign Affairs (*utrikesnämnden*), Council concerning Political Contributions (*partibidragsnämnden*) and one concerning the Swedish National Bank (*Riksbanken*).

The Council on Legislation (*lagrådet*), comprising current and former justices of the Supreme Court and the Supreme Administrative Court, provides advisory opinions to the Government as to the constitutionality and general suitability of proposed legislation.[8] Standing parliamentary committees can also submit legislative proposals for review to the Council on Legislation. Under Article 21 of the eight chapter of the Instrument of Government, the Parliament is to obtain a preliminary ruling from the Council with respect to:

1   A proposed constitutional act concerning freedom of the press and media;
2   A proposed statute limiting public access to documents;
3   A proposed statute affecting certain chapter two rights of the Instrument of Government, namely industrial action, rights to property, intellectual property rights, limitations in chapter two rights for citizens or non-citizens (Articles 14–16, 20 and 25, respectively);
4   A proposed statute with respect to data processing of personal data;
5   A proposed statute concerning the municipalities' right to tax or imposing an obligation upon municipalities;
6   A proposed statute concerning government regulations, the administration of justice or of the government; and
7   A proposed statute changing or repealing an act as set out under the above points 1–6.

According to Article 22, the Council is to assess:

1   The manner by which the proposed law relates to the constitutional acts and legal system generally;

---

8   The Council on Legislation is also regulated by the Act on the Council on Legislation (*lag 2003:333 om Lagrådet*). The Council's opinions are available in Swedish at its website at lagradet.se.

2   The manner by which the various provisions within the proposed legislation relate to one another;

3   Whether the proposed law fulfills the requirements of legal certainty;

4   Whether the proposed law is framed so that it can be deemed to satisfy its stated objectives; and

5   Any potential problems likely to arise with the application of the proposed law.

The Parliament is not bound to follow the opinion of the Council and the failure to obtain the Council's opinion as to a proposed act's constitutionality currently does not bar its implementation.

The Parliamentary Ombudsmen (*Justitieombudsmännen*, JO or *Riksdagens ombudsmän*) were originally created in 1809 as a check against any unauthorized use of power by the King and now serve as a check against such an exercise by the authorities under the Government, but not the Government itself or individual ministers. The Parliamentary Ombudsmen are to supervise the application of the laws and can direct criticism against actions taken by a court, or other national or local authority.[9] Matters can be brought to their attention by complaints filed by individuals or the ombudsmen themselves can initiate audits of governmental authorities. About 7,000 complaints are filed annually with the ombudsmen. The ombudsmen are elected by the parliament for a four-year period and often are already justices. The common response by JO for errors found is public criticism, however, opinions as issued by JO are not legally binding. JO can also prosecute a public employee for the crimes of misconduct in office or another crime in service, as well as initiate disciplinary proceedings against public employees for more serious mistakes committed while in public service.

In addition to the Ombudsmen, the Parliament can hold the Government accountable through the "parliamentary question". With this institution, an interpellation or question can be addressed by a Parliamentary member to a minister relating to the performance of official duties. The Parliament's standing constitutional committee is also empowered to criticize the

---

9   For more information on the Parliamentary Ombudsmen, *see* their website at jo.se.

Government or ministers. One more direct check the Parliament has against the Government is a vote of no confidence (*misstroendeförklaring*).

1.1.2 THE GOVERNMENT

Article 6 of the first chapter of the Instrument of Government states that the "Government governs the realm" and is accountable to the Parliament. The Government is charged with drafting the national budget, submitting legislative bills, administering justice and heading government agencies. The Speaker of the Parliament submits a candidate for Prime Minister, which proposal is put to a parliamentary vote under Article 4 of chapter six of the Instrument of Government. The Prime Minister, once elected by a simple majority in the Parliament, appoints (and dismisses) the other ministers comprising the Government. Under the current rule of negative parliamentarism, the sitting Government (*expeditionsregering*) continues to sit until a new government is formed. No express support of the Parliament is required, with only a vote of no confidence dissolving the Government unless a new government is formed.

Ministers do not have the power to issue directives. Consequently Sweden is not a system of ministerial rule. All decisions taken by the Government are to be taken collectively, and the ministers are accountable to the Government. Under the Instrument of Government, the Government is accountable to the Parliament. The Parliament can declare that a prime minister no longer enjoys its confidence and thereby can dismiss the Government as a whole, or simply an individual minister.

The Government has direct legislative powers with respect to promulgating regulations (*förordningar*) regarding the enactment of legislation, and also in areas not explicitly defined as under the jurisdiction of the Parliament by the Instrument of Government. The Government is responsible for approximately 400 public authorities and agencies.[10] To this end, the

---

10 There are an additional 600 private organizations providing services as outsourced by government authorities. *See* the Government inquiry, GETTING THINGS DONE – A PROPOSAL FOR A MORE EFFECTIVE STATE ADMINISTRATION (*Styra och ställa – Förslag till en effektivare statsförvaltning* SOU 2008:118). The report issued by the inquiry includes a summary chapter in English of its review of state administration. This report is available at the website of the Government Offices of Sweden at regeringen.se.

Government has been delegated legislative authority to issue government regulations as set out under Article 7 of the eighth chapter of the Instrument of Government. The only sanction that the Government can impose legislatively for a failure to follow government regulations, however, is fines. The Parliament can strengthen government regulations by legislating penalties of imprisonment and/or criminal fines as sanctions for violations of specific government regulations.

The Government has subdelegated extensive legislative authority to the government agencies to issue regulations. The primary task of the agencies is to ensure the implementation of decisions as taken by the Parliament and Government. The agencies are responsible to the Government and fall under various government ministries. Agencies are to act independently, free from political influence, however, and ministers are not to attempt to influence individual agency decisions.

The Government has an ombudsman comparable to that of the Parliament, the Chancellor of Justice (*Justitiekanslern*, JK or *regeringsombudsman*), an office created in 1713 by King Karl XII.[11] The Chancellor as appointed by the Government has a life-time state position (*med fullmakt*). This entails that the Chancellor sits in office until reaching the mandatory retirement age, transferring to a different comparable office or until removed for cause. The Chancellor has jurisdiction over the courts and national and local authorities as well as over their respective personnel. The Chancellor is charged with several different tasks, including acting:

- As legal counsel for the Government;
- As the State's representative in trials and other legal disputes;
- On complaints and claims for damages against the State and determining amounts of financial compensation, if any, for such claims;[12]

---

11   The duties of the Chancellor are set forth in the Act Concerning Supervision by the Chancellor of Justice (*lag 1975:1339 om Justitiekanslerns tillsyn*) and the Ordinance Concerning the Duties of the Chancellor of Justice (*förordning 1975:1345 med instruktion för Justitiekanslern*). For more information on the Chancellor, *see* its website at jk.se.
12   A decision by the Chancellor, however, is not binding on the courts if a plaintiff decides instead to litigate the issue.

- As the Government's ombudsman in the supervision of authorities and civil servants, and taking action in cases of abuse of office;
- To ensure that freedom of the press and other media is not transgressed and is the sole public prosecutor in cases regarding offences against freedom of the press and other media; and
- As the guardian for the protection of privacy in different fields.

The Chancellor is also empowered to appeal decisions by county administrative boards under the Public Camera Surveillance Act as part of the duties of safeguarding individual privacy. Approximately 8,600 matters were filed with the Chancellor's office in 2011. Of these, 2,700 concerned claims for damages arising from state actions, particularly unlawful imprisonment (*frihetsberövanden*), 2,400 concerned legal aid, 1,200 were with respect to supervisory issues and public authorities, 97 concerned threats to ethnic groups, 450 concerned freedom of the press and expression and 1,200 camera surveillance. Compensation was granted in ninety percent of the cases alleging unlawful imprisonment as handled in 2011 (1,333 of 1,451 cases) and Sweden paid a total amount of over SEK forty million in damages in such cases.

1.1.3 ELECTIONS AND POLITICAL PARTIES

General elections are held every four years on the second Sunday in September. Parliamentary, municipal and county/regional elections are held on the same day. Votes are cast for political parties to represent voters at three different levels: municipalities (*kommun*), county councils (*landsting*) and the national level. European Union elections are held on the other hand every five years and on a different day.

To be eligible to vote in the municipal and county council elections, a voter must be at least 18 years of age and a resident of the municipality and county concerned. Swedish citizenship is not required in order to vote in municipal and county elections, but voters must either be citizens of another EU Member State or Nordic country and registered in Sweden at the time of the election, or be registered as a permanent resident in Sweden for the last three years. Swedish citizenship is required to vote in the national elections.

Votes are most often cast for a political party, which in turn determines the individuals who are to fill the various posts according to the party lists. A party must have a threshold of at least 4 % of the votes cast nationally, or 12 % of the votes cast in a voting district, in order to receive a seat in the national parliament. The direct election of individual candidates (*personval*) began to be tentatively allowed in 1998 and is now possible under fairly limited circumstances.[13] In the majority of cases, however, the candidates for political office are not elected individually, but rather chosen by the parties according to party lists after the votes are tallied.

There are currently eight political parties represented in Parliament. The two major political parties historically are the Social Democrats (*socialdemokraterna*)[14] and the Conservative Party (*moderaterna*).[15] The other political parties include the Liberal Party (*folkpartiet*),[16] the Centre Party (formerly the farmer party, *centerpartiet*),[17] the Left Party (formerly the Communist Party, *vänsterpartiet*),[18] the Christian Democrats (*kristdemokraterna*),[19] the Swedish Green Party (*miljöpartiet*)[20] and the Swedish nationalist party, *Sverigedemokraterna*.[21] The parties tend to act in blocks, often forming either a conservative/non-socialist block or a socialist block. The conservative block can comprise, for example, the Centre Party, Liberal Party, Conservative Party and Christian Democrats. The socialist block historically has consisted of the Social Democrats and the Left Party. The Green Party is often part of the socialist block, but in some geographic areas the Green Party holds the balance of power and can choose either block

---

13 With respect to the Parliament, eight percent of the voters for one party in a voting district (*valkrets*) have to vote for the individual who must also be on the party list. There are 29 national voting districts and the individual chosen by a political party for a certain voting district does not have to reside in that district.

14 For information on the Social Democrats in English, *see* its website at socialdemokraterna.se.

15 For information on the Conservative Party in English, *see* its website at moderat.se.

16 For information on the Liberal Party in English, *see* its website at folkpartiet.se.

17 For information on the Centre Party in English, *see* its website at centerpartiet.se.

18 For information on the Left Party in English, *see* its website at vansterpartiet.se.

19 For information on the Christian Democrats in English, *see* its website at kristdemokraterna.se.

20 For information on the Swedish Green Party in English, *see* its website at mp.se.

21 For information on the *Sverigedemokraterna*, *see* its website at sverigedemokraterna.se.

to achieve an objective. The Green Party on the national level has previously committed itself to supporting the socialist block with the local chapters free to decide how they wish to align themselves. The Social Democrats were in power (along with their respective allied parties) for the majority of the twentieth century, beginning in the 1930's up to 2006, with only two short breaks in 1976–1980 and 1994–1998. The conservative block has now in a third longer break been in power since 2006.

1.2 Local Government

The tradition of local government dates back long before Sweden was forged into a nation state by King Gustav Vasa.[22] Heads of families gathered regularly at councils of one hundred (*ting* or *thing*) to settle disputes. This strong local power did not give way until the monarchy amassed greater power during the 17th century. Local church parishes were still charged with certain duties such as poor relief and vagrancy control. The Municipalities Act of 1862 separated the secular and ecclesiastical administrations, reestablishing the significance of secular local government. The objective of having decisions taken as closely as possible to those affected by the decisions can also be seen as a product of geography and population. Geographically Sweden is the fifth largest European country after Russia, the Ukraine, France and Spain, but population-wise, has only 9 million inhabitants, resulting in vast sparsely populated territories.

The system of local governance is protected constitutionally in the first chapter of the Instrument of Government. Article 1 there states that "Swedish democracy is … to be realized through a representative and parliamentary polity and through local self-government." Article 7 of the same chapter states that "Sweden has municipalities and county councils." The decision-making power in these local authorities is exercised by elected assemblies. The local authorities, both municipalities and county councils, may levy taxes in order to finance their local operations.

The Local Government Act (*kommunallag* 1991:900) defines the roles of municipalities (*kommuner*) and county councils (*landsting*), which

---

22 *See* Sören Häggroth et al., SWEDISH LOCAL GOVERNMENT – TRADITIONS AND REFORMS (The Swedish Institute 1993).

according to its first paragraph are to "take care of those matters as stated in this law and other specific regulations on the principles of democracy and the self-determination of municipalities." Municipalities are responsible for matters relating to the residents of the municipality and their immediate environment as discussed further in Chapter Six below.

There are presently twenty-one counties (*län*), each headed by a county administrative board (*länsstyrelse*) and a governor (*landshövding*).[23] The county administrative boards and governors are not elected but deemed part of the State's local administration. Health and dental care, as well as regional collective transportation, are managed on the county level by county councils (*landsting*) and county council assemblies (*landstingsfullmäktige*).[24] The council representatives are elected on the regional level. Several county councils can cooperate voluntarily as a region.

Each county is further divided into municipalities, today numbering 290.[25] The municipalities are headed by a municipal assembly (*kommun-fullmäktige*) elected locally and headed by a municipal council (*kommun-styrelse*) appointed by the municipal assembly. No general hierarchical exercise of power exists between municipalities, counties and regions, as each is delegated different areas of responsibility. The Parliament and other national authorities can set requirements that local authorities must follow. For example, the municipalities are responsible for primary education and schools, but must fulfill certain nationally-set standards. However, enforcing national standards is complicated as sanctions are seen to impinge on the municipalities' right of self-determination. One example of this can be seen where a municipality decides to give financial support to a local enterprise, which support can be in violation of national or EU regulations. The Government can request that the municipality demand the return of the

---

23 For more information on the county administrative boards in English, *see* their joint website at lst.se.

24 For more information on the county councils, *see* their website at skl.se.

25 The population of Sweden in 2011 was 9.48 million and the average population of a Swedish municipality was 15 000, with actual numbers varying from 2 431 in Bjurholm to over 864 324 in Stockholm. The county councils have an average population of 424 000 with the largest being Stockholm County Council, with over 2 million inhabitants. The average municipal tax for 2011 was 31.55 %. For these statistics in English, *see* the government agency, Statistics Sweden at scb.se.

monies from the enterprise,[26] but can experience difficulties with enforcing such a demand as it can be deemed by the municipality as a violation of the municipalities' right to self-determination. This can become even more complicated if the municipal support provided was in violation of EU law. Sweden as a Member State then can be seen to be in violation of EU law despite demands by the Government for the municipality to have the funds returned and the municipal decision annulled.

There are approximately 42 000 political assignments in the 290 municipalities and 3 500 political assignments in the 20 county councils and regions. This entails that approximately 0.5 % of the population in Sweden holds a political assignment in a municipality or county council. In county councils, 42 % of the members are women, county council assemblies, 47 % and in the municipalities, 40 %. Approximately one-half of the members in the county councils and in municipal political assignments are between 50 and 65 years old. Only approximately 5 % are between 18 and 29 years old and close to 10 % are older than 65 for both county councils and municipalities.[27]

1.3 The Judicial System

Swedish courts are to be independent of the Parliament as well as all other governmental authorities according to Article 2 of chapter eleven of the Instrument of Government, the chapter in the constitutional act governing the courts generally. This requirement of independence is also found in Article 6 of the European Convention for the Protection of Human Rights and Fundamental Freedoms ("European Convention"), effective as law in Sweden since 1 November 1998. The courts fall under the administration of the Ministry of Justice and its agency, the National Courts Administration.[28]

There is no general right of judicial review in Sweden, only a limited one. The courts are empowered under Article 14 of the eleventh chapter to disregard a legal provision in conflict with a constitutional act only in the

---

26 This would be under the Act on the Application of EC Competition and Subsidy Rules (*lag 1994:1845 om tillämpning av Europeiska unionens statsstödsregler*).
27 This information is taken from the website of the county councils at skl.se.
28 For more information in English on the National Courts Administration and on the judicial system in general, *see* its website at domstol.se.

case at hand. Prior to 2011, if the provision was enacted by the Parliament or Government, the courts could disregard the provision only if it was manifestly, on its face, in contradiction to one of the constitutional acts (*uppenbarhetsrekvisit*). This requirement of "manifestly" was removed as of 1 January 2011.

Sweden has two parallel court systems, the general courts and the administrative courts. The general courts comprise fifty-three district courts (*tingsrätt*), six courts of appeal (*hovrätt*)[29] and the Supreme Court (*Högsta domstolen*). The administrative courts comprise twelve administrative district courts (*förvaltningsrätt*, formerly *länsrätt*), four administrative courts of appeal (*kammarrätt*) and the Supreme Administrative Court (*Högsta förvaltningsdomstolen*, formerly *Regeringsrätten*).

There are also specialized courts with specific jurisdictions, such as the Labor Court (*Arbetsdomstolen*),[30] the Market Court (*Marknadsdomstolen*),[31] the Court of Patent Appeals (*Patentbesvärsrätten*),[32] the five land and environment courts (*mark- och miljödomstol*) and the Land and Environment Court of Appeal (*Mark- och miljööverdomstolen*), the seven maritime courts (*sjörättsdomstol*), the three migration courts (*migrationsdomstol*) and the Higher Migration Court (*migrationsöverdomstol*).

Some of these specialized courts are tied into the general or administrative court systems, such as the Court of Patent Appeals. Others have no connection whatsoever with the general or administrative courts. For example, the Labor Court is often the court of first instance as well as the sole appellate court in cases concerning the social partners, with the Supreme Court having no general jurisdiction over its decisions. The Supreme Court can technically grant a petition to vacate a judgment of the Labor Court (*resning*), but has yet to do so.

---

29 The first court of appeal, *Svea hovrätt*, was established in 1614 to administer justice on behalf of the King. The Supreme Court was established in 1789 by King Gustav III to replace the right of appeal to the King's Council.

30 For more information in English on the Labor Court, *see* its website at arbetsdomstolen.se.

31 For more information in English on the Market Court, *see* its website at marknadsdomstolen.se.

32 For more information in English on the Court of Patent Appeals, *see* its website at pbr.se.

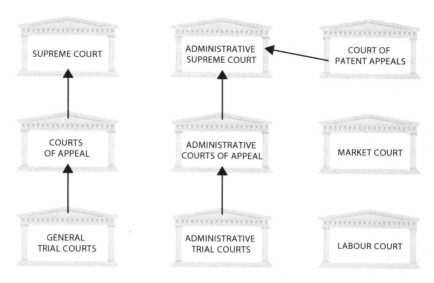

DIAGRAM 1.1 The Court System.

Permanent judges are appointed by the Government. They are to have law degrees and traditionally have gone through a series of clerkships beginning at a district court (general or administrative) for a period of two years, and then at an appellate court for one year. These three years are followed by at least one additional probationary three-year period as a judge trainee, two years of which are at the district courts and the final year at an appellate court as a member of a judging panel. Once appointed as a permanent judge, a judge can sit on the bench until 65-years old, but has the right to voluntarily stay until the age of 67-years. Judges can only be removed from the bench for serious crimes.

The Government appoints the justices to the supreme courts. The Parliament does not have any veto power with respect to these appointments. Prior to 2011, vacancies were not announced, but now they are publicly open for applications. A justice must be a permanent judge as mandated by Article 1 of the eleventh chapter of the Instrument of Government. Sixteen justices currently sit on the Supreme Court and nineteen on the Supreme Administrative Court.

Lay judges can be included with legally trained judges in certain judging panels as defined by statute at both the district and appellate courts levels. However, there are no lay judges at the supreme courts. Lay judges are politically appointed for four-year terms. In contrast to juries in England and the United States, lay judges vote on both questions of law as well as questions of fact. Lay judges do not, however, adjudicate in all types of cases. For example, in the district courts lay judges only adjudicate in criminal and child custody cases, but not in criminal arraignments. Lay judges also do not sit in the judging panels for most civil cases, such as those concerning tort or contractual claims.

1.4 The Legal System

The Swedish legal system over time has been influenced by several different legal systems, including the Canon law system during the Middle Ages, French law after the Revolution and American law. German law, however, has influenced Swedish law in three different waves, beginning with the German Hansa law of the Hanseatic League during the 14th century, German-Roman law in the 17th century and German law again in the 19th and first half of the 20th century. German law historically was the most influential foreign law in Sweden. This is now changing in light of Sweden's membership in the European Union and the subsequent requirements of Member State legislative harmonization. EU law now can be seen as having the greatest impact on Swedish law in modern times. This is evidenced by the rate of recent legislative amendments made in Swedish law. In 2007 there were an estimated 1,270 laws and 2,300 regulations applicable in Sweden. Of these, approximately 1,150 were amended in some form by the Parliament that year, with the passage of 24 new laws and 278 new regulations. In 2008, there were 1,200 laws and 2,200 regulations, of which approximately 600 were amended.

Although traditionally thought of as a civil law system, the Swedish legal system fits neither the category of a civil law or common law country perfectly. It is not perfectly civil as it does not have a complete codification such as the *Bürgerliches Gesetzbuch* ("BGB") or the Code Napoleon. The most recent Swedish general codification, more of a compilation, was enacted in 1734, parts of which are still valid law today. There are, on the other hand, codes (*balkar*) concerning specific topics, such as the Code of Judicial Procedure, the Environmental Code, the Penal Code and the Marriage Code. In contrast, certain areas of law, such as perfecting security interests in chattels (*sakrätt*), are almost entirely regulated by case law with little or no statutory provisions. However, Sweden does not either fit perfectly within the common law designation, particularly in light of the perception of the role of the judiciary.

This mixture of statutory and case law, the perceived role of the judges, and the degree of self-regulation built into the legal system, are characteristic of that referred to as the Nordic legal family.[33] The Nordic legal family is seen as distinct from the Anglo-American, Germanic and Romanist legal families and is often referred to as a "third" way between common law and civil law systems. The countries within the Nordic legal family as a rule do not have complete codifications such as the BGB and Code Napoleon but also invoke case law in a manner different from the Anglo-American systems.[34] The reason why the legal systems within this family partly fall within the civil law systems is the perception of the role of the courts. The courts theoretically are simply to determine the intent of the legislator[35] and not make law. The Swedish legal system consequently is based on a separation of political function, but not a separation of political power.

Another unique aspect of the legal systems found within the Nordic family is that quasi-legislative power is often delegated to private organizations, the most apparent of these in the areas of labor and employment law with respect to the social partners, the employer and employee organizations. The premise

---

33 For more on the Nordic legal family, see Chapter 19 in Konrad Zweigert and Hein Kötz, AN INTRODUCTION TO COMPARATIVE LAW (3rd ed. 1998).

34 The Nordic family is seen to consist presently of Denmark, the Faroe Islands, Greenland, Finland, Åland, Iceland, Norway and Sweden. These countries have historical roots and co-operations dating back to the Kalmar Union in place from 1397–1521. Today these countries belong to the Nordic Council, a parliamentary co-operation body formed in 1952. The Nordic Council drafts model legislation to be adopted by the Nordic countries, such as the Contracts Act, the Sale of Goods Act and the Commission Act. For more information on this body, *see* its website at norden.org.

35 When interpreting legislation, the aim of the court is to determine the intent of the legislator. The singular form of legislator is used intentionally, with the approach being divining the intent of the single lawmaker, as opposed to perceiving the legislature as a group of individuals with different, and at times, contradictory interests and intents.

behind this more or less implicit delegation of law-making authority resulting in the absence of statutory regulation is that these organizations are closer to the actual problems arising in their areas and consequently are perceived to have a better understanding of both the problems and possible solutions. Self-governance and self-regulation are very strong aspects of this model, as can be seen in not only the areas of employment and labor law, but also in landlord tenant law, contract law, insurance law and corporate law.

Within the Swedish legal system, areas of law are often first categorized as either public or private law, much as in the Roman law tradition. Public law concerns issues between the political power, the state, counties and munici-palities, and the individual. Private law concerns the relationship between two private parties. A major distinction between public and private law is that public law is mandatory (*tvingande*), while private law is seen as having a gap-filling function (*dispositiv*) in most cases. Certain provisions in private law, however, are mandatory. Even if certain private law provisions, mostly consumer protection provisions, are mandatory, the parties are still free to agree to the contrary. The party negatively affected by such an agreement then has to exercise her rights under the mandatory law to have the agreement voided, consequently rendering these protections in private law more quasi-mandatory than mandatory.

An example of this quasi-mandatory nature can be given with respect to consumer protection legislation. If a consumer has entered into an agreement waiving the protective legislation, the consumer must assert the rights granted under the legislation despite the agreement, as no state agency does so *sua sponte* on behalf of that consumer under the consumer acts.[36]

---

36   The Consumer Agency (*Konsumentverket*) has the authority under a specific act, the Act on Certain Contract Clauses in Consumer Relationships (*lag 1994:1512 om avtalsvillkor i konsumentförhållanden*) to forbid companies from invoking certain unconscionable contract clauses or using certain marketing materials, but this authority is not granted under the Consumer Sale of Goods Act (*konsumentköplag 1985:716*). For more information in English as to the Consumer Agency, *see* its website at konsumentverket.se.

TABLE 1.1 The Traditional Distinction of Public and Private Law.

Public Law (*offentlig rätt*)	Private Law (*privaträtt* or *civilrätt*)
Criminal Law (*straffrätt*)	Family Law (*familjerätt*) • Marriage Law (*äktenskapsrätt*) • Inheritance Law (*arvsrätt*)
Procedural Law (*processrätt*)	The Law of Obligations and Property (*förmögenhetsrätt*)
Constitutional Law (*statsrätt*)	The Law of Obligations (*obligationsrätt*) • Contract Law (*avtalsrätt*)
Municipal Law (*kommunalrätt*)	– General Contract Law – Specialized Contract Law
Administrative Law (*förvaltningsrätt*) • General Administrative Law • Administrative Procedural Law • Specialized Administrative Law – Tax Law (*skatterätt*) – Environmental Law (*miljörätt*) – Competition Law (*konkurrensrätt*) – Securities Law (*börsrätt*) – Social Security Law (*socialförsäkrings-rätt*)	– Sales Law (*köprätt*) – Law on Gifts (*gåvorätt*) • Law on Business Organizations (*bolagsrätt*) • Tort Law (*skadeståndsrätt*) The Law of Property • Real Property Law (*fastighetsrätt*) – General Real Estate Law – Specialized Real Estate Law • Third party rights to property (*sakrätt*)

The boundary between mandatory and gap-filling in certain cases can be somewhat blurry as legislative acts regarding private law can have elements of a purely public law nature. For example, the Companies Act (*aktiebolagslag* 2005:551) as well as the Land Code (*jordabalk* 1970:994), contains sections regarding criminal sanctions for violations of certain provisions of these laws.

1.4.1 SOURCES OF LAW

A fundamental cornerstone in the Swedish legal system is the doctrine of the hierarchy of legal sources (*rättskälleläran*). This doctrine provides an order of precedence for the different legal sources that traditionally has been seen as:

1   The Constitution as comprising the four distinct constitutional
    acts (*grundlagar*);
2   Legislation (*lagstiftning*): parliamentary acts (*lagar*), government
    regulations (also referred to as ordinances, *förordningar*) and agency
    regulations (*föreskrifter*);
3   Legislative preparatory works (*förarbeten*);
4   Case law (*rättspraxis*);
5   General principles of law (*allmänna rättsprinciper*);
6   Custom and usage; and
7   Legal scholarship (*doktrin*).

A brief description of each of these categories is given below. This ranking is
often mandatory in public law with respect to the constitution and legislation,
however after that the courts are fairly free to decide their focus. Deviations
from the general hierarchy described above can also be made in specific areas
of private law in which the parties have been given the right to contract out
of certain statutory regulations, for example, contract law. In such cases, the
agreement between the parties, or the contract, has the highest precedence to
the extent it is not in contravention to mandatory statutory regulation. If the
contract does not resolve a specific issue, then the hierarchy as above kicks
in, with the default statutory regulation the next source of law. However, if
the private law legislation is mandatory, for example with respect to certain
consumer protections, the contract is voidable to the extent it deviates from
the protections to the disadvantage of the consumer.

   Another complication with this traditional hierarchy of legal sources has
been EU law and how it fits into this equation. The implementation of EU
law in Sweden is insured by the EU doctrines of the supremacy of EU law
over Member State law as well as principle of direct effect, and the duty of
loyal cooperation by the Member States. In brief, Sweden has the obligation
to enact and enforce EU law over Swedish law in certain areas, and in cases
of uncertainty, the lower courts may, but the highest courts must, request
a preliminary ruling from the Court of Justice of the European Union as
to potential conflicts in accordance with Article 267 of the Treaty on the
Functioning of the EU ("TFEU").

   It can be mentioned here that the establishment of a similar hierarchy
of legal sources on the Union level specifically with respect to the role of

legislative preparatory works has been on the agenda of certain actors as a potential Swedish contribution to EU law.[37] In contrast, the position of EU law in the Swedish hierarchy of legal sources has not been consistently affixed by all Swedish scholars. These EU principles, as well as the different types of legal acts at the European Union law level, are discussed further below in Chapter Three.

The Constitution

Constitutional law has been presented above with respect to allocation of political power and is presented in greater depth in the next chapter with respect to the rights of individual as primarily against state power. It suffices to restate here that there is no one document called the constitution within the Swedish legal system, but rather that perceived of as the constitution is the four separate acts: The Instrument of Government, the Act of Succession, the Freedom of the Press Act and the Fundamental Law on Freedom of Expression.

Legislation

The legislation comprises parliamentary acts, government regulations and agency regulations. The parliamentary acts tend to be written in broad terms with little detail, more in the style of framework legislation. For example, the Contracts Act has only twenty-three sections excluding those concerning agency. The Torts Liability Act is another example of a broad statute, in which key principles such as determining standards of negligence and causality are not defined but rather left to the courts to define. In addition, many areas of the law are not regulated by legislation, reflecting the very conservative approach to legislating in Sweden, very similar to the physician's oath, "do no harm."

All Swedish parliamentary acts and government regulations are published annually in the series *Svensk författningssamling* ("SFS"), beginning in

---

37 *See, for example,* Ulf Öberg, *Tre lösa trådar: mer om förarbeten, statens processföring vid EG-domstolen och det gemenskapsrättsliga uppenbarhetsrekvisit,* SvJT 4/2003 at 505.

1825.[38] Each parliamentary act or government regulation is given an SFS number, which is the year of passage followed by its chronological number as addressed by the Parliament that year. For example, the Land Code has the SFS designation of 1970:994, meaning that the Land Code was passed (not necessarily came into effect) in 1970, and the measure was the 994th one voted on by the Swedish Parliament in 1970. An act can be amended after its adoption, but this generally will not be reflected in the title of the act or its SFS number, unless the amendments are considered so extensive that the act is given a new SFS number. Instead, the paragraph or section as amended will have an SFS number at the end of that paragraph or section, respectively, indicating the year of the enactment of the amendment and its chronological order.

Agency regulations are published by their respective agency according to the agency's internal designations. Most agency regulations are available through the Internet today. Examples of agency regulations are those published by the Work Environment Authority under the designation AFS, which can be ordered from the agency or downloaded as PDF files from its website at av.se. Another example is the regulations as issued by the Tax Authority, under the designation SKVFS which can also be downloaded from its site at skatteverket.se.

Several statutory compilations are privately published annually. The most well-known of these, THE LAWS OF THE REALM OF SWEDEN (*Sveriges Rikes Lag*), first published in 1861, has three main sections. The first section contains the Swedish constitution and the European Union treaties. The second section is divided into the individual codes (*balkar*). These codes follow an order loosely mirroring the course of the life of an individual. The first code is the Marriage Code (*äktenskapsbalk*), followed by the Parental Code (*föräldrabalk*), the Inheritance Code (*ärvdabalk*) and then the Land Code (*jordabalk*), the Environmental Code (*miljöbalk*) and the Town Land Use Code (*byggningabalk*). After the individual has married, started a family, inherited her parent's land and built a house, she goes into trade. The next codes concern going into business, the Commerce Code (*handelsbalk*), followed by the Penal Code (*brottsbalk*), the Code of Judicial Procedure

---

38 Two useful free resources in Swedish for Swedish statutes and legislative history are the websites notisum.se and lagen.nu.

(*rättegångsbalk*) and ending with the Execution [of Judgments and Debts] Code (*utsökningsbalk*), a somewhat jaundiced view of an individual's life ending in crime and bankruptcy. Parts of the 1734 Code are still valid law and are contained within several of the above codes. The third section (*bihanget*) of the compilation is an assortment of statutes chosen for their topicality and presented in chronological order, with the first one dating from 1904.

Legislative Preparatory Works

The legislative preparatory works, *travaux préparatoires,* have a high degree of authority in the Swedish legal system. In certain areas, the authority of the legislative preparatory works is almost as high as the legislation itself, at least in reality if not in theory. The detail lacking in the statutory language is often supplied by the legislative preparatory works.

If a question is not answered in the text of the legislation, the court will often check whether the issue was addressed in the legislative preparatory works. An example that can be mentioned here is the definition of "employee" under the employment legislation. The Employment Protection Act does not include a definition of "employee" in its text. The Labor Court has relied in its cases instead on a definition of employee as set out in a 1975 Government Inquiry Report when faced with the issue of determining whether an individual is an employee or independent contractor.[39]

The dignity of a specific legislative preparatory work is a reflection of both the stage in the legislative process at which the work was generated, as well as the author of the work. The legislative process is begun by a motion made by a political party, parliamentary member or the Government as to enacting legislation. The Government drafts a mandate (*kommittédirektiv*) that is then given to a ministry (*departement*) or an *ad hoc* committee of persons deemed to be experts in the field. A report is generated, either a ministerial report (*departementspromemoria*) or an inquiry report (*Statens offentliga utredningar,* SOU) including proposed legislation.[40] The report is submitted

---

39 *See* AD 1982 no. 172 *citing* Government Report 1975:1, in particular at 722–723.

40 The more recent government inquiries are available as pdf-files at the website of the Government Offices of Sweden. Almost all government inquiries now have English summaries for those persons interested in current Swedish legislative issues.

back to the Government, which then sends the report to institutions and organizations for comment (*remiss*), chosen either for their expertise or connection to the topic. Comments are sent back to the Ministry, which then assesses any comments, makes any perceived necessary adjustments, and sends its report to the Government.

The Government then sends the proposal to the Council on Legislation (*lagrådsremiss*), which submits its comments to the Government. The Government makes any necessary adjustments and then submits a legislative bill (*proposition*) to the responsible parliamentary standing committee (*utskott*),[41] which issues a report (*utskottsbetänkande*). The parliamentary committee either accepts the proposal or makes amendments to it, and then submits it to the Parliament. The Parliament then votes on the legislative bill. If passed, the act is published in SFS.

This significant reliance on legislative preparatory works is facilitated by the fact that most of the documents generated in this process have been published and easily accessible in many public libraries since the mid-1800's. In addition, many of the legislative preparatory documents are now freely accessible at the Parliament's website at riksdagen.se or the Government's website at regeringen.se. As seen from this procedure, reliance on the legislative preparatory works raises certain democratic issues, as the Parliament (legislator) votes only on the legislative text, and not on the commentaries and different documents generated during the process. This aspect of a democratic deficit has long been seen as one of the reasons for the English exclusionary rule with respect to legislative preparatory works.

Under the Swedish system, the legislative bill and the opinions of the standing committees are the documents nearest in time to the actual legislation and usually given great significance. However, in certain

---

41 The names of the parliamentary standing committees are officially abbreviated as follows:

AU	Labor Market	MJU	Environmental and Agricultural
CU	Private Law	NU	Industry and Trade
FiU	Finance	SfU	Social Insurance
FöU	Defense	SkU	Taxation
JuU	Justice	SoU	Health and Welfare
KrU	Cultural Affairs	TU	Transportation
KU	Constitution	UbU	Education
		UU	Foreign Affairs

3 Either a ministerial report
(*departementspromemoria*)
or inquiry report (SOU)
is generated including
proposed legislation.

4 Government
circulates report for
comment (*remiss*).

2 Government drafts a
mandate (*kommittédirektiv*)
which is then given to a
ministry (*departement*)
or an ad hoc committee
of experts.

5 Comments (*yttrande*)
submitted to the
Government which makes
appropriate changes.

1 Motion for legislation
made by a political party,
a parliamentary member
or the Government.

6 Government sends
proposed bill to the Council
on Legislation (*lagrådet*)
if deemed necessary for
comment and appropriate
adjustments then made
by the Government.

10 The Government issues
the law if passed which is
then published in SFS.
The Government can also
issue regulations
(*förordningar*) as to enactment
of the legislation.

7 Government submits
Legislative Bill (*proposition*)
to appropriate standing
parliamentary committee
(utskott) for its report
(*utskottsbetänkande*).

9 The Parliament
votes on the bill
(*riksdagskrivelse*)

8 Parliamentary Committee
(*riksdagsutskottet*) approves
the bill for vote as is or
makes amendments and then
submits the bill to the Parliament

DIAGRAM 1.2 The Legislative Process.

situations, comments written by a legal scholar in the field addressing a specific topic within their expertise can be deemed to have great weight. There is no fixed order by which the legislative works are to be relied upon by the courts, and the courts are fairly free to pick and choose, even to the point of relying on legislative preparatory works for repealed legislation when the legislative preparatory works for the current legislation contain no direct answer. For example, the Labor Court in certain cases has relied on the legislative preparatory works to the 1974 Employment Protection Act when the preparatory works for the 1982 Employment Protection Act did not specifically address the issues in the case.[42]

---

42 *See, for example*, AD 2000 no. 26.

Case Law

Given the tendency towards broad statutory language, reliance on legislative preparatory works at times can be perceived to be a necessity by the courts. It must be kept in mind, though, that this still is a question of legislative preparatory works as recognized by the courts in their judgments. This entails that case law in reality is extremely important. In addition, certain areas of Swedish law are almost entirely regulated by case law with few statutory provisions, such as standards of negligence in tort. There is no strict requirement that a court must follow case law such as in the English legal system with *stare decisis*. The practice, however, is that the lower courts typically follow the decisions of the higher courts. The fallout of this less than strict requirement of *stare decisis* is that Swedish lawyers do not often perceive the same need to make sharp distinctions in the cases between the *ratio decidendi* or holding of a case, and that which is simply *obiter dictum* or dictum as stated by a court.[43]

The effects of the Europeanization of the legal systems are also palpably felt here. As example, the Supreme Court in a 2010 case, NJA 2010 p. 168, found that the Swedish tax penalty (*skattetillägg*), which can be assessed and the taxpayer then criminally tried and sanctioned again with imprisonment and fines, was not in violation of the protections against double jeopardy (*ne bis in idem*) found in Article Six of the European Convention on Human Rights. Several of the trial courts refused to follow this decision by the Supreme Court, and in 2010 the Haparanda trial court sent the question to the EU Court of Justice for a preliminary ruling on the question in Case C-617/10, *Hans Åkerberg Fransson*. The Court of Justice heard the case in January 2012 in Grand Chambers. This type of questioning by a trial court of a Swedish Supreme Court decision was basically unheard of even twenty years ago .

As discussed above in Section 1.3 and in further detail in the subsequent Chapters Four and Six, there are two parallel court systems in Sweden, the general courts and the administrative courts, along with several specialized courts. The general courts consist of the trial courts, courts of appeal and the

---

43 *See, for example*, Hans-Heinrich Vogel, *Sources of Swedish Law* in Michael Bogdan, ed., SWEDISH LEGAL SYSTEM (Norstedts Juridik 2010) at 34.

Supreme Court. The decisions of the Supreme Court (*Högsta domstolen*) have been published in a series entitled *Nytt Juridiskt Arkiv* ("NJA") since 1874. The cases are referred to by year and volume page number, not by case number and almost never by the names of the parties. A complete citation to a case decided by the Supreme Court consequently is simply NJA 2005 p. 462, which is a case decided in 2005 and found in the volume for the year 2005 starting on page 462. Note that even though each case in NJA has a reference number, this reference number is not used in the proper citation of the case, but only for the less important decisions that are mentioned as notes at the end of the reporter. The cases of the courts of appeal are not published as a rule, but certain decisions are published in the reporter, *Rättsfall från hovrätterna* ("RH"). Some cases of the courts of appeal are published on-line.[44] Decisions by trial courts are not published in any series but occasionally are available through an on-line service.

The administrative courts comprise the administrative district courts, the administrative courts of appeals and the Supreme Administrative Court. The decisions of the Supreme Administrative Court are as of 2010 published in the series, *Högsta förvaltningsdomstolens årsbok* ("HFD", formerly *Regerings-rättens årsbok*/RÅ), by year of decision and reference (not page) number. A typical modern citation for a decision by the Supreme Administrative Court is HFD 2011 ref. 73. Decisions by the administrative appellate courts and the administrative district courts are not published, but some cases from the administrative appellate courts are available on-line.

There are two specialized courts in Sweden whose decisions are published as a rule: The Labor Court's decisions are published in the series *Arbetsdom-stolens domar* ("AD"), beginning in 1929, which was the first active year of that court. The Labor Court's judgments are cited based on year and case number in the reporter, AD, for example, AD 2007 no. 45. The decisions of the Market Court are published in *Marknadsdomstolens avgöranden* ("MD") and cited as MD year and case number, for example, MD 1975:22.

---

44 For example, these decisions, as well as those of the administrative appellate courts, can be found in the on-line service Zeteo.

General Principles of Law

Another legal source is that referred to as general principles of law, or the "unwritten law." These general principles of law function in many ways in the same manner as common law principles. In fact, certain of these principles exist in both civil law and common law systems, such as *pacta sunt servanda* (the contract is to be kept). These principles are not stated in any legislative text explicitly, but are deemed to have been relied upon by the legislator, and consequently the courts, when interpreting certain legal issues. A second example of such a principle is that of unjust enrichment as embedded in the general principles of law, *negotiorum gestio* and *condictio indebiti*. The first, *negotiorum gestio,* allows a party who has provided an unsolicited service to receive compensation for the service under certain circumstances, mostly related to emergency situations. The second, *condictio indebiti*, gives a party who has made payment to a wrong party, or has paid the correct party too much, the right to retrieve the payment or excess, respectively, in most situations.

Custom and Usage

Custom and usage is another source of law within the Swedish hierarchy of legal sources. There are several different types of custom and usage captured in this category. One distinction that can be drawn is between custom and usage in private law, and the routines established by government authorities in public law. As to the latter, the routines can be seen as a source of law to the extent they do not deviate from the statutory texts.

Custom and usage can be established in private law on several different levels: custom and usage generally (*sedvanerätt*), commercially (*handelsbruk*), in a specific sector (*branschpraxis*), or between the parties to a contract (*partspraxis*). However, in contrast to public law, custom and usage can have a dignity in certain areas of law higher than that even of the statutory text. This is evidenced by Section 3 of the Sale of Goods Act, which states that the act is not applicable to the extent anything to the contrary can be seen to follow from the contract, custom and usage between the parties or commercial practices or any other general custom and usage that can be seen as binding the parties. The simplest way to establish custom and usage in private law is by its incorporation into standard contracts or previous contracts between the parties.

In public law, custom and usage can refer to typical routines or interpretations by a government authority (*myndighetspraxis*). An example of a controversial interpretation by the Social Insurance Agency was denying compensation for treatment provided outside of Sweden when such treatment was not used within Sweden.

Legal Scholarship

The final legal source in this hierarchy is legal scholarship. One can speak here of professor-made law fairly consistent with the German legal tradition. There is no legislation in certain areas of Swedish law and the reliance by the courts on treatises by professors at times is significant.

The legal academic tradition in Sweden has been greatly influenced by German legal academic traditions, as well as by Scandinavian Legal Realism, both of which are reflected not only in the substantive content of the scholarship, but also in the approach taken. Many Swedish legal scholars perceive their task to be similar to that of a master gardener, creating order and pruning a bit where needed, but not encouraging change, as "law" is to be made solely by the legislator.

1.4.2 SCANDINAVIAN LEGAL REALISM

The impact of the political ideology as adopted by the Social Democrats, the predominant ruling political party in Sweden during almost all of the twentieth century, cannot be overexaggerated when assessing Swedish legal institutions and its legal system. Another significant ideological influence on the understanding of the law and its role in Swedish society is Scandinavian Legal Realism, arising during this same period. Legal realism is a theoretical approach to the law that developed separately in the United States and in Scandinavia. An essential tenet of both legal realisms is that all law is made by human beings and, thus, is subject to human foibles, frailties and imperfections. Scandinavian Legal Realism, however, developed in a direction different from that of its American counterpart, rejecting the concept of natural law, arguing that legal concepts and terminology should be based on experience, observation and experimentation and thus, be "real."

Professor Axel Hägerström (1868–1939) of the Department of Philosophy at Uppsala University started the Uppsala School of Legal Theory and is seen as a forefather to Scandinavian Legal Realism. Professor Hägerström, and later Danish Philosopher and Jurist Alf Ross (1899–1980), had the objectives of eradicating the distorting influences of metaphysics from legal thinking and building a stable philosophical foundation for a scientific knowledge of the law separate and distinct from morals. Hägerström and Ross rejected natural law tenets such as "rights" and "duties," arguing that they basically are meaningless as they cannot be scientifically verified or proven.[45] The object of legal scholarship is "legal science."

Ross expressed this sentiment in his book, ON LAW AND JUSTICE: "The legal rule is neither true nor false; it is a directive [for judges]."[46] As to natural law, Ross stated:

> Like a harlot, natural law is at the disposal of everyone. The ideology does not exist that cannot be defended by an appeal to the law of nature. And, indeed, how can it be otherwise, since the ultimate basis for every natural right lies in a private direct insight, an evident contemplation, an intuition. Cannot my intuition be just as good as yours? Evidence as a criterion of truth explains the utterly arbitrary character of the metaphysical assertions. It raises them up above any force of inter-subjective control and opens the door wide to unrestricted invention and dogmatics.[47]

Scandinavian legal realism has influenced the legal education, thinking and research conducted in Sweden since its inception. Teaching at Swedish law faculties historically has been focused on the positivistic study of the physical law, *de lege lata*, while the study of the philosophy of law and the social function of law, *de lege ferenda*, has been more limited. The focus of the legal education traditionally has been to train judges, to equip them as technicians with specialist knowledge of legal documents and interpreting the intent of

---

45 *See* Alf Ross, *Tû-Tû*, 70 Harv.L.Rev. 812 (1957).
46 *See* Ross, ON LAW AND JUSTICE (1959) at 2.
47 Ibid. at 261.

the legislator. The study of law as within society falls outside legal science and historically has been relegated to a large extent to other academic disciplines, such as philosophy, history, sociology, political science and economics. In many legal debates spanning such issues, a common rebuttal is that the argument presented is not law, but rather legal sociology, legal policy, legal history, etc., the death knell to its validity from a legal scientific perspective.[48]

1.5 The Education and Regulation of Lawyers

There is no monopoly of a legal bar in Sweden, entailing that the title of lawyer (*jurist*) is not protected. Any individual wishing to provide legal advice may do so even without having undergone any legal education. However, most practicing lawyers have law degrees. Students begin the study of law directly at university and receive a Master of Laws (*juris kandidat*), LL.M., after four and one-half years of law studies. One-half of the students studying law in Sweden have been women for well over the past decade, with 53 % in 1997 and 61 % in 2007 women.[49] Approximately 17 % of the partners in law firms in Sweden are women, while associates are 57 % women (2010).

Despite the absence of a monopoly, there is a bar association in Sweden, the Swedish Bar Association (*Sveriges advokatsamfund*),[50] founded in 1887 and today having approximately 4 400 members, of which twenty-five percent are women. Members in good standing with the Swedish Bar Association

---

48 For this description, *see* Göran Skogh, *Law and Economics in Sweden,* ENCYCLOPEDIA OF LAW AND ECONOMICS (Edward Elgar Publishing 2000) at 371. For more on Scandinavian Legal Realism, *see* Jes Bjarup, *Scandinavian Realism* available at the website of the International Association for Philosophy of Law and Social Philosophy (IVR) Encyclopaedia of Jurisprudence, Legal Theory and Philosophy of Law at ivr-enc.info. *See also* Patricia Mindus, A REAL MIND: THE LIFE AND WORK OF AXEL HÄGERSTRÖM (Springer 2009) and Max Lyles, A CALL FOR SCIENTIFIC PURITY: AXEL HÄGERSTRÖM'S CRITIQUE OF LEGAL SCIENCE (Stockholm 2006).

49 This statistic is available at the website of the women's group, Hilda, within the Swedish Bar Association at advokatsamfundet.se.

50 The Bar Association is regulated by Chapter Eight of the Code of Judicial Procedure and also by the Bar's Charter as ratified by the Government, most recently amended in 2003. For more information in English on the Swedish Bar Association, *see* its website at advokatsamfundet.se. English translations of Chapter Eight of the Code of Judicial Procedure, the Charter of the Swedish Bar Association and the Code of Conduct for Members of the Swedish Bar Association are available at its website.

have the privilege of using the title *advokat*, translated in this work as licensed attorney. The use of the title *advokat* without being a member of the Bar Association is a criminal offense. Certain legal advisors must be licensed attorneys as required by law. These include bankruptcy trustees, public defenders and supervising legal counsel as paid for by the state to victims of crimes (*målsägandebiträde*).

To become admitted to the Swedish Bar Association, the applicant under JP 8:2[51] must:

1   Be domiciled in Sweden or another state in the European Union, the European Economic Area or Switzerland;
2   Have passed the examinations prescribed to qualify for appointment as a judge, in Sweden it is the Masters of Law (*juris kandidat*);
3   Have completed the practical and theoretical training of at least three years necessary to practice as a Member of the Bar Association;
4   Have gone through the course for and passed the bar examination as given by the Bar Association;
5   Have established a reputation as a person of integrity; and
6   Be considered in general suitable to practice as a Member of the Bar Association.

Certain exceptions can be granted with respect to these requirements. On the European Union law level, two directives have had an impact as to membership requirements, Council Directive 89/48/EEC on a general system for the recognition of higher-education diplomas awarded on completion of professional education and training of at least three years duration, and Directive 98/5/EC of the European Parliament and of the Council to facilitate the practice of the profession of lawyer on a permanent basis in a Member State other than that in which the qualification was obtained, the "Establishment Directive." These have generally meant that an individual fulfilling either the education or experience requirements necessary in her Member State

---

51 The citation system used here is reference first by chapter then section. For example, JP 8:9 is the ninth section of the eighth chapter of the Code of Judicial Procedure. If the sections are not renumbered with each chapter, or if there are no chapters in the act or ordinance, reference is then made simply to the section, such as Section 5 of the Contracts Act.

to become a bar association member there is also to be seen as fulfilling the comparable requirements in Sweden if she can prove knowledge of Swedish law. A registration process is also available under which an Advocate from another EU country, who has registered with the Bar Association and worked continuously for three years in Sweden, can apply to become a member.

As to suitability, a person who is declared bankrupt, under a guardianship, barred from acting as counsel due to a past criminal history or for providing legal advice in the assistance of a criminal act, cannot become a member of the Bar Association. A denial of membership can be appealed to the Supreme Court.

Professional judges, court officers, public prosecutors and bailiffs may not be members of the Bar Association. Neither may a person working for an individual who is not a member of the bar association become a member unless an exemption is granted. Consequently, in-house counsel, or attorneys working for accounting firms, as a rule, cannot be members of the Bar Association. Law professors are also typically not members. A member is also prohibited from entering into a partnership with a person who is not a member.

The public functions performed by the Bar Association include setting membership requirements and deciding admissions, supervising and taking disciplinary actions against members. The Bar Association has a body of decisions in which certain duties and ethical obligations have been developed. The most important duties are those of loyalty to the client, observing professional independence, and confidentiality. There is also a general duty for members to practice law in accordance with the general standards developed by the Bar Association (*god advokatsed*).[52]

Based on the principles developed in its decisions, the Bar Association has issued ethical rules of conduct as to certain topics, for example in relation to clients, courts and opposing parties, Rules for Attorney Practice (*Regler för advokatverksamhet*), the most recent version from 2011. A compilation of the decisions by the disciplinary board of the Bar Association was also issued in 2010, *Advokatetik – en praxis genomgång*. Sanctions for violations of the rules include issuing statements, warnings, a warning combined with a fine,

---

52 These guidelines, *Vägledande regler om god advokatsed* (2010), are available in Swedish at the website of the Swedish Bar Association at advokatsamfundet.se.

temporary revocation of membership or permanent disbarment. Fines can be between SEK 1 000 and 50 000. A disciplinary action may not be appealed, with the exception of disbarment, which can be appealed to the Supreme Court. The Chancellor of Justice can request that disciplinary action be taken against a member by the Bar Association. A member who has deliberately committed a wrongful act or omission in practice, or otherwise behaves dishonestly, is to be disbarred. Disbarment does not, however, entail that the individual can no longer practice law, simply that the title *advokat* can no longer be used by that individual.

There is a criminal sanction for providing legal advice used to facilitate a crime. The Act Prohibiting Legal or Financial Advice in Certain Cases (*lag 1985:354 om förbud mot juridiskt eller ekonomiskt biträde i vissa fall*) prohibits giving professional advice or assistance of a legal or financial nature to an individual that can be seen as facilitating a crime not constituting attempt, preparation, conspiracy or complicity. The provision of such advice or assistance can be criminally sanctioned by fines or up to two years of imprisonment. However, the sanction for providing the advice cannot be higher than the criminal sanction for the crime facilitated. A prohibition as to providing legal or financial advice can be issued against such an individual for up to ten years with respect to more serious crimes. The prohibition is to be noted in a register maintained by the Swedish Companies Registration Office (*Bolagsverket*).[53] A person violating the prohibition can be sanctioned by an extension of the prohibition for up to five years, and imprisonment up to a maximum of two years, or fines or both.

---

53 For information on the Swedish Companies Registration Office in English, *see* its website at bolagsverket.se.

CHAPTER 2

Individual Rights under the Constitution

Chapter One above described the institutions of political power, the judiciary and the legal system as set out mainly in the Instrument of Government. This chapter focuses on the exercise of state power with respect to the individual as set out in the constitutional acts, the Instrument of Government, the Freedom of the Press Act, and the Fundamental Law on the Freedom of Expression.

The role of the constitution and the limits of constitutional rights have been renewed topics of debate in Sweden since its membership in the European Union in 1995, particularly in light of the enactment of the European Convention on Human Rights and Fundamental Freedoms ("European Convention") as Swedish legislation effective 1998. This chapter first addresses the individual rights of access to public documents and the freedoms of the press and expression, then goes on to the second chapter of the Instrument of Government delineating individual rights in the form of human rights, ending with the European Convention.

There has been a long constitutional tradition in Sweden with respect to individual rights, at least with respect to limiting the exercise of royal power as against the classes represented in the Parliament. Certain scholars date Swedish constitutional tradition back to Magnus Eriksson's Letter of Proclamation in 1319 (*Frihetsbrev*), which bound the crown to govern by rule of law, assure due process, and allow new taxes to be imposed only after consultation with the Royal Council.[1] The first "Instrument of Government" was drafted in 1634, arguably simply as a safety precaution to allow for a continued

---

1   *See* generally Roger Congleton, IMPROVING DEMOCRACY THROUGH CONSTITUTIONAL REFORM – SOME SWEDISH LESSONS (Springer 2003).

government administration in the absence of Swedish kings during war. The second Instrument of Government in 1719 after the death of King Karl XII marked the beginning of a period lasting until 1772, referred to in Swedish history as the "Age of Liberty" (*frihetstiden*). The power of the King was diminished, giving greater political authority to the central administration and the Parliament. The third Instrument of Government was drafted by the politically strong King Gustav III in 1772, giving greater political power back to the king and marking the end of the Age of Liberty.[2] The fourth Instrument of Government, adopted in 1809 after King Gustavus IV was removed from the throne for losing Finland to Russia, again redistributed the political power. This time the distribution was based more, but not completely, on a separation of power in line with Baron de Montesquieu's political theory, between the King, Parliament, the Supreme Court and the National Bank.[3]

The constitutional protection of freedom of the press in Sweden has also historically reflected the balance of power between the Parliament and king. The first act was adopted in 1766 during the Age of Liberty. The act granted broad protections as to freedom of the press and was one of the oldest, if not the oldest, legislative acts in Western society establishing such freedoms. The 1766 act prohibited censorship and abolished printing licenses as well as established the right of public access to public documents (*offentlighetsprincipen*). The King, after regaining power, repealed the act through the 1772 Instrument of Government. Subsequent acts were passed, again reflecting the balance of power between the Parliament and king, with the 1812 Freedom of Press Act in place until the present act was adopted in 1949.

2.1 Access to Public Documents and Freedom of the Press

Areas that the current Freedom of the Press Act regulates include access to public documents, freedom from censorship, the right to anonymity, the right

---

2   The 1772 Swedish Instrument of Government also encompassed Finland and was not formally replaced in Finland until Finland's first constitutional act, the 1919 Instrument of Government.

3   At this time, justices of the Supreme Court were appointed by the King.

to the production and dissemination of printed material, and offences against these rights as defined under the act. The current act is based on freedom from prior censorship by the state, imposing liability after publication for any abuses of this freedom on those persons designated as responsible under the act.

The rights granted under the Freedom of the Press Act and the Fundamental Law on the Freedom of Expression can only be restricted by another constitutional act, in contrast to many of the rights granted in the second chapter of the Instrument of Government discussed below, which in certain cases can be restricted by a simple majority of the Parliament. However, the right to access public documents may be limited by a law passed by a simple majority of the Parliament if falling within one of the enumerated categories.

2.1.1 ACCESS TO PUBLIC DOCUMENTS

Public access to government documents became an issue as early as the 18th century, when access to public documents was viewed as a central instrument for checking the activities of political power. Under the current right of public access to government documents, most documents received or generated by a public authority, whether on the municipal, regional or state level, are to be available to individuals without any undue delay. Many see this institution as one of Sweden's strongest contributions to the European Union as seen from Regulation 1049/2001 enacted during the Swedish presidency, granting Union citizens and member state residents a right of access to the documents of the European Parliament, Council and Commission.

The right of access to public documents can be restricted by law under Article 2 of the second chapter of the Freedom of the Press Act if necessary with regard to:

- National security or relations with foreign states or international organizations;
- National financial, monetary or foreign exchange policies;
- Inspection, control or other supervisory activities by public authorities;
- Preventing or prosecuting crimes;
- Public economic interests;

- The protection of personal privacy or financial information; or
- The preservation of animal or plant species.[4]

This listing is meant to be exhaustive and Parliament may not legislate restrictions falling outside the scope of this list. Further statutory restrictions based on this listing are found in the Public Access to Information and Secrecy Act (*offentlighets- och sekretesslag* 2009:400).

The Freedom of the Press Act defines those documents that are to be deemed public documents, a delineation necessary to allow government authorities to conduct business without having all drafts and other unfinished documents becoming public prematurely. To be classified a public document, the document must either be received by a government authority or generated by one. If generated, the document does not become public until final or until archived. Consequently, working materials are not to be considered public documents while still works in progress.

Not all documents become accessible to the public, even if they fulfill the requirements of received or generated and final. Certain documents are classified as confidential in accordance with the Public Access to Information and Secrecy Act. Two main types of classifications exist under this system of confidentiality, those documents deemed public which must be individually assessed as to confidentiality, and those documents of a more sensitive nature that are automatically deemed confidential and must be individually assessed as to whether they should be public (*omvänd sekretess*).

The Public Access to Information and Secrecy Act also states that certain legal entities in which a municipality has a controlling interest are also to be seen as authorities with respect to these rights. The same is not true, however, for those legal entities controlled by the state. A necessary consequence of the right of public access is that all public documents received by public authorities are registered in a public register and archived for a certain period of time.

---

4   This last exception is based on the circumstance that as so many statistics are kept in
    Sweden, poachers looking to illegally acquire certain animal or plant species, such as
    rare bird eggs or orchids, could simply find their locations from the public documents.
    This exception was added to deter this type of unlawful conduct. *See* Legislative Bill
    1975/76:160 at 109.

Each public employee presented with a request of access is to make an individual determination as to the confidentiality of that document. In other words, documents are not simply stamped confidential for a period of time after which the document becomes a part of the public domain. Each categorization needs to be reassessed with every request. Consequently, a stamp put on a document classifying it as confidential is only a reminder that the document contains confidentially sensitive information and may be confidential. Confidentiality is limited to a maximum of seventy years and if the information concerns an individual, seventy years after that person's death. If possible, the document is to be produced with all the sensitive information deleted.

When requesting access to a document, the individual requesting the document needs not state her identity or the purpose for which the document is being requested, and is entitled to a copy of the document up to nine pages free of charge. Otherwise, the individual has the right to view the document at the offices of the government authority, or have it copied for a fee as set by law. The person requesting access to a document does not need to provide the document's registration number or name, but must provide sufficient enough information so that the authority can identify the document. If a government authority denies a request of access to a public document, the individual can appeal the denial to the administrative courts. However, parties who are the subjects of the information in the documents have no standing to contest access issues.

2.1.2 FREEDOM OF THE PRESS

Each Swedish citizen is guaranteed freedom of expression including the freedom to disseminate information and express views and opinions through speech, publications or depictions under the first article of the second chapter of the Instrument of Government. Non-citizens mostly have the same constitutional protections in this area. According to the first article of the first chapter of the Freedom of the Press Act, freedom of the press "is understood as the right of every Swedish citizen to publish written materials, without prior hindrance by a public authority or other public body." Any criminal prosecution based on content must be before a court of law and only if the written material "contravenes an express provision of law enacted to preserve public order without suppressing information to the public." In other words, unlawful censorship both prior to and after publishing is prohibited. This freedom from censorship is balanced by the imposition of liability after publication upon disclosed authors or those persons designated as responsible parties under this Act as further discussed below.

Certain statutory limitations with respect to freedom of the press are constitutionally permitted as stated in Article 9 of chapter one in the Freedom of the Press Act. These limitations relate to advertisements concerning alcohol, tobacco, health and the environment, as well as the disclosure by professional credit agencies of private information. Article 10 was added in 1998 prescribing that the protections granted under the act were not applicable to depictions of children in pornographic pictures falling within the definition of a criminal offence. This article was amended in 2010 to better protect children up to the age of eighteen years regardless of sexual development. Commercial messages are also not considered to be covered constitutionally by the right of freedom of speech or expression to the same extent, which is why the Market Court can impose sanctions on commercial actors with respect to certain types of advertising.

Every Swedish citizen or legal person has the right to produce printed materials as set out in the fourth chapter of the Freedom of Press Act. Certain non-citizens are also granted rights, but these can be limited by statute. Any material printed in Sweden is to clearly state the name of the designated responsible party and copies are to be furnished to certain libraries and archives.

Each Swedish citizen has the right to disseminate printed material freely under the sixth chapter of the Act with the exception of the public display or unsolicited mailings of pornography, or the dissemination to minors of printed materials that can be seen as having a detrimental or imperiling effect on the morals of youth.

A distinction is made in the act between periodicals and printed materials. Periodicals published in Sweden are to be published by Swedish citizens or legal persons having a designated responsible editor who is a Swedish citizen domiciled in Sweden as stated in the fifth chapter of the Freedom of the Press Act. In accordance with the Act on Regulations in the Area of Freedom of the Press and Media (*lag 1991:1559 med föreskrifter på tryckfrihetsförordningens och yttrandefrihetsgrundlagens områden*), periodicals published in Sweden may be owned by resident aliens or foreigners with citizenship in a country that is a member of the European Economic Area ("EEA").[5] Such owners do not have, however, constitutional protection under Swedish law. Regardless of the nationality of the owners, certificates of no impediment as to publishing have to be obtained prior to a periodical being published in Sweden.

2.1.3 RIGHT TO ANONYMITY

Certain categories of persons are protected under the Freedom of the Press Act in order to insure freedom of expression, in particular the freedom of public employees to express or disclose information their employers may not want made public (*meddelarfrihet*). The name of the author of a work does not need to be disclosed as guaranteed by Article 1 of the third chapter of the Act. This right of anonymity extends to authors as well as to persons who have communicated information to authors, journalists or editors that is printed, as well as a publisher of printed materials that are not periodicals.

This right of anonymity also results in a duty of non-disclosure by responsible parties as to the identities of these persons. Disclosure of the identity of an author or information source is permitted only if the person communicating the information has consented to the disclosure, the information concerns an offence against the Freedom of Press Act, or if disclosure is deemed to be of exceptional significance by a court. There is also an incumbent duty placed on authorities under the fourth section of the third chapter to not investigate the source of information that the authority preferred not to be made public except to the extent required to prosecute crimes under the Act as well as not to retaliate for any disclosures made. Unlawful disclosure of an identity, unlawful intentional investigation of identity or sources or other unlawful measures can result in penal sanctions of up to one-year imprisonment. If anonymity is invoked with respect to publications that are periodicals, the responsible publisher is liable for the

---

5   The European Economic Area ("EEA"), created in 1994, allows Iceland, Liechtenstein and Norway to participate in the EU internal market without EU membership. In exchange, they are obliged to adopt all EU legislation related to the single market, except laws within the fields of agriculture and fisheries.

lawfulness of the publication. If the author chooses to disclose her identity, the author is then responsible.

2.1.4 OFFENCES UNDER THE FREEDOM OF PRESS ACT

The counterbalances to the freedoms given in the Freedom of the Press Act are the criminal offences based on misuses of these freedoms as also defined in the same act. The criminal offences set out in the seventh chapter of the Freedom of Press Act generally fall into four categories:

- Criminal violations against freedom of the press comprising unlawful statements as defined in Article 4, and unlawful public disclosures under Article 5;
- Criminal violations committed by persons other than designated responsible parties according to Article 3;
- Criminal violations of the regulations such as an unlawful disclosures of an identity; and
- Criminal violations committed by public employees.

Damages can only be awarded under the Freedom of Press Act for the crimes defined by the Act. Offences against freedom of the press as delineated in Articles 4 and 5 can be tried by a jury, one of the very few types of cases in Sweden in which a jury is used. To be deemed an offence against freedom of the press, the statement or disclosure must fall within the listings in Articles 4 and 5 and also be criminal as defined under a different statute. In addition, those parties designated as responsible under the act are the only ones responsible under these paragraphs. This system of exclusive liability was designed to hold the persons most knowledgeable and also the final actors culpable. The assumption is that with periodicals at least, authors may not be familiar with the regulations under the Act, while the designated persons are held by law to be knowledgeable.

Unlawful statements as defined in Article 4 are mostly crimes against the state, including high treason, instigation, espionage, unauthorized trafficking in confidential information, negligent disclosure of such information, insurrection, treason, betrayal, sedition, negligence resulting in national harm, and the dissemination of false information jeopardizing national security. Another category of acts included in Article 4 are crimes against public order, such as incitement, threats against minority groups, crimes against civil liberties and unlawful depictions of violence. Other crimes listed in the article include defamation, insult, unlawful threats, threats against public servants and obstruction of justice.

Unlawful disclosures deemed offences against freedom of the press as defined in Article 5 include the intentional disclosure of a confidential document, the disclosure of information in violation of a duty of confidentiality under the Public Access to Information and Secrecy Act, and the disclosure of information during war or the immediate threat of war. Individuals are seldom convicted under this paragraph, as they need not only to be the party designated as responsible under the Freedom of the Press Act, but also at the same time need to be a public employee receiving documents or information through their public employment.

Despite the system of exclusive liability with respect to the designated responsible parties as to crimes under the Freedom of the Press Act, other parties can be guilty of offences under the Act. These are set out in Article 3. For example, if a person provides information, or assists with a presentation intended to be printed as author or other copyright holder, or as publisher, and either commits a certain type of crime such as high treason, unlawfully discloses a public document or intentionally violates a duty of confidentiality, this is seen as an offence under Article 3. The crimes listed in the first paragraph of Article 3 include high treason, espionage, aggravated espionage, aggravated unauthorized access to confidential information, insurrection, unlawful possession of information, riot, treason or betrayal of country, or any attempt, preparation or conspiracy to such a crime. The second paragraph names the intentional unlawful release of public documents not generally accessible or in violation of a public agency's decision. The third paragraph addresses the intentional failure to follow a duty of confidentiality as prescribed by law. The double requisite also exists here, the act has to fall within the scope of Article 3 and also has to be defined as a crime or unlawful by other legislation.

The third category of crimes under the act encompasses crimes other than those against freedom of the press. These crimes are violations of other statutory regulations, entailing that parties other than those designated as responsible can be held liable for the actions. Included in this category are the unlawful disclosures of sources and the failure to include sources of origin, to acquire a certificate of publication or to provide archive copies.

The final fourth category of crimes under the Freedom of the Press Act includes crimes committed by public servants including censorship, obstructing an informer's access to the media, impermissible inquiry as to an informer's protected identity, and the refusal to respect or the obstruction of the public right of access to public documents.

2.2 The Fundamental Law on Freedom of Expression

The Fundamental Law on Freedom of Expression concerns freedom of expression in media other than print. It is the most recent of the constitutional acts, intended to mirror the Freedom of Press Act in most ways, including those acts seen as offences, simply expanding the media addressed. Every Swedish citizen is guaranteed the right as against the public authorities to publicly express thoughts, views and sentiments "on sound radio, television and certain similar transmissions, public displays of materials from a database, and in films, video recordings, sound recordings and other technical recordings" in the furtherance of the free exchange of opinions, information and artistic creation under the first article of the first chapter. The following media are deemed to be encompassed by this definition: TV and radio programs, films and video films, compact discs and sound recordings, computer discs and computer games, Internet newscasts, mass mailings by e-mail, databases used for print on demand processes and web broadcasts initiated by the sender.

The Fundamental Law on Freedom of Expression shares much of the same construction as the Freedom of the Press Act, including the right to expression, the right to anonymity, prohibition against censorship, protection for informers, exclusive liability for designated parties, a list of criminal offences and the use of juries.

2.3 Individual Rights and the Instrument of Government

The Instrument of Government adopted in 1974 to replace the one of 1809 was to embody the constitutional changes that had successively occurred during that interim. The 1809 Instrument of Government had long since failed to reflect the realities of Swedish constitutional law. This discrepancy between the reality of the political situation and the marginalization of the outdated Instrument of Government is seen by certain scholars as giving rise to a sort of "anti-constitutionalism." The constitution did not and should not reign in popular sovereignty. Power had been transferred from the King to the Parliament decades previously absent any constitutional basis in a manner inconsistent with the 1809 Instrument of Government.

A second departure consciously taken from the 1809 Instrument of Government was the decision to change the balance of political power from that of separation of power to a separation of function. Parliament is to be the sole legislator as seen from the portal paragraph of the 1974 Instrument of Government: "All public power in Sweden emanates from the people." As a result of this focus on majoritarianism, a comparatively weak court system was created with only limited powers. This is also clear from the fact that the third branch of political power, after the legislative and executive branches, is not generally perceived of as the judicial branch in Sweden, but rather the press.

Article 16 of the 1809 Instrument of Government had actually addressed certain fundamental rights and freedoms, proclaiming that the King should:

[M]aintain and further justice and truth,

[P]revent and forbid inequity and injustice,

[N]ot deprive nor allow any person to be deprived of life, honor, personal liberty or well-being without a lawful trial or sentence, and

[That] no person [should] be deprived of property, whether chattels or real, without a warrant and judgment in the manner as prescribed by Swedish law,

[T]hat no person's peace should be disturbed in his home,

[T]hat no person should be extradited from one place to another,

[T]hat no person should be forced to act in violation of his conscience but rather be protected and able to freely exercise his religion as long as he did not disturb the public peace or cause public disturbance.

The King was also to ensure that every person sentenced was judged by a court having jurisdiction over that person. This article, and the rights therein contained, had roots extending back to Magnus Eriksson's Letter of Proclamation in 1319, evidencing a fairly unbroken constitutional tradition as to certain individual rights of over six hundred years.

2.3.1 THE 1974 INSTRUMENT OF GOVERNMENT

A parliamentary committee was appointed in 1938 to oversee Article 16, but its findings were not acted upon in the direct aftermath of World War II. A new committee was charged with modernizing the constitution as a whole, but its 1963 proposal including a separate chapter on fundamental rights was criticized. A new committee was formed in 1966, first presenting a proposal that did not include a separate chapter on fundamental rights and freedoms. The predominant political view, much in line with a communitarian approach to law, was that such rights and freedoms were unnecessary in a welfare state. This omission was also criticized, and the Government was forced to include a separate chapter addressing individual rights. The draft was adopted in 1974 and the rights expanded already by 1976.

The role of the rights as cataloged in chapter two, however, was greatly debated in certain circles. Those legal scholars in favor of a weak judicial system argued that chapter two rights should be more of a policy declaration as were certain of the rights in chapter one, and not meant to serve as any legal basis for a remedy. Instead, the chapter two rights should be deemed to serve as guidelines for the Parliament in its legislative work, this view giving precedence to the principles of parliamentary rule and popular sovereignty. Others envisioned chapter two rights as created for the protection of individuals at the behest of individual. These different views are reflected in the legislative preparatory documents for the 1974 constitution. The emphasis in the final second chapter as to limiting the rights therein contained, embodies the compromise finally reached. The absence in general of any separation of powers or any restrictions on political power, for example in the form of judicial review, also reinforces this compromise.

More recently, a greater recognition of human rights can be seen as emerging in the case law, arguably due to the requirements of European law. Significant amendments were made to the Instrument of Government in 2010, for the purposes of modernizing the Instrument of Government, as well as simplifying its language and making it in general more accessible. The chapter two rights were amended for the purpose of further strengthening and clarifying the individual's protections against violations of freedoms and rights.

The rights as enumerated in the second chapter of the Instrument of Government are not based on an understanding of absolute rights independent of state authority, but rather of rights as granted by state authority within the Constitution and only to the extent as laid down by it.[6] Individual rights are primarily dealt with in the first two chapters of the Instrument of Government.

These rights are expressed as either positive or negative rights.[7] Under the theory of positive and negative rights, a negative right is a right not to be subjected to an action by another human being, or group of individuals, such as a state, usually in the form of abuse or coercion. A positive right is a right to be provided with something through the action of another person or the state. In theory a negative right forbids certain actions, while a positive right requires certain actions.

The first chapter of the Instrument of Government sets out several positive rights, establishing that the public power is to be exercised with respect to the equal worth of all persons and for the freedom and dignity of the individual. It goes on to state that public authority should particularly safeguard the rights to work, housing and education, as well as promote social welfare, security and a good living environment with a particularly focus on environmental sustainability. Democracy is to guide the community, and each individual is to be able to participate in society with the right to not be unlawfully discriminated against on the basis of sex, color, national or ethnic origins, language, religion, disability, sexual orientation, age or other circumstances.

---

6   For this discussion, *see* Elizabeth Palm, *Human Rights in Sweden* in Hugo Tiberg, et al., SWEDISH LAW – A SURVEY (Juristförlaget 1994) at 62.

7   This designation between positive and negative rights is invoked in public international law under a three generational theory as first proposed by Karel Vasak in the 1970's, based loosely on the French constitutional principles of liberty, equality and fraternity. First generation rights are traditional or negative rights, such as freedom of the press. Second generation rights are positive rights in that the state has to act to secure them, such as a right to education or housing. The third generation of rights is group rights, such as the right to recognition of a language or a cultural heritage.

The rights of children are to be respected. The Sami people[8] specifically, as well as other ethnic, linguistic and/or religious minorities, are to be given the opportunity to retain and develop their own cultures and communities. These individual rights as stated in the first chapter, however, are explicitly not viewed as binding with the exception of the equal treatment principle and the protection of local government.[9]

2.3.2 CHAPTER TWO RIGHTS

The rights and freedoms granted in chapter two concern the relationship between the individual and the state, with the exception of Article 14 as discussed at the end of this section found by the Labor Court to be applicable between the social partners. The applicability of the other chapter two rights as between two private parties, referred to in German as *Drittwirkung,* has not yet been resolved by the Swedish courts.

The articles in chapter two can be seen as in two main groupings: the individual rights of Swedish citizens and non-citizens, the restriction of the rights of Swedish citizens and non-citizens. The rights as granted under chapter two can be loosely arranged within four groupings: intellectual freedoms, physical freedoms, legal rights, and property rights.

Intellectual Freedoms

According to Article 1, every individual (regardless of citizenship) is to be guaranteed the following rights and freedoms in relation to public institutions:

---

8   This is a strengthening under the 2010 amendments from the previous wording of "ought to be given." For information about the Sami people in English, see the Sami Information Center at eng.samer.se. The Sami Parliament (Sametinget) website is at sametinget.se, the Swedish Sami National Organization ("SSR") at sapmi.se and the Sami party at samerna.se.

9   See Joakim Nergelius, *Constitutional Law* in Michael Bogdan (ed.), SWEDISH LEGAL SYSTEM (Norstedts Juridik 2010) at 42.

TABLE 2.1 Instrument of Government Chapter Two Rights.

I. Individual Rights

Intellectual Freedom

Art. 1(1) Freedom of Expression*	Art. 1(5) Freedom of Association*
Art. 1(2) Freedom of Information*	Art. 1(6) Freedom of Religion
Art. 1(3) Freedom of Assembly*	Art. 18 Right to a Public Primary Education,
Art. 1(4) Freedom of Demonstration*	Academic Freedom

Physical Freedoms

Art. 2 Freedom from Coercion as to Divulging Opinions	Art. 6 Prohibition against Searches of Persons, Houses or Correspondence*
Art. 3 Freedom from being Registered without Consent Based only on Political Opinion**	Art. 7 Prohibition against Deportation**
Art. 4 Prohibition against the Death Penalty	Art. 8 Prohibition against Unlawful Incarceration* and Right to Move Freely**
Art. 5 Prohibition against Corporal Punishment, Torture and Medical Procedures to Obtain Information	

Legal Rights

Art. 9 Right to a Judicial Hearing without Delay as to Incarceration	Art. 13 Prohibition as to Laws that Discriminate on the Basis of Sex unless to achieve equality or with respect to the military
Art. 10 Prohibition as to Retroactive Application of Penal and Tax Laws	Art. 19 Prohibition as to Any Law in Conflict with the European Convention.
Art. 11 Prohibition as to Courts Established only for One Case. Judicial Proceedings are to be Public (*)	
Art. 12 Prohibition as to Laws that Discriminate on the Basis of Ethnic Origins, Color or Similar Circumstance, or Sexual Orientation	

Property Rights

Art. 14 Right to Take Industrial Action	Art. 16 Right to intellectual property of authors, artists and photographers
Art. 15 Right to Compensation and Lawful Expropriation	Art. 17 Limitations in Commerce only Lawful to Protect the Public. Sami's right to reindeer herding also protected.

II. Restrictions as to Individual Rights

Art. 20 Rights that Can Be Restricted by Law*	Art. 24 Restrictions as to Freedom of Assembly and Demonstration
Art. 23 Restrictions as to Freedom of Expression and to Information	

III. Individual Rights and Non-Swedish Citizens

Art. 25 Restricting the Rights of Non-Swedish Citizens.

* Those rights that can be limited by law under Article 25 as discussed below with respect to non-Swedish citizens.
** Those rights accruing only to Swedish citizens.

1   Freedom of expression including the freedom to disseminate
    information and express thoughts, opinions and views, whether orally,
    pictorially, in writing, or in any other way;
2   Freedom of information including the freedom to obtain and receive
    information and otherwise have access to public statements made by
    other individuals;
3   Freedom of assembly including the freedom to organize and attend
    meetings for the purposes of disseminating information or expressing
    views or for any other similar purpose, or for the purpose of presenting
    artistic works;
4   Freedom to demonstrate including the freedom to organize and take
    part in public demonstrations;
5   Freedom of association including the freedom to associate with others
    for public or private purposes; and
6   Freedom of religion including the freedom to practice a religion alone
    or in the company of others.

These freedoms are deemed to form the basis for the democratic cornerstone
of public awareness. All children encompassed by a requirement of
compulsory schooling are entitled under Article 18 to free primary education
at a public school. The public institutions are also responsible for providing
undergraduate and graduate higher education. Academic freedom is also
protected under this Article.

Physical Freedoms

There are several freedoms expressed within chapter two having to do with
what is termed here as physical freedoms. The first is contained in Article 2,
in that no individual, in relation to public institutions, is to be coerced into
divulging an opinion in a political, religious, cultural or similar context.
Individuals are also protected from being coerced into participating in
meetings concerning the formation of opinions, demonstrations or other
manifestations of opinion, or to belonging to a political, religious or other
association concerning such opinions.

Public records may not be kept solely on the basis of political opinions
of Swedish citizens without consent as prescribed by Article 3. Every citizen

is to be protected against violations of personal privacy resulting from the registration of personal information by means of automatic data processing.[10]

Capital punishment is prohibited in Article 4 and corporal punishment and torture in Article 5. Every individual is also to be protected under Article 6 against other types of physical violations, as well as against bodily searches, searches of residences and other such invasions of privacy, examinations of mail or other confidential correspondence, and against eavesdropping and recordings of telephone conversations or other confidential communications. In addition, the individual is to be protected as against the state with respect to significant incursions in personal privacy if such occur without consent and entail the monitoring or surveying of the individual's personal circumstances.

No Swedish citizen may be deported from or refused entry into Sweden as stated in Article 7. Nor may a Swedish citizen who is or has previously been domiciled in Sweden be deprived of citizenship unless she, at the same time, becomes a citizen of another state, either through her own express consent or due to employment in public service. Despite this protection, children under the age of eighteen can be required to have the same nationality as one or both parents. A person born a dual citizen and permanently domiciled in another country can by statute be deemed to forfeit Swedish citizenship at or after the age of eighteen years unless she applies for a continuation of her citizenship.

Every individual is protected from unlawful deprivations of personal liberty under Article 8. Swedish citizens are guaranteed freedom of movement within Sweden including the right to leave the country. In the event a public authority other than a court of law has deprived an individual of her liberty on account of a criminal act or suspicion of having committed a crime, she is entitled to have the matter examined by a court of law without undue delay under Article 9. This right does not include, however, the enforcement by Sweden of a penal sanction involving deprivation of liberty as imposed by another state. If taken forcibly into custody for reasons other than a crime or suspicion of a crime, the individual is likewise entitled to have the matter

---

10 This right is more explicitly regulated in the Personal Data Privacy Act (*person-uppgiftslag* 1998:204), based on Directive 95/46/EC. An English translation of this act is available at the website of the Data Inspection Board at datainspektionen.se/in-english/legislation.

examined without undue delay by a court of law or a comparable tribunal as chaired by a permanent judge.

Legal Rights

Certain legal rights are guaranteed under chapter two. Every individual is protected against the retroactive application of criminal and tax laws and sanctions in Article 10. The Parliament has the power to levy taxes or charges retroactively where the Government, or a committee of the Parliament, had already submitted a proposal to this effect to the Parliament at the time of the levy.

Article 11 prohibits the formation of courts of laws or tribunals based on acts already committed, or for a particular dispute or otherwise for a particular case. Article 11 also mandates that all proceedings in courts of law be fair and held within a reasonable time, as well as open to the public.[11]

Article 12 contains a prohibition against the unfavorable treatment of individuals belonging to a minority group by reason of ethnic origins, color or similar circumstance, or with respect to sexual orientation. Article 13 prohibits the same with respect to sex, with an exception for efforts to promote equality between men and women or acts relating to compulsory military service or other similar official duties unless for affirmative action reasons.

Article 19 prohibits the enactment of any laws or regulations in violation of the rights as granted under the European Convention.

Property Rights

There are also several protections with respect to property and/or commercial rights. Under Article 14, labor unions, employers and employer associations are entitled to take industrial action unless provided otherwise by an act of law or a collective agreement. The Swedish Labor Court has rigorously upheld this right. In contrast, the right of association to belong to a labor union has been only applied historically to the positive right of association by the Labor

---

11   This is the main rule. However, certain proceedings, such as those concerning sexual crimes and particularly those committed against children, can be held in closed chambers in a procedure as set out in JP 5:1.

Court, not encompassing the negative right of association, the right to not belong. Article 14 is addressed further in Chapter Sixteen concerning labor law, but is unique in this catalogue of rights in that it gives constitutional protections as between two private parties.

State limits as to issues of expropriation are set out in Article 15, which prescribes that the property of each individual is to be guaranteed so that no one can be compelled by expropriation or other such taking to surrender property to a public institution or a private subject, or tolerate restrictions by public institutions of the use of land or buildings, other than those necessary to satisfy compelling public interests. A person forced to surrender property by expropriation or other such taking is guaranteed compensation for her loss. Such compensation is also to be guaranteed to any person whose use of the affected land or buildings is restricted by the public institutions in such a manner that it is substantially impaired or harmed significantly in relation to the value of the affected part of the property. Compensation is to be determined according to principles laid down in law.

Article 15 also includes the right for all persons to have access to nature under this article through a right of public access. This right was established by custom already in the Middle Ages and is discussed further in Chapter Eleven below under the presentation concerning real property. Every person is guaranteed access to nature in accordance with the right of public access as balanced against the property owner's right of quiet enjoyment.

Authors, artists and photographers are guaranteed the rights to their works under Article 16 in accordance with statutory regulations. Restrictions affecting the right to a trade or to practice a profession may be introduced as prescribed by Article 17 only in order to protect compelling public interests and never solely to further the economic interests of a particular person or enterprise. The right of the Sami population to practice reindeer husbandry is to be regulated by law.

2.3.3 ABSOLUTE V. QUALIFIED CHAPTER TWO RIGHTS

Certain of the chapter two rights are absolute (*absoluta rättigheter*) in that they cannot be restricted except by an amendment of the Instrument of Government. These absolute rights include freedom of religion, the prohibition against capital punishment and torture, as well as against medically invasive procedures invoked to extort or suppress information. Several are explicitly tied to citizenship. Citizens cannot be deported from Sweden, barred from re-entry or deprived of citizenship except as consistent with the Instrument of Government. Citizens are also to be protected against the registration of their opinions without consent.

Other rights as granted in chapter two are not absolute, in other words, they are qualified rights (*kvalificerade rättigheter*) and can be restricted by legislation as passed by a simple majority of Parliament. These rights generally include freedom of expression, information, assembly, demonstration, association, movement and protections against bodily searches, searches of homes or correspondence.

The designation as qualified rights and the procedure with respect to adopting lawful limitations are set out in Articles 20–24. Certain statutory restrictions of qualified chapter two rights are permitted under Article 20. These are with respect to certain of the rights and freedoms referred to in Article 1, namely freedom of expression, information, assembly, demonstration and association, unlawful searches in Article 6, unlawful deprivation of liberty in Article 8, and public access to judicial proceedings in Article 11. These restrictions can only be to the extent provided for in Articles 20 to 25 as discussed below. These restrictions may only be imposed as prescribed by Article 21 to satisfy a purpose deemed as acceptable in a democratic society. A restriction of a chapter two right is never to go beyond that necessary taking into regard its purpose. Nor may it be carried so far as to constitute a threat to the free formation of opinion, one of the cornerstones of democracy. No restrictions may be imposed based solely on political, religious, cultural or other similar opinions.

The freedoms of expression and information may be restricted under Article 23 taking into account national security, the national supply of goods, public order and public safety, the good name of the individual, the sanctity of private life, and the prevention and prosecution of crimes. Freedom of expression may also be restricted with respect to commercial activities. Otherwise, the freedoms of expression and information may only be restricted for significant reasons. In assessing the extent of the restrictions, particular regard is to be paid to the importance of the widest possible freedom of expression and information in political, religious, professional, scientific and cultural matters. Any statutory provision regulating in detail a specific manner of disseminating or receiving information regardless of content is not to be deemed a restriction of the freedom of expression or information.

The freedoms of assembly and demonstration may be restricted in accordance with Article 24 for the interests of preserving public order and public safety at meetings or demonstrations or to insure traffic flow. These freedoms may otherwise only be restricted with respect to national security or in order to combat epidemics. Freedom of association may be restricted only in respect to organizations whose activities are of a military or quasi-military nature, or whose activities constitute persecution of a group comprising a particular race, color, or ethnic origin.

A proposed legislative bill containing restrictions of a right as enumerated in chapter two can be tabled under Article 22 for a year if so moved by at least ten parliamentary members. The motion to table may be quashed and Parliament may adopt the proposal providing that it has the support of at least five-sixths of those voting.

The right to table a bill containing such restrictions is not applicable to any bill proposing the extension of an already existing act for a period not exceeding two years. This procedure is also not applicable to any bill concerned simply with:

1   A prohibition of the disclosure of matters which have come to a person's knowledge in the public service, or in the performance of official duties, where confidentiality is mandated taking into regard the interests under Article 2 of the second chapter of the Freedom of the Press Act including:
    • National security or relations with foreign states or international organizations;
    • National financial, monetary or foreign exchange policies;
    • Inspection, control or other supervisory activities by public authorities;
    • Preventing or prosecuting crimes;
    • Public economic interests;
    • The protection of personal privacy or financial information; or
    • The preservation of animal or plant species.
2   House searches and similar invasions of privacy; or
3   The deprivation of liberty as a penal sanction for a specific act.

The standing parliamentary constitutional committee has the jurisdiction to determine on behalf of the Parliament whether this procedure is applicable to a specific legislative bill.

2.3.4 NON-CITIZENS AND CHAPTER TWO RIGHTS

Instead of the two categories of rights as created for Swedish citizens, those rights that are absolute and those that are qualified, the rights as set out in the second chapter of the Instrument of Government for non-Swedish citizens are placed into three categories, absolute rights protected to the same degree as for Swedish citizens, qualified rights, and those rights not applicable to non-citizens.

Those rights and freedoms that can be qualified for non-Swedish citizens are set out in Article 25:

1. Freedoms of expression, information, assembly, demonstration, association and religion (Article 1);
2. Protection against being coerced into divulging opinions (Article 2, sentence one);
3. Protection against physical violations in cases other than those involving the death penalty (Article 4), corporal punishment, torture and invasive medical procedures (Article 5), protection against body searches, house searches and other such invasions of privacy, and against violations of confidential communications as well as invasions of privacy due to monitoring or survey of personal information without consent (Article 6);
4. Protection against unlawful deprivations of liberty (Article 8, sentence one);
5. The right to have any deprivation of liberty other than one based on a criminal act or suspicion of a criminal act reviewed by a court of law (Article 9(2) and (3));
6. The right to public court proceedings (Article 11(2));
7. The right of authors, artists and photographers to their works (Article 16);

8   The right to conduct business (Article 17);
9   Protection of academic freedom (Article 18(2)); and
10 Protection against invasions based on political, religious,
    cultural or other such opinions (Article 21).

Restrictions by law of the rights contained in this second category are subject to the parliamentary right to table the proposal for a year if invoked by
ten parliamentary members as set out in Article 22. The motion to table can
be quashed by a qualified majority of five-sixths of the Parliamentary votes.
The right to table cannot be invoked, however, if the proposal concerns an
extension of an already existing law for at the most two years. The standing
parliamentary constitutional committee is also to determine on behalf of
the Parliament whether the right to table is appropriate with respect to the
proposal.

The rights that are absolute for non-citizens can be identified as those
rights and protections in chapter two beginning with "[e]very individual"
(*var och en*). These consequently are not dependent upon citizenship status.
To determine the absolute rights for non-citizens, one has to compare these
rights to those listed above as to rights that can be limited for non-Swedish
citizens. The third category of rights is those rights not available to
non-Swedish citizens. Those rights reserved only for Swedish citizens
begin with a reference to a Swedish citizen in the article. Few protections
are reserved only to citizens after the amendment to the Instrument of
Government in 2010, namely those prohibiting the registration of political
opinions without consent (Article 3), prohibiting deportation (Article 7) and
guaranteeing free movement (Article 8). One of the objectives with the 2010
amendments was to narrow the gap between the article two rights of Swedish
citizens and those of non-citizens.

2.4 The European Convention

The European Convention[12] was signed in Rome in 1950 by the Council of Europe,[13] which Sweden has been a member of since its inception in 1949.[14] Sweden ratified the convention in 1952. The Convention was one of the first concrete human rights conventions in the wake of World War II, drafted almost directly after the 1948 United Nation Universal Declaration of Human Rights. The implementation of the system regarding the protections under the European Convention required two additional acts by the signatories, recognition of the Council's jurisdiction to receive individual applications, which Sweden was the first to do in 1951, and a declaration accepting the jurisdiction of the European Court of Human Rights, which Sweden did not do until 1966. The European Convention did not have effect as Swedish law until 1998.

2.4.1 DUALISM IN SWEDEN

The status of the European Convention upon Sweden's signing was uncertain in Swedish law, as the issue of whether Sweden had a monistic or dualistic system with respect to international obligations was not clear. This issue remained uncertain until two cases presenting claims under the European Convention were decided almost two decades later by the Supreme Court and the Supreme Administrative Court in 1973 and 1974, respectively.[15] These courts ultimately determined that Sweden had a dualistic system, and consequently, individuals could not raise claims under the Convention as it had neither been incorporated nor transformed into Swedish law. These

---

12 For more on the European Convention and Sweden, *see* Iain Cameron, An Introduction to the European Convention on Human Rights (6th ed. Iustus 2011). For more on the Convention and the European Court of Human Rights, *see* the Council's website at echr.coe.int.

13 At that time, the Council of Europe consisted of ten Member States: Belgium, Denmark, France, Ireland, Italy, Luxembourg, Netherlands, Norway, Sweden and the United Kingdom. It now consists of 46 Member States. *See* the Council of Europe website at coe.int.

14 *See* Legislative Bill 1949:214 (*Kungl. Maj:ts proposition till riksdagen angående godkännande av Sveriges anslutning till Europarådet*).

15 *See* NJA 1973 p. 423 and RÅ 1974:121.

judgments, referred to as the "transformation judgments," established the principle that foreign treaties had to be incorporated or transformed into Swedish law before Swedish citizens could cite them as a direct basis for a remedy. Incorporation entails that the international treaty or convention itself must be enacted as Swedish legislation, while transformation entails that the Parliament in some fashion must either translate the document into Swedish or reformulate it to better-fit Swedish law. There is no rule as to which of these two procedures is to be applied at any given point, with the Parliament making that decision on an ad hoc basis.

The 1973 Swedish Supreme Court case also raised an interesting question of interpretation. When Sweden signed the Convention, the legislative preparatory works stated that the parliamentary investigation demonstrated no need for Sweden to amend its laws as Swedish laws were already in conformance with the requirements of the Convention. The Supreme Court, when addressing issues raised under the Convention almost twenty years later in the 1973 case, stated that as Parliament had twenty years ago found Swedish law to be in compliance with the Convention upon signing, Swedish law could not later be found by the Swedish Supreme Court to be in conflict with the requirements of the Convention. This stance by the Supreme Court in essence meant that the Swedish Parliament was to be the ultimate arbitrator as to the content of the Convention, as opposed to the European Court of Human Rights, the institution charged by the Council with this task.

Swedish government agencies originally did not take the obligations under the Convention into consideration when assessing different procedures and regulations, an omission backed up by the opinion of the Parliamentary Ombudsmen that agencies were not required to do so up to the early 1990's.[16] This stance was based on the mistaken assumption by Sweden when ratifying the Convention in 1952 that the civil rights referred to in the Convention referred to private law, rights between private parties, in Swedish *civilrätt*, and not to public law issues.[17]

One of the primary obstacles to acceptance of the European Convention in the Swedish context was the resulting judicial protection of human rights,

---

16 *See* JO ämbetsberättelse 1991/92 p. 153.

17 *See* Cameron (2006) at 90 *citing* Legislative Bill 1990/91:176 at 3 and Olle Mårsäter, FOLKRÄTTSLIGT SKYDD AV RÄTTEN TILL DOMSTOLSPRÖVNING (Uppsala 2005).

placing the power of the courts above that of the Parliament. This was seen primarily by the Social Democrats as a shift away from majoritarianism with its emphasis on the power of the Government and of the democratically elected legislature. The concept of judicial review was also generally controversial in the Swedish legal system, resulting in the system of a limited power by the courts to simply declare a parliamentary act "manifestly" (removed as of 2011) not in compliance with the constitution not applicable to the case at hand.

The Convention was not enacted as Swedish law, a requirement under dualism, until 1994, effective 1998.[18] This enactment of the convention as Swedish legislation was predominantly due to the requirements of pending membership in the European Union set for 1995. The European Convention was not enacted as a constitutional act, but is given protection by Article 19 of the second chapter of the Instrument of Government prescribing that "laws or other provisions may not be adopted which contravene Sweden's undertakings under the European Convention."

The more recent approach to the European Convention by the Swedish courts can be seen in a 2005 case.[19] In that case, a pastor had been criminally prosecuted for hate speech due to denigrating statements he had made regarding homosexuality. He appealed the judgment to the Swedish Supreme Court, claiming that the Swedish law making certain types of speech directed against certain groups criminal as hate speech was in violation of his right to freedom of religion and speech as guaranteed under the European Convention. The Supreme Court, after reviewing the case law of the European Court of Human Rights, found that the Swedish criminal statute did limit the pastor's right to freedom of religion under the European Convention and vacated the criminal judgment.

An unprecedented procedural situation arose recently with respect to the Swedish civil tax penalty. The Swedish Supreme Court, in a 2010

---

18 *See* The Act on the European Convention on Human Rights and Fundamental Freedoms (*lag 1994:1219 om den europeiska konventionen angående skydd för de mänskliga rättigheterna och de grundläggande friheterna*).

19 NJA 2005 p. 805. An English translation is available at the website of the Swedish Supreme Court at www.hogstadomstolen.se/Domstolar/hogstadomstolen/ Avgoranden/2005/Dom_pa_engelska_B_1050-05.pdf.

judgment,[20] was faced with the question whether the Swedish tax penalty was in violation of the protection against double jeopardy as provided by the European Convention. A tax penalty is assessed in cases in which the taxpayer was found by the Tax Authorities to have incorrectly filed taxes. In addition, the taxpayer could be sentenced to criminal penalties in the forms of imprisonment and/or fines for the same behavior. The Swedish Supreme Court reasoned that there was not clear support in the case law of the European Court of Human Rights that the tax penalty was in violation of the prohibition against double jeopardy. Despite this decision by the Supreme Court, the issue was brought again to different trial courts. One of these trial courts sent the question to the Court of Justice for a preliminary decision in 2010, which the Court heard in Grand Chambers at the beginning of 2012.

Regardless of the outcome of the decision by the Court of Justice, this series of cases set up an unprecedented situation in which the trial courts did not follow a judgment of the Swedish Supreme Court but instead sent the issue to the Court of Justice for a final determination. This demonstrates not only that the trial courts are looking to the case law of the European Union courts in their decisions, but also placing a greater emphasis on human rights and the protection of such, even to the extent that it can be seen as an act of judicial defiance.

2.4.2 THE PROTECTIONS UNDER THE EUROPEAN CONVENTION

Another source of individual rights within the Swedish legal system is the European Convention. The European Convention as originally drafted has been strengthened and modernized by the promulgation of protocols, to date fourteen in number, with the most recent from 2004.[21] Forty-seven countries have signed the convention, covering approximately 800 million people. The protections as granted under the European Convention and the protocols are briefly summarized below.

As can be assumed from a cursory reading of the list below, many of the protections in the European Convention and its protocols have not been

---

20 NJA 2010 p. 168.

21 The texts of the Convention and of the Protocols are available at the website of the Council of Europe at conventions.coe.int.

problematic in the Swedish context, particularly with respect to the total prohibition as to capital punishment. The death penalty for civilian crimes was abolished in Sweden in 1921 and for war crimes in 1973. Other articles, however, have posed new challenges to the Swedish legal system and legal thought.

TABLE 2.2 Rights and Freedoms under the European Convention and Protocols.

Rights and Freedoms under the European Convention and Protocols	
The European Convention	
Article 2	Right to life protected by law, death penalty to be imposed in criminal cases by a court
Article 3	Prohibition against torture and inhuman or degrading treatment or punishment
Article 4	Prohibition against slavery, servitude and forced labor
Article 5	Right to liberty and security of person with no person deprived of liberty except by law
Article 6	Right to a fair trial in any civil or criminal case before an independent and impartial tribunal established by law, presumption of innocence until proven guilty
Article 7	No punishment except as imposed by law
Article 8	Right to respect for private and family life
Article 9	Freedom of thought, conscience and religion
Article 10	Freedom of expression
Article 11	Freedom of assembly and association
Article 12	Right to marry
Article 13	Right to an effective remedy under law
Article 14	Prohibition against discrimination
Protocol 1	
Article 1	Protection of property and expropriation by law with due compensation
Article 2	Right to education
Article 3	Right to free elections
Protocol 4	
Article 1	Prohibition against imprisonment for debt
Article 2	Freedom of movement for all persons lawfully within a territory, including the right to leave
Article 3	Prohibition as to deportation of nationals
Article 4	Prohibition as to the collective deportation of non-citizens

Protocol 6	
Article 1	Abolition of the death penalty except in times of war

Protocol 7	
Article 1	Procedural safeguards relating to the deportation of non-citizens
Article 2	Right of appeal in criminal matters to a higher tribunal unless a misdemeanor
Article 3	Compensation for wrongful criminal conviction
Article 4	Prohibition against double jeopardy
Article 5	Equality between spouses

Protocol 12	
Article 1	General prohibition of discrimination, guaranteeing the enjoyment of legal rights without discrimination on any ground such as sex, race, color, language, religion, political or other opinion, national or social origin, association with a national minority, property, birth or other status as well as prohibition against discrimination on these grounds by public authorities

Protocol 13	
Article 1	Abolition of the death penalty in all cases

2.4.3 THE PROTECTIONS IN THE SWEDISH CONTEXT

Upon the Swedish ratification of the convention in 1952, the Parliamentary inquiry found that Sweden fulfilled all the obligations under the convention and that there was no need to amend Swedish law in any respect. This can be seen as reflectedive of the "export" approach taken by Sweden with respect to human rights, that the convention was primarily for other countries and the protections need not be "imported" into Sweden.[22] One of the more problematic areas in the Swedish context has been the protections as granted under Article 6 guaranteeing objective judicial scrutiny in civil and criminal cases. As administrative law falls outside this definition in the Swedish system, the assumption by Sweden at the time of its signing was that the right to a court hearing did not extend to administrative law issues as they

---

22 *See* Cameron (2006) at 15.

were not "civil rights" as found in private law.[23] The lack of judicial review has now been partially remedied by amendments to administrative procedural regulations as seen in Chapter Six below.

The requirement of an objective court in Article 6 has also raised questions concerning the tribunals created as alternatives to the general courts in Sweden, most of which in essence are arbitration panels with members appointed by the central organizations in that sector. This issue has been brought up in several cases, particularly with respect to the composition of the Housing Court, which the European Court of Human Rights found not to be an objective court as required by Article 6,[24] and the Labor Court, which the Court found to fulfill the requirements of an objective court in the case at hand.[25]

The remedies, if any, to be granted by Swedish courts for violations of the European Convention have been another topic of much debate. No specific statutory regulation was adopted in Sweden with respect to this issue. Reopening cases as decided by administrative agencies is now possible

---

23 Some of the cases concerning Sweden raising issues of "civil" matters subject to judicial review under Article 6 include *Sporrong and Lönnroth v. Sweden*, European Court of Human Rights, judgments dated 23 September 1982 and 18 December 1984, App. Nos. 7151/75 and 7152/75 (expropriation proceedings with respect to two property units of 25 and 12 years respectively a taking a civil matter), *Pudas v. Sweden*, European Court of Human Rights, judgment dated 27 October 1987, App. No. 10426/83 (revocation of driving status as taxi driver a civil matter), *Skärby v. Sweden*, European Court of Human Rights, judgment dated 25 May 1990, App. No. 12258/86 (refusal of a grant an exception to a zoning regulation a civil matter), *Mats Jacobsson v. Sweden*, European Court of Human Rights, judgment dated 21 May 1990, App. No. 11309/84 (construction prohibitions as to a property unit and changes in zoning regulations a civil matter), *Bóden v. Sweden*, European Court of Human Rights, judgment dated 27 October 1987, App. No. 10930/84 (expropriation proceedings a civil matter), *Tre Traktörer Aktiebolag v. Sweden*, European Court of Human Rights, judgment dated 7 July 1989, App. No. 10873/84 (revocation of alcohol retail license a civil matter), and *Allan Jacobsson v. Sweden*, European Court of Human Rights, judgment dated 22 June 1989, App. No. 11179/84 (successive building prohibition a civil matter).

24 *See Langborger v. Sweden*, European Court of Human Rights, judgment dated 22 June 1989, App. No. 11179/84.

25 *See AB Kurt Kellermann v. Sweden*, European Court of Human Rights, judgment dated 26 October 2004, App. No. 41579/98.

under both the Code of Judicial Procedure and the Administrative Judicial Procedures Act. Awarding monetary damages for state action arguably could be seen as precluded by Section 3:7 of the Tort Liability Act which bars claims against the state for enactment or a failure to enact a statute or government regulation. In two cases, the Swedish Supreme Court found that Swedish courts had the jurisdiction to impose damages on the State for harm caused to the plaintiffs to the extent necessary for Sweden to be seen as fulfilling its obligations under the European Convention.[26] The Supreme Court in a later case found, however, that damages could not be imposed on a private party for violations of the European Convention.[27]

---

26 *See* NJA 2005 p. 462 and NJA 2007 p. 295.
27 *See* NJA 2007 p. 747.

CHAPTER 3

European Union Law

The law of the European Union ("EU"), Union law, creates an outer boundary for the legislation of the Member States in the areas delegated to the Union. Originally formed as a cooperation after World War II to help maintain peaceful relationships between its Member States, the European Union has undergone radical and swift changes in recent decades. Initially consisting of six Member States, as of 2012, there are now twenty-seven Member States covering approximately one-half a billion people in Europe. However, the most dramatic change has not been in the physical enlargement of the Union, but rather its focus.

Begun as a cooperation of coal and steel markets, the Union, in the form of the European Economic Community ("EEC"), extended its reach to the creation of a common market based on four freedoms of movement regarding goods, services, persons and capital, in a manner reminiscent of the expansion of legislative power by Congress under the commerce clause of the American federal constitution. From this platform of a common market, the treaties began to incorporate social and political areas under the European Community ("EC"). The Lisbon Treaty in 2009 further strengthened individual fundamental rights within the Member States and as against the Union. The EU has emerged as an extensive economic, political and social cooperation, as concerned with fundamental human rights as with the free movement of goods in the now single market.

Sweden joined the European Union on 1 January 1995. Swedish membership in such an association was controversial. Sweden has prided itself on having a long tradition of neutrality in the international arena dating back to 1814, after Sweden lost Finland to Russia, having recently gained Norway. Swedish membership in the European Union began to be seen as more attractive during the 1990's for three reasons: The end of the cold war and the dismantling of the Soviet Union made the apparent neutrality of Sweden less a key factor, Sweden's generally weaker economy at that time, and the fact that though legislation and decisions were taken on the domestic Swedish level to be consistent with Community demands as prescribed in the EEA agreement, Sweden had no influence internally in the European Communities without formally being a member. A referendum was held on 13 November 1994 and 52.1 % of the votes were cast for membership.

Sweden had several conditions upon which its membership was contingent, one of which was that the Community had to maintain the same level of human rights as that found in Sweden.[1] Two other conditions as asserted by Sweden were that Swedish collective agreements in the labor market would be honored and that the Swedish crown would be retained as currency. These latter conditions were not explicitly taken up in the Accession Treaty.[2]

The Swedish Instrument of Government had to be amended to allow the delegation of lawmaking authority to the European Communities and now in the current form, the European Union. The first paragraph of Article 6 of the tenth chapter after its most recent amendment in 2010 states:

> Parliament may transfer a right of decision-making that does not affect
> the fundamental principles of the [Swedish] form of Government within
> the framework of cooperation for the European Union. Such transfer pre-
> supposes that the protection of rights and freedoms in the field of coopera-

---

1   For criticism as to the tenability of this requirement, *see* Ulf Bernitz, *The European Constitutional Project and the Swedish Constitution* in SCANDINAVIAN STUDIES IN LAW – CONSTITUTIONAL LAW, Vol. 52 (Stockholm 2007) at 49 and 58. Bernitz points to the fact that the European Convention was not adopted as Swedish law until the year before EU membership in 1994, effective November 1998, so that there was no explicit protection of the European Convention in Sweden at the time this manifestation was adopted. The discussion as to the issue of the protection of human rights in the legislative preparatory works can be found at Legislative Bill 1993/94:114 at 32 and in the report by the parliamentary constitutional standing committee in 1993/94:KU21 at 27. The series in which this article is printed, SCANDINAVIAN STUDIES IN LAW, began in 1957 with volumes issued several times a year with articles written in English as to various legal topics. Information and older articles are available at its website at scandinavianlaw.se.

2   The Treaty of Accession of Austria, Finland and Sweden, OJ 1994 C 241, signed 24 June 1994 and coming into force 1 January 1995.

tion to which the transfer relates corresponds to that afforded under this Instrument of Government and the European Convention for the Protection of Human Rights and Fundamental Freedoms.

A decision to transfer such legislative authority has to be approved by a qualified majority of three-fourths of the Parliamentary votes cast as by at least one-half of the members of parliament. Such a decision may also be taken in accordance with the procedure prescribed for the enactment of a constitutional act. The transfer cannot be effected until the Parliament has approved it in accordance with the procedure set out in Article 3 of the tenth chapter of the Instrument of Government as regarding international agreements.

The following presentation first reviews the historical background of the EU through the succession of its treaties, beginning with the Treaty of the European Steel and Coal Community. The present EU structure and institutions most affecting EU lawmaking are described thereafter, followed by a brief overview of the different types of EU legal instruments and the legislative processes.

3.1 The Emergence of the Union

The development to the European Union as well as the expansion of its jurisdiction is reflected in the progression of its treaties. The development of the social platform of the EU[3] can be seen as a reflection of the line of development of the economic cooperation between the Member States and the evolution of its constitutional law. The original focus, of a treaty on the steel and coal markets, has given way to a European Union based on the rule of law and fundamental human rights through a process in which market rights have been invoked to strengthen constitutional and civil rights.

---

3 The designation of EU law, EC law or Community law was somewhat blurred prior to the Lisbon Treaty. Many scholars used "EC law" or "Community law" for the European Union under Maastricht as the law technically was still based on the EC Treaty. After the Lisbon Treaty and the removal of the pillars, EU law or Union law are the only correct current designations.

3.1.1 THE ORIGINS: THE PERIOD FROM 1951 TO 1986

Addressing social issues of any dimension was not uppermost in the minds of the original drafters of the first treaties ultimately establishing the EU. The "Treaty of the European Coal and Steel Community," also known as the "ECSC Treaty" or the "Treaty of Paris," signed in 1951 and in force 1952,[4] created a common European market in coal and steel, two vital resources, held by France and Germany, used in waging wars. The common market was called the European Coal and Steel Community (the "ECSC"), the first of the European communities. France, the Federal Republic of Germany, Italy and the Benelux countries, Belgium, the Netherlands and Luxembourg, agreed that "world peace can be safeguarded only by creative efforts commensurate with the dangers that threaten it," and that Europe could "be built only through practical achievements which will first of all create real solidarity, and through the establishment of common bases for economic development."[5] The ECSC Treaty created a High Authority, a Commission, a Common Assembly, a European Parliament, a Special Council of Ministers, a Council, as well as the Court of Justice and a Consultative Committee.

Six years later, the "Treaty establishing the European Economic Community," referred to as the "EEC Treaty" or the "Treaty of Rome" was signed, creating the second of the communities. The third community was created with the "Treaty Establishing the European Atomic Energy Community" (the "Euratom"), also signed by the original six members in 1957, coming into force in 1958. These two treaties are referred to collectively as the "Treaties of Rome" and with these treaties, the three European Communities, the ECSC, the EEC and the Euratom, were created.

The EEC Treaty extended the market sectors from simply coal and steel to all economic sectors in the Member States, creating a common economic market. This integration of all economic sectors was to be achieved in a period

---

4   The Treaty establishing the European Coal and Steel Community expired 23 July 2003. This first treaty is not published in the official journals. For the text of this treaty as well as the others cited below, *see* the official website of the European Union at http://eur-lex.europa.eu under founding treaties.

5   *See* the second and fourth paragraphs of the preamble to the ECSC Treaty.

of twelve years, by 1970, through the establishment of the four freedoms of movement of goods, persons, capital and services. A Social Policy Title was included in the EEC Treaty, and common community policies were agreed upon with respect to certain key areas to insure these freedoms of movement: a common agricultural policy,[6] a transportation policy,[7] and a commercial policy.[8] A common market operating at maximum efficiency with the removal of all impediments was seen as benefiting everyone, consumers, workers and employers alike, in turn improving the internal economies of the Member States. In addition, the EEC Treaty designated the Parliamentary Assembly and the Court of Justice as single "common" institutions instead of each community duplicating these institutions.

The very first provision having a social dimension was Article 119 of the Treaty of Rome (later Article 141 EC Treaty and now Article 157 TFEU) dealing with issues of discrimination. France worked for the inclusion of Article 119 proscribing equal pay for women and men in the draft of the treaty as France had had equal pay provisions in place since World War II and at that time, one of the smallest pay differentials between women and men.[9] France argued that it could not compete with the price of goods from countries in which women were paid less than men.[10] This "market distortion" or "social

---

6 *See* EEC Treaty, Articles 38–43.

7 *Id*. at Articles 74–75.

8 *Id*. at Articles 110–113.

9 Catherine Barnard, EC EMPLOYMENT LAW (3rd ed. Oxford 2006) at 7 *citing* Budiner, LE DROIT DE LA FEMME A L'ÉGALITÉ DE SALAIRE ET LA CONVENTION NO. 100 DE L'ORGANIZATION INTERNATIONALE DU TRAVAIL (Librairie Générale de Droit et de Jurisprudence, Paris 1975).

10 The drafting of Article 119 was also inspired by the United Nation's specialized agency, the International Labor Organization ("ILO") Convention No. 100, Equal Remuneration Convention of 1951, incorporating the principle of equal remuneration for men and women workers for work of equal value. *See* Barnard at 22. The ILO conventions have influenced both EU and Swedish law. For more information on the ILO, *see* the ILO website at ilo.org.

dumping" was argued to be an impediment to the free movement of goods.[11] Article 119 has been referred to as the "slender historical thread" upon which the constitutional dimension of the EU's gender regime hangs.[12] Issues of equality and discrimination were arguably not taken up again seriously in the treaties until the Amsterdam Treaty, a gap of over forty years.

The Merger Treaty, signed in 1965 and entering into force in 1967,[13] merged the executive bodies, the Councils and Commissions, of the three different European Communities, the ECSC, the EEC and the Euratom, into single "common" institutions similar to the Court of Justice, completing the unification of the institutions of the communities. In addition, a "common" budget was introduced.

From this time forward, the EEC became the most prominent of the three communities. The Treaty of Luxembourg, signed in 1970, granted the European Parliament certain budgetary powers.[14] The United Kingdom, Denmark and Ireland joined the Communities in 1973.[15] The Treaty of Brussels, signed in 1975,[16] strengthened the European Parliament's powers by granting it the right to reject the budget. The citizens of the Member States

---

11 Article 119 was to be implemented by the Member States by 1961, the end of the first transitional stage. In *Defrenne II*, the Court gave Article 119 direct effect both vertically and horizontally, however, not retroactively from 1962 but rather from the date of the judgment, 1967, *see* Case C-43/75, *Gabriella Defrenne (No. 2) v. Societe Anonyme Belge de Navigation Aerienne Sabena* [1976] 1 ECR-455, Celex No. 61975J0043 at para. 40. The non-retroactive application of Article 119 by the Court has been attributed to the consideration the Court took to the arguments of Ireland and the UK that retroactivity from 1962 would expose many employers to claims of unequal pay spanning more than a decade, forcing many employers into bankruptcy. *Defrenne (No. 2)* at 480–81.

12 Jo Shaw, *Gender Mainstreaming and the EU Constitution*, EUSA REVIEW, Vol. 15, No. 3 (2002) at 3, available at eustudies.org.

13 The Merger Treaty, OJ 1966 152, Celex No. 165F/PRO/PRI/13, signed 8 April 1964 and coming into force 1 July 1967.

14 The Treaty of Luxembourg ("Treaty amending certain Budgetary Provisions"), OJ 1971 L 2, signed 22 April 1970 and coming into force 1 January 1971.

15 The Treaty of Accession of the United Kingdom, Ireland and Denmark, OJ 1972 L 73, signed 22 January 1972 and coming into force 1 January 1973.

16 The Treaty of Brussels ("Treaty Amending Certain Financial Provisions"), OJ 1977 L 359, signed 22 July 1975 and coming into force 1 June 1977.

directly elected the European Parliament for the first time in 1979. Greece became a member in 1981[17] while Portugal and Spain joined in 1986.[18]

The Single European Act ("SEA")[19] was signed by the now twelve Member States in 1986, "moved by the will to continue the work undertaken on the basis of the Treaties establishing the European Communities and to transform relations as a whole among their States into a European Union."[20] The European economic cooperation was extended into a political cooperation with SEA introducing several new areas of responsibility: the internal market, social policy, economic and social cohesion, research and technological development as well as environmental issues. SEA introduced a legislative procedure for cooperation between Parliament and the Council giving Parliament real, if limited, legislative powers, addressing the concern that had been expressed with respect to Parliament's lack of real power and the ensuing democratic deficit. Social elements, however, were not specifically addressed, raising the criticism of a Europe existing without its citizens, instead of for them.[21] All Member States except the United Kingdom signed the Community Charter of Fundamental Social Rights of Workers in 1989, which was in the form of a political declaration not having legally binding effect.

3.1.2 TOWARDS THE EUROPEAN UNION

The movement towards greater integration as well as the expansion of the social and political cooperation became stronger during the 1990's. The single European common market came into effect in 1992. Two major treaties were signed during this decade, the Maastricht Treaty establishing the EU and the European Community in the singular as well as the Amsterdam Treaty, which further strengthened the political and social objectives set out in the

---

17 The Treaty of the Accession of Greece, OJ 1979 L 291, signed 28 May 1979 and coming into force 1 January 1981.
18 The Treaty of Accession of Spain and Portugal, OJ 1985 L 302, signed 12 June 1985 and coming into force 1 January 1986.
19 The Single European Act ("SEA"), OJ 1987 L 169, signed 28 February 1986 and coming into force 1 July 1987.
20 First paragraph of the preamble to the SEA.
21 Barnard at 9.

Maastricht Treaty while also giving greater legislative power to the European Parliament.

The Maastricht Treaty (1993)

The "Treaty on European Union together with the treaty establishing the European Community" ("Maastricht Treaty" or "EU Treaty") was signed in 1992 and came into force in 1993.[22] It established a European Union based on the European Communities (ECSC, EEC and Euratom), marking "a new stage in the process of creating an ever closer union among the peoples of Europe, in which decisions are taken as closely as possible to the citizen."[23]

The EU now had a single institutional structure, consisting of the European Council, the European Parliament, the Council, the Commission, the Court of Justice and the Court of Auditors. The EEC Treaty was officially renamed the "Treaty establishing the European Community" ("EC Treaty") in accordance with Article G(1) of the EU Treaty. The renaming of the EEC to the EC was to reinforce the change of focus from economic issues to issues concerning the environment, industrial strategy, education, consumer affairs, health and social welfare. The United Kingdom opted out of health and social welfare harmonization until 1997.[24]

As set out by the Maastricht Treaty effective 1993, the EU comprised three pillars forming its basic structure. The first pillar was the Community pillar, corresponding to the three Communities: the European Community, the European Atomic Energy Community and the former European Coal and Steel Community. The second pillar was devoted to common foreign and security policy, which came under Title V of the EU Treaty. The third pillar was devoted to police and judicial cooperation in criminal matters under Title VI of the EU Treaty.

---

22 The Treaty on European Union ("Maastricht Treaty"), OJ 1992 C 191, signed 7 February 1992 and coming into force 1 November 1993.

23 Title 1, Common Provisions, Article A of the Treaty on European Union.

24 The stance of the United Kingdom and its reluctance to go forward with social issues through the EU at this time has been referred to as "two-speed Europe" or "variable geometry." *See* Barnard at 15.

Community lawmaking procedures were invoked with the first pillar and intergovernmental procedures in the other two. The objectives as set out in the Treaty were to be pursued by the establishment of a single market and an economic and single monetary policy.

The European Council had already launched plans for an Economic and Monetary Union ("EMU") in 1989 based on the Euro, and the Maastricht Treaty consolidated them. The groundwork for future proposals as to expanding the social platform and constitutional changes can be seen as beginning with Maastricht. Two years after the signing of the Maastricht Treaty, Sweden, Austria and Finland became members of the European Community, bringing the total number of Member States to fifteen.[25]

The Amsterdam Treaty (1999)

The Treaty of Amsterdam, signed in 1997 and coming into force in 1999,[26] was perceived as "a step forward in the process of European integration ... a system which is more effective, more open to dialogue with the people of Europe, more democratic and more geared to the outside world."[27] The Amsterdam Treaty codified, amended and renumbered the EU and EC treaties in efforts to achieve greater transparency. Certain legislative procedures were changed, again strengthening Parliament's role and addressing the issue of the democratic deficit. Included among the former areas of legislation in which a co-decision was to be taken by the Parliament and the Council were Article 12(6) prohibitions against discrimination, Article 18 (8a) free movement of EU citizens, Article 141(3)(formerly Article 119) implementation of equal pay for equal work.

A movement towards a more constitutional basis for EU and Community policies can be seen in the Amsterdam Treaty in the amendments to the

---

25 The Treaty of Accession of Austria, Finland and Sweden, OJ 1994 C 241, signed 24 June 1994 and coming into force 1 January 1995.

26 The Treaty on Amsterdam, OJ 1997 C 340, signed 2 October 1997 and coming into force 1 May 1999.

27 Remarks of Marcelino Oreja, Member of the Commission responsible for institutional affairs and a negotiator of the Amsterdam Treaty with respect to the treaty, *see* The European Commission, *Entry into Force of the Amsterdam Treaty*, Press Release, 28 April 1999.

EU and EC Treaties. Article 136 EU Treaty was amended by Article One of the Amsterdam Treaty to include the recognition of the "fundamental social rights as defined in the European Social Charter signed at Turin on 18 October 1961 and in the 1989 Community Charter of the Fundamental Social Rights of Workers."[28] The 1989 Community Social Charter was included in the Amsterdam Treaty, with the United Kingdom finally signing the Charter. The Amsterdam Treaty again expressly confirmed the protection of fundamental rights through the application of EU law, which until then had been a matter primarily for the Court of Justice case law. In addition, the concept of EU citizenship was further developed in the Amsterdam Treaty. A system of political sanctions was also established in the Amsterdam Treaty as to serious and persistent violations by Member States of the founding principles of the EU, namely freedom, democracy, human rights and rule of law.

Special prominence was given to balanced and sustainable development as well as the objective of a high level of employment with a mechanism set up to coordinate Member States' policies on employment. This emphasis on a high level of employment and social protection within the EC Treaty was seen as a shift in the emphasis of the EU from measures protecting those in employment to addressing the high levels of unemployment in Europe.[29] The delegation of power to the Community legislator through Articles 13, 137 and 141 EC Treaty to take action in the area of equal opportunities and equal treatment was seen as constituting "an explicit embodiment of the Court's statement that the elimination of discrimination based on sex forms part of fundamental rights."[30]

Work was begun on a Charter of Fundamental Rights of the European Union in 1999. The objective of the Charter was to clarify the rights of EU citizens, not by explicitly establishing new rights, but rather by consolidating

---

28 The European Social Charter was drafted by the Council of Europe in 1961, and has been revised most recently in 1996. For the text of the charter and its history, *see* the Council of Europe website, available at coe.int.

29 Barnard at 25.

30 Proposal for a directive of the European Parliament and of the Council on the implementation of the principle of equal opportunities and equal treatment of men and women in matters of employment and occupation (recast version) Com(2004) 279 Final at 2.

the rights already existing in other sources, including the EU treaties and the case law of the Court of Justice and the European Convention.

3.1.3 THE EU AT THE TURN OF THE NEW MILLENNIUM

One of the major goals of the EU in the new millennium was the ratification of a constitution to entirely replace all the treaties. The Treaty of Nice, signed in 2001 and coming into force 2003,[31] was drafted to reform the institutions of the EU prior to the fifth enlargement of membership. The then fifteen Member States, the original six of Germany, France, Italy and the Benelux countries, followed by the United Kingdom, Denmark, Ireland, Greece, Portugal, Spain, Austria, Finland and Sweden, were facing a possible enlargement of twelve additional Member States: Bulgaria, Cyprus, the Czech Republic, Estonia, Hungary, Latvia, Lithuania, Malta, Poland, Romania, Slovakia and Slovenia.[32]

The Nice Treaty set out to simplify certain legislative procedures with respect to the doubling of EU members, replacing requirements of unanimity in certain areas with a lower requirement of a qualified majority. A new division of tasks between the Court of Justice and the Court of First Instance (after Lisbon renamed the General Court) was also enacted. With the accession of the ten new members, the Treaty of Athens addressed certain specific considerations without any major changes. The EU and EC Treaties were amended by the Treaties of Nice and Athens and issued in consolidated form in 2002, incorporating all changes to the treaties until 2002.[33]

---

31 The Treaty on Nice, OJ 2001 C 80, signed 26 February 2001 and coming into force 1 February 2003.

32 Ten of these were then accepted with the membership of Bulgaria and Romania postponed until 2007. The Treaty concerning the accession of the Czech Republic, the Republic of Estonia, the Republic of Cyprus, the Republic of Latvia, the Republic of Lithuania, the Republic of Hungary, the Republic of Malta, the Republic of Poland, the Republic of Slovenia and the Slovak Republic to the European Union ("Treaty of Athens"), OJ 2003 L 236, signed 16 April 2003 and coming into force 1 May 2004.

33 Treaty Establishing the European Community ("EC Treaty") (consolidated text), OJ 2002 C 325 and Treaty on European Union ("EU Treaty") (consolidated text), OJ 2002 C 325.

The focus of treaty efforts after this was on the ratification of a constitutional treaty. Two different versions were proposed, and both failed to gain the unanimity necessary. The first draft constitutional treaty was ambitious, with the objective of replacing all other treaties and also having:

- The inclusion of the Charter of Fundamental Rights as drafted in 1999 in the text of the Treaty;
- A new definition of the EU to replace the current "European Community" and "European Union";
- A new presentation of the distribution of powers between the Union and the Member States;
- A revised institutional framework addressing the respective roles of the European Parliament, the Council and the Commission; and
- More effective decision-making procedures.

The first draft constitutional treaty was rejected by France and the Netherlands. As it had to be ratified by all then twenty-five Member States to be binding, this created a deadlock.

3.1.4 THE LISBON TREATY

A second constitutional treaty was drafted with more modest objectives, the Lisbon Treaty, and approved by the heads of the Member States in December 2007. The structure of the treaty was built around four objectives, a more democratic and transparent Europe, a more efficient Europe, a Europe of rights and values, freedom, solidarity and security, and a Europe as an actor on the global stage. Ireland rejected it in June 2008, entailing a second deadlock. In October of 2009, Ireland accepted the Lisbon Treaty, which came into force two months later on 1 December 2009.

The Lisbon Treaty, although presented as modest in its design, has brought about quite substantial changes. First is the fact that the EU is now definitively a legal person, allowing for the EU to enter into agreements and sign treaties. The Lisbon Treaty comprises in actuality two amended treaties, the Treaty on the European Union ("TEU")(formerly Maastricht of 1992) and the Treaty on the Functioning of the European Union ("TFEU")(formerly Treaty of Rome of 1956) and appendices such as the Charter on Human Rights discussed

© THE AUTHOR AND STUDENTLITTERATUR

below. The Treaty of Lisbon consequently amended the existing EU and EC treaties without replacing them. Given space constraints, only highlights under the four objectives will be raised here.

A more democratic and transparent Europe:

- Strengthened roles for the European Parliament and the national parliaments;
- More opportunities for citizens to have their voices heard through the citizens' initiative;
- Clearer definitions of the competence at the European and national levels; and
- A procedure for withdrawal from the Union: The Treaty of Lisbon explicitly recognizes for the first time the possibility for a Member State to withdraw from the Union

A more efficient Europe:

- Simplified working methods and voting rules, streamlined and modern institutions for a EU of 27 members;
- Effective and efficient decision-making: qualified majority voting in the Council is extended to new policy areas to make decision-making faster and more efficient with a double majority from 2014;
- More stable and streamlined institutional framework:
  - President of the European Council elected for two and one-half years,
  - New composition of the European Parliament, and
  - Clearer rules on enhanced cooperation and financial provisions;
- EU's ability to act in several policy areas of major priority for Union and its citizens is enhanced, particularly in the policy areas of freedom, security and justice, such as for combating terrorism or crime.

A Europe of rights and values, freedom, solidarity and security:

- Charter of Fundamental Rights introduced into European primary law;
- Preservation and reinforcement of the four freedoms as well as the political, economic and social freedom of European citizens;

- Union and Member States are to act jointly if a Member State is the subject of a terrorist attack or the victim of a natural or man-made disaster;
- Solidarity in the area of energy is also emphasized;
- Union receives an extended capacity to act on freedom, security and justice to fight crime and terrorism; and
- New provisions on civil protection, humanitarian aid and public health also aim at boosting the Union's ability to respond to threats to the security of European citizens.

Europe as an actor on the global stage:

- Europe's external policy tools now combined, both when developing and deciding new policies, giving the EU legal status in relations with its partners worldwide;
- The High Representative for the Union in Foreign Affairs and Security Policy, also acting as Vice-President of the Commission, is to increase the impact, coherence and visibility of the EU's external actions;
- The European External Action Service is to provide back up and support to the High Representative; and
- European Security and Defense Policy will preserve special decision-making arrangements but also pave the way towards reinforced cooperation amongst a smaller group of Member States.

Thus the changes brought about by the Lisbon Treaty to the European Union in essence have been quite extensive.

3.2 The Structure of the EU

The Treaty of Lisbon changed the face of the EU. Merging the three pillars as set out in the Maastricht Treaty into one, the EU was given status as a legal person with the view of "enhancing the efficiency and democratic legitimacy of the Union and to improving the coherence of its action." Several European institutions are now key to the legislative and enforcement processes and are presented below: The European Council, the Court of Justice of the European Union, the Court of Auditors, the Commission, the Council of Ministers, the European Parliament, the Economic and Social Committee and the Committee of Regions.

The Union enjoys the competences conferred on it by the Member States under the Lisbon Treaty, while all other competences continue to be within the purview of the Member States. The "principle of conferred powers" is to guarantee that the Union does not extend its competence at the expense of the Member States without their prior agreement. The Lisbon Treaty includes the possibility to give competence in an area back to the Member States.

The relation between the Union and its Member States as to competence is described in Articles 3–6 TFEU as being of three different types:

- Exclusive Union jurisdiction (where the Member States have relinquished all possibility of taking action);
- Concurrent or shared jurisdiction (the most common); and
- Supporting actions (the EU's sole task is to coordinate and encourage action by Member States).

The principles of subsidiarity and proportionality, as well as the new role of national parliaments in the legislative procedure, as discussed below, function to ensure compliance with this distribution of governance.

Under Article 3 TFEU, the Union's exclusive competence includes the:

- Customs Union;
- Establishment of competition rules necessary for the functioning of the internal market;
- Monetary policy for Member States which use the Euro ("€") as legal tender;
- Conservation of the biological resources of the sea as part of the common fisheries policy;
- Common trading policy; and the
- Execution of international agreements.

Shared competence between the Union and its Member States under Article 4 TFEU includes the areas of the:

- Internal market;
- Social policy with regard to specific aspects defined in the treaty;

- Economic, social and territorial cohesion;
- Agriculture and fisheries except for the conservation of the biological resources of the sea;
- Environment;
- Consumer Protection;
- Transportation;
- Trans European Networks;
- Energy;
- Area of freedom, security and justice;
- Joint security issues with regard to aspects of public health as defined in the Lisbon Treaty;
- Research, technological development and space; and
- Development cooperation and humanitarian aid.

The Economic and Monetary Union ("EMU") of the EU was reaffirmed by the Lisbon Treaty. Sweden is a member of the EMU but has not participated in its third stage, entailing that the Swedish currency is the Swedish crown and not the Euro. Great Britain and Denmark, two of the other Member States still not having the Euro as currency, negotiated explicit exceptions to the Euro in their signing of the Maastricht Treaty. Denmark, though not adopting the Euro, has tied the Danish crown to it, resulting in a *de facto* acceptance of the Euro. Maastricht was already in effect when Sweden joined the communities and Sweden has no explicit grant of exception to adopting the Euro. A referendum was held in Sweden regarding whether the Euro should become Swedish currency, and 56 % of the voters voted no. Neither is the Swedish crown tied to the Euro. As Sweden does have obligations under EMU, the political compromise has been for the EU to find that Sweden does not meet the financial conditions necessary for the adoption of the Euro, the reason given for why Sweden and the most recent member countries have not yet officially adopted the Euro.[34] The Euro is currently used as the currency for 330 million people in seventeen countries.

---

34 *See* the EU website of the European Commission regarding economic and financial affairs at http://ec.europa.eu/economy_finance/euro/countries/sweden_en.htm.

3.3 EU Lawmaking Institutions

As can be seen from the progression of the treaties described above, not only have the size and scope of the EU changed considerably since the original steel and coal union, but also the institutions themselves. The core institutional actors with respect to EU law after the Lisbon Treaty are seven: the European Council (*Europeiska rådet*), the Court of Justice of the European Union (*Europeiska unionens domstol*) and the General Court (*Europeiska unionens tribunal*), the Court of Auditors, the Commission (*Europeiska kommissionen*), the Council of Ministers (*Ministerrådet*), the European Parliament (*Europaparlamentet*), and the Economic and Social Committee and the Committee of Regions.

Each of these institutions has all undergone significant alterations since their inception. Many of the institutional changes were made to address the democratic deficit originally existing with the very weak European Parliament having basically only consultative power in contrast to the very strong Council.

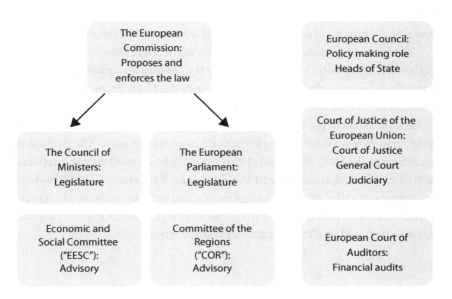

DIAGRAM 3.1 The EU Institutions.

3.3.1 THE EUROPEAN COUNCIL

Under the Lisbon Treaty, the European Council[35] gained status as an EU institution distinct from the Council of Ministers. The European Council originally was created in 1974 as an informal forum for discussions between Heads of State or Government and rapidly developed into a body setting goals and courses of action for the Union. The European Council acquired formal status in the 1992 Treaty of Maastricht, which defined its function as providing the impetus and general political guidelines for the Union's development. The European Council today comprises the Heads of State or Government of the Union's Member States, its own president and the president of the European Commission, consequently having twenty-nine members. The High Representative also participates in its work. The European Council meets twice every six months.

The European Council defines the general political direction and priorities of the European Union, setting the strategic priorities of the Union and managing any crises that may arise. Under an emergency break procedure established in the Lisbon Treaty, a Member State may refer debated legislation from the Council of Ministers to the European Council if the Member State is outvoted in the Council of Ministers. In this sense, the European Council has a final say as to whether to go forward with certain legislation.

The European Council also has a key role in the suspension of membership rights, changing voting systems as under the treaties' bridging clauses, and in appointments including the Commission, the High Representative and members of the Board of the European Central Bank.

The President of the European Council is appointed for a two and one-half year term by a qualified majority of the European Council. The President coordinates the work of the European Council, hosts meetings and reports activities after each meeting to the European Parliament. The President also represents the Union on foreign policy and security matters when such representation is required. Certain of the meetings of the European Council are also televised in efforts for greater transparency.

---

35 For more information on the European Council, *see* its website at european-council.europa.eu.

3.3.2 THE COURT OF JUSTICE OF THE EUROPEAN UNION

The Court of Justice has been a major actor historically in the development of EU law. This is the case with respect to both substantive and procedural law, and also with respect to both the economic and social platforms as evidenced by its jurisprudence beginning already in the 1970's. Established by the ECSC Treaty in 1952 with six justices, the Court now has twenty-seven justices, one from each Member State. The Court may sit *en banc*, in a Grand Chamber of thirteen justices, or in panels of five or three justices.

The Court also has eight advocates-general to assist it in deciding cases, presenting opinions arguing for certain results in cases from objective and impartial stances. The justices and advocates-general are appointed by the governments of the Member States for renewable six-year terms. If a case is not seen to raise any new issues of law, the Court can decide that an opinion by an advocate-general is not necessary.[36] If an opinion is submitted, the Court is not compelled to follow it.

Judgments by the Court are decided by a majority. Dissenting opinions are not given, nor are the votes of the Court included in the judgment. This anonymity was purposefully created to reduce pressures on the justices to act in accordance with national demands as opposed to EU interests.[37] To alleviate the Court's increasing caseload, the General Court (prior to the Lisbon Treaty, the Court of First Instance) was created in 1989.

The Court of Justice has jurisdiction in five types of cases:

1 Reference for a preliminary ruling brought under Article 267 TFEU;
2 Actions for failure of a Member State to fulfill an obligation under Article 258 TFEU;
3 Actions for annulment of a EU law under Article 263 TFEU;
4 Actions for failure of a EU institution to act under Article 265 TFEU; and
5 As a court of last instance in cases decided by the General Court, i.e., regarding competition law, trade mark law and

---

36 Article 20 of the Statute of the Court of Justice. The statute, and other information about the EU courts, is available at their website, curia.europa.eu.
37 Síofra O'Leary, EMPLOYMENT LAW AT THE EUROPEAN COURT OF JUSTICE (Hart Publishing 2002) at 59.

design law cases (originally decided by Commission or OHIM respectively).

The majority of cases heard by the Court falls within one of the first two categories, a request for a preliminary ruling or a failure by a Member State to act.

In a request for a preliminary ruling, a Member State's court of final instance is to present an issue of law to the Court as to interpreting and applying Union law. The Court has jurisdiction only to rule upon issues of law and not on issues of fact in preliminary rulings.[38] The national court then takes the decision of the Court and applies it to the case at hand.

3.3.3 THE EUROPEAN COURT OF AUDITORS

The European Court of Auditors is a separate court from the above courts, and purposefully so. It was established by the Treaty of Brussels of 1975 and is the EU Institution that carries out the audit of EU finances. As external auditor, it is to contribute to improving EU financial management and act as an independent watchdog as to the financial interests of the Union and ultimately its citizens.[39]

3.3.4 THE EUROPEAN COMMISSION

The European Commission is the executive body of the EU, charged with implementing and enforcing Union law. It has in essence a monopoly on proposing legislation falling within the framework of the ordinary legislative procedure. The Commission also represents the EU internationally, negotiating agreements between the EU and other countries. At present there are twenty-seven commissioners, one from each EU Member State. The Commission is reviewing whether a system creating a maximum number of commissioners can be enacted.[40]

---

38 O'Leary at 67–81.

39 For more information on the Court of Auditors, *see* its website at eca.europa.eu.

40 For more information on the Commission, *see* its website at ec.europa.eu.

The Commission, Member States and individuals can bring actions with respect to the implementation of Union law to the European courts. However, the Commission is charged with enforcing Union law in contrast with the Member States and individuals. An example of this system at work can be seen in the case of Sweden and the Parental Leave Act (*föräldrale-dighetslag* 1995:584). Sweden had revised its Parental Leave Act in 1995 making the changes it deemed necessary for compliance with Council Directive 92/85/EEC on the introduction of measures to encourage improvements in the safety and health at work of pregnant workers and workers who have recently given birth or are breastfeeding ("Pregnancy Directive"). The right to a transfer and leave due to certain conditions during a pregnancy was extended for reasons of health and safety to women recently giving birth. The unconditional right to six weeks of leave for women immediately prior to or after the birth of a child was extended to seven weeks.

Sweden did not, however, make this leave mandatory, but instead kept it as a right. The specific requirement of an obligatory two-week maternal leave as prescribed in the Pregnancy Directive had been considered unnecessary in Sweden based on the findings of the legislative committee.[41] Nothing in the Swedish labor market indicated to the committee that women, who had recently given birth or who were nursing, had difficulty in taking maternal leave under the current legislative scheme. The requirement of a mandatory maternal leave was considered foreign and not motivated with respect to the view of women taken by Swedish legislation as a whole. Ninety-eight percent of all women with children took leave in connection with the birth of a child, and the remaining two percent were assumed to take sick leave instead. A Swedish practice, that women who had recently given birth took maternal leave, was found to exist by the committee. A mandatory requirement was viewed as unnecessary to fulfill the requirements of the directive, and the present legislation was deemed sufficient.

The European Commission in accordance with Article 226 EU Treaty (now Article 258 TFEU) gave formal notice to Sweden in December of 1998 for the failure to legislate a mandatory two-week maternal as required under Article 8 (2) of the Pregnancy Directive. As support for its interpretation of

41 SOU 1994:41 at 195.

the need for mandatory legislation to comply with Article 8.2, the European Commission stated:

> The two weeks of mandatory maternal leave are necessary for the health of the mother and the child, and to secure and protect against the pressuring of women to work until the last minute or to return to work too early. They also guarantee that women wishing to work late into their pregnancy, or to return immediately to work, must be away at least two weeks due to health reasons.[42]

In its response to the Commission dated 25 February 1999, the Swedish Government argued that according to Swedish legislation, employers cannot deny employees the right to maternal leave for a period of up to fourteen weeks. The efficacy of the Swedish legislation, the Government argued, was demonstrated by the fact that the practice exists in Sweden that women who have recently given birth utilize their right to take maternal leave and that Sweden fulfilled the requirements of the Directive.

The Commission responded on 6 August 1999 with a reasoned opinion in accordance with Article 226 EU Treaty, repeating verbatim the reasons given above for the mandatory nature of the leave. In addition, the Commission rejected Sweden's argument that the directive was implemented through practice, relying on *Commission v. The Netherlands*[43] and *Commission v. France*[44] for the proposition that a practice mirroring the protections mandated by a directive does not excuse the omission of legislating the protection. The Commission argued that legislation was required to insure that individual persons are conscious of their rights and able to assert them. As a result, the Commission found Sweden still to be in violation of the Directive.

In the response to the reasoned opinion submitted by the Swedish Government on 30 September 1999, Sweden stated that Swedish legislation

---

42 Letter dated 30 December 1998 from Pádraig Flynn, European Commissioner, addressed to Swedish Minister Anna Lindh.

43 Case C-339/87, *Commission of the European Communities v. The Kingdom of the Netherlands* [1990] ECR I-851, Celex No. 61987J0339.

44 Case C-167/73, *Commission of the European Communities v. French Republic* [1974] ECR-359, Celex No. 61973J0167.

created the right for women, not the obligation, to a maternal leave. However, as the Commission found Sweden to be in violation of the directive, a legislative proposal would be drafted in the fall of 1999, submitted to the Parliament in March of 2000 and enacted as law by 1 July 2000.[45] This gives an example of the enforcement power that can be exerted by the Commission with respect to EU law. If Sweden had not conceded and amended its legislation, the Commission is empowered to bring Member States to the Court of Justice in accordance with Article 258 TFEU.

3.3.5 THE COUNCIL OF MINISTERS

The Council of Ministers, also referred to as the Council of the European Union,[46] originally had the final decision-making authority on most EU legislation. Today the Council adopts legislative acts in most cases through the ordinary legislative procedure (formerly the co-decision procedure) with the European Parliament, a bi-cameral process invoked in 83 areas and is described in Diagram 3.2 below. The measures adopted by the Council can take the form of regulations, directives, decisions, common actions or common positions, recommendations or opinions. The Council also can adopt conclusions, declarations or resolutions. The Council also adopts the Union's budget together with the European Parliament.

The Member States meet within the Council of the European Union. Depending on the issues to be addressed on the agenda, each country is represented by a minister responsible for that area, for example, the minister of foreign affairs, finance, social affairs, transport or agriculture. However, the heads of the respective governments of the different Member States (not the heads of state) attend the top meetings. The presidency of the Council is held by each Member State on a rotational basis for six months. The number

---

45 The Act on Amending the Parental Leave Act (*Lag 2000:580 om ändring i föräldra-ledighetslagen 1995:584*), Legislative Bill 1999/2000:87 *Obligatorisk mammaledighet*, Bet. 1999/2000:AU8, Rskr. 1999/2000:231.

46 The Council of Ministers, previously referred to as the Council of the European Communities, is not the same body as the European Council or the same body as the Council of Europe, located in Strasbourg and the author of the European Convention and the European Social Charter of 1961. For more information on the Council of Ministers, *see* its website at consilium.europa.eu.

of votes each Member State can cast in the Council was originally set out by the Treaty of Nice.

Current distribution of votes for each Member State:

Germany, France, Italy, United Kingdom	29
Spain, Poland	27
Romania	14
Netherlands	13
Belgium, Czech Republic, Greece, Hungary, Portugal	12
Austria, Bulgaria, Sweden	10
Denmark, Ireland, Lithuania, Slovakia, Finland	7
Cyprus, Estonia, Latvia, Luxembourg, Slovenia	4
Malta	3
Total	*345*

The object of the decision determines whether a simple majority, qualified majority or unanimity is required. A qualified majority currently is reached if either of the two following conditions is met:

- A majority of Member States approve (in some cases, a two-thirds majority); or
- A minimum of 255 votes is cast in favor of the proposal, out of a total of 345 votes.

In addition, a Member State may ask for confirmation that the votes in favor represent at least 62% of the total population of the Union. If this is not found to be the case, the decision will not be adopted. The Lisbon Treaty expanded the use of qualified majority voting in the Council of Ministers by having it replace unanimity as the standard voting procedure in almost every policy area outside taxation and foreign policy.

Effective 2014, there will be a requirement of a double qualified majority: A qualified majority will be reached when at least 55% of all Member States, who comprise at least 65% of EU citizens, vote in favor of a proposal. When the Council of Ministers is acting on a proposal not from the Commission or the High Representative,[47] 72% of the Member States will be required while the population requirement will remain the same.

The Council is also to help coordinate Member State policies, for example, in the economic field; develop common foreign and security policy on the basis of strategic guidelines set by the European Council; and conclude international agreements on behalf of the Union. Certain Council deliberations, for example on legislation, are now to be televised in efforts at greater transparency.

3.3.6 THE EUROPEAN PARLIAMENT

The European Parliament[48] was originally one of the weakest institutions as established by the Treaty of Paris in 1951. Initially elected by the national legislatures of the Member States, the Parliament was directly elected by European citizens for the first time in 1979. Elections are now held every five years and every EU citizen is eligible to vote. The Parliament has three main functions: to legislate in accordance with the ordinary legislative procedure, adopt the budget and approve the nominations of commissioners. Broadcasts of parliamentary procedures are available at the Parliament's website to increase accessibility for EU citizens.

The Lisbon Treaty expanded the ordinary legislative procedure (formerly co-decision procedure) to an additional forty fields, for a total now of 83, further cementing the strength of the parliament. The change in the name of the procedure, from co-decision to ordinary, was also to emphasize that this is now the main process with respect to legislation and that the European Parliament is a main actor.

The Parliament presently has 754 members elected directly by the citizens of the 27 Member States. Sweden has 20 parliamentary members. The Lisbon Treaty changed the way by which Member State seats are apportioned.

---

47 The Treaty of Lisbon created a High Representative of the Union for Foreign Affairs and Security Policy in the effort to ensure greater coordination and consistency in EU foreign policy. The High Representative is in charge of the External Action Service as also created by the Treaty of Lisbon, essentially the common Foreign Office for the Union.

48 For more information on the European Parliament, *see* its website at europarl.europa.eu.

Instead of an exact number (as was the case in each previous treaty), the Lisbon Treaty gives power to the Council of the EU, acting unanimously on the initiative of the Parliament and with its consent, to adopt a decision fixing the number of seats for each Member State. Moreover the Lisbon Treaty provides for the number of seats to be successively reduced proportionate to the number of citizens of each Member State, referred to in Eurospeak as degressive proportionality. The maximum number of seats to be aimed for in the future in the Parliament is 750 in addition to the President of the Parliament regardless of the number of Member States.

3.3.7 THE EESC AND COR

The European Economic and Social Committee ("EESC")[49] and the Committee of Regions ("CoR")[50] are two consultative bodies included in the ordinary legislative procedure in order to have input from stakeholders. The EESC (originally the Economic Social Committee under the Treaty of Rome) has branded itself as the bridge between Europe and organized civil society. Members come from either the social partners (employer or employee organizations), or from a diverse group of perceived stakeholders ranging from farmers to youth organizations. The CoR comprises of 344 members with the task of providing the EU with inputs from the regional and local levels of the Member States.

3.3.8 THE SOCIAL PARTNERS WITHIN THE EU

The last of the actors involved in the ordinary legislative process are the social partners. The increasing participation by the social partners in the EU legislative process in many ways parallels the increased participation of the European Parliament, both in efforts for greater democracy and transparency on the EU level. Three stages of participation by the social partners can be discerned beginning in 1985. During the first period from 1985 to 1991, the

---

49 For more information as to the EESC, a body of 317 members set up in 1994 under the EU Treaty, *see* the EESC website, available at http://eesc.europa.eu.

50 For more information as to the CoR, also with 317 members, *see* the CoR website, available at cor.europa.eu.

activities of the social partners resulted principally in the adoption of joint opinions, resolutions and declarations, all soft law documents non-binding in nature.

In the second stage, from 1991 to 2001, an agreement signed between the social partners was subsequently integrated into the Protocol on Social Policy in 1991, and then annexed to the Maastricht Treaty and incorporated into Articles 138 and 139 of the EC Treaty (now Articles 154-55 TFEU). The third and present stage can be seen as commencing with the "Joint Contribution" presented by the European cross-industry social partners in December 2001 to the Laeken European Summit, moving towards an increasingly independent and autonomous European social dialogue, as confirmed by the Barcelona summit.

The Commission has recognized six social partners within the European Social Dialogue process. The original three were the Federation of European Business ("BUSINESSEUROPE"), formerly the Union of Industrial and Employers Confederation of Europe ("UNICE"), the European Labor Union Confederation ("ETUC") and the European Centre of Public Enterprises ("CEEP"). BUSINESSEUROPE represents more than twenty million small, medium and large companies active in Europe, employing over 106 million employees in all. Members include 41 central industrial and employers' federations from 35 countries.[51] ETUC represents sixty million European workers, 82 national labor union confederations in 36 countries as well as eleven European Industry Federations.[52] CEEP is the international employers' association consisting of public enterprises and organizations in over seventeen countries.[53] The three more recently recognized social partners are the European Association of Craft, Small and Medium Sized Enterprises ("UEAPME"),[54] Eurocadres[55] and the European Confederation of Executives and Managerial Staff ("CEC").[56]

---

51 For more information on BUSINESSEUROPE, *see* its website at businesseurope.eu.
52 For more information on ETUC, *see* the ETUC website at etuc.org.
53 For more information on CEEP, *see* its website at ceep.eu.
54 For more information on UEAPME, *see* its website at ueapme.com.
55 For more information on Eurocadres, *see* its website at eurocadres.org.
56 For more information on CEC, *see* its website at cec-managers.org.

Social dialogue can take two main forms – a bipartite dialogue between the European employers and labor union organizations, or a tripartite dialogue involving interaction between the social partners and the public authorities that takes place generally at a cross-industry level. Under the process now set out in Articles 153 and 154 TFEU, the social partners can be consulted in the legislative process; to date this has happened almost thirty times.[57] Three "cross-sector" framework agreements have been concluded, Council Directive 96/34/EC implementing the framework agreement on parental leave concluded by the social partners, Council Directive 97/81/EC concerning the framework agreement on part-time work concluded by UNICE, CEEP and ETUC, as well as Council Directive 99/70/EC concerning the framework agreement on fixed-term work concluded by ETUC, UNICE and CEEP. The social partners have also concluded voluntary agreements on telework (2002), work-related stress (2004), and on harassment and violence at work (2007).

3.4 EU Law

The constitutional law of the EU is defined by the treaties (*fördrag*) forming its jurisdiction. The different governing bodies within the EU promulgate, interpret and enforce Union law through secondary legislation in the form of regulations (*förordningar*), directives (*direktiv*), decisions (*beslut*) and case law (*rättspraxis*). The treaties, regulations, directives, decisions and case law constitute the "hard law" of the Union, the binding law. In addition to these legal sources, there are other documents perceived as the "soft law" of the Union, non-binding instruments such as working papers, declarations and recommendations. These latter instruments cannot be cited in court as legally compelling, but are persuasive with respect to issues of interpretation and policy.

An additional complication arising when assessing legal issues under EU law is whether the provision in question is immediately binding, has direct effect or simply can be seen as persuasive. For example, regulations are always binding on the Member States. Direct effect, however, is a term of

---

57 *See* European Commission, *Social Dialogue,* available at its website at ec.europa.eu/social.

art in EU law, meaning that a provision in a treaty or directive after certain requirements are fulfilled, will create rights that a national Member State court must protect and which can also form the basis for judicial review. The test for whether a treaty provision has direct effect was first set out by the Court in *van Gend & Loos*.[58] A treaty provision is to be given direct effect if it either is "clear and unconditional" or requires legislative intervention by the Member States. Direct effect in its turn can be either vertical or horizontal. Vertical direct effect exists when an individual can cite the treaty provision or directive as against a Member State. Horizontal direct effect creates rights between private parties and is more restrictively applied to treaty regulations and not at all to directives to date.[59]

3.4.1 THE PRIMARY LEGISLATION: THE EU TREATIES

Total consensus by the Member States is required with respect to the adoption of treaties, as seen with the Lisbon Treaty process. The two core treaties of the European Union after the Lisbon Treaty comprise the Treaty on the European Union ("TEU") and the Treaty on the Functioning of the European Union ("TFEU"). They establish the constitutional boundaries between the EU, the Member States and EU citizens.

The Treaty on the European Union/TEU has six titles: Common provisions, democratic principles, provisions on the institutions (European Parliament, the European Council, the Council of Ministers, the European Commission, the Court of Justice of the European Union, the European Central Bank, the Court of Auditors and the High Representative of the Union for Foreign Affairs and Security Policy), enhanced cooperation, general provisions on the Union's external action and specific provisions on the common foreign and security policy, and final provisions including establishing legal personhood for the EU, treaty amendment procedures,

---

58 *See* Case C-26/62, *NV Algemene Transport- en Expeditie Onderneming van Gend & Loos v. Netherlands Inland Revenue Administration* [1963] ECR-3, Celex No. 61962J0026.

59 *See* Case C-152/84, Andrea Francovich and Danila Bonifaci and others v Italian Republic [1991] ECR I-5357, Celex No. 61990CJ0006.

applications to join the EU, ratifications. TEU is in force for an unlimited period of time.

The Treaty on the Functioning of the European Union/TFEU has seven sections. The first addresses principles including the basis of the treaty and legal status, competencies, social principles, public access to documents, and respect of church status under Member State law. Part two takes up protections against discrimination and for Union citizenship, with part three setting out Union policies and internal actions. Part four delineates associations with overseas territories and part five, EU external action (foreign policy). Part six further elaborates the institutional provisions as set out in TEU, including legislative acts and procedures and the budget process. Part seven concerns issues such as territorial application, the seat of institutions, effects of certain treaties as well as accession.

Thirty-seven protocols are attached to TEU and TFEU addressing different issues such as the role of national parliaments in the EU, the application of principles of subsidiarity and proportionality, the statute of the Court of Justice of the European Union, and accession by the EU to the European Convention. Two annexes are also attached to the two treaties, as well as sixty-five declarations. Needless to say, the sought after simplicity of having only two treaties has been muddied by the accompanying documents.

3.4.2 THE CHARTER OF FUNDAMENTAL RIGHTS OF THE EUROPEAN UNION

The Charter of Fundamental Rights of the European Union, signed and proclaimed in 2000 by the European Parliament, European Commission and the European Council, became Union law through Article 6(1) TEU.[60] It is the first formal EU document to combine in a single text the entire range of civil, political, economic and social rights and certain "third generation" rights such as the right to good administration or the right to a clean environment. The Charter's prime objective is to make rights more visible to EU citizens by assembling existing rights previously scattered over a range of sources including the European Convention on Human Rights and Fundamental

---

60 For more on the Charter, *see* eucharter.org

Freedoms and other Council of Europe, United Nations and International Labour Organisation agreements.

The Charter has seven titles. The first six titles address dignity, freedoms, equality, solidarity, citizen rights and justice, with the seventh title concerning the interpretation and application of the Charter. The Charter applies to the EU institutions (European Commission, European Parliament, European Council, the Council of Ministers, the Court of Justice of the European Union, European Court of Auditors and European Central Bank) and bodies set up under secondary legislation (such as Europol, Eurojust, the European Economic and Social Committee, and the Committee of the Regions). The Charter also applies to EU Member States when acting within the scope of EU law.[61]

3.4.3 THE EU AND THE EUROPEAN CONVENTION

The European Convention was signed in Rome in 1950 by the members of the Council of Europe, including five of the six founders of the EU. Alleged violations of the convention are brought to the European Court of Human Rights in Strasbourg. The Convention has now been adopted by all EU Member States. The EU as an entity could not previously formally accede to the European Convention as the Court of Justice[62] had found in 1996 that there was no treaty provision that empowered the Community to do so. This has changed with the Lisbon Treaty and the accession process of the Union is currently underway.

The Court of Justice in the 1960's was naturally initially reluctant to address issues containing more of a human rights' dimension given the economic focus of the original treaties. By the 1970's, however, the Court began to evaluate issues and treaty rights against the background of fundamental rights as included in the European Convention, particularly with respect

---

61 The interpretation of protocol 30 to the Lisbon Treaty on the Application of the Charter of Fundamental Rights of the European Union to Poland and the United Kingdom, and endorsed by the Czech Republic upon signature of the Lisbon Treaty, is open to whether the Charter can be enforced in courts of those member states.

62 See, for example, *Opinion 2/94 on Accession of the Community to the ECHR* [1996] ECR 1-1759.

to actions by Community institutions and Member States. The Court held that fundamental rights ranked as general principles of EU law based on two sources: the constitutional traditions of the Member States as well as international treaties as entered into by the Member States, particularly the European Convention. For example, when assessing whether a regulation restricting the planting of grape vines could be viewed as interference with the right to own property, the Court stated:

> Fundamental rights form an integral part of the general principles of the law, the observance of which is ensured by the court. In safeguarding those rights, the [Court] is bound to draw inspiration from constitutional traditions common to the Member States, so that measures incompatible with the fundamental rights recognized by the constitutions of those states are unacceptable in the Community. International treaties for the protection of human rights on which the Member States have collaborated or of which they are signatories, can also supply guidelines that should be followed within the framework of Community law.[63]

The Court went on to find that the Regulation could not be seen as in violation of the right to own property as set out in the European Convention.

The European Parliament, the Commission and the Council signed a Joint Declaration in 1977 in which they undertook to continue to respect fundamental rights as arising from these two sources identified by the Court of Justice, the constitutional traditions of the Member States as well as the European Convention. Article 6 TEU explicitly states that "[t]he Union shall respect fundamental rights, as guaranteed by the European Convention ... and as they result from the constitutional traditions common to the Member States, as general principles of EU law."[64]

---

63 The Court found it to be a permissible restriction in view of the rights granted under the European Convention, see Case C-44/79, *Liselotte Hauer v. Land Rheinland-Pfalz* [1979] ECR-3727, Celex No. 61979J0044. The first case raising this issue of the European Convention and its relationship to Community law was Case C-11/70, *Internationale Handelsgesellschaft mbH v. Einfuhr- und Vorratsstelle für Getreide und Futtermittel* [1970] ECR-1125, Celex No. 61970J0011.

64 *See* Article 6(2) EU Treaty, formerly Article F.2 EU Treaty.

3 EUROPEAN UNION LAW

Before the Treaty of Amsterdam entered into force, the powers of the Court of Justice did not extend to this article. The amendments made in the Treaty of Amsterdam ensured that Article 6(2), now Article 6 TEU, is within the jurisdiction of the Court, which now has the explicit, as opposed to the assumed, power to decide whether the institutions have failed to respect fundamental rights. An example of this can be seen in a decision issued by the General Court, evaluating the actions of the Commission as against Article 6(2) of the European Convention under which any person charged with a criminal offence is to be presumed innocent until proven guilty according to law.[65]

3.4.4 THE SECONDARY LEGISLATION

The secondary legislation as promulgated by the EU institutions described above is the third major source of EU law after the treaties and international agreements. According to Article 288 TFEU, the institutions, in order to exercise the Union's competences, are to adopt regulations, directives, decisions, recommendations and opinions. The binding legal instruments are in the form of regulations, decisions, directives and case law.

Regulations are instruments issued by the Council in conjunction with the European Parliament or solely by the Commission. Regulations are directly applicable and having immediate effect in all Member States without any further action required by the Member States. A regulation consequently has general immediate application.[66]

Directives are issued by the Council in conjunction with the European Parliament in accordance with the ordinary legislative procedure described above, or solely by the Commission. If the subject-matter of the proposed directive is seen as contentious, it is to go through the ordinary legislative procedure. The main purpose of directives is to harmonize Member State

---

65 *See* Case T-22/02, *Sumitomo Chemical Co. Ltd. v. Commission of the European Communities* [2005] ECR II-04065, Celex No. 62002A0022.

66 One of the first regulations issued was Council Regulation (EC) No. 1408/71 of 14 June 1971 on the application of social security schemes to employed persons and their families. For a thorough analysis of this regulation as well as the Court's subsequent case law, *see* Vicki Paskalia, FREE MOVEMENT, SOCIAL SECURITY AND GENDER IN THE EU (Hart 2007).

© THE AUTHOR AND STUDENTLITTERATUR

national legislation. A directive is binding, as to the result to be achieved, upon each Member State to which it is addressed, but the Member States are to determine the most suitable means of enacting the directive in the national legal system. A directive is given vertical "direct effect," in other words, can be invoked by a private citizen against a Member State in the national courts, if the period for enactment by the Member State has expired and the Member State has taken no or an incorrect action. The directive must also be sufficiently precise, confer a right upon which a citizen can base a claim, and unconditional. Directives are not given horizontal direct effect. The giving of direct effect to the directives is a product of the case law, and not expressly included in the founding treaties.[67]

A decision ruling on a specific matter can be taken either by the Council alone, the Council in conjunction with the European Parliament, or solely by the Commission. A decision is binding in its entirety upon those specific parties to whom it is addressed. Though not binding on third parties, decisions can be seen to give guidance as to the stances adopted by the institution, for example, decisions of the Commission with respect to mergers or anti-trust issues.

3.4.5 GENERAL PRINCIPLES OF EU LAW

In addition to the primary and secondary EU legislation, certain overarching principles are applied in interpreting and enforcing EU law. These include the principles of subsidiary, proportionality, necessity and loyal cooperation. Certain of these principles are now grounded in the treaties, while others have been only developed in the case law. A few are mentioned here, but this listing is not by any means exhaustive.

The principle of subsidiarity is defined in Article 5 TEU and is intended to ensure that decisions are taken as closely as possible to the citizen and that constant checks are made as to whether action at the Union level is

---

67 *See Van Gend en Loos* and also Case C-41/74, *Yvonne van Duyn v. Home Office* [1974] ECR-1337, Celex No. 61974J0041. *See also* Case C-152/84, *M. H. Marshall v. Southampton Area Housing Authority (No. 1)* [1986] ECR-723, Celex No. 61984J0152 and Case C-188/89, *A. Foster and others v. British Gas plc.* [1990] ECR I-3313, Celex No. 61989J0188.

justified in light of the possibilities available at national, regional or local levels. Specifically, the EU is not to take action (except in areas falling within its exclusive competence) unless doing so is more effective than an action taken at the national, regional or local levels. The principle of subsidiarity is closely bound to the principles of proportionality and necessity, which require that any action by the Union should not go beyond that which is necessary to achieve the objectives of the Treaty.

Like the principle of subsidiarity, the principle of proportionality as also found in Article 5 TEU regulates the exercise of powers by the EU, seeking to set actions taken by the EU institutions within specified boundaries. Under this principle, the involvement by EU institutions must be limited to that necessary to achieve the objectives of the Treaties. In other words, the extent of the action must be kept within the aim pursued. When various forms of intervention are available to the Union, where the effect is the same, the approach providing the greatest freedom to the Member States and individuals is to be taken.

The principle of loyal cooperation is set out in Article 4(3) TFEU, requiring Member States to take appropriate measures, whether general or particular, to ensure fulfillment of the obligations arising out of the Treaty or resulting from action taken by the institutions of the Union. Member states are also to facilitate the achievement of the Union's tasks and abstain from any measure that could jeopardize the attainment of the objectives of the Treaty. The principle of the conferral of competence as set out in Article 5 TFEU can be seen as an explicit principle emphasizing that the competences not granted to the Union remain with the Member States.

Other legal institutions that have been vital in insuring the efficacy of EU law have been the principle of direct effect as discussed above, the doctrine of supremacy of EU law and member state liability for breaches of EU law.

3.4.6 THE SOFT LAW OF THE EU

In addition to the treaties and secondary law as discussed above, there are instruments which are not considered binding, categorized instead as "soft law," such as Council Resolutions and Commission Recommendations. However, many objectives as set out in soft law documents eventually became incorporated into the hard law documents such as directives and even treaties. For example, sexual harassment was first taken up in the 1984 Recommendation on the Promotion of Positive Action for Women[68] and later was incorporated in the 2006 Discrimination Directive. Even if the soft law is not binding, it gives a good indication of approaches being taken by policy makers that may later come to fruition.

3.4.7 THE LEGISLATIVE PROCEDURES

In line with the expansion of parliamentary power, the ordinary legislative procedure (formerly the co-decision procedure), with respect to regulations and directives, gives the same legislative power to the European Parliament and the Council of the European Union under Article TFEU 294 in eighty-three areas. However, special legislative procedures still exist in certain fields, such as common external tariffs.

The ordinary legislative procedure

Along with the Council of Ministers and the Parliament, two other advisory instances are in place with respect to the ordinary legislative procedure: The national Member State parliaments, and then the European Economic and Social Committee/EESC representing sectors impacted by EU law and the Committee of Regions/CoR. Before the European Commission proposes new legislative initiatives, it is to conduct an impact assessment as to the initiative with respect to its potential economic, social and environmental consequences. Impact assessments are seen as giving political decision-makers information as to the advantages and disadvantages of possible policy options. To this end, an Impact Assessment Board was created within the Commission in 2006.

After making the impact assessment evaluation, in the ordinary legislative procedure, as seen in the flowchart below, the Commission sends the proposal to Parliament/EP" and the Council, Member State national

---

68 Council Recommendation 84/635/EEC of 13 December 1984 on the promotion of positive action for women, OJ 1984 L 331/34, Celex No. 31984H0635.

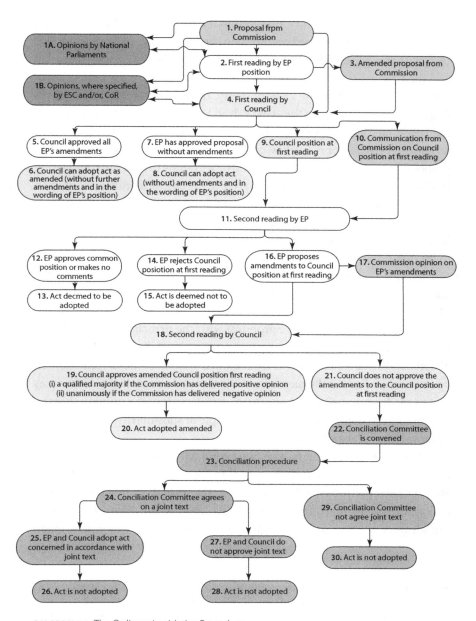

DIAGRAM 3.2 The Ordinary Legislative Procedure.

This flowchart of the ordinary legislative procedure as established in Article 294 TFEU is taken from website of the European Commission at http://ec.europa.eu/codecision/stepbystep/diagram_en.htm.

parliaments, the EESC and CoR. National Parliaments[69] then have eight weeks to send their reasoned opinions on the compliance of draft legislative texts with the subsidiarity principle to the Council, the European Parliament and the Commission. Under the early warning system for the protection of subsidiarity created by the Lisbon Treaty, the national parliaments are to flag potential problems. In the event a draft legislative act's compliance with the subsidiarity principle is contested by one-third of the votes allocated to national parliaments (yellow cards), the Commission is to review the proposal and decide to maintain, amend or withdraw the act, also motivating its decision. This threshold is one-quarter in the case of a draft submitted on the basis of Article 76 TFEU in the area of freedom, security and justice. If contested by a simple majority of the votes allocated to national Parliaments (orange cards), the Commission has to re-examine the proposal. If it chooses to maintain the draft, the Commission has to justify its position by means of a reasoned opinion. The reasoned opinions of the Commission and the national Parliaments are submitted to the co-legislator. The Council of Ministers and the European Parliament are to take into consideration the compatibility of the legislative proposal with the principle of subsidiarity, taking particular account of the reasons expressed and shared by the majority of national Parliaments as well as the reasoned opinion of the Commission. If, by a majority of 55% of the members of the Council or a majority of the votes cast in the European Parliament, the co-legislator is of the opinion that the proposal is not compatible with the principle of subsidiarity, the legislative proposal is to be abandoned.

After the first reading by the Council of Ministers and the European Parliament, and after taking into account the opinions submitted by Member State national parliaments, EESC and CoR, the second reading is held. After two readings, if the Council of Ministers and the European Parliament cannot agree, the proposal is brought before a Conciliation Committee made

---

69 All proposals from the Commission, initiatives from a group of Member States, initiatives from the European Parliament, requests from the Court of Justice, recommendations from the European Central Bank and requests from the European Investment Bank for adoption of a legislative act are to be sent to the national Parliaments at the same time as they are sent to the co-legislator (Council of Ministers and the European Parliament).

up of an equal number of representatives of the Council of Ministers and the European Parliament. Representatives of the Commission also attend the meetings of the Conciliation Committee and contribute to the discussions. When the Committee has reached agreement, the agreed upon text is sent to the European Parliament and the Council of Ministers for a third reading, after which they can adopt it as a legislative text. The final agreement of the two institutions is essential if the text is to be adopted as a law. Even if a joint text is agreed on by the Conciliation Committee, the European Parliament and the Council of Ministers can still reject it.

Special legislative procedures

A few remaining areas invoke special legislative procedures where Parliament has either the right of consent to a Council of Ministers' measure, or vice-versa. In a few cases, the former consultation procedure still applies, whereby the Council of Ministers needs only to consult the European Parliament before voting on a Commission proposal. The Council of Ministers then is not bound by the Parliament's position but only by the obligation to consult.

CHAPTER 4

Procedural Law and Arbitration

Procedural law in the Swedish system is primarily set out in the Code of Judicial Procedure (*rättegångsbalk* 1942:740),[1] which encompasses both civil and criminal procedure. However, criminal procedure is supplemented by provisions outside the Code of Judicial Procedure. In the same vein, administrative judicial procedure has its own judicial procedural act, with the Code of Judicial Procedure then having a gap-filling function. To further complicate this system, certain of the specialized courts, such as the Labor Court, have their own sets of procedural rules, again with the Code of Judicial Procedure filling in any gaps, while other specialized courts simply follow the rules in this Code.

This chapter and the next two concern procedure. This chapter takes up the general characteristics of the rules of procedure as found in the Code, and then focuses on civil litigation and arbitration. Chapter Five focuses on criminal law and procedure, with the understanding that the general rules as discussed below in certain cases can also be applicable with respect to criminal procedural matters. Chapter Six discusses administrative law and judicial procedure, and here again the reader must keep in mind that the provisions as presented below can be applicable in the absence of any specific administrative regulation in accordance with the canon of statutory construction, *lex specialis.*

---

1   An English translation of the Swedish Code of Judicial Procedure is available at the Government Office of Sweden website at sweden.gov.se. An English/Swedish and Swedish/English legal glossary is available from the website of the Court Administration Authority, GLOSSARY FOR THE JUDICIAL SYSTEM (*Ordlista för domstols-väsendet*) at domstol.se.

The Code of Judicial Procedure ("JP") was enacted in 1942 to replace the 1734 code and has been amended continuously since that year. It is divided into seven parts:

TABLE 4.1 The Code of Judicial Procedure.

Part One: The Court System

Chap. 1 Trial Courts	Chap. 6 Court Records
Chap. 2 Courts of Appeal	Chap. 7 Prosecutors and Police
Chap. 3 The Supreme Court	Chap. 8 Licensed Attorneys
Chap. 4 Judges	Chap. 9 Sanctions, Fines and Police Escort
Chap. 5 Public Attendance and Order	

Part Two: General Procedure

I. Proceedings in Civil Cases

Chap. 10 Jurisdiction	Chap. 15 Interlocutory Measures
Chap. 11 Parties and Representatives	Chap. 16 Voting
Chap. 12 Legal Counsel	Chap. 17 Judgments and Decisions
Chap. 13 Legal Actions and Filing	Chap. 18 Litigation Costs
Chap. 14 Joinder and Third Parties	

II. Proceedings in Criminal Cases

Chap. 19 Jurisdiction	Chap. 26 Interlocutory Measures
Chap. 20 Right to Prosecute	Chap. 27 Seizures
Chap. 21 Defendant and Defenses	Chap. 28 Searches of Premises and Persons
Chap. 22 Victim Claims	Chap. 29 Voting
Chap. 23 Preliminary Investigations	Chap. 30 Judgments and Decisions
Chap. 24 Arrest and Detention	Chap. 31 Litigation Costs
Chap. 25 Travel Prohibitions and Reporting	

III. General Provisions

Chap. 32 Statutes of Limitations and Defenses	Chap. 34 Procedural Impediments
Chap. 33 Pleadings and Service	

Part Three: Evidence

Chap. 35 Evidence generally	Chap. 39 Inspections
Chap. 36 Examinations of Witnesses	Chap. 40 Experts
Chap. 37 Examinations of Parties	Chap. 41 Preservation of Evidence
Chap. 38 Written Evidence	

Both civil and criminal cases are encompassed by the Code, but as can be seen, certain chapters are applicable only to civil cases, others only to criminal ones. Approximately one- half of the fifty-nine chapters are generally applicable to both types of cases. Those chapters governing civil procedure are discussed here, while those regarding criminal procedure are addressed in the next chapter concerning criminal law and procedure.

4.1 General Characteristics of Procedural Law

Four principles are deemed to be the cornerstones of Swedish judicial procedural law, both civil and criminal. The first is the principle of concentrated proceedings (*koncentrationsprincipen*) as set out in JP 43:11, "the trial, if possible, is to continue without interruption until the case is ready for determination." Postponements and recesses are granted only by way of exception. The second principle is that of public access (*offentlighetsprincipen*) as defined in JP 5:1, also discussed above in Chapter Two. Court hearings as a rule are to be public. However, with respect to certain sensitive circumstances and information, such as concerning sexual crimes against children, the court can order that the trial be held behind closed doors.

The third principle is that any judgment issued by the court on the merits is to be based on the evidence as presented at trial where a trial has been held (*omedelbarhetsprincipen*) as prescribed by JP 17:2. The last of these cornerstone principles is the principle of oral presentation (*muntlighetsprincipen*), prescribing that the case is not to be decided on the written pleadings and documents submitted, but rather on that which the parties have orally presented at trial, both with respect to the evidence and arguments. The court is to decide the case based only on this oral presentation.[2] Previously this meant that any written documents introduced as evidence had to be read aloud, at the same time as there was a ban prohibiting the parties from reading aloud any arguments they wished to present. An exception to this principle now exists in JP 43:5 in the event the court finds that a written summary would facilitate the understanding of the issues in the case or be of benefit to the proceedings. In addition, a party has the right to read written submissions aloud under certain conditions. Evidence can now also be submitted without reading it aloud if the court finds such to be appropriate under JP 43:8. These recent amendments reflect that which had become the practice in many cases. For example, the parties and court could agree that bank statements could simply be submitted rather than having to read the entire statements aloud. These amendments reflected the necessity of being able to present written evidence in a more efficient manner in complicated cases, for example money laundering cases. Otherwise, reading all the evidence aloud is excessively time consuming, increasing the costs of litigation and overburdening the court docket.

---

2   One of the reasons for adopting this principle was to ensure that any observers present at a trial would have the same information as the parties and the court, *see* Legislative Bill 1986/87:89 at 219.

There are several other principles that significantly affect the course of litigation in Sweden. According to the constitution, all individuals are to be treated equally by the courts (*likhetsprincipen*). Another overarching principle is *jura novit curia,* "the court knows the law." This principle does not exist in the Code, but is very strong in the legal culture. The parties argue the facts to the court, but the parties are not required to argue/plead the law, as the court is assumed to know the law. This is true today regardless of whether it is a legal question arising under Swedish law, Union law or applicable international conventions. There is a minimum requirement that the parties state the factual basis for their claims.

4.1.1 EVIDENCE

With respect to both civil and criminal cases, the main rule is that there are no restrictions with respect to the admissibility of evidence. Both legally qualified and lay judges assess the relevance and weight of all the evidence "in accordance with the dictates of conscience" with everything admissible as set out in JP 35:1. The court can reject certain evidence if it is deemed to be irrelevant, unnecessary or without effect in the case. The court can also find that other evidence should be used instead if the latter poses considerably less difficulty or expense, or where the evidence in question cannot be produced despite reasonable efforts and that the judgment should not be further delayed.

4.1.2 EVIDENTIARY PRIVILEGES

Even if there are no general evidentiary rules, there are certain privileges that are recognized in chapter thirty-six of the code. These are mainly with respect to evidence received in certain professional contexts. Included here as professionals with a privilege are members of the bar association, doctors, priests, dentists, midwives, nurses, psychologists, psychotherapists, family counselors[3] and assistants, as well as licensed patent representatives. Privilege was also extended in 2012 to mediators on the Regional Rent

---

3   Those family counselors falling within the scope of the Social Services Act (*social-tjänstlag* 2001:453) have this privilege.

and Tenancy Tribunals, as well as to mediators in private cases in order to encourage settlements. All individuals falling within the above groups may only be called to give evidence with regard to information confided in the practice of their profession or anything to which they have become privy to in conjunction therewith, where such disclosures are permitted by law or consent has been given by those individuals protected.

Counsel in court proceedings, assistants and defense attorneys may be called to give evidence about information confided to them in the provision of their services during a case only if the party they are representing consents. Information categorized as confidential under the Public Access to Information and Secrecy Act may only be provided as evidence if permitted by law or with the consent of the individual. The privilege may be found inapplicable by a court in criminal cases where the crime is deemed to be of a more serious nature as stated in JP 36:5, except with respect to priests and defense attorneys.

4.1.3 PRIORITY STATUS

The Act on Prioritized Status before the Court (*lag 2009:1058 om förturs-förklaring i domstol*) addresses problems arising due to litigation or administrative delays. According to this act, a case or matter before a governmental authority that has been unreasonably delayed is to be given a priority status on the docket at the request of the petitioner. The court is to make the assessment as to unreasonably delayed taking into consideration:

1 The complexity of the case or matter;
2 The conduct of the parties during the processing of the matter or case;
3 The conduct of the governmental authority or court during the processing of the matter or case; and
4 The significance of the dispute for the petitioner.

The court is to address such a petition expeditiously and the court's order granting or denying such a request cannot be appealed.

4.2 Civil Litigation

The Swedish civil procedural rules can be seen as creating a defendant friendly forum. This conclusion is based on several different aspects of the regulations as discussed below: The requirement of the definitiveness of the pleadings, the limited opportunities to amend pleadings, the limited discovery mechanisms available to the parties, which also only come into play after the pleadings have been submitted, as well as the allocation of legal costs and fees with the losing party paying both sides' trial costs and fees in the majority of cases. This combination of rules can be seen as increasing the economic risks for plaintiffs in bringing and prosecuting claims successfully. Even the principles discussed above as to the oral presentation of evidence and admission of all evidence can be seen as rules increasing trial costs, a factor more easily borne in the majority of cases by defendants, particularly in cases where consumers, employees or subvendors are plaintiffs.

The first distinction in the Code of Judicial Procedure as already mentioned above is between criminal and civil cases. With respect to civil cases, these in turn are categorized as either dischargeable (*dispositiv*) or non-dischargeable cases (*indispositiv*). Dischargeable cases, constituting the majority of civil cases, are those cases that can be settled freely by the parties without the need of judicial approval of any settlement. Non-dischargeable cases are those civil cases in which a settlement by the parties is not automatically permitted but must be reviewed by the court. Non-dischargeable civil cases are mostly within the area of family law, such as child custody and marital divorce cases. In many family law cases, the court is to take into account not only the interests of the parties, but also of specific third parties, such as minor children. In practice, agreements between the parents usually are approved by the courts unless specific reasons exist for not doing so from the perspective of any children involved.

Dischargeable cases are further categorized based on the amount at issue in the case. If the amount in dispute is less than one-half of the statutory price base amount (*prisbasbelopp*),[4] the case is treated as a small claims case. As a small claims case, certain provisions as discussed below are not applicable to the same degree. For example, a more experienced law clerk can decide some of these cases. This is in order to expedite procedures in the interest of resolving issues quickly and cheaply. The focus of the presentation below is on that which is typical for civil dischargeable cases.

4.2.1 THE PRE-TRIAL PHASE

Swedish civil litigation is divided into two main phases, the pre-trial phase (*förberedelse*) and the trial phase (*huvudförhandling*). The court makes the determination when a case is ready for trial. During the pre-trial phase, the court is expected to take an active role in the management of the case and in getting the parties to resolve issues and if possible, settle. At trial, the court is to assume a more passive role, particularly in non-family law cases, and the parties are to present the factual circumstances in the case.

The Complaint and Summons

A civil case begins with the plaintiff filing a complaint (*stämningsansökan*) setting out the plaintiff's claims (*käromålet*). The complaint is filed with the court along with a request for a summons (*stämning*) as well as by paying the required filing fee.[5] Plaintiffs previously could only file complaints individually, but a limited opportunity now exists for class actions

---

4   Beginning in 2011, the statutory price amount to which many legislative issues are tied is established in the Social Insurance Code (*socialförsäkringsbalken 2010:110*). As the statutory price amount is determined annually, it acts as an index, allowing certain thresholds to be raised or lowered, such as here with the amount at stake in litigation, or parental leave compensation, without having to amend various pieces of legislation. The statutory price base amount for 2012 is SEK 44 000. There is also a statutory higher base amount (*förhöjda prisbasbeloppet*) with the same function, which was SEK 44 900 for 2012. The statutory price base amount was formerly referred to as the statutory base amount (*basbelopp*), and prior to 2011 was established under the now repealed National Insurance Act (*lag 1962:381 om allmän försäkring*).
5   The fee for 2012 is SEK 450. For a listing of the different fees, *see* the Court Administration Authority's website at domstol.se.

(*grupptalan*).[6] If the defendant is a Swedish resident, the main rule is that plaintiff is to file the complaint with the court having physical jurisdiction over the defendant. If the defendant is an individual, the proper court is the one in whose territory the individual has her registered place of residence, if a legal person, where the board of directors has its registered office. Specific rules exist with respect to certain types of claims, for example a dispute arising under an employment agreement can be filed at the court where the plaintiff employee has her place of residence. Certain venues are compulsorily, for example with respect to real estate cases, the court having jurisdiction over the real estate is the only proper court.

The complaint is to be in writing and contain defined claims according to JP 42:1, a detailed account of the circumstances forming the basis for the claims, and a listing of the evidence to be produced to support the claims, as well as the basis for the court's jurisdiction. Written evidence is to be submitted at the time the complaint is filed, but can also be submitted later.[7]

The requirement of defined claims is fairly high. The complaint is filed on the basis of fact, not belief as is the case, for example, in certain United States jurisdictions. Filing based on fact means that the claims in general have to be so sufficient on their face that a default judgment can be rendered. This entails a defined monetary amount for damages as well as whether the claim is for monetary, declaratory or injunctive relief. A party can, however, reserve the right to adjust certain monetary amounts, for example with respect to damage amounts, but that right has to be actively reserved. The right to amend the pleadings under the Code is fairly limited, with the applicable provision in JP 13:3 beginning by stating that a complaint that has been filed may not be amended. Certain limited exceptions are given to this main rule. For example, amendments are permitted:

---

6   For an English translation of the Act on Group Proceedings (*lag 2002:599 om grupprättegång*), *see* the website of the Government Offices at sweden.gov.se.

7   Certain other information must always be included in any submission to the court as set out in JP 33:1(2), including the party's social security number and occupation, work and residential mailing addresses or other addresses at which the party can be served, work and residential telephone numbers or other information of importance with respect to the service of documents.

- Where a circumstance occurring during the litigation or brought to the knowledge of the plaintiff as a result of the litigation requires a remedy other than the one originally pled;
- Where a clarification of the legal relationship between the parties during the litigation can lead to certain declaratory relief now being pled; or
- Where plaintiff wishes to add a claim based on the primary one already pled, or even a new remedy based on an original claim.

A modification of the complaint to limit claims already made, or to cite new evidence without changing the original claims, is not viewed as an amendment of the complaint.

In the event the complaint is deemed by the court to be insufficient on its face, the court can order plaintiff to remedy that deficiency. The failure to do this or to pay the filing fee can result in a dismissal of the case by the court without prejudice (*avvisa käromålet*). A complaint is also to be dismissed where there is a procedural impediment, such as if the court does not have jurisdiction.

Where the complaint is not dismissed, the court issues a summons and serves the defendant with the complaint and an order to submit an answer within a certain period of time. The defendant can be ordered to file an answer upon penalty of default judgment (*tredskodom*) in dischargeable cases. As soon as the complaint is served upon the defendant, the court begins the pre-trial phase of the case, which is regulated by the provisions in chapter forty-two of the Code of Judicial Procedure.

The Answer

A written answer (*svaromål*) is to be submitted by the defendant at this stage. When the code was originally enacted in 1942, the answer was to be presented orally at a pre-trial conference, consistent with the principle of oral presentations as discussed above. As this caused too many complications, the code was amended to allow for written answers. Certain objections and requests have to be included in the answer in order to be preserved, for example, objections as to the court's jurisdiction, or requests that a foreign plaintiff provide security for the legal costs and fees of the case.

The defendant is to address the plaintiff's claims in the answer and the degree to which the claims are admitted or contested, as well as the evidence to be produced. If the claims are contested, the defendant is to state the grounds as well as the circumstances for the objections. Written evidence is to be submitted with the answer, but can also be submitted at a later date. The answer is also to include any procedural objections.

Dismissal

The court can dismiss the case without prejudice as already discussed above where the complaint is insufficient and plaintiff fails to supplement it, or for example, where the complaint is based on *pactum turpe,* in other words, an illegal or immoral agreement (for example, a gambling debt). Other reasons for dismissal include improper venue, lack of jurisdiction, lack of standing or legal capacity, or the failure of a party to attend court proceedings. *Lis pendens,* that a lawsuit concerning the issue is already in progress, or *res judicata,* that the issue has already been finally decided in a judgment between the parties, can also be grounds for dismissal. Other grounds include failure of service or that a valid arbitration agreement exists between the parties precluding litigation. Certain of these grounds must be asserted by the defendant for the case to be dismissed, while for others the court has a duty to assess the issues *sua sponte.*

The Pre-Trial Conference

The case is to be managed in light of the objectives of an expeditious and inexpensive resolution. As soon as appropriate, a case schedule is to be drafted and the parties are to be bound by the schedule. If the parties cannot follow the schedule, they are to immediately inform the court of this. During the pre-trial phase, the parties are to clarify the claims and any objections and factual circumstances, the degree to which the parties disagree as to the facts, the evidence to be presented and that which is to be proven by each piece of evidence. The court is also to determine if any further investigation needs to be conducted before the case can be decided, and preferably, whether a settlement can be reached. An overwhelming majority of all civil dischargeable cases brought to the general courts are settled.

As soon as the written answer is received, the court is to hold a pre-trial conference (*muntlig förberedelse*) attended by both parties as ordered upon penalty of default judgment in dischargeable cases. If both parties fail to attend the conference, the case can then be dismissed without prejudice. The proceedings during the conference are to be oral, and the parties are only allowed to read written arguments aloud if the court finds that this would facilitate an understanding of the case. The court can prepare a list of questions to be addressed by the parties during the conference. The court is to manage the conference so that all the issues can be resolved, making further conferences unnecessary. In certain cases, the court can order the parties to finally prepare their arguments and state the evidence to be cited by a certain date, after which no new circumstances or evidence can be cited without cause. Minutes of the conference are to be kept by the court.

Prior to or after the pre-trial conference, the court can draft a written summary of the claims, objections, circumstances and evidence in the case if doing so would be beneficial to the management of the case. The court can give the parties an opportunity to respond to the summary or to submit materials in support of or against the summary. The options of mediation and settlement are also to be again explored by the court.

With respect to the production of evidence, the court can order that certain evidence be accessible at trial, that an expert opinion be obtained, that written evidence be produced, and that objects be made available for inspection upon penalty of fine. However, the full array of discovery mechanisms between the parties at the pre-trial stage such as those existing, for example, in the United States, in the form of interrogatories, admissions of facts, depositions, inspections and document production are not as available and cannot be enforced by the courts to the same degree in the Swedish system. The more limited enforcement mechanisms in the Swedish judicial system are in part a product of the fact that the parties' legal representatives are not officers of the court, nor necessarily members of the bar association.

Depositions of the parties and witnesses are not held, and witness testimony is typically not available until given at trial. There is a general duty obligating a party holding relevant evidence to produce it. The court can grant a request by a party during the pre-trial phase to interrogate the other party or another person as to whether they have documents in their possession and if so, which documents those are (*editionsförhör*). However, the enforcement mechanism for the court is only fines.

A civil dischargeable case takes about two years to come to trial. During the pre-trial phase, the parties can bring motions, for example, for summary judgment, production of documents or seizing property. The court at this stage can resolve the case by issuing a default judgment, a summary judgment, confirm a settlement, or by issuing judgment if a trial is deemed patently unnecessary based on the investigation in the case.

4.2.2 THE TRIAL

The main provisions governing civil trials are found in chapter forty-three of the Code of Judicial Procedure. During trial (*huvudförhandling*), the judging panel is to consist of three legally qualified judges, unless an expedited procedure is invoked or the parties consent to only one judge. The judging panel in certain family law cases is one legally qualified judge and three lay judges. One legally qualified judge is also sufficient in small claims or less complicated cases. The trial is to be held in one continuous session if possible, and in the majority of cases, be open to the public. The proceedings are to be held orally, with written submissions permissible only if the court finds that this facilitates the proceedings.

The trial begins by the parties presenting their claims and objections. After this, the evidence is introduced. The parties can testify under an attestation of truth (*sanningsförsäkran*), which is less than an oath (*ed*). The difference between these two is the criminal sanctions invoked for failure to tell the truth under an attestation and under oath. The latter is classified as the crime of perjury (*mened*) with the risk of a greater penal sanction than that following from failure to tell the truth under an attestation. Witnesses can be examined by the parties, but judges are also allowed to pose questions and even conduct examinations. However, the court is not to provide tactical assistance to the parties in the presentation of their arguments.

Arguments, circumstances or evidence cited for the first time at trial are not to be taken into consideration if the court finds that the party was attempting by the late submission to delay the trial or unduly surprise the other party, or has acted unjustly or grossly negligently. After the evidence has been presented, the parties give their closing statements.

The last segment in a civil trial is that the parties submit petitions as to their legal costs and fees. Sweden applies the English rule with respect to trial costs and fees, which means that as a general rule, the losing party pays the prevailing party's trial costs and fees as seen in chapter eighteen of the Code. Though this rule sounds simple, in practice it can become fairly complicated. If the prevailing party caused unnecessary litigation, the court can order that the prevailing party instead is to pay the losing party's fees and costs, or that each party should bear its own costs. For example, if the plaintiff has petitioned for damages of SEK 1 million, but the court has awarded only SEK 100 000, the court can find that the plaintiff won the case, but that defendant need not pay costs and fees as plaintiff only received one-tenth of that pled. In addition, this rule is applied so that if plaintiff prevails at the trial court level, but defendant appeals and prevails at the appellate court, plaintiff may be forced to pay defendant's costs and fees for both the trial and the appellate litigation. In certain other cases, for example those presenting new, uncertain or difficult legal issues, the court can decide that each party is to bear its own costs.

4.2.3 LEGAL AID

Individuals are eligible for public financial legal aid for certain types of cases and up to certain income levels under the Legal Aid Act (*rättshjälpslag* 1996:1619). Financial legal assistance is limited in civil cases. In certain more urgent matters an individual can be eligible for two hours of advice by a licensed attorney or associate. There is a ceiling of one hundred hours of legal work for eligible cases that can be extended in certain circumstances. Most individuals are expected to obtain legal assistance insurance as part of a home or business insurance policy, with most of these policies having ceilings as to the legal costs and fees covered.

Certain state subsidies are available from the Legal Aid Authority (*Rättshjälpsmyndigheten*)[8] as to legal costs, but mostly only in criminal or family law matters. The individual, if receiving a subsidy, still has to pay an amount varying from two to forty percent of the legal costs and fees.

---

8   For more information in English on this agency, *see* its website at rattshjalp.se.

An individual with an income of more than SEK 260 000 (2012) annually according to the Legal Aid Act is not eligible for any state subsidies as to legal assistance.[9] Even if eligible, the subsidy covers only the individual's legal costs and fees. If that person loses the case, she still has to pay the other party's legal costs and fees herself.

4.2.4 THE JUDGMENT AND APPEAL

The case is to be decided by a judgment based on that presented during the trial as set out in chapter seventeen of the Code. Only those judges who have participated in the entire trial may participate in the judgment. The court is not bound by any law cited by the parties, but the court is bound by any claims and admissions made by the parties and the grounds cited thereto in dischargeable cases. Admissions are routinely made by the parties as to certain aspects of the amounts of damages requested, for example, with respect to interest. Thus in a case where plaintiff has requested damages of SEK 20 000, defendant can deny liability, but at the same time, admit that if liability were to be found, the amount of liability should be SEK 10 000. Thus if the court finds liability, the court cannot then impose liability for less than SEK 10 000. If the court awards an amount closer to that as admitted by defendant than that pled by the plaintiff, the allocation of trial costs and fees may be decided other than in accordance with the English rule as discussed above.

The judges are to deliberate as soon as possible after the completion of the trial, either the same day or the next workday, and if possible, issue the judgment immediately. The written judgment is to contain certain information: The court, time and date of the issuance of the judgment, the parties and their representatives or assistants, the judgment in the case (liable or not liable), the parties' claims, objections and allegations of facts

---

9   When this income amount was set in 1996, almost 90 % of the Swedish population fell under this limit. The economic standard for Swedish households increased 36 % from 1999 to 2012. The average yearly salary in 2012 was SEK 366 900, meaning that considerably less than one-half of the population today is eligible for such subsidies. For this statistic and others concerning Sweden, *see* the website of the government authority charged with keeping statistics, Statistics Sweden at scb.se.

and that which was proven in the case. If the parties have the right to appeal, information about the appeal process is to be included in the judgment. The judges do not issue judgments *seriatim*, but instead the court drafts one judgment. Concurring and dissenting opinions are allowed to be included in the judgment by special minutes attached to the judgment.

Appeal to a Court of Appeal

Chapter forty-nine of the Judicial Code governs appeals generally, and chapter fifty, appeals in civil cases. The parties previously had an almost automatic right to appeal to the courts of appeal with no requirement as to pleading the existence of either a question of law or an incorrect finding of fact.[10] This distinction was not even made in most cases, and a completely new trial was held before the court of appeal, arguably to give the parties the chance to better hone their arguments. This has been modified by a reform that took place in 2008.

The request for leave to grant an appeal is to be in writing and submitted to the trial court issuing the judgment being appealed within three weeks of the issuance of the judgment. Where one party has appealed the judgment, the other party has an additional week in which to also file an appeal. The appeal now is to include information as to the judgment being appealed, which portions of the judgment are being appealed and why they are incorrect according to the petitioner, the circumstances being cited as support for the appeal and the evidence to be presented and that which is to be proven. If new evidence is to be presented, cause must be shown as to why it was not presented at trial. If the party wishes a new inspection or new examination, this is to be cited as well as the reasons for such a request stated.

The recent reform has changed procedures at the appellate level in an endeavor to achieve greater judicial economy. First, the court of appeal no longer has to take up and review all the trial evidence again as if it were the

---

10 The threshold as to appeal to the courts of appeal previously instead was a certain monetary amount at issue in the case. Leave to appeal had to be granted for dischargeable civil cases concerning an amount less than one time the statutory base amount under the former wording of JP 49:12, otherwise appeal was automatic for amounts above that level.

court of first instance. Instead, the court of appeal needs only take up the evidence anew if it finds doing so is significant to the case as stated in JP 35:13. In addition, recordings[11] of witness testimony at the trial level can be used by the court of appeal unless new issues are raised and new witness testimony is found necessary. The new rules are to increase the ability of the court of appeal to decide cases without having a second full-blown trial, with the objective of the court of appeal's hearing to be a review of the trial court's judgment (*överprövning*) and not, as before, to be holding a completely new trial (*omprövning*).

Appeal to the Supreme Court

A party can petition for leave to appeal a judgment of a court of appeal to the Supreme Court. Leave to appeal is to be granted under JP 54:10 only if a Supreme Court judgment in the case would be of significance in the application of the law or if particular reason exists, for example, grounds to vacate the judgment. Leave to appeal can be limited to only a specific issue in the case. The petition to grant leave must be filed within four weeks of the issuance of the judgment being appealed and filed with the court of appeal whose judgment is being appealed.

The Supreme Court may decide appeals without a hearing with respect to issues of precedent (*prejudikatfrågor*), affirmations of decisions of the courts of appeal, appeals of a decision in which a court of appeal was the court of first instance, as well as cases in which the entire court is to render the judgment *en banc*, or where nine members are to render judgment. The Supreme Court can affirm, reverse, amend or vacate a judgment and remand the case to the court below to decide consistent with its judgment.

Extraordinary Judicial Remedies

Three extraordinary judicial remedies are available to petitioners: vacating a judgment for procedural or substantive grounds, tolling the procedural statute of limitations, or vacating a judgment for judicial error. Vacating

---

11 These are digital or tape recordings. Court stenographers are not used in Swedish trials, so consequently transcripts of trial proceedings are not routinely created.

a judgment for procedural or substantive grounds includes where a judge or court employee commits a criminal act or violation of office, or a legal representative or legal counsel commits such a crime, and the act has had an effect on the outcome of the case. Another ground is where written evidence or witness testimony was falsified and this has had an effect on the outcome of the case. Evidence not presented previously can also be a ground for vacating a judgment if its introduction would likely have led to a different result and the party shows cause for not bringing it earlier. The final ground is where the application of the law that is the basis of the judgment is in obvious violation of a statute. A petition to vacate on the basis of the first three grounds is to be filed within one year of the party receiving knowledge as to the circumstance forming the basis for the request to vacate. A petition to vacate based on an incorrect application of the law in a civil case is to be filed within six months of the judgment becoming final.

The Supreme Court has the right to toll the procedural statute of limitations in cases where the right to appeal has been barred as the time has expired, basically the three-week statute of limitation discussed above. Petitioner must show good cause for the failure to bring the appeal within the correct time. Such a petition can be brought at the earliest three weeks after the expiry of the period, and at the latest one year after the statute of limitations has expired.

The third remedy available is vacating a judgment on the basis of judicial error. Grounds for such relief include where a case has been decided despite a procedural impediment or where some other legal error occurred during the trial that can be assumed to have had an effect on the judgment. Such appeals must be brought within six months of the date the judgment became final. Another ground here is where a judgment has been rendered against a party not correctly served and thus not able to present a defense. Such an appeal must be brought within six months of the individual becoming aware of the judgment. The fourth ground is where a judgment is drafted so poorly that how the court has decided the matter cannot be determined.

4.2.5 ENFORCEMENT OF JUDGMENTS

The judgment becomes final when the regular time for appeal has expired. When the judgment becomes final, it acts as a bar to further suits between the parties as to these claims due to *res judicata*. Once a judgment is final, it can be enforced. In some cases, a judgment may also be enforced, at least partially, even if an appeal is pending. For example, a judgment for payment (including legal fees) may be enforced unless the party ordered to pay provides security for the payment of the judgment during the appeal.

A national agency, the Enforcement Authority (*Kronofogden*), is empowered to enforce court judgments in the absence of voluntary compliance.[12] The Enforcement Authority also has the authority to enforce both state and private unpaid debts upon the application of a creditor in a summary process. This Authority also supervises bankruptcies as discussed further below in Chapter Ten.

4.2.6 PRIVATE INTERNATIONAL LAW

The conflict of laws, referred to in the European context as private international law (or international private law), is the body of rules each state has adopted in order to regulate situations crossing national borders and thus involving a "foreign" element. In other words, there must be a connection to more than one legal system for the rules of private international law to apply.

Private international law in Sweden is only partially legislated, the regulations consisting of a combination of statutory and case law. Several of the statutes incorporate international conventions to which Sweden is a party under its system of dualism. The European Union also has several legal instruments governing private international law issues, particularly with respect to choice of law, and the recognition and enforcement of judgments within the EU.

Conflict of laws (choice of law) issues are governed by:

- Rome Convention on the Law Applicable to Contractual Obligations 1980;
- Rome I Regulation No. 593/2008 on the law applicable to contractual obligations;
- Rome II Regulation No. 864/2007 on the law applicable to non-contractual obligations (*i.e.*, torts and delicts);

---

12 For more information on the Enforcement Authority in English, *see* its website at kronofogden.se.

- Regulation No. 662/2009 establishing a procedure for the negotiation and conclusion of agreements between Member States and third countries on particular matters concerning the law applicable to contractual and non-contractual obligations; and
- Rome III Regulation No. 1259/2010 implemented enhanced cooperation in the area of the law applicable to divorce and legal separation.

A case involving a conflict of laws can be seen as having different analytical stages, the first of which is characterizing the cause of action, i.e. determining the relevant legal concepts at the heart of the dispute. Once the appropriate characterization has been determined, the court will apply the relevant set of jurisdictional rules to the dispute, deciding whether the court has jurisdiction. Once jurisdiction is established, the corresponding choice of law rule is to be applied. After the applicable law is decided, that law will be applied by the forum court to reach its judgment.[13]

Two main categories of actions as addressed by the private international law rules can be seen as those involving family law issues (including wills and succession) and private law issues (civil and commercial law), including *inter alia* contracts, debtor-creditor rights and tort issues. These categories are also reflected in the EU regulations. Each of these categories has different rules, some of which are incorporated in the general statutes, others can exist in specific statutes addressing conflict of laws in that area. Within the scope of the general EU regulations, the specific rules can only be found in EU directives and international conventions. In the Swedish commercial arena, for example, choice of law is taken up in sections 79–87 of the Bills of Exchange Act (*växellag 1932:130*). As to a contract regarding the sale of movable goods, these issues are taken upon in the Act on the Law Applicable

---

13 The principle of *jura novit curia* also applies to international cases. It is, however, possible for a Swedish court to order the parties to prove the content of the foreign law under JP 35:2.

to the Sale of Goods (*lag 1964:528 om tillämplig lag beträffande internationella köp av lösa saker*).[14]

There is also a general principle of Swedish private international law that a provision of foreign law should not be applied if its application is manifestly incompatible with the fundamentals of the Swedish legal system, *i.e.*, an *ordre public* assessment. This does not occur very often. There are also provisions of Swedish law that protect important Swedish policies and thus must be applied regardless of the applicable law. The determination of which provisions of Swedish law are internationally mandatory is usually a matter for the courts to make on an *ad hoc* basis. One example is the employment protection found in the Swedish Employment Protection Act (*lag 1982:80 om anställningsskydd*) governing unlawful employment terminations.[15]

Finally, the prevailing party may want to enforce the judgment in a state other than the forum state, which will involve the task of securing cross-border recognition and enforcement of the judgment. Cross-border enforcement and/or recognition of a judgment may naturally also be relevant in a "purely" national dispute, such as where assets are situated abroad.

Legal instruments addressing recognition and enforcement within the EU include:

- Brussels I Regulation No. 44/2001 on jurisdiction and the recognition and enforcement of judgments in civil and commercial matters;

---

14 The origins of these provisions are the 1930 Geneva Convention Providing a Uniform Law For Bills of Exchange and Promissory Notes, and the 1955 Hague Convention on the Law Applicable to International Sale of Goods, respectively. Regarding the interrelation between uniform laws such as the 1980 United Nations Convention on Contracts for the Sale of Goods ("CISG") and choice of law rules in contract such as the Rome Convention, *see further* Carolina Saf, *A Study of the Interplay between the Conventions Governing International Contracts of Sale* (1999) available at the Pace Law School CISG Institution's website at cisg.law.pace.edu/cisg/biblio/saf.html.

15 *See*, for example, the Labor Court's decision in AD 1976 no. 101, in which the Court found that an agreement between the parties that all agreements under the employment agreement would by tried in Switzerland was not applicable when plaintiff was a Swede and worked in Sweden, thus the Swedish Employment Protection Act should apply instead.

- Brussels II bis Regulation No. 2201/2003 on jurisdiction and the recognition and enforcement of judgments in matrimonial matters and the matters of parental responsibility;[16]
- European Enforcement Order Regulation No. 805/2004; and
- European Payment Order Regulation No. 1896/2006.[17]

The recognition and enforcement of Member State judgments has been seen as a key with respect to European integration.

4.3 Arbitration

As seen in the procedural rules above, alternative dispute resolution ("ADR") mechanisms such as settlement (*förlikning*) and mediation (*medling*) are alternatives to litigation that the courts are to encourage. ADR is a large part of the legal approach in Sweden generally. One example is the permanent mediation authority, the National Mediation Office (*medlingsinstitut*), created by the state to negotiate solutions in the labor market prior to the taking of industrial action.[18]

Arbitration (*skiljeförfarande*) has also been a long accepted alternative to litigation, in many cases the preferred alternative for several reasons. The first of these is that due to the right of public access, documents filed with a court as a rule become public documents, accessible to any party most of the time, unless deemed confidential under the Public Access to Information

---

16 Council Regulation (EC) No. 2201/2003 of 27 November of 2003 repealed the earlier Brussels II Regulation (EC) No. 1347/2000 in force as of 1 March 2001 on jurisdiction and the recognition and enforcement of judgments in matrimonial matters and the matters of parental responsibility for children of both spouses, in effect extending its scope to include all matters of parental responsibility. This latter regulation is referred to as either BII revised, BIIr or BII bis; bis meaning approximately encore.

17 The European Judicial Network in Civil and Commercial Matters, under the European Commission, has a website listing the different choice of law rules for the different member states. The Swedish rules and procedures can be found at http://ec.europa.eu/civiljustice/applicable_law/applicable_law_swe_en.htm.

18 For more information on the National Mediation Office in English, *see* its website at mi.se.

and Secrecy Act. Even that system is not foolproof, as the assessment of confidentiality is made with each request for the document. Another aspect of arbitration that has been perceived as advantageous is that the parties to the dispute are allowed to choose the persons who are to arbitrate the dispute. Another significant advantage is that arbitration can be set up to be quicker than litigation. Furthermore, an arbitration award may be easier to enforce in other countries than a court judgment. Disadvantages with arbitration can be seen as the costs and that certain areas of the law have been impoverished as little case law is then developed.

The first statutory provisions in Sweden referring to arbitration date back to 1359 and the first arbitration act was adopted in 1887. The current Arbitration Act (*lag 1999:116 om skiljeförfarande*) is primarily gap-filling legislation, entailing that the parties are free to contract out of most of its provisions.[19] There is, however, an element of consumer protection in the act. An arbitration agreement is not binding on consumers if entered into prior to the dispute arising. Exceptions to this rule are given with respect to certain landlord tenant agreements, land lease agreements and insurance agreements.

Arbitration is a procedure that can be prescribed in detail by legislation, or as contracted for between the parties orally or in writing. It can be part of a general contract between the parties as to future disputes, or it can be an agreement in itself as to present or future disputes.[20] The Arbitration Act states that the parties are free to agree to arbitrate in matters they are free to settle, such as to the existence of a fact, contract interpretation or civil sanctions of competition law violations as between the parties. The act has adopted the competence-competence doctrine, which means that the arbitrators are authorized to rule on challenges to their jurisdiction, as well as the doctrine of separability, which means that an arbitration clause that

---

19 An English translation of the 1999 Arbitration Act is available at the website of the Arbitration Institute of the Stockholm Chamber of Commerce at sccinstitute.com under library and then legislation.

20 Model arbitration clauses in both Swedish and English are available at the website of the Arbitration Institute of the Stockholm Chamber of Commerce at sccinstitute.com.

is part of a contract is to be treated as an agreement separate to the contract itself.

A valid arbitration agreement between the parties can act as a bar to litigation. If a complaint has been filed in the courts, the defendant must raise this defense immediately or else it is deemed waived. However, the courts will enforce arbitration agreements and awards, and can also hear motions as to interlocutory measures, such as seizing property for payment.

Any person possessing legal capacity can be an arbitrator, the only requirement being that she be impartial. An arbitrator can be discharged from her duties based on the appearance of partiality where she or a party close to her is a party to the dispute, or is a member of a board of directors or similar organization, and has an interest in its outcome. An arbitrator can also be discharged where she has taken a position in the dispute as an expert, or helped in the preparation or presentation of the case, or has received or demanded compensation in violation of the Act. Any person appointed as an arbitrator has a duty of disclosure as to circumstances that can be deemed to be a conflict of interest.

The parties are free to determine the number of arbitrators, and if they do not, the Act prescribes three. Each party then chooses one arbitrator, and the two arbitrators choose the third. The rules governing arbitration proceedings are entirely decided by the parties, and can be as complicated as litigation, or as simple as meeting at a neutral location, for example Stockholm, with each party presenting a ten-minute oral argument and the award being immediately issued by the arbitrator. The Arbitration Institute of the Stockholm Chamber of Commerce, a permanent arbitration institute, has two sets of procedural rules that can be adopted by the parties, one for normal arbitration proceedings and another for simplified arbitration proceedings (*förenklat skiljeförfarande*) with only one arbitrator.

Arbitration proceedings are invoked when one party submits a request for arbitration to the other party. These proceedings as set out in the Act are optional, in that the parties are free to contract out of them. Under the Act, the request invoking arbitration is to be in writing and include an express request for arbitration, a statement as to the issue as covered by the arbitration agreement to be resolved, and the party's choice of arbitrator if permitted to choose one. If there is more than one arbitrator, the arbitrators chosen by the parties are to choose the chairperson. The dispute is to be handled in an impartial, practical and expeditious manner. The parties are to determine the place of the proceedings and if not, the arbitrators are to decide.

According to the Act, the claimant is to include the claims as to the issue in the request for arbitration, as well as the circumstances. The respondent is then to reply by stating her position with respect to the claims and any other circumstances. New claims can be presented as long as they fall within the scope of the arbitration agreement. Arguments can be presented either orally or in writing, and each party is to have access to any documents submitted to the arbitrators. The decision of the arbitrators is to be in the form of a signed written arbitration award (*skiljedom*) stating the place and date of the award. The award is to be immediately delivered to the parties and is the ultimate determination of the issue between the parties. Normally an arbitration award may not be challenged on questions of law or fact. It can be set aside for limited reasons, such as where an award is granted as to issues that could not be arbitrated, is granted under an invalid arbitration agreement or in the presence of irregularities in the arbitration proceedings. The parties are jointly and severally liable to pay the costs of the arbitration and the fees for the arbitrators.

When making the choice whether to arbitrate or litigate, certain issues should be assessed. Arbitration proceedings can be completely confidential, which in many cases is seen as an advantage over the principle of public access as applied in judicial proceedings. The parties can choose arbitrators and cannot choose judges presiding in litigation. However, arbitrators in Sweden are often judges. No conflict of interest is seen to exist under Swedish law for judges to be paid and act as private arbitrators. The allocation of trial costs and fees is also an aspect that should be addressed when deciding whether to litigate or arbitrate. The losing party in arbitration can be ordered to pay the prevailing party's costs and fees. Naturally, the parties are free to decide otherwise, which is often done, for example, with consumers. In disputes where one party has significantly greater access to financial and legal resources than the other, for example a manufacturer as against a consumer, forcing the consumer to bring a case to arbitration can be seen as onerous.

A well-drafted arbitration clause usually contains a floor as to the value in dispute, in that conflicts up to a certain value should be litigated and not arbitrated. This is done because it is less expensive to litigate such issues in Sweden than to arbitrate. The state pays for the courts, judges and the administration. In addition, certain types of uncontested claims can be directly executed by the Enforcement Authority, entailing no need for litigation at all. If the dispute concerns simply payment, arbitration costs may be an unnecessary expense particularly in light of the expediency of the Enforcement Authority's procedures. Within the European context, well-drafted arbitration clauses also include reference to the language in which the arbitration is to be conducted, the location of the arbitration, whether it is to be submitted to a permanent arbitration institute, and the rules to be applied.

CHAPTER 5

Criminal Law and Procedure

Five basic objectives are deemed to underlie penal systems generally: Retribution, individual deterrence, societal deterrence, rehabilitation and reparation. The balance of these different objectives has been changing in Sweden during recent decades. Before the 1970's, retribution was a dominant theme. During the 1970's, retribution was marginalized with the need for rehabilitation placed in the forefront (*behandlingslinjen*). A reform in 1989 forged a new balance with a "Neo-classical" approach (*nyklassicismen*), in which the objective now is to achieve proportionality between the criminal act and its criminal sanction.

Once an individual has paid for her crime, in other words, served her sentence, an unauthorized disclosure of past criminal activity can be seen as defamation, as the truth is not an absolute defense in Sweden. Private parties are not allowed to keep registers of criminal convictions unless permission has been granted to do so by the Data Inspection Board (*Datainspektionen*). For example, insurance companies are not allowed to keep registers of insured drivers who been convicted of driving under the influence of alcohol or narcotics unless they have permission to do so. Only the police can lawfully keep registers of criminal convictions, and public access to such registers is not allowed as a rule under the Police Register Act (*lag 1998:620 om belastningsregister*) and the Personal Data Act (*personuppgiftslag 1998:204*).[1] Naturally, the courts keep records of criminal judgments.

---

1   An English translation of the Personal Data Act is available at the website of the agency charged with the enforcement of the act, the Data Inspection Board, at datainspektionen.se.

The Swedish Penal Code (*brottsbalk* 1962:700),[2] encompassing thirty-eight chapters, is divided into three main parts.

TABLE 5.1 The Penal Code.

Part One: General Provisions	
Chap. 1 Crimes and Criminal Sanctions	Chap. 2 Jurisdiction

Part Two: Crimes	
Crimes Against Persons and Property	
Chap. 3 Crimes Against Life and Persons	Chap. 8 Theft and Robbery
Chap. 4 Crimes Against Personal Liberty	Chap. 9 Fraud
Chap. 5 Defamation	Chap. 10 Embezzlement
Chap. 6 Sexual Offences	Chap. 11 Crimes Against Creditors
Chap. 7 Crimes against the Family	Chap. 12 Crimes Inflicting Public Damage
Crimes Against the State and Public Order	
Chap. 13 Crimes Involving Public Danger	Chap. 18 Crimes Against the Head of State
Chap. 14 Crimes of Falsification	Chap. 19 Crimes Threatening National Security
Chap. 15 Perjury, False Prosecution and Other Untrue Statements	Chap. 20 Crimes concerning the Misuse of Office
Chap. 16 Crimes against Public Order	Chap. 21 Crimes by Members of the Armed Forces
Chap. 17 Crimes against Public Operations	Chap. 22 Treason
General Provisions	
Chap. 23 Attempt, Preparation, Conspiracy and Complicity	
Chap. 24 Defenses to Criminal Liability	

Part Three: Sanctions	
Chap. 25 Fines	Chap. 32 Repealed
Chap. 26 Imprisonment	Chap. 33 Credit for Arrest and Custody
Chap. 27 Probation	Chap. 34 Concurrent Sentencing
Chap. 28 Probation with Supervision	Chap. 35 Sentencing Ceilings
Chap. 29 Sentencing	Chap. 36 Forfeiture of Property
Chap. 30 Choice of Penal Sanction	Chap. 37 Supervisory Boards
Chap. 31 Commitment to Care	Chap. 38 Criminal Procedure

---

2   An English translation of the Penal Code is available at the website of the Government Offices at sweden.gov.se.

According to Section 1:1 of the Penal Code ("PC"), "a crime is an act as described in this code or other law or regulation and for which a criminal sanction as stated [within the code] is prescribed." Consequently, the Penal Code is one statutory source of criminal law, but several major categories of crimes are not encompassed within the code but are found elsewhere, including criminal acts as defined by the Tax Crimes Act (*skattebrottslag* 1971:69), the Act on Penal Law for Narcotics (*narkotikastrafflag* 1968:64),[3] the Traffic Crimes Act (*lag 1951:649 om straff för vissa trafikbrott*), the Genocide Crimes Act (*lag 1964:169 om straff för folkmord*), and the Act on Social Benefit Fraud (*bidragsbrottslag* 2007:612). Consequently, many of the most serious crimes are not included in the Penal Code. Specific statutes can also regulate criminal penalties for specific crimes, such as the Act on Penalties for Smuggling (*lag 2000:1225 om straff för smuggling*).[4] A third category is crimes not set out in the Penal Code or specific criminal statutes, but rather in private law statutes. For example, the Land Code contains several paragraphs concerning criminal offenses in the form of illegally brokering apartments and the Companies Act (*aktiebolagslag* 2005:551) also includes criminal provisions.

5.1 Criminal Law

About one and one-half million crimes are reported annually in Sweden, of which approximately forty percent are solved.[5] Crimes committed in Sweden are to be tried under Swedish law by Swedish courts. Certain crimes committed outside of Sweden also fall within the jurisdiction of Swedish law and the Swedish courts, for example where the perpetrator of a crime committed elsewhere is a Swedish citizen, becomes one, or has permanent residency in Sweden. Jurisdiction also exists where the perpetrator is not a Swede but physically in Sweden, and the crime according to Swedish law has

---

3   An English translation of the Act on Penal Law for Narcotics is available at the website of the Government Offices at sweden.gov.se.

4   An English translation of the Act on Penalties for Smuggling is available at the website of the Government Offices at sweden.gov.se.

5   These statistics are from the Swedish National Council for Crime Prevention (*Brotts-förebyggande rådet*, Brå) and are available at its website, bra.se.

a sanction of at least six months imprisonment. Jurisdiction, as the main rule, is not to be exercised in Sweden if the act is not criminal in the country in which it was committed, or the only criminal sanction is a fine. Neither can the defendant be sentenced to a higher sanction in Sweden than that imposed by the country in which the act was committed.

A fundamental principle in criminal law is that individuals must be convicted and sentenced in accordance with law (*legalitetsprincipen*).[6] This is espoused in Article 10 of the second chapter of the Instrument of Government, and again in Section 5 of the Act Concerning the Enactment of the Penal Code (*lag 1964:163 om införande av brottsbalken*). This principle entails that the courts cannot impose criminal liability by applying criminal statutes retroactively, by analogy or interpreting criminal statutes extensively. However, the courts can to some extent look to the legislative preparatory works when interpreting a penal law. The courts are to be objective (*objektivitetsprincipen*) and when interpreting a statute, the courts are to choose the interpretation more favorable to the defendant, setting the defendant free rather than convicting (*hellre fria än fälla*) in cases of uncertainty. When assessing the sufficiency of the evidence, the court is also to find for the defendant in cases of doubt, with the prosecutor having the burden of proof of beyond a reasonable doubt (*utom allt rimligt tvivel*).

5.1.1 THE ELEMENTS OF A CRIME GENERALLY

Crimes are defined in PC 1:1 as those acts defined as criminal by the code or other statute for which a sentence in accordance with the Penal Code is to be assessed. Criminal acts have objective and subjective requisites, both of which must be proven for an individual to be criminally convicted. Many of the crimes listed in the Penal Code have three degrees: aggravated (*grövt*), normal (*normalgrad*), and lesser (*ring*), reflecting different levels of violence or harm, or other factors, with respect to the crime committed.

---

6   *Nullum crimen sine lege* and *nulla poena sine lege*.

Objective Requisites

The objective requisites of a criminal act are those as set out in the statute. For example, murder is defined in PC 3:1 simply as the taking of another's life. Thus the two objective requisites are taking and another's life. Certain crimes focus on the result, requiring a physical harm (*effektdelikt*) such as murder and battery. Some crimes replace the requirement of a harm with the requirement of a danger, which can be a requirement of an actual danger (*konkret fara*) such as with arson of a building at the time inhabited by persons, or a hypothetical danger (*abstrakt fara*) such as can be the case with sabotage endangering public safety. There must be causality between the criminal act and the harm or danger. Other crimes focus more on the behavior, requiring an act or omission (*beteendedelikt*) such as insubordination.

Subjective Requisites

The subjective requisite is either in the form of intent or negligence. As a main rule, an act is to be considered criminal under the Penal Code only if committed intentionally. Self-intoxication or similar conduct does not negate the requirement of intent. Where nothing is stated in the Code or statute as to intent or negligence, intent is required. Negligence results in criminal liability only when expressly stated as such in the Penal Code. For example, the crime of negligent manslaughter is defined in PC 3:7 as where a person "due to negligence causes another's death." Thus the objective requisites are causes and another's death, and the subjective requisite is negligence.

The requirement of intent in the Swedish system is not interpreted to mean that a person has to be deemed legally capable of forming an intent. For example, juveniles or persons suffering from mental disorders are not found to be lacking the capacity to form the intent required to be found guilty. Juveniles or adults suffering from a mental disorder can thus be found to have intentionally committed an act. However, juveniles under the age of fifteen years cannot be criminally prosecuted. A mentally disturbed person can be prosecuted, but cannot be criminally sanctioned even if found guilty. Legal persons as a rule also cannot be criminally sanctioned as the requirement of intent is deemed to require an individual. Corporations can be found to have committed certain criminal acts for which there are civil sanctions such as fines or forfeiture of property.

There are three general categories of intent when assessing this issue: direct intent (*direkt uppsåt*), indirect intent (*indirekt uppsåt*) and reckless intent (*likgiltighetsuppsåt*). Direct intent exists, for example, where an individual intends to murder a specific person and then murders that person. Indirect intent can be seen to exist where the individual places a bomb on a train to kill A, but also ends up killing everyone else on the train. Indirect intent then exists with respect to all the persons killed except A, whom the individual had the direct intent to kill. Reckless intent exists where the individual did not mean to kill anyone, but rather simply wanted to derail a train, was aware of the risks involved and indifferent to the fact that someone might die.

Another general principle in Swedish criminal law is that the individual's intent must cover all the subjective requisites (*täckningsprincipen*). This has been problematic with respect to sexual crimes as defined in the sixth chapter of the Penal Code. For example, rape is defined in PC 6:1 as where a person, who "through battery, or otherwise through violence or threat of a criminal act forces another person to sexual intercourse or to perform or tolerate a sexual act that with respect to its degree of violation and the circumstances in general can be seen as comparable to rape." The objective requisites that the prosecutor must prove then become the use of violence or threat of a criminal act, and forcing another to sexual intercourse. The prosecutor must then also prove beyond a reasonable doubt that the defendant had the intent to use violence or threat, and that the defendant had the intent to force another to sexual intercourse. Defendants often successfully argue they did not know the sexual act was not consensual and the prosecutor is unable to prove the lack of consent, as understood by the defendant, beyond a reasonable doubt.

5.1.2 ATTEMPT, PREPARATION, COMPLICITY, CONSPIRACY AND FAILURE TO REPORT

Chapter twenty-three of the Penal Code contains provisions as to attempt (*försök*), preparation (*förberedelse*), complicity (*medverkan*) and conspiracy (*stämpling*) with respect to crimes. Attempt to commit a crime, preparation and conspiracy are not general criminal actions. Instead, statutory provisions must explicitly impose criminal liability. For example, attempted murder, manslaughter, infanticide and battery are crimes as stated in PC 3:11. Chapters three through twenty-two of the Penal Code all end with provisions listing those crimes in which criminal liability is imposed for attempt, preparation, complicity or conspiracy. Criminal liability for attempt, preparation or conspiracy is not to be imposed where the individual voluntarily interrupts the act and no crime was committed.

Criminal attempt is defined as where the defendant has begun a course of action leading to a crime, but has not yet completed the crime. The course of action must entail a risk that the crime can be completed, or that any absence of such a risk was perceived by the individual as simply temporary. Criminal preparation is defined as where an individual, with the intent to commit or facilitate a crime, provides or receives monies for a crime or to cover the costs for committing a crime, or procures or provides objects particularly for the purpose of assisting in committing a crime. Criminal conspiracy is where a person, in connection with another, decides to commit or solicit, or offers to commit, a criminal act.

Complicity is where a party encourages another through advice or by deed (*råd eller dåd*) to commit a crime. In contrast to attempt or preparation, complicity is a general crime, applicable to each of the crimes contained in the Penal Code as set out in Section 23:4. In those crimes defined outside of the Penal Code, liability for complicity can only be imposed with respect to criminal actions for which imprisonment is the sanction.

The omission to report a crime is also criminally punishable if such a duty is explicitly set out by statute. The omission has to be in a situation where a report could have been made as to a crime in progress without danger to the individual or anyone close to her. Parents can also be found criminally liable for a failure to control a child or ward in their care or under their control from committing a crime if this could have been done without danger to themselves or anyone close or by reporting it.

5.1.3 CRIMINAL DEFENSES

Lawful defenses to criminal acts are set out in chapter twenty-four of the Penal Code, but can also be found in other statutes. Several have been created in the case law. The first general defense in the Penal Code is self-defense (*nödvärn*), defined to exist where a criminal attack is imminent or has been commenced against a person or property, where a person through violence or the threat of violence has obstructed the repossession of property while caught in a criminal act, where a person has unlawfully forced or attempted to force entry into a dwelling, or where a person has refused to leave a dwelling when ordered to do so. The violence used in self-defense cannot, however, exceed that necessary in the situation taking into account the nature of the criminal act, the object of the self-defense and the circumstances in general. The right to self-defense is also seen to cease when the attack ends.

Necessity (*nöd*) is another general self-defense. This is where an act is taken due to a danger to life, health, property or another important interest protected by law. Consent (*samtycke*) is also a permitted defense in certain cases, such as an injury received in boxing, but not, for example, with respect to murder. With many crimes, such as theft, the lack of consent is also a required element of the crime. The duty to obey an order (*lydnad*) can also be invoked as a defense in certain cases, particular in the use of violence by police officers. A mistake as to the law can be a defense where the individual's mistake is based on a mistake made by a public authority when publicly issuing the legal provision or for another reason that is manifestly excusable. Specific defenses include the use of violence by police in certain situations as well as by military personnel in cases of mutiny.

5.1.4 STATUTE OF LIMITATIONS

The statute of limitations for crimes is based on the criminal sanction. If the highest sanction for the crime is one year in prison, the defendant has to be detained or served with the criminal complaint within two years. If two years imprisonment is the highest sanction, then the statute of limitations is five years. Imprisonment of eight years has a statute of limitations of ten years, and if imprisonment is for a defined number of years over eight, the statute of limitations is fifteen years. If the sentence can be lifetime, then the statute of limitations is twenty-five years. As of 2010, several crimes are now never barred by the statute of limitations: murder, crimes against humanity, genocide and certain terrorist acts, as well as an attempt at any of these crimes. If several crimes are committed, the statute of limitations does not expire until the end of the period for the most severe of the group of crimes.

5.2 Criminal Sanctions

Criminal sanctions (*brottspåföljder*) under Swedish law consist of two categories: criminal penalties (*straff*) involving either imprisonment (*fängelse*) or criminal fines (*böter*), and other criminal sentences (*andra brottspåföljder*) comprising of probation (*villkorlig dom*), probation with supervision (*skyddstillsyn*), institutionalized treatment for substance abuse or psychiatric care (*särskild vård*) and institutionalized care for juveniles

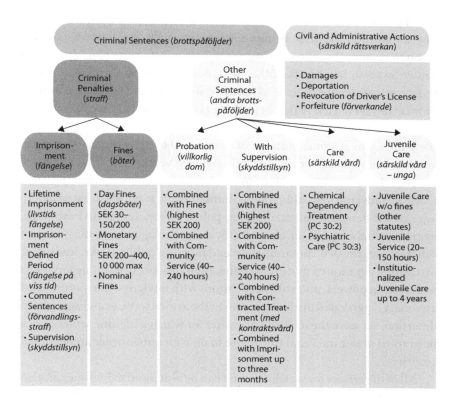

DIAGRAM 5.1 Criminal Sentencing Structure (reprinted with permission from the author, Josef Zila).

(*särskild vård av unga*). Civil and administrative actions can also be a consequence of a criminal act, for example liability for damages, deportation, driver's license revocation and forfeiture of property. Imprisonment is deemed the most serious of these sanctions.

5.2.1 CRIMINAL PENALTIES

The catalogue of criminal offenses in the Penal Code can be categorized as those crimes for which only imprisonment is a sanction, those for which either imprisonment or criminal fines can be imposed, and those for which only criminal fines can be imposed.

Imprisonment is either for life or for a certain defined maximum amount of years or months, these being eighteen, ten, eight, six, four, two or one, or up to six months. Life imprisonment is the most severe penalty allowed under Swedish law. Unlike other sentences, life imprisonment is for an indeterminate length of time. When a person sentenced to lifetime imprisonment has served ten years, the individual can petition to have the sentence commuted to a defined number of years. The court may only commute a life sentence to a defined number of years equal to or below the maximum sentence allowed in Sweden, currently eighteen years.[7]

The crimes for which lifetime imprisonment is a sanction under the Penal Code include: murder, kidnapping, human trafficking, aggravated arson, aggravated destruction endangering public safety, aggravated sabotage, aggravated sabotage of air or sea traffic endangering public safety, airport sabotage, aggravated contamination endangering public safety, leading or instigating aggravated mutiny, sedition, high treason, disloyal negotiations with foreign powers, unlawful negotiations with foreign powers, aggravated espionage, aggravated insubordination in the armed services and aggravated desertion. As seen, the majority of crimes for which a lifetime sentence can be granted under the Penal Code have to do with public order and national security.

All of the crimes for which a person can be sentenced to lifetime can also in the alternative have a sentence of up to ten years, and several eighteen

---

7   This and other information in English is available at the website of the Swedish Prison and Probation Service at kriminalvarden.se.

years, of imprisonment under the Penal Code. Crimes punishable by life or a maximum of eighteen years in prison include: Murder, kidnapping, aggravated arson, public destruction, aggravated sabotage, crimes against folk groups, unlawful possession of weapons, unlawful obstruction of air traffic, spread of poison, mutiny and aggravated mutiny, treason and aggravated espionage.

The following crimes can entail a sentence of up to ten years (without lifetime imprisonment): intentional manslaughter, aggravated assault, unlawful deprivation of liberty, unlawful coercion resulting in jeopardy, aggravated rape, aggravated robbery, instigating violent riot and armed threat to public order. Imprisonment of up to eight years can be sanctioned for aggravated sexual exploitation of a minor, arson, destruction endangering public safety, aggravated money counterfeiting, aggravated perjury and instigating war.

Crimes entailing imprisonment of up to six years include infanticide, reckless manslaughter, lesser kidnapping, aggravated coercion, aggravated violation of integrity, rape, aggravated sexual exploitation, aggravating procurement of sexual services, aggravated theft, robbery, aggravated fraud, aggravated extortion, aggravated use of criminal proceeds, aggravated swindling, aggravated embezzlement, aggravated breach of duty to a principal, aggravated creditor fraud, contamination posing a public danger, aggravated contamination posing danger to animals or plant, aggravated forgery, leading or instigating mutiny, mutiny, aggravated obstruction of justice, sedition, unlawful threat or coercion as to public opinion, unlawful negotiations with foreign powers, espionage, aggravated misuse of office, aggravated bribery, aggravated violence against a superior in the armed forces and lesser treason.

Approximately fifty crimes have a sanction of up to four years imprisonment, ninety have the sanction of up to two years imprisonment and only fifteen have the sanction of up to one-year imprisonment. Slightly over fifty crimes have the sanction of up to at most six months imprisonment.

Criminal fines are to be paid to the state and can be ordered in several different ways. Variable (day) fines (*dagsböter*) are assessed based on the defendant's income and other circumstances for a certain number of days from 30 to 150, within an economic range beginning with SEK 50 depending on the income of the individual, and a total minimum of SEK 750 after any adjustments. Variable fines are based on income so that wealthier defendants are not perceived of as getting off too easily, and the fines for poorer defendants are not too onerous. Fixed fines (*penningböter*) can be awarded as total amounts between SEK 200 and 4 000. Nominal fines can also be assessed according to guidelines (*normerade böter*) for each crime, with a minimum amount of SEK 100.

5.2.2 OTHER CRIMINAL SENTENCES

In certain cases, the courts can decide on criminal sentences other than imprisonment or fines, such as probation, probation with supervision, institutionalized chemical dependency or psychiatric care, or a juvenile sentence. Probation is simply that the defendant is sentenced to good behavior. If the defendant violates this, she can be sentenced to prison instead. Probation can be combined with fines or community service. Probation with supervision can entail electronic monitoring. The convicted person then is monitored twenty-four hours a day with the aid of an ankle transmitter. Persons sentenced to a maximum of six months can apply for this type of sanction. Approximately 3 000 persons serve their sentences by electronic monitoring. Probation with supervision can also be combined with fines, community service, contracted care or imprisonment of up to three months.

Institutionalized care is an alternative to imprisonment or fines for persons who are chemically dependent, as well as for persons suffering from mental disorders. Juveniles can be sentenced either to social services care with or without fines, community service or institutionalized care for up to four years.

5.2.3 CIVIL AND ADMINISTRATIVE ACTIONS

Other consequences of a criminal conviction can arise falling outside of criminal law and into civil or administrative law instead. The defendant can be found liable to pay compensatory damages for losses as caused by the criminal act to persons or property. Certain property of the convicted party can be forfeited, or a driver's license revoked. For non-Swedish citizens, it can be a question of deportation in certain cases.

5.3 Criminal Procedure

The Code of Judicial Procedure as discussed in the previous chapter also governs proceedings in criminal cases, both through the general regulations and the chapters specific to criminal procedure, at the police, prosecutor and judicial levels. In addition, several chapters in the Penal Code also address criminal judicial procedural issues.

Criminal cases are typically delineated by the fact that it is the state prosecuting an individual for a violation of the law resulting in harm to the society (*allmänt åtal*) and sanctioned, for example, by imprisonment or fines. Rape, though a crime perpetuated on an individual, has been politically deemed harmful to society. Crimes in Sweden can be categorized as one of three types. The first two are crimes where the prosecutor has the discretion to prosecute (*åklagarbrott*) and crimes where the consent of the victim is necessary for prosecution to protect the victim from any further invasions of privacy (*angivelsebrott*). In both these categories, the victim (*målsägande*) has the right to prosecute the case if the prosecutor decides not to pursue it. The third category is those cases in which the victim of the crime has the sole right to prosecute the case, for example with respect to criminal slander. Prosecutions as driven by the victim (*enskilt åtal*) are very rare.

In a case prosecuted by the state, both the state criminal action and the victim's claim for damages can be and usually are tried in the same litigation. This is in contrast, for example, to systems in which the criminal case is tried separately from the civil tort claim for victim damages. The reasons for including the tort claim in the criminal prosecution are judicial economy and alleviating the situation of the victim by not forcing her to go through two trials. However, when these two actions, the criminal and tort, are combined into one, the civil tort claim is often tried under the same standard of proof as the criminal case, beyond a reasonable doubt, as opposed to the typical civil tort claim burden of proof, the preponderance of the evidence. This means that if the defendant is found not guilty, liability for damages in tort is usually not imposed on the defendant in the criminal case, unless the prosecutor or attorney representing the victim (*målsägandebiträde*) at the same time has alleged damages based on negligence. By pleading both criminal intent and negligence, the court can find defendant not guilty of the criminal act, but still be liable for damages due to negligence. However, this seldom occurs.

Damages if awarded are in addition to any fines assessed. The Crime Victims Support and Compensation Authority (*Brottsoffermyndigheten*) is in charge of state compensation to victims of crime.[8] Liability for the payment of damages resulting from a crime first rests the defendant, then any applicable insurance coverage, and then with the state in certain but not all cases.

5.3.1 THE CRIMINAL INVESTIGATION PHASE

Chapter twenty-three of the Code of Judicial Procedure regulates the course of the criminal investigations. A criminal pre-investigation can begin when the police or prosecutor receive knowledge of criminal activity. If it is a more serious crime, the police are to report it to the prosecutor. If the crime is obviously insignificant and the perpetrator would only be sentenced to a fine, the police need not report the crime to the prosecutor at all (*rapporteftergift*). For crimes that are not serious (*enkel beskaffenhet*), the police initiate and conduct the investigation, with the prosecutor being notified after the investigation is completed.

If the criminal investigation is submitted to the prosecutor, the prosecutor is to initiate an official investigation (*förundersökning*) as quickly as possible. Once the official investigation is commenced by the prosecutor, certain decisions as taken by the authorities, mainly the police and the prosecutor, can be appealed to the administrative courts. The criminal trial is held, in contrast, before the general courts.

The investigation is to be conducted in line with the objectives of determining whether a crime has been committed, identifying any person who can reasonably be suspected of committing the crime, and deciding whether sufficient reason exists to file a criminal complaint. The investigation is also to prepare the case in a manner so that it can be presented in one continuous session at trial. The prosecutor has a duty to conduct the investigation objectively and expeditiously, taking into consideration circumstances that speak both for and against the suspect.

---

8   For more information in English on the Crime Victim Support and Compensation Authority, *see* its website at brottsoffermyndigheten.se.

Examinations

One of the tools available during the investigation is the examination of witnesses and suspects (*förhör*). The police have the right to require any witnesses present at a crime scene to accompany the police to the station to be examined. The police also have the right to summon persons upon penalty of fine to an examination. Individuals are not required to undergo more than six hours of examination. A juvenile cannot be required to participate for more than three hours. A suspect can be required to remain an additional six hours if this is considered particularly important, and if a juvenile, only an additional three hours. After the examination with the suspect is concluded, or after twelve hours have passed, the suspect can immediately leave. In the event the police want to detain the suspect for further examination, the prosecutor must approve the suspect's arrest and the court thereafter must issue a detention order.

No person can be compelled to make statements or answer questions at an examination. However, the prosecutor can request the court to be allowed to examine the person as a witness (*vittne*) already during the investigation. The person conducting the examination is not permitted to provoke a confession or statement by using incorrect information, promises, threat, duress or other unlawful measures. The police can also request that a witness be brought in for questioning. The person in charge of the examination has the authority to decide who can be present at the examination, including a reliable witness to the proceedings and a representative for the person being interrogated. If it is the suspect, the suspect has the right to have counsel present if she so requests. Counsel for the victim can also be present if the victim is being examined, as well as a support person if such a presence is not negative to the investigation. Minors under the age of fifteen years have a right to a custodian being present if such will not interfere with the investigation.

Searches and Seizures

The regulations regarding searches can be found in chapter twenty-eight of the Code of Judicial Procedure. The police can conduct searches of residences and offices of individuals suspected of committing more serious crimes. Searches of other premises can only occur if a crime has been committed, or a suspected arrested there, or if there is particular reason to believe that evidence can be found there. An order to search is to be issued by the investigative leader, the prosecutor or a court. It is to be granted only where the reasons for the measure outweigh the potential violation or general harm that the measure could cause the suspect or another party.

Body searches can also be conducted of the suspect and certain other persons, extending to any bags, packages or other objects on their person. A person subjected to a body search can be detained for six hours, and if particular reason exists, an additional six hours. A DNA saliva test can be taken of a suspect of a crime for which imprisonment is a sentence.

Property can also be seized under the regulations in chapter twenty-six of the Code where there is a reasonable suspicion of a crime, and a risk that the suspect will dispose of property, for example, to avoid paying criminal sanctions in the form of variable fines. An order to seize property is to be issued by a court, but the prosecutor can seize property pending the order. Property can also be seized as evidence under the provisions of chapter twenty-seven. Electronic eavesdropping and videotaping can occur within certain parameters during an investigation with respect to crimes sanctioned by a minimum prison sentence of two years. Any person subject to such measures is to be informed of the measure as soon as possible after the investigation no longer can be jeopardized by such disclosure, and at the most, one month after the investigation has been closed.

If the police violate the rights of an individual during a search or seizure, that evidence is admissible at trial and the individual can file a complaint with the Chancellor of Justice or a Parliamentary Ombudsman. If either finds a violation, a public criticism can be issued. Only the Chancellor of Justice can grant a claim for damages. An individual can also sue the state through the Chancellor. The sanction of police conduct by declaring certain evidence inadmissible at trial if obtained in violation of a person's constitutional rights is not invoked in Sweden.

Pre-Trial Custody

The provisions regulating custody, arrest and detention are found in chapter twenty-four of the Code of Judicial Procedure. The police have the authority to place an individual in custody (*gripande*) for compelling reasons in the absence of a judicial detention order. Private individuals also have the power to immediately seize suspects in the process of committing crimes or fleeing a crime scene, or any persons posted as wanted for committing a crime, if the crime has imprisonment as a sanction.

In all other cases, the prosecutor makes the decision to arrest a suspect (*anhållningsbeslut*) and can hold a suspect in arrest without a judicial order for at the most three days. The decision to arrest is also to be assessed under the principle of proportionality and in addition, the suspect must be reasonably suspected on probable cause of committing a crime having a sanction of at least one-year imprisonment. A suspect is to be arrested only with respect to more serious crimes and where it can be assumed that the suspect will not appear at trial, will tamper with or destroy evidence or jeopardize the investigation, or continue in criminal activity. Suspects can also be arrested for less serious crimes if it is significant that the suspect be taken into custody awaiting further investigation.

The prosecutor is to apply for a judicial detention order (*häktningsbeslut*) immediately after the arrest and the court is to address the request within four days. The detention of suspects has been an area in which Sweden has received criticism by the European Court of Human Rights under Article 5 of the European Convention concerning the right to liberty and security of person, as extended periods of time could elapse with a suspect in arrest without a detention order.[9] The requirement now is that the prosecutor normally is to request judicial approval the same, or at least, the next, day after the arrest under JP 24:12. If the prosecutor fails to do this, the suspect is to be released.

If the court issues a detention order, the suspect is to remain in jail until either the reasons for the detention no longer exist (for example, the investigation is complete and the suspect can no longer destroy evidence), the case is dismissed or judgment has been rendered. There is no bail or bond system under which a suspect can be released before trial. The prosecutor can also decide that the suspect should be put in isolation, with contacts to the outside world limited while in custody if there is a perceived risk that evidence

---

9   *See Skoogström*, European Court of Human Rights, judgment dated 28 September 1984, App. No. 8582/79 and *McGoff v. Sweden*, European Court of Human Rights, judgment dated 26 October 1984, App. No. A/83.

could be tampered with or destroyed or the investigation impeded.[10] The prosecutor can order that the suspect be placed in isolation, with minimum contacts only with counsel, and no access to television or newspapers.[11] If such a decision is taken, the prosecutor needs to file for judicial approval on the same or next day as the decision was made. The court is to issue its approval within one week.

The authority of the prosecutor to limit the contacts of the accused with the outside world is based on the premise that such contacts would allow suspects to try to destroy or tamper with evidence. The counterbalance to this detention is that if the individual is found innocent, or the case dismissed, the individual is entitled to damages from the state for unlawful detention. Damages for unlawful arrest can include compensation for loss of income and other costs, as well as for pain and suffering. According to the Chancellor's guidelines, the average amount of damages for simply pain and suffering awarded for the first month is SEK 30 000.[12]

Instead of being detained in custody, the suspect can be required by the prosecutor or a court under chapter twenty-five of the Code to periodically register with the police. A travel prohibition can also be put in place forbidding the suspect from leaving a certain geographic area or the country. The suspect can also be ordered to be at home at certain times during the day.

Right to a Public Defender

If the suspect is placed into custody, according to Section 21:3a of the Code of Judicial Procedure, the suspect has the right to a public defender (*offentlig försvarare*) if she so requests. The same section prescribes that a public defender is to be appointed if the suspect has need of one taking into

---

10 Fifty-eight people committed suicide in jail in Sweden between 1998–2008, and for those same years, eighteen suicides were committed in Swedish prisons. There were 108 suicide attempts in jails in 2008. Thirty thousand individuals are taken into pre-trial arrest annually, on average about 2 500 per month in Sweden. These statistics are available at the website of the Swedish Prison and Probation Service at kriminalvarden.se.

11 See The Jail Act (*häkteslag 2010:611*).

12 For this information in Swedish, *see* the website of the Chancellor of Justice at jk.se.

consideration the criminal investigation or if it seems probable that the eventual criminal sanction will be imprisonment. A public defender is also to be appointed if particular reasons merit such an appointment taking into consideration the suspect's personal circumstances or the circumstances in the criminal case. A public defender can be appointed by the court even against the wishes of the suspect. If the suspect already has a defense attorney, a public defender is not to be appointed.

Right to the Investigation Materials

If the police or prosecutor have grounds for a reasonable suspicion (*skäligen misstänkt*) that a suspect has committed a crime, they must inform the suspect of this at the next examination. After this notification, the suspect has the right to access the materials gathered during the investigation and be continually notified as to the course of the investigation.

Decision to Prosecute

The prosecutor when investigating and prosecuting a case has a duty to be objective and present evidence that speaks in favor of the defendant. If during the course of the investigation the prosecutor finds that the evidence is not sufficient for a successful prosecution, or that the costs of the proceedings are too high, the prosecutor can terminate the investigation. Even where the evidence is sufficient, the prosecutor can decide to not prosecute the case (*åtalsunderlåtelse*). The prosecutor is free to do this where it has been shown that the suspect most likely committed the crime, for example, by confessing to the crime, and the sentence would only be fines or probation, or where the crime was committed by a juvenile or a person suffering from a mental disorder.

The prosecutor also has the authority with respect to lesser crimes to assess criminal sanctions of fines and/or probation if the defendant confesses to the crime and agrees to the sanction. These agreed upon sanctions are reported in the police register. Aside from this admission of minor crimes, there is no plea bargaining system in Sweden.

5.3.2 THE TRIAL

When determining whether to file the criminal complaint, the prosecutor must assess not only whether the evidence is sufficient for a prosecution, but also the appropriateness of a prosecution (*lämplighetsprövning*). Under the Penal Code, certain crimes require prosecution only where there is reason from a public interest perspective to do so, such as the crime of the unlawful deprivation of custody of children. The decisions of a prosecutor to either lay down an investigation or not prosecute a case can be appealed by the victim. If a question of new information or evidence, the prosecutor is to herself reassess the decision. Otherwise, the appeal is filed with the Prosecutor's Office and a head prosecutor is to handle the appeal. An appeal of the latter decision can be filed with the National Prosecutor's Office. Approximately 2 400 decisions were appealed to the Prosecutor's Office in 2011.

If the prosecutor decides to go forward with the criminal case, any requests by the prosecutor with respect to how the court should handle the case must be included in the criminal complaint. The prosecutor is also under a duty to file a written report summarizing the investigation to the court. A pre-trial conference can be held if deemed beneficial, but the main rule is that the case simply goes to trial when ready.

The court is bound by the pleadings of the prosecutor to the extent of the description of the criminal conduct and actions by the defendant cited (*gärningsbeskrivning*) as fulfilling these necessary criminal requisites, but not as to the actual crime alleged. For example, if the prosecutor has only pled assault, the court can find the defendant guilty of a lesser or higher degree of assault if the requisites for the lesser or higher offense are fulfilled by the acts included in the prosecutor's description of the criminal acts.

At trial, the judging panel in criminal cases typically consists of one legally qualified judge and three or five lay judges. One legally qualified judge without any lay judges is considered sufficient where the case concerns a crime with a sanction of six months imprisonment and/or a fine, and the sanction is assessed in advance to only entail a fine. The court can decide a case without an oral hearing where neither party has requested a trial, or where a trial is deemed unnecessary with respect to the case, for example with respect to offences such as shoplifting or speeding tickets. If the case involves a juvenile, an oral hearing has to be held.

If the defendant does not have defense counsel, the defendant can request that the court appoint a public defender who initially is paid by the state. If the defendant is found guilty, defendant can be liable to repay the defense fees and costs. If the only possible sanction is a fine, or if the court finds the case to not be complicated, the court may choose to not appoint a public defendant.

A criminal trial is conducted much as a civil trial, with the prosecutor and defense attorney making opening statements and then presenting evidence. The four general principles of procedural law discussed in the previous chapter, namely that all evidence and arguments are to be presented orally, that all evidence is to be presented in one continuous hearing upon which the judgment is to be based, and that court hearings are to be public, are applicable in criminal trials. The main rule with respect to evidence is that everything is admissible. Under Section 35:1 of the Code of Judicial Procedure, the court is to assess all the evidence submitted according to conscience. Under Section 35:7, the court has the authority to reject evidence concerning issues not relevant to the case, evidence that is not necessary or without effect, can be replaced with less effort by other evidence or cannot be introduced without unreasonably delaying the trial. Privileges, such as attorney-client privileges, can also be invoked as discussed in Section 4.1.2 of the previous chapter.

Neither the victim nor the defendant is permitted to testify under oath during the trial as prescribed by JP 36:1. Close relatives to the defendant are also not to be compelled to testify. Other witnesses can be compelled to testify upon penalty of being found guilty of perjury (*mened*) or negligent testimony (*ovarsam utsaga*). All examinations of witnesses, as well as of the defendant and the victim, can be digitally recorded unless there are specific reasons for not doing so. In addition, the court can find that the parties or witnesses do not need to personally appear in court, but can make an appearance via videoconference or by telephone.

After the evidence in the trial has been presented, personal information as to the defendant is to be submitted. This personal information is used as a basis for determining the criminal sentence if the defendant is found guilty and includes information as to the defendant's previous criminal record as well as personal circumstances, including family life, substance abuse, and any other physical or psychological factors that should be considered. After that, closing arguments are given by the parties followed by the submission of legal costs and fees. Judgment can be given directly after closing arguments, but also within three weeks after the trial and deliberations. Judgment is issued both orally and in writing. When a guilty judgment is issued, the court at the same time issues the sentence.

5.3.3 SENTENCING

Sentencing is not a separate procedure held after a finding of guilt in the Swedish system, but the criminal sentence is determined at the same time as the finding of guilt, and the criminal sentence is given with the criminal judgment of guilty. When determining the criminal sanctions within the alternatives available, the court typically follows a three-step procedure. The first step is to establish the range of criminal sanctions for the crime, taking into account both aggravating and mitigating circumstances.

Aggravating circumstances can include whether the defendant intended much more serious consequences than those resulting from the criminal act, the degree of any ruthlessness or exploitation, the degree of criminal activity, and whether the actions were directed at a person of a minority background. Mitigating circumstances can include provocation, diminished control or judgment, or strong human compassion. In addition, the court can take into consideration whether defendant was physically injured and to what degree, if defendant attempted to minimize any damage, if the defendant turned herself in voluntarily, whether defendant would be deported for the crime, whether the sanction would pose an excessive hardship due to defendant's age or health, whether the crime was committed a long time ago, or whether any other reasons exist to impose a lesser sentence.

The second step for the court is to determine which criminal sanction to impose, whether a criminal penalty or other criminal sentence. A first distinction is made with regard to those defendants who are juveniles or mentally disturbed. Juveniles under the age of fifteen years cannot be sentenced to any criminal sanctions and should not be prosecuted. Juveniles between the ages of fifteen and eighteen years can be sanctioned, but imprisonment is to be the exception. Individuals cannot be sentenced to life for crimes committed prior to turning twenty-one years of age. At this stage, institutionalized treatment for juveniles or those suffering from mental disturbances can be chosen.

The court can also in the typical case decide whether imprisonment should be imposed. In choosing the sanction, imprisonment is to be deemed more severe than probation. No person is to be sentenced to more than one sanction for one crime as a rule, but probation can be combined with criminal fines and/or community service. If a person has been convicted of a crime in both Sweden and another country, the determination of the Swedish sentence is to take into consideration other sentences imposed elsewhere.

The third stage in sentencing is finally determining the sentence. The court here can look at other circumstances not taken up in the first two stages, such as the risk for recidivism. Aspects of fairness can also be taken into account, including defendant's need of medical care, age or other factors.

Sentences for several crimes are not imposed consecutively, but concurrently. The sentence for several crimes can be imprisonment if one of the crimes has imprisonment as a sanction. The length of a sentence of imprisonment can exceed that of the longest sentence in a group of crimes, but with certain ceilings. If the longest sentence available for one of the crimes is eight years or more, the total sanction cannot exceed that by more than four years. If defendant is convicted for a number of crimes, the sentence may not be less than the minimum sanction for the most serious of the crimes. In certain cases, it can be advantageous for the defendant to admit to as many crimes as possible, as the sum of the sentence cannot exceed these ceilings. For example, if the defendant is convicted of manslaughter, and has also assaulted two other persons, the defendant can confess to the two other assaults and receive only an additional four years added to the sentence. After serving two-thirds of the sentence, defendant is entitled to parole unless certain particular reasons exist for not granting it. In addition, any time spent in pre-trial custody is to be deducted from the sentence.

About 5 000 individuals are currently serving sentences in prison in Sweden, 93 % of whom are men. Forty-two percent of those incarcerated in 2010 were first time offenders. Seventy-two percent of all individuals incarcerated are Swedish citizens and twenty-eight percent foreign citizens. During the 1990's, only 30 persons had been sentenced to lifetime imprisonment, today approximately 159 persons are serving life terms.

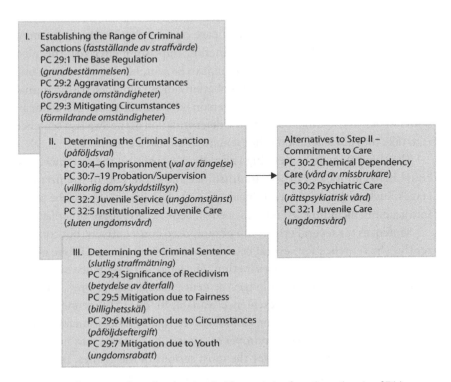

I. Establishing the Range of Criminal
Sanctions (*fastställande av straffvärde*)
PC 29:1 The Base Regulation
(*grundbestämmelsen*)
PC 29:2 Aggravating Circumstances
(*försvårande omständigheter*)
PC 29:3 Mitigating Circumstances
(*förmildrande omständigheter*)

II. Determining the Criminal Sanction
(*påföljdsval*)
PC 30:4–6 Imprisonment (*val av fängelse*)
PC 30:7–19 Probation/Supervision
(*villkorlig dom/skyddstillsyn*)
PC 32:2 Juvenile Service (*ungdomstjänst*)
PC 32:5 Institutionalized Juvenile Care
(*sluten ungdomsvård*)

Alternatives to Step II –
Commitment to Care
PC 30:2 Chemical Dependency
Care (*vård av missbrukare*)
PC 30:2 Psychiatric Care
(*rättspsykiatrisk vård*)
PC 32:1 Juvenile Care
(*ungdomsvård*)

III. Determining the Criminal Sentence
(*slutlig straffmätning*)
PC 29:4 Significance of Recidivism
(*betydelse av återfall*)
PC 29:5 Mitigation due to Fairness
(*billighetsskäl*)
PC 29:6 Mitigation due to Circumstances
(*påföljdseftergift*)
PC 29:7 Mitigation due to Youth
(*ungdomsrabatt*)

DIAGRAM 5.2 Sentencing Procedure (reprinted with permission from the author, Josef Zila).

5.3.4 APPEALS

Leave to appeal a judgment or sentence in a criminal case follows the rules generally applicable in civil cases. Both parties have the right to appeal in a criminal case, in other words, the defendant has the right to appeal a finding of guilty or the sentence imposed, and the prosecutor can appeal a judgment of not guilty or the sentence. The prosecutor even has the obligation to appeal a judgment of guilty if circumstances arise in the defendant's favor. A request for leave to appeal is to be filed in writing with the trial court issuing the judgment within three weeks of its date. The other party then has an additional week to appeal. If the petitioner is being detained, appeal proceedings are to be held expeditiously.

A court of appeal can decide the case without a trial if it is apparent that the appeal is without any merit. The court of appeal can also decide the case without a trial where the issue can be satisfactorily investigated and the prosecutor has appealed in a manner favorable to the defendant. Other grounds for deciding the appeal without a trial can include where only the defendant has appealed and the claim has been accepted by the other party, where no reason exists to sanction the defendant with more than fines and/or probation, where the parties have requested that the case be decided without a trial, or where neither of the parties objects to the case being decided without a trial.

The court of appeal is to review the judgment of the trial court, and no longer has to conduct an entirely new trial as was the rule before the 2008 amendments. Digitally recorded witness examinations from the trial court are to be reviewed. Supplemental witness examinations can be held, but new witness examinations are to be held only by way of exception. The trial court recordings are to be deemed sufficient in order to conduct an assessment as to the credibility of the witnesses.

Requests for leaves to appeal criminal judgments of the courts of appeal follow the same general rules as those in civil cases. Leave to appeal to the Supreme Court is only granted where the issue is of precedential value or a serious error has been committed.

Extraordinary Judicial Remedies

The same three extraordinary judicial remedies exist with respect to criminal cases as civil cases: tolling the procedural statute of limitations (*återställande av försutten tid*), vacating a judgment for judicial error (*domvilla*) or vacating a judgment for procedural or substantive grounds (*resning*). The Supreme Court has the right to toll the statute of limitations in cases where the petitioner can show good cause for the failure to bring the appeal within the correct time, usually the three week window, when such a petition is brought at the earliest three weeks, and at the latest, one year after the statute of limitations has expired. Vacating a judgment on the basis of judicial error includes grounds where a judgment is issued despite a procedural impediment or other procedural trial error, such as failure to serve, that can be assumed to have affected the judgment, or where the judgment is so poorly drafted that its content cannot be ascertained.

As to vacating a criminal judgment due to procedural or substantive error, the four grounds are the same as in civil cases: Where a judge or employee of the court commits a criminal act or violation of office, or a legal representative or legal counsel commits such a crime, and the act has had an effect on the outcome of the case; where evidence was falsified and that can be seen to have affected the outcome of the case; where there is new evidence if its introduction would likely have led to a different result and the party can show cause for not bringing it earlier; or where the judgment is in obvious violation of the law. There is an additional ground when appealing a criminal judgment, where a judge or prosecutor had a conflict of interest and that conflict was not obviously without significance in the case. The statute of limitations is again one year or six months depending upon which of these grounds is cited.

The judgment becomes final when the normal time for appeal has expired. When the judgment becomes final, it can act as a bar to further criminal prosecution of the acts adjudicated as *res judicata*, and also at that point of time be enforced. Civil remedies for tort damages may, however, still be brought if not decided in the criminal trial.

CHAPTER 6

Administrative Law and Procedure

A major delineation in the Swedish legal system is between public law and private law, public law governing matters between the state and individuals, private law regulating the relations between two private parties. Public law is furthered categorized into penal law as discussed in the previous chapter, constitutional law on the national level, municipal law on the local level, and administrative law. This chapter concerns the latter two areas of public law, which to some extent overlap.

This categorization is also reflected in the three tiers upon which the different decision-making bodies are placed: The Parliament, on the first tier, is bound as discussed in Chapters One and Two by the constitutional acts and the Riksdag Act. Its exercise of political power is perceived as falling within the area of constitutional law. The second tier comprises the administrative authorities including municipal assemblies, county councils and national government authorities. The courts are the third tier, including the general, administrative and special courts. Measures and decisions taken by the bodies on the second and third tiers fall within the areas of administrative law and procedure.

Administrative law in its turn is categorized as either general administrative law as generally applicable to all administrative agencies on the two bottom tiers, or specialized areas of administrative law applicable only within specific areas of law, such as tax law. The specialized areas of administrative law are many, as the Swedish welfare system literally takes care of its citizens from the cradle to the grave. Major specialized areas of administrative law include the provision of health care (socialized in Sweden), preschool, education (primary and secondary), the assessment of taxes, social security in cases of unemployment, sickness, disability, parental leave and pensions, and the provision of social benefits. Each of these areas is regulated by legislation and in many cases, agency regulations, as is the case, for example, with the assessment of taxes as regulated by the Income Tax Act (*inkomstskattelag* 1999:1229) and the regulations of the Tax Authority (*skatteföreskrifter*). The focus of the discussion in this chapter, however, is simply on municipal law, general administrative law and administrative judicial procedural law.

6.1 Municipal Law

The municipalities and county councils are governed by the Local Government Act (*kommunallag* 1991:900).[1] The activities of municipalities are financed through government subsidies, municipal real estate taxes and municipal income taxes. Municipal income taxes, including those paid to the county councils, can vary from municipality to municipality, the average being thirty-two percent.[2] Monies raised from municipal taxes comprise approximately seventy percent of a municipality's income. In certain cases, revenues raised in wealthier municipalities can be redistributed at the national level to less wealthy municipalities.

By law, the municipalities are to offer certain services to their members. A member of a municipality is a person who is registered as living there, owns real property within the municipality or is to pay municipal taxes to that municipality. The services municipalities are to offer include childcare, preschool, primary education, library services, Swedish as a second language courses, social services including family services, elderly care, care for the disabled, construction and city planning, health and environmental protection, garbage and waste removal, emergency services such as firefighting, water and sewage, emergency planning, collective transportation and public housing. Overall, municipalities and county councils employ more than one million people, corresponding roughly to one-fourth of the total employment in Sweden. Municipalities employ approximately 760 000 people and county councils employ around 260 000. Women represent just

---

1   An English translation of the Local Government Act can be found at the website of the Government Offices at sweden.gov.se.

2   More information about municipalities can be found at the website of the central organization of municipalities, country councils and regions, the Swedish Association of Local Authorities and Regions, SALAR, at skl.se.

over eighty percent of the total employment figure for municipalities and county councils.[3]

Each of the 290 municipalities has a locally elected municipal assembly (*kommunfullmäktige*). Only municipal residency for three years (not Swedish citizenship) is required to participate in the local elections held every four years. The municipal assembly has the tasks of adopting the municipal budget and setting taxes, determining which administrative boards are needed and appointing auditors to audit the activities of the municipality. The municipal assembly also appoints the municipal council (*kommunstyrelse*).

The municipal council decides in principle all major decisions for the municipality. The meetings are held monthly, minutes of the meetings are to be kept, and both are to be public. The municipal council is the central administrative body and is assisted in its work by a number of committees, *e.g.* an education committee and a social welfare committee. As a rule, an administrative organization is also attached to each committee: for example, a social welfare office is attached to the social welfare committee. The municipal council decides issues in many areas including education, preschool, elder care, roads, water and sewage and energy. The municipalities also issue various types of licenses, for example construction permits and alcohol serving licenses.

Certain central principles are to be applied by the municipalities when making decisions either on the general or individual levels. First, decisions are to be taken as close as possible to the source (*självstyre*) as expressed in the first paragraph of the first chapter of the Local Government Act. Second, municipalities are to treat their residents equally (*likhetställighetsprincipen*) unless there are objective reasons for different treatment. Last, municipalities are not to make retroactive decisions to the disadvantage of their residents unless for specific reasons.

Municipalities are permitted to operate non-profit businesses to provide facilities, housing or services to residents. In addition, municipalities may outsource certain matters to corporations, partnerships, cooperative enterprises, foundations or individuals. However, matters concerning the exercise of political power by the municipality may only be outsourced in accordance with the provisions of the Instrument of Government and under

---

3   This information is taken from the website of the central organization for county
    councils at skl.se.

Parliamentary decision. Municipalities may also enact measures for the purpose of promoting business in the municipality. They are also required to give financial support to political parties as represented in the municipal assembly.

Municipal decisions may be appealed in one of two ways. The first is an appeal based on the procedural legality of the decision as set out in the Local Government Act (*laglighetsprövning* or *kommunalbesvär*). This type of appeal can only be made by a resident of the municipality. The second is an appeal by an individual affected negatively by a decision of a municipality or one of its organs under the Administrative Procedures Act (*förvaltningsbesvär*). This type of appeal can be on either procedural or substantive grounds. These avenues of appeal are very different, but certain decisions can be appealed through either routes depending upon the standing of the parties. For example, a building permit can be appealed by a resident of the municipality with respect to its legality. It can also be appealed by the individual party negatively affected by the decision as an administrative appeal. The latter type of appeal is discussed under Section 6.3 below.

With respect to the first type of appeal, every municipal resident (and no one else) has the right to appeal certain municipal decisions in writing to an administrative district court on the procedural ground of legality. The decision is to be found unlawful by the court if it has been taken in a manner inconsistent with the procedural rules for such decisions, if the subject matter of the decision is outside the jurisdiction of the municipality or decision-making body, or if the decision is in conflict with a statute or other legislation. Exceptions with respect to the latter two grounds are given for certain budgetary decisions.

If a court finds the decision unlawful, the court may not substitute it with a different decision. The statute of limitations for such appeals is three weeks from the date the decision was made public by the municipality on its public notice board. After this period expires, a petitioner who has already filed a complaint cannot amend it. This right of appeal by municipal residents is seen as a counter-check to the exercise of political power by the municipality. An example of this could be where a municipality takes a decision to increase the pay of members sitting on a municipal board retroactively. The decision can then be appealed by a municipal resident to the administrative court, which could find it to be unlawful.

6.2 General Administrative Law

Sweden has a long history of central administration going back to King Gustav Vasa. Cardinal Richelieu's successor, Cardinal Mazarin, once remarked that if all the ministers of Europe were on the same ship, the helm would be handed over to Sweden's Chancellor Axel Oxenstierna (the author of the 1634 Instrument of Government). Sweden maintained its reputation of having a high degree of administrative competence over the next several centuries.

A reform of the administrative system was undertaken in the 1970's with the adoption of the Administrative Procedures Act (*förvaltningslag* 1971:290, now 1986:223)[4] and the Administrative Judicial Procedures Act (*förvaltnings-processlag* 1971:291). The first act sets out the procedures with respect to matters brought to the administrative authorities, the second governs the procedures with respect to the administrative courts.

Another aspect of the reform begun in the 1970's concerned the administrative court system itself. There was formally only the Supreme Administrative Court and one administrative court of appeal, *Kammarrätten,* until the 1970's. Two and then finally four administrative courts of appeal were successively established. Administrative district courts were more formally established in the 1980's as evolving from the county administrative courts and more specialized administrative courts such as those treating worker's compensation cases. However, the judicial administrative system was not in sync until the 1990's. In other words, the trial courts did not have the same areas of jurisdiction as the appellate courts until that decade. Before that, the areas of jurisdiction of the different courts varied. In the new millennium, the number of administrative trial courts was reduced, with the trial courts and the Supreme Administrative Court changing their names.

The right to a judicial appeal has been secondary, or sometimes almost non-existent, in the Swedish administrative law model. The main rule traditionally has been that a decision of an authority is to be appealed to the authority itself, and then to that authority's supervisory authority, and finally, to the Government. This system was derived from the medieval Swedish right

---

4   A state inquiry in 2010 has proposed replacing the 1986 act, with most of the changes argued as necessary to keep up with the developments of European law (Union law and the European Convention).

of an individual to petition the king. A party having an issue or problem arising under the administration would turn to the highest organ in the administration, historically the king and in modern times, the Government.

With Sweden's Europeanization, in other words, membership in the European Union as well as its obligations under the European Convention, this tradition has been challenged. Sweden has not succeeded in gaining acceptance for its model on the European level, but rather has been forced to adopt its model accordingly. The most recent case exposing this dissonance is from 2009 in which the European Court of Human Rights found against Sweden: A woman participating in an employment program was removed from the program for her failure to meet the program's conditions, and thus lost her unemployment subsidy. She appealed the decision to the Labor Market Board (*Arbetsmarknadsstyrelsen*), the supervisory authority for the authority making the decision, alleging that she had been sick and even hospitalized during her periods of absence, but otherwise had fulfilled the requirements of the program. The Labor Market Board found that the petitioner had not participated in the program to the degree required and thus that the decision was correct. The Board's decision could not be appealed, which the European Court of Human Rights found to be a violation of Article 6 of the European Convention.[5]

The administrative courts originally heard only appeals of adminis-trative decisions. Such types of decisions often, with only few exceptions, did not involve any concrete counter-party, for example neighbors appealing a building permit. The courts acted as both arbiters of the law and as defense for the state, a position similar to that of the King historically. Petitioners were placed somewhat in a vacuum by the courts being both arbiters and representing the state, as in such cases, no counter arguments were presented by an opposing party. Petitioners not only had to present and argue their claims, but also rebut hypothetical arguments never presented by any respondent.

This background also influenced the formation of administrative procedures generally. As stated above, the administrative courts acted in a manner reminiscent of a type of supervisory authority. The courts can

---

5   This board has now been replaced by the Public Employment Service (*Arbets-förmedling*). For the judgment in the case, *see Mendel v. Sweden*, European Court of Human Rights, judgment dated 7 April 2009, App. No. 28426/06.

place themselves in the stead of an administrative authority and have the same authority as such – an independent duty to investigate with the ability to initiate new investigations, the right to both vacate a decision of an administrative authority and also to issue a new decision in its place. The only limitation of the authority of the courts is that the assessment may not go beyond that as alleged by the parties in the case, unless it is to the benefit of the individual. Judicial assessments are to encompass both appropriateness and lawfulness with respect to the decision being appealed. The procedures originally were based only on the writings submitted, but an increased opportunity for oral hearings has developed again due to Sweden's obligations under the European Convention.

The Administrative Procedures Act serves as a floor setting out minimum procedural standards to be followed by administrative agencies and the courts. As it is a general law, more specific regulations in other laws take precedence over those in the Act in cases of conflict, with the explicit exception of the provisions regarding appeals as protected by Article 6.1 of the European Convention. An amendment was passed in 1995 making administrative and municipal judicial procedures two-party processes, with the administrative authority or municipality making the decision defined by law as the counter-party to the petitioner.

Under the Administrative Procedures Act, every administrative authority has a duty of service in the form of suitably providing information, guidance, advice and other similar assistance to individuals in questions regarding areas in the operations of the authority. Questions as posed by an individual are to be responded to as quickly as possible. If the individual has sought help from the wrong authority, that authority is to help the individual identify the correct authority.[6]

Certain general principles of law are also applicable with respect to both the decision-making levels of agencies as well as the courts when later

---

6   The duty of service also includes keeping visiting and telephone hours so that individuals can contact the authority, and informing the public as to these hours. Each authority is to be open at least two hours each working Monday through Friday in order to be able to receive and register public documents as well as receive requests for public documents kept by that authority. Individuals should also be able to contact authorities by facsimile and email, with answers being provided in the same manner.

assessing such decisions. That all individuals are to be treated equally is one such fundamental principle. The principle of proportionality (*proportionalitetsprincipen*) entails that a decision can be taken by an authority on behalf of the community only after taking into consideration its effects on the individuals. Another principle is that investigations by the authorities are to be conducted to the extent necessary as seen from the nature of the dispute and that the authority has the ultimate responsibility with respect to the investigation (*officialprincipen*). Decisions are to be taken in accordance with the law (*legalitetsprincipen*). A last principle that can be mentioned here (this listing is by no means exhaustive), is that the treatment of the issue is to be documented.

6.2.1 INITIATING AN ADMINISTRATIVE ACTION

Every administrative case involving an individual as a party is to be handled simply, expeditiously and at the least cost possible without jeopardizing legal certainty. Authorities are to take into consideration their own ability to obtain information and statements from other authorities where such is necessary. Authorities are to communicate in a manner that is easy to understand and facilitate the individual's contacts with authorities. The authorities have a duty to help each other within the framework of their operations, but this is often limited by the rules regarding confidentiality.

A matter or claim brought before an authority can be seen to comprise different stages, at which the authority has different obligations under the act. The first stage is where a claim is initiated. This can occur through an application for a right, such as a building permit, or the registration of a complaint, such as the lack of child daycare in a municipality. An authority can also initiate a claim, for example reporting a restaurant's failure to follow sanitary regulations. The claim is then processed and investigated by the authority that ultimately issues the decision.

6.2.2 ASSISTANCE IN BRINGING CLAIMS

An individual bringing a claim or matter has the right to have a representative or assistant present during the administrative proceedings. However, the individual can still be requested to participate in certain proceedings personally. If the representative or assistant demonstrates a lack of skill or knowledge, or is unsuitable in any other manner, the authority may dismiss the representative or assistant. Authorities are to provide non-Swedish speakers with interpreters, as well as provide assistance for persons who are hearing or speech impaired.

6.2.3 PROCEEDINGS

Administrative proceedings are often conducted in writing, in contrast with the oral proceedings in the general courts, with the right to an oral hearing historically very limited. The lack of oral proceedings was found to be in conflict with the rights granted under Article 6 of the European Convention. Individuals now are to have the right to provide information orally in cases concerning the exercise of governmental power against an individual (*myndighetsutövning*) if such can be done taking into consideration administrative working procedures. In other cases, the authority can decide as to having an oral hearing taking into account whether it is easier for the individual. An authority can request information or opinions from other authorities or persons (*remiss*) if necessary to decide an issue. The request needs to state the matter and the time by which a response is desired.

Information received in a form other than a public document is to be recorded by authorities in matters concerning the exercise of governmental power against an individual. An applicant, claimant or other party has the right of access to information received in such a case in compliance with the Public Access to Information and Secrecy Act. A matter cannot be decided unless the applicant, claimant or other party has been notified as to information received from other persons in the matter and has been given the opportunity to respond. An authority can issue a decision despite a failure to divulge this information if the decision is not negative to the individual, if the information lacks relevance, if the measure is apparently not necessary, where the implementation of a decision would be made considerably more difficult or if the decision cannot be postponed. An authority can also issue a decision despite this if the matter concerns employment, acceptance to voluntary education, grading, the allocation of educational grants or the comparable and it is not a decision by a higher instance after an appeal.

6.2.4 CONFLICTS OF INTEREST

An individual is to recuse herself from deciding a matter if certain conflicts of interest are deemed to exist (*jäv*). If the matter directly concerns the person, her spouse, parents, children or siblings, or any other person close to her or if the decision can be expected to result in particular gains or harm to the person or anyone close to that person, or if the person has acted as a representative or counsel of a party in the case, she is to recuse herself from the matter. If the decision is on appeal to an authority that previously had participated in the case, the authority is to recuse itself. There is also a general rule that where particular circumstances exist in the case giving rise to a question of whether the person can be impartial in adjudging the issue, that person is to be recused.

A person found to have a conflict of interest is not to make a decision in the case. She can, however, take certain actions if appointing a replacement would result in an undue delay. A person having knowledge of a conflict of interest is to divulge such information voluntarily. If a conflict of interest arises, the authority is to decide the matter as quickly as possible. The person in question may participate in the assessment of the conflict of interest only if the authority needs that person to fulfill a quorum and no other person is available.

6.2.5 DECISIONS

A decision (*beslut*) as issued by an authority has to state the reasons upon which the decision is based in cases invoking the exercise of governmental power against the individual. Such reasons can be omitted, for example, where the decision is not to the disadvantage of an individual. If the persons making the decision cannot reach a consensus, the chairperson has the deciding vote and dissenting opinions can be noted. The petitioner, claimant or other party is to be informed of the content of the decision unless it is obviously unnecessary to do so. The authority can decide whether notification is to be orally, by letter or by service.

Only a negative decision can be appealed by a party. The first step that must be ascertained is whether the authority has issued a decision within this definition. The authority makes the first assessment, in that a decision must include information as to the possibility to appeal. If the authority has included this information, the authority has determined that it is such a decision. However, certain cases have arisen in which the authority has not considered the decision to be such, and the court despite this has found it to be an appealable decision.[7] The second assessment that needs to be made is whether the decision is positive or negative to the interests of the individual affected. Individuals can only appeal decisions that are negative to their interests.

6.2.6 APPEALS

An administrative decision negatively affecting an individual's interest can be appealed to the authority making the decision for a correction (*självrättelse*) or to a supervisory authority if such exists, as happened in the 2009 case above. A decision containing an obvious mistake as a consequence of a clerical or numerical error by the authority or another party can be corrected by the authority issuing the decision. Prior to making the correction, the authority is to give any interested party the opportunity to make a statement where the matter concerns the exercise of governmental power against an individual and the measure is necessary.

In the event an authority finds that a decision it has issued is manifestly incorrect due to new circumstances or other reasons, the authority is to change the decision if it can do so quickly and simply without negative consequences to an individual. This duty exists even where the decision has been appealed. An appeal is to be dismissed as moot where the authority changes the decision as requested by the petitioner. If the authority changes the decision in a manner other than as requested by petitioner, the appeal is to be deemed to include the modified decision. An authority has the power to delay the implementation of a decision (*inhibition*) until the appeal is decided.

Three types of judicial appeals are available with respect to administrative decisions, an appeal of a municipal decision by a municipal resident to an administrative court as discussed in the previous section, an appeal of an

---

7   In the case, RÅ 2006 ref. 43, the authority had sent a letter, which in actuality contained a decision that was appealable, as found by the Supreme Administrative Court.

administrative decision to an administrative court, and judicial review of a decision by the Government. The first two are taken through the administrative court system, the latter directly to the Supreme Administrative Court. There are also certain procedural rules applicable to specific types of cases, such as decisions with respect to involuntary institutionalization.

Even if the issue of the right to a judicial appeal today can arguably be deemed to be resolved, Swedish law may still be seen as not completely fulfilling the requirements of the European Convention and EU law in those cases in which an action by an authority is not deemed to be a decision negatively affecting the interests of an individual. As such actions fall outside the scope of judicial appeal, these rights have not been guaranteed. The administrative courts have the jurisdiction only to review decisions negatively affecting the interests of an individual, and not other decisions or measures taken by authorities.

6.3 Administrative Judicial Procedure

Criminal cases, though falling within public law, are brought to the general courts as discussed in the preceding Chapter Five under the provisions of the Code of Judicial Procedure. Certain administrative law issues, as a main rule, fall within the jurisdiction of the administrative courts, comprising administrative district courts, the administrative courts of appeal and the Supreme Administrative Court, and are governed by the Administrative Procedures Act (*förvaltningslag* 1986:223). The procedure for cases brought to these courts is set out in the Administrative Judicial Procedures Act (*förvaltningsprocesslag* 1971:291). In the absence of regulation with respect to an administrative judicial procedural issue, the administrative courts are to turn to the Code of Judicial Procedure for guidance. When doing this, the administrative court must make the assessment of whether the case is more civil or criminal in its nature, and then turn to the relevant sections in the Code of Judicial Procedure. This determination is not always simple, particularly in more invasive types of cases such as the involuntary institutionalization of an individual. There are over five hundred different types of administrative cases that can be brought to the administrative courts, everything from tax cases to appeals of police decisions in criminal cases to building permits.

The Administrative Judicial Procedures Act concerns the procedures to be followed by the administrative courts, paralleling in many ways the Code of Judicial Procedure. However, the two supreme courts have entirely different areas of non-overlapping jurisdiction, which system previously was not totally coordinated. The case bringing this incongruence to its head was *Stallknecht,* concerning an incorrectly paid agricultural subsidy. The petitioner attempted to bring an appeal in the mid-1990's through both court systems, which attempts were dismissed by both supreme courts for lack of jurisdiction in deference to the other (*negativ kompetenskonflikt*).[8] The petitioner ultimately brought the case to the European Court of Human Rights arguing that the failure of both courts to exercise jurisdiction was a violation of Article 6 of the European Convention.[9]

The Administrative Judicial Procedures Act governs the procedures before the administrative courts. Appeals through the administrative courts historically have been based on written submissions, with the right to oral proceedings fairly recently expanded due to the requirements under Article 6 of the European Convention. The act is a general act, entailing that any provision in a more specific statutory act or government regulation has precedence over those in this act. Another remedy now available as Sweden was found in to be in violation of Article 6 of the European Convention is that the Supreme Administrative Court can hear appeals of Government decisions under the Act on Legal Review of Governmental Decisions (*lag 2006:304 om rättsprövning av vissa regeringsbeslut*).

6.3.1 APPEALS OF ADMINISTRATIVE DECISIONS

An appeal of an administrative decision is generally to be heard by an administrative district court. Since 1998 and the *Stallknecht* case, the administrative district courts are to have general jurisdiction in appeals of administrative decisions. If the decision can be appealed, as a rule it is to be to the administrative district courts. Section three of the Administrative Judicial Procedures Act states, however, that where another Swedish

---

8 *See* NJA 1994 p. 657 och RÅ 1995 ref. 58.
9 The petitioner ultimately settled with the Swedish Government and withdrew the lawsuit.

provision or the right to appeal as mandated by the European Convention or EU law proscribes otherwise, the general rules, including any prohibitions as to appeals, must give way.

A petition to appeal a decision by an authority or bring any other matter to the administrative court is to be in writing and state the grounds for the appeal. It is to be filed with the authority that issued the decision generally within three weeks of the date the individual received the authority's decision. The authority receiving the appeal is to determine whether the appeal was filed in the correct time. If late, the authority can dismiss the appeal unless the delay was due to the authority's incorrect information regarding appeals. With respect to an appeal of a decision by an administrative authority, that authority will be deemed to be the respondent in the case as filed by the individual.

Petitions are to be signed by the petitioner or her representative and include the claims, the circumstances upon which the claims are based, the decision being appealed, and if a right of appeal is to be granted, and the circumstances upon which such a right of appeal can be granted. In addition, the petitioner ought also to state the evidence to be cited and that which is to be proven by the evidence.[10]

The petitioner can have a representative or assistant present at any hearings. The court has the right to dismiss the representative or assistant if that person is shown to be incompetent, unknowledgeable or unsuitable for the case. If the representative or assistant is an attorney as licensed by the Swedish Bar Association, its board of directors is to be notified of such an action. The representative is also to produce a power of attorney demonstrating her authority in the matter. The court can request that the petitioner provide supplemental information within a certain period of time where the initial application or appeal is too incomplete for a decision to be issued.

---

10 Information to allow the service of documents is also to be included in the petition, such as the person's social security or organization number, residential and employment address and telephone number (if unlisted, it need only be included upon the request of the court) as well as where necessary, another address or other information so that the person can be served documents.

If the court finds that it does not have jurisdiction in the case but that a different court does, the documents in the case are to be transferred over to that court if the petitioner has no objections or no other reasons exist not to do so. The documents in the case will be deemed received by the latter court on the same day that the first court received them.

6.3.2 THE PROCEEDINGS

The court is to insure that the matter is sufficiently investigated, and if need be, guide the parties as to that which needs to be further investigated. The court can also deny requests for unnecessary investigations. The proceedings are to be in writing. Oral proceedings can be held with respect to certain issues if advantageous to the investigation or if beneficial to a speedy resolution of the case. Oral proceedings are to be held in the administrative district and appellate courts if the individual has so requested. Oral proceedings are to then be held if deemed relevant and no specific reasons exist against having them.

The respondent is to receive documentation concerning an application or appeal and is to file a written answer within a designated time. Such notification is not necessary where there is no reason to assume that the case will be granted either wholly or partially, if the notification is obviously unnecessary, if the respondent is an administrative authority and the notification is unnecessary, or if notification would make the enforcement of a decision considerably more difficult.

The respondent's answer is to identify the case and include whether the respondent admits or denies the claims or measures at stake, the reasons for any denial and the evidence to be cited by the respondent. The petitioner is to be given the opportunity to respond in writing to the respondent's answer unless deemed unnecessary. The court can also order a response to the answer upon penalty of further judicial proceedings without the response. The court can also request a statement by the administrative authority previously deciding in the matter.

The petitioner and respondent are to be summoned to an oral hearing if one is held. Petitioner can be ordered to be present personally upon penalty of fine or further proceedings. The administrative authority representing the public can also be ordered to be present upon penalty of further proceedings.

Petitioner and respondent can also participate in the oral proceedings either through sound or video transmissions. Private individuals present at the oral proceedings can request compensation for travel costs and lodging from public funds where the court finds such compensation to be fair. Proceedings are to be public, but the court may order closed doors if information is to be divulged that is to be kept confidential under the Public Access to Information and Secrecy Act.

Minutes are to be kept of the oral proceedings including an account of the proceedings and the investigation conducted therein. Notations are to be made of that presented during the proceedings concerning the claims, admissions, objections in law or fact and attestations. Before the case is to be decided, the parties are to be notified of any information provided by other parties and given the opportunity to respond in most cases.

6.3.3 EVIDENCE

Written documentation and physical objects cited as evidence are to be provided to the court without delay and consistent with the provisions regarding written evidence as found in the Code of Judicial Procedure. If a party cites evidence that it does not produce, the court may order production of the evidence upon penalty of further proceedings without taking the evidence into consideration. The court can order an inspection of premises or of objects not suitable to be produced in court. The court can also obtain opinions from expert witnesses and order the examination of witnesses or expert witnesses.

6.3.4 THE JUDGMENT AND FURTHER APPEALS

The court is bound by the claims of the parties in the case with respect to the judgment issued. However, the court can decide outside the scope of the claims to the advantage of a private individual if such can occur without harm to the interests of another private individual. The decision issued by the court is to be based on the documents in the case as well as other information provided during the proceedings and include the reasons for the decision as well as any dissenting opinions. The procedures for an appeal, where possible, are to be included in the judgment.

The rules as to appealing a judicial administrative judgment vary depending upon the decision at issue. A grant of leave to appeal to the Supreme Administrative Court is to be given if a decision in the case can be seen as important to the development of the law or if particularly compelling reasons exist, such as grounds to vacate a judgment (*resning*) or that the outcome in an administrative court of appeal obviously was the result of a gross omission or gross mistake. If the procedural statute of limitations has run, leave to appeal can be granted for a circumstance constituting a valid excuse in exceptional cases.

6.3.5 JUDICIAL REVIEW OF A GOVERNMENT DECISION

A decision by the Government that cannot be appealed in any other manner can be directly appealed to the Supreme Administrative Court (*rättsprövning*) under the Act on Judicial Review of Government Decisions. This form of appeal previously included all types of administrative decisions for which there was no route of judicial appeal in any form. The issue then arose whether the Administrative Procedures Act or the Act on Judicial Review would have precedence. This issue was resolved by removing jurisdiction over all administrative decisions from the latter act, allowing for jurisdiction to be based simply on the Administrative Procedures Act.

Under the Act on Judicial Review of Government Decisions, any individual can bring an action concerning a Government decision affecting the individual's civil rights under the European Convention. An innovation here is that environmental organizations are granted standing under the act to also bring certain claims. The petition has to be filed with the Supreme Administrative Court within three months of the date of the Government's decision and cite the law the petitioner believes to have been violated by the decision. If the petitioner so requests, an oral hearing can be held by the Court if it deems such to not be unnecessary. If the Court finds the decision to be in violation of a right, the decision is to be nullified. The Court can also remand the matter to the Government.

PART II

The Basics

As discussed in the first chapter, the initial classification in Swedish law is between public and private law. Private law is then classified as either the law concerning property and obligations having monetary values (*förmögenhetsrätt*) or family law (*familjerätt*) including the law of inheritance (*arvsrätt*), the latter two covered in the following chapter. A third category can be identified as overarching these two categories, legal personhood and capacity.

The first category, the law concerning property and obligations, is further divided into the law of obligations (*obligationsrätt*) concerning the legal relationships between persons, and the law of property (*sakrätt*) concerning the legal relationship between persons and things. These distinctions are based on Roman law. All these categories are quite broad, but the law concerning persons and property in certain areas has less statutory regulation in Sweden compared to the law of obligations. Since this area of law is outside the law of obligations, the parties typically are not as free to contract out of it as they have no contract to begin with in general. Chapter Eleven addresses property law generally, while the law of debtors, creditors and security interests in property is addressed separately in Chapter Ten.

The law of obligations in its turn includes contract law (*avtalsrätt*) and the law of torts (*utomobligatorisk skadeståndsrätt*). Contract law is divided into general contract law (*allmän avtalsrätt*), discussed in Chapter Nine, and specific areas of contract law (*speciell avtalsrätt*), some of which are taken up in Part Three such as sales, and landlord/tenant law. The law of torts is addressed in Chapter Twelve below.

Those areas of law falling within the law of obligations are characterized by the prevalence of statutory provisions that can be contracted out of by the parties. This number has been diminishing in modern times, with a greater recognition of the unequal bargaining powers of certain parties to a contract, for example, consumers or tenants, as well as the mandatory nature of certain EU law provisions.

In the areas of private law where freedom of contract prevails, the courts first look to the agreement between the parties when trying to resolve an issue. If the agreement is silent, or does not provide any clear guidance, the courts then look to the legislation, confirming its gap-filling function. After that, the courts can turn to the legislative preparatory works, case law, custom and usage on different levels (including general, industrial and between the parties), general principles of law that greatly resemble common law principles, and finally, the legal scholarship.

The courts apply certain interpretative approaches and rules when assessing these different legal materials. They can take either a restrictive (*restriktiv*) or literal (*bokstavlig*) approach, or an expansive (*extensiv*) approach, to interpreting sources. The courts can even apply a different law by analogy (*analogi*). However, the Swedish courts are not as predisposed to apply case law by analogy. This goes to the heart of the perception of the courts, that their task is to interpret the legislator's intent but not to make law. Where a statute is not clear on its face, the court will try to determine the intent of the legislator by turning to the legislative preparatory works. This in turn can also be done either restrictively or expansively. With the more restrictive approach, the court will rely solely on that stated in the legislative preparatory works (*objektiv teleologisk metod*). A more expansive approach is where the court changes the question from "what did the legislator intend" to "what would the legislator have intended if faced with the specific issue at hand" (*subjektiv teleologisk metod*).

In addition to these approaches, there are also canons of construction (interpretation) that can be applied by the courts. A few examples of textual canons are:

- *Expressio unius est exclusio alterius*: The expression of one suggests the exclusion of others;
- *Noscitur a sociis*: A thing is known by its associates, a general term is to be construed to be similar to more specific terms in a series; and
- *Ejusdem generis*: When specific words of description are used, followed by general words, the latter are to be limited in meaning so as to embrace only the former.

There are few rules as to which method or interpretive rule the courts must use, the only firm one being that criminal laws are to be interpreted restrictively. With respect to private law issues, the courts have fairly free hands.

This part two takes up the framework of the private law system, beginning with family law and then moving on to the law governing persons and property, ending with tort and insurance law.

CHAPTER 7

Family Law

Three major statutory codes establish the framework for family law in Sweden, the Marriage Code, the Parental Code and the Inheritance Code. The primary regulations as established in these codes are discussed below in the areas of marriage and cohabitation, children, parents and guardianships, and the law of wills and inheritance.

7.1 Marriage and Spouses

Marriage, in Sweden as elsewhere, historically has been a legal institution between men and women. As of 1 May 2009, however, marriage is available to both heterosexual as well as homosexual couples.[1] The portal paragraph of the Marriage Code (*äktenskapsbalk* 1987:230) now states that "[t]he regulations governing living in marriage are to be found in this Code." Individuals that have entered into a marriage with each other are spouses, and a marriage is dissolved either through death or divorce.

The Marriage Code comprises eighteen chapters. Certain rights and obligations as between the spouses are set out in the first chapter of the Marriage Code.[2] Under this chapter, spouses are to show each other faithfulness and respect, and together take care of the home and children, consulting with each other and working for the best interest of the family.

---

1   Prior to this date, homosexual couples could enter into a registered partnership under the Act on Registered Partnerships (*lag 1994:1117 om registrerat partnerskap*). The latter act is repealed as of 1 May 2009 and those homosexual couples living as registered couples can choose either to marry or to continue to live as registered partners. Registered couples are to be treated as spouses for all purposes under the act.

2   There is no sanctioning system under the Marriage Code for a failure of a spouse to perform these rights and obligations. These are rather policy declarations (*program-förklaring*).

Each spouse is to own her own property and be liable only for her own debts. The spouses are to divide any expenses and tasks between them, and if necessary, provide each other with the information necessary to assess the family's financial situation.

TABLE 7.1 The Marriage Code.

Part One: General Provisions	
Chap. 1 Marriage	

Part Two: The Commencement and Dissolution of Marriage	
Chap. 2 Marital Impediments	Chap. 4 Marriage Ceremony
Chap. 3 Review of Marital Impediments	Chap. 5 Dissolution of Marriage

Part Three: The Financial Relationship between Spouses	
Chap. 6 Maintenance	Chap. 10 The Marital Estate
Chap. 7 Spousal Property	Chap. 11 Shares in the Estate
Chap. 8 Gifts between Spouses	Chap. 12 Adjustments of the Shares
Chap. 9 Estate Division	Chap. 13 Legal Effects of the Division

Part Four: Judicial Procedures in Marital Cases	
Chap. 14 Divorce and Maintenance Cases	Chap. 17 Estate Executor
Chap. 15 Validity of a Marriage	Chap. 18 General Provisions
Chap. 16 Registration	

The rights and obligations between spouses in the first chapter of the Marriage Code at first glance might appear somewhat unusual taken out of their historical context. The endeavor in Sweden since the 1970's has been to facilitate the work of women. Employment in general in the 1970's had increased by 390 000 jobs, of which 380 000 jobs were held by women, many of whom were working part-time in the then expanding public sector.[3] Despite this, women still had almost total responsibility in the private sphere for home and the care of children. The word *jämställdhet* (equality between

---

3   *See* SOU 1978:38 at 39 and Legislative Bill 1978/79:175 *med förslag till lag om jämställdhet mellan kvinnor och män i arbetslivet, m.m.* at 13–15.

the sexes) began to be used in earnest, coined to denote a demarcation from term used for equality in society as whole, *jämlikhet. Jämställdhet* focused exclusively on equality between the sexes, marking a shift from issues of women's rights to societal issues between women and men. Theoretically, this was to free both sexes from the roles society historically had forced on them, giving women and men equal rights as well as equal responsibilities as to both paid and unpaid work.

To this end, one of the first acts in the 1970's with respect to *jämställdhet* was the transition begun in 1972 and completed by 1991 from family-based to individual-based income taxation.[4] Spousal maintenance obligations were also in essence abolished. The rights to paid parental leave for both parents and to child daycare were established. The right of women to have equal access to employment was the last step taken as legislated in 1978. The approach taken politically, and consequently, legally, has been that if men and women share equally in both paid and unpaid work, women will be equal with men in all aspects. This ideology is reflected in the duties as set out for spouses in the first chapter of the Marriage Code.

7.1.1 MARITAL IMPEDIMENTS

Several legal impediments to marriage are listed in the Marriage Code. Persons already married, or registered as a partner to a third party, may not marry. A minor under the age of eighteen years may not marry unless permission has been granted by the appropriate county administrative board (*länsstyrelse*) after a hearing is held. Such permission is to be given only for exceptional reasons.

Marriage may also not be entered into between persons who are of direct lineal descent, for example, between a parent and a child or between siblings. Half-siblings may marry with the consent of the appropriate county administrative board. Adopted children are to be considered the same as biological children with respect to these rules, but adopted siblings can marry with

---

4   For a criticism in Swedish of the theoretical neutrality of this taxation system and its contribution to *jämställdhet*, see Åsa Gunnarsson, *Myten om vad den könsneutrala skatterätten kan göra för jämställdheten*, 2000 SKATTENYTT 487.

the consent of the county administrative board. First cousins may marry without consent.

Prior to the marriage ceremony, one of the parties is to request an assessment as to whether any impediments to the marriage exist. The Swedish Tax Authority conducts the assessment and issues a certificate of no impediments to the marriage, which is valid for four months.[5]

7.1.2 THE MARRIAGE CEREMONY

The marriage ceremony is to be officiated by an authorized civil servant or religious leader and held in the presence of witnesses. The Swedish Church and other religious congregations must receive permission to officiate over marriage ceremonies from the Legal, Financial and Administrative Services Agency (Kammarkollegiet).[6] Individuals have a guaranteed right to a civil ceremony, but do not have an automatic right to a religious ceremony. In other words, a religious officiator can refuse to marry a couple, for example, due to their different religions or because one of the individuals is divorced.

The officiator is to check that there is a valid certificate of no impediments to the marriage prior to conducting the ceremony. Both persons have to be physically present at the marriage ceremony as marriage by proxy is not allowed. The individuals are to express their consent to the marriage to the officiator. Certain different texts must be included in the ceremony, depending upon whether the ceremony is civil or religious. After the ceremony has been completed, the officiator declares the couple married. She provides the couple with a marriage certificate and notifies the Tax Authority of the marriage.

Prior to the marriage ceremony, the couple is to decide if they wish to change their last names. Women in Sweden have been taking the last names of their husbands since the late 1700's, and the overwhelming majority of women still do so today. The provisions regarding changing last names, as

---

5 Prior to 1991, the Swedish Church, as a state authority, kept the records of births, residency, civil status and deaths dating back to the 1600's of those individuals living in Sweden (*folkbokföring*). The Tax Authority as of 1991 now keeps these records.

6 The requirements for qualification are found in the Act on the Right to Officiate over Marriage Ceremonies within Religions Organizations (*lag 1993:305 om rätt att förrätta vigsel inom trossamfund*). For more information on the Legal, Financial and Administrative Services Agency, *see* its website at kammerkollegiet.se.

well as those concerning the names of children, are found in the Name Act (*namnlag* 1982:670). The spouses can choose to keep their own names, or take one of the spouse's last names or create a double name. The rules as to completely new names are strict in Sweden. An individual is not free to simply take a last name already in use, such as Carlson, unless the consent of all users of that name in Sweden is obtained.[7]

7.1.3 THE FINANCIAL RELATIONSHIP BETWEEN SPOUSES

Each spouse has legal control of her property and is responsible for her own debts under the Marriage Code.[8] Spouses have a legal duty to provide each other with the information necessary for assessments of the family's financial status. The spouses are to enjoy the same standard of living while married. In the event a spouse is not economically able to support her own personal needs, the other spouse has a legal duty to provide that needed. If the spouses have children, they are both to contribute to the financial and physical needs of their children.

As a rule, property in Sweden is owned individually. Joint ownership of property can be in the form of tenants in common as regulated by the Act on Co-tenancy (*lag 1904:48 p. 1 om samäganderätt*). Real property and chattels can be owned by spouses as co-tenants, and unless otherwise contracted, each co-tenant has an equal share in the property. The heirs of each spouse as a co-tenant directly inherit the property owned as co-tenants from the spouse. This is a fairly rare form of property ownership outside of real property. Joint tenancy, whereby the tenants own the property together,

---

7   This rule acts as a bar for nationalized citizens to taking Swedish names. Statistics Sweden keeps statistics at their website, scb.se, as to the number of persons having certain last names. For example, 2 263 persons in Sweden in 2011 have the name of Carlson, 284 the name Karlson, 30 021 the name Carlsson and 193 090 the name Karlsson. The only way for a nationalized citizen to obtain a Swedish last name is to marry a person having a Swedish name, or by inventing a new name that sounds Swedish, such as Qarlson.

8   However, if the Enforcement Authority executes a judgment or debt as to the chattels of one spouse, the assumption is that all property in the home is that of the debtor spouse and can be seized for the execution. The other spouse has to prove that the property belongs to her and not the debtor spouse.

and upon the death of one tenant, the other automatically receives complete ownership of the property, and the property is not included in the estate of the deceased, does not exist as a form of property ownership in Sweden. Despite the fact that perhaps only one of the spouses is officially listed as owner to the joint residence of the spouses, the owner spouse may not dispose freely over the joint residence unless the consent of the non-owning spouse has been obtained.

Even though the spouses own their own property, for purposes of the marital property estate, property is characterized as either marital property (*giftorättsgods*) or separate property (*enskild egendom*). The marital property constitutes the marital estate to be divided between the spouses upon the dissolution of the marriage under a system referred to as a deferred community property regime (*giftorättssystem*). The spouses are free to enter into marital property agreements at any time categorizing marital or separate property as one type or the other (*äktenskapsförord*). Such agreements must in writing and registered with the Tax Authorities. In the same manner, gifts between spouses of a disproportionate value, when taking into consideration the donor's financial circumstances, must be registered with the Tax Authorities in order to be valid as against third parties. The rules for registering agreements between spouses as to property distribution as well as gifts were set in place in order to protect third-party creditors.

7.1.4 DISSOLUTION OF MARRIAGE

Marriage is dissolved by death or by divorce. Spouses who are in agreement to a divorce can obtain a divorce as quickly as the court system allows. However, if only one of the spouses wishes to divorce, the law imposes a six-month waiting period. In addition, if either of the spouses has custody of a child under the age of sixteen years residing with them, there is also a six-month waiting period, even if the spouses are in agreement. The commencement of the waiting period begins the day the court has received the petition for divorce. No waiting period is required where the spouses have lived separately for at least two years.

The municipalities have the responsibility for providing counseling services to couples requesting such support under the Act on Social Services (*socialtjänstlag* 2001:453). These services can be used prior to any separation between spouses or cohabitees, during a separation and also to resolve issues arising after divorce or separation. The services are provided confidentially, with all information or documents generated classified as confidential and not public. The counselors also have a privilege of confidentiality as discussed in Chapter Four in relation to giving witness testimony at trial.

After the expiration of the waiting period, one of the spouses must file a request for divorce within six months, otherwise the petition is dismissed. There is no requirement of fault with respect to divorce proceedings in Sweden, so that the parties do not have to cite any reason for requesting a divorce. After a divorce, the spouses are free to either retain their married names or revert to the name they had prior to the marriage.

7.1.5 THE DIVISION OF THE MARITAL PROPERTY ESTATE

A division of the marital property estate can be invoked voluntarily during the marriage, but in most cases, it is executed because of the dissolution of the marriage, either due to divorce or death. The first step is to identify the property of the spouses as either marital or separate property. Any assets that are not separate property are considered marital property. A second distinction within marital property is that property exempted as personal property.

Separate property is defined in Section 7:2 of the Marriage Code and can be created in one of two ways: either through a valid marital property agreement between the two spouses, or an agreement with a spouse and a third party as to the separate nature of the property. Examples of the later include wills, gifts, insurance or pension policies as stemming from third parties. Any surrogate property derived from separate property that is kept separate from the spouse's marital property remains separate property. If the surrogate property is not kept separate, it becomes marital property. For example, if a spouse sells a painting that was separate property and places the funds in the other spouse's bank account, the funds become marital property.

Each spouse gets to exempt personal property from the marital estate. Two categories of personal property are defined under Section 10:3 of the Marriage Code. The first is property of a personal nature that can be exempted to a reasonable extent. This includes clothing and other items of personal use as well as personal presents. Damage awards for personal injuries and interest accrued thereon are also to be exempted. One of the motivating factors for this exemption was the situation in which a spouse who was the victim of domestic abuse would be forced to share any personal injury award with the abusive spouse (who had been ordered to pay the compensation). Now such awards are exempted as personal property.

The second category of personal property constitutes personal rights that cannot be transferred. Three main types of property rights are included in this category, intellectual property rights, rights to future income and pension rights. Pensions are a significant category of personal property exempted from the marital estate. Three main types of pensions exist in Sweden, state pensions,[9] employment (occupational) pensions and individual pensions. The primary state pension by law is not marital property. The state pension each spouse is eligible to receive is based only on their own income, not the income of the family.[10] The possibility exists to transfer a portion of the state pension from one spouse to the other, but only for one year at a time. This transfer cannot be effected retroactively, and there is an administrative fee amounting to 8 % of the amount transferred.[11] Most employment pensions are personal property. Such policies are often drafted to reflect this family law designation by including a provision in the pension agreement that it cannot be transferred, thus rendering it personal property. After a 1989 amendment to Section 10:3 of the Marriage Code, these types of pensions can be entirely or partially included in the marital estate "if taking into consideration the length of the marriage, the financial circumstances of the spouses, and the circumstances in general, it would be unfair to exempt the pension from the marital estate." The legislative preparatory works to this section emphasize, however, that this exemption is to be applied restrictively.

A division of property need not take place if neither of the spouses has any marital property or neither of the spouses has requested a division. Otherwise, the marital property of each spouse is tallied individually as set

---

9   Public pensions are administered by the Swedish Pensions Agency. More information on this agency is available at its website, pensionsmyndigheten.se.

10 Section 15:16 of the Act on Income-Based Pensions (lag 1998:674 om inkomstgrundad ålderspension).

11 This high fee is imposed due to the fact that women live longer than men. Prior to 2009 the fee was 15 %. As different fees cannot lawfully be imposed on one group based on sex, it is imposed upon any individual transferring pension monies.

out in the tenth chapter of the Marriage Code. After each spouse's marital property has been identified, the value of the property is totaled, and then any personal debts (and one-half of any joint debts) that the spouse has are deducted from that spouse's total. The two totals are then summed together and divided equally between the spouses.

Two examples of marital property estate distributions are given in Table 7.2 below. In the first example, Astrid will need to transfer property worth 100 000 to Johan.

TABLE 7.2 Two examples of marital property estate distributions.

Example 1:			
Astrid		Johan	
		[Separate Property	1 000 000]
Marital Goods	600 000	Marital Goods	300 000
Debts	100 000	Debts	0
Total	500 000	Total	300 000
Marital Property Estate 500 000 + 300 000 = 800 000/2 = 400 000			
Of the marital property, each receives:			
Astrid: 400 000		Johan: 400 000	

Example 2:			
Astrid		Johan	
		[Separate Property	1 000 000]
Marital Goods	600 000	Marital Goods	300 000
Debts	100 000	Debts (student loans)	600 000
Total	500 000	Total	0
Marital Property Estate 500 000 + 0 = 500 000/2 = 250 000			
Of the marital property, each receives:			
Astrid: 250 000		Johan: 250 000	

This second example is somewhat more complicated. If Johan's debt had been related to his separate property, the rule is that the debt would need to be first deducted from the separate property. Here the debt is student loans, so they are deducted first from the marital property as stated in Section 11:2 of the Marriage Code. Astrid will need to transfer property worth SEK 250 000 to Johan.

The Marriage Code provides for a rigorously equal division of the property between spouses. If within a period of three years prior to the divorce, one of the spouses has substantially decreased their amount of marital goods, for example by giving property away without the consent of the other spouse, that spouse's marital property is to be computed as if the property were still in the hands of that spouse.

Another deviation that can be made from an equal division between the spouses is where the court finds that such a division would be too onerous for the wealthier spouse (*skevdelning*) as stated in Section 12:1 of the Marriage Code: "To the extent it is unfair, taking into consideration particularly the length of the marriage but also the financial circumstances of the spouses, that one spouse in the estate division is to transfer property to the other in accordance with chapter eleven [of the Marriage Code], the division of the estate can be made instead so that the first spouse can retain more of his or her marital goods." This rule was adopted to protect wealthier spouses in short-term marriages. The legislative preparatory works discuss a five-year limit, that after five years of marriage, all marital property is to be equally divided. If the parties have been married one year, one-fifth of both spouses' marital property is to be included in the marital property estate and after two years, two-fifths and so on.

Another exception to the rules as stated above is with respect to the mutual residence. If one of the spouses owns the mutual residence, but the other spouse is found to be in greater need of the residence, the latter spouse can be allotted the mutual residence in the division of the marital estate despite the fact she is not the owner. The spouse found to be in greater need must, however, financially compensate the other spouse for her share in the residence.

7.1.6 MAINTENANCE OBLIGATIONS AFTER DIVORCE

Each spouse is responsible for her own support after a divorce. The right to spousal maintenance technically exists under the sixth chapter of the Marriage Code, but only for limited periods of time (more than three years is the exception), and only in extreme cases.[12] Spouses have no right to maintain the same standard of living after a divorce.

Maintenance is typically to be paid monthly, but cannot judicially be ordered retroactively for more than three years, or executed more than three years after payment was due. In addition, the court is empowered to modify a judgment so that the paying spouse can pay a lesser amount, but cannot modify a judgment to increase the amount of maintenance. The amount of spousal maintenance as awarded by court judgment is usually tied to follow the changes made in the statutory base amount.

7.2 Cohabitees

Almost one-third of the couples in Sweden cohabit without marrying, and the legal rights provided in such relationships by the Act on Cohabitees (*sambolag* 2003:376) are limited.[13] Cohabitees (*sambor*) are two unmarried persons living in a couple relationship, heterosexual or homosexual, with a mutual household under marriage-like conditions. There is no defined period of time that has to be fulfilled as to living together, but the assessment is made on a case-by-case basis of the circumstances as a whole. One circumstance that is significant is whether the couple has mutual children.

The relationship is entered into formlessly, but dissolved less formlessly in that a division of the mutual home (*gemensam bostad*) and household goods (*bohag*) similar to that for spouses can be requested by one of the cohabitees. The term "mutual" does not imply mutual ownership, but only that the home has been acquired for the mutual use of the cohabitees. Only the mutual home and household goods (and any related secured debts) are included in the division of the estate. A cohabitation relationship as recognized under the act is dissolved when either party marries, when they move apart, when one

---

12 See, however, Margareta Brattström, *Spouses' Pension Rights and Financial Settlement in Cases of Divorce* in SCANDINAVIAN STUDIES IN LAW Vol. 50 (2007) at 331.

13 For the history of cohabitation in Sweden and Swedish law, *see* Göran Lind, COMMON LAW MARRIAGE: A LEGAL INSTITUTION FOR COHABITATION (Oxford 2008) comparing the Swedish institution of cohabitation with Anglo-American common law marriage.

of the cohabitees dies or when a cohabitee requests a division of the mutual home and household goods. No division of property occurs unless one of the cohabitees requests such within one year from the separation of the parties.

There is a general public misunderstanding that cohabitees have the same legal rights as spouses, but this is far from the case. Significant differences include the fact that the parties do not have any property rights with respect to each other except relating to the mutual residence and household goods. There are even limitations with respect to what is considered the mutual residence and household goods, for example, vacation homes are explicitly not included, neither are household goods used only by one cohabitee. There is no duty to support each other during the cohabitation, and there is no right to the same standard of living for cohabitees.

Cohabitees are free to enter into a property agreement as to the distribution of property between them. This agreement does not have to be registered with a court, but must be in writing and signed by both parties. The same limitation exists here, however, as for spouses, in that the owner of the mutual residence cannot dispose of it without the other cohabitee's consent. After a separation, the cohabitee in greater need of the mutual residence has the right to take it over, but only after buying the other party out.

Cohabitees do not inherit from each other under the law. They can be beneficiaries under a will to the extent the other cohabitee is free to dispose of her property, as discussed below, basically after any children of the testator have received their mandatory statutory portion if they wish to exercise their rights to such. The father of any children born in a cohabitation relationship has to register paternity with an acknowledgement of paternity (regardless of the length of the cohabitation and the number of previous mutual children) as opposed to a spouse, who is presumed to be the father and is automatically granted child custody rights. Cohabitees also cannot adopt children jointly, only individually.[14]

---

14 *See* NJA 1976 p. 702 upholding this principle. A legislative investigation was conducted as to changing the legislation to allow cohabitees to adopt jointly, *see* More Modern Adoption Rules (*Modernare adoptionsregler*, dir. 2007:150). On the European level, *see Emonet and Others v. Switzerland*, European Court of Human Rights, judgment dated 13 December 2007, App. No. 39051/03 concerning Swiss adoption provisions for cohabitees similar to those in Sweden. The European Court of Human Rights found them to be in violation of Article 8 of the European Convention.

7.3 The Relationship between Parents and Children

The legal relationship between parents and children, as well as the rights of children, are addressed in the Parental Code (*föräldrabalk* 1949:381). Sweden has signed the United Nation's Convention on the Rights of the Child,[15] but has not yet enacted it as legislation nor transformed it as required under dualism for it to become Swedish law. Thus the Convention on the Rights of the Child is binding for Sweden as between signatory countries, but individuals cannot directly assert rights under it. This is not to say that the Convention on the Rights of the Child has not affected Swedish law. One of the overriding principles in the law governing the relationship between parents and children is the best interest of the child (*barnets bästa*), which is often interpreted as the right of a child to equal care by two parents.

TABLE 7.3 The Parental Code.

Part One: The Parents and Child	
Chap. 1 On paternity and maternity	Chap. 4 Adoption
Chap. 2 Establishing paternity	Chap. 5 The child's name
Chap. 3 Paternity lawsuits	
Part Two: The Care of Children	
Chap. 6 Custody, residence and visitation	Chap. 7 Maintenance obligations
Part Three: The Legal Capacity of Children	
Chap. 9 The legal capacity of children	
Part Four: Guardianship Generally	
Chap. 10 Guardian of a child	Chap. 14 Appointed guardians
Chap. 11 Guardians ad litem and guardians	Chap. 15 Preservation of rights in an estate
Chap. 12 Guardianships generally	Chap. 16 Supervision of guardians
Chap. 13 Parental guardianship	Chap. 19 Municipal supervisor of guardians
Part Five: Judicial Proceedings	
Chap. 20 Trial procedures	Chap. 21 Enforcement of Judgments and orders

---

15 For more information on the Convention in Sweden, *see* the website of Children's Ombudsman, the government authority charged with protecting the rights of children in Sweden at barnombudsmannen.se.

The Parental Code compromises twenty-one chapters which can be roughly divided into five topics, the first three directly relating to children, namely issues arising at birth, the care and later emancipation of children.

The fourth area of regulation, guardianship, concerns the guardianship of persons regardless of age and is addressed separately in section 7.4 below. The fifth section concerns judicial procedures in these types of family cases.

7.3.1 THE PARENTS OF THE CHILD

There is a very strong presumption in Swedish law that the husband of a woman who has given birth to a child is the father of that child (*faderskaps-presumption*). This presumption was adopted in order to protect the sanctity of marriage from claims by third parties. The husband has the right to bring a suit to determine paternity, as does the child, but where the biological father is not the husband, he has no standing to bring a lawsuit. This presumption of fatherhood is not, however, applicable to cohabitees as discussed above.

A court can find that a husband is not the father of a child under three circumstances: where it has been shown that the mother has had sexual intercourse with another man during the time the child was conceived and it is probable that the other man is the biological father, where it is genetically shown that the husband is not the father, or where the child was conceived prior to the marriage or when the spouses lived separately and it is not probable that the spouses had sexual intercourse with each other during the time the child was conceived. If the husband accepts another man's acknowledgement of paternity, the husband will be deemed to not be the father of the child. Any acknowledgement of paternity is always to be confirmed by the mother in writing.

If the parents are not married, the paternity of a child is to be established either by a voluntary acknowledgement of paternity or court judgment. An acknowledgement of paternity is to be in writing, witnessed by two persons and confirmed by the mother in writing unless a guardian has been appointed for the mother. The acknowledgement of paternity must also be approved by the municipal social welfare committee (*socialnämnden*).

If paternity is to be established by court judgment, the court is to declare a man the father if such is established through genetic testing, or if it is established that the man had sexual intercourse with the woman during the period in which the child was conceived, or during the same period, the woman was artificially inseminated with his sperm, and it is probable that the child is his.

The phenomenon of artificial insemination has led to the most recent amendments to the Parental Code. A 2006 act took away the possibility for a court to declare a man the father of a child where the man was a sperm donor in accordance with the Act on Genetic Privacy (*lag 2006:351 om genetisk integritet*). If a woman is artificially inseminated with sperm with the consent of her husband or cohabitee, the husband or cohabitee is to be declared the father of the child if it is found probable that the child was conceived as a result of the insemination. Where a woman is artificially inseminated with another woman's egg, she is to be considered the mother, and if this is done with the consent of her spouse or cohabitee, he is to be the father. If the woman is in a lesbian relationship, and the artificial insemination has occurred with the consent of her spouse, the other woman is to be deemed a parent to the child.

As the best interest of the child has been interpreted to mean two parents, the municipal social welfare committees are obligated to try to determine the identity of the second parent, whether paternity or in the case of a lesbian couple, parenthood, for all children in Sweden. The committee is also to insure that such a relationship is legally confirmed either voluntarily or by court judgment. As paternity is assumed for married couples, this issue mainly arises with respect to children born to unmarried women. The committee has a mechanism to insure cooperation by the mother, namely that certain social benefits can be withheld for a failure by the mother to cooperate with respect to determining paternity or parenthood.[16]

---

16 A child is considered to not have a right to certain state child maintenance subsidies (*underhållsstöd*) if the child permanently resides with the mother and she, without reasonable cause, obviously omits to take or cooperate in measures to have paternity or parenthood established in accordance with the provisions in the Parental Code, *see* Section 8 of Chapter 18 of the Social Insurance Code.

7.3.2 ADOPTION

The provisions concerning adoption are set out in the fourth chapter of the Parental Code. A court is to assess an adoption petition taking into account the suitability of the adoption. In assessing suitability, the court is to take into consideration the will of the child in light of the child's age and degree of maturity. The adoption can only be approved if it is advantageous to the child and the applicant has raised or wishes to raise the child, or other reasons exist to find the adoption appropriate due to the personal relationship between the child and applicant. The petition is not to be granted if the court finds that compensation for the adoption has been promised or a contract related to economic support for the child exists. A lump payment for support, however, is permitted if the amount has been paid to the municipal social welfare committee where the child is to live.

A person who has reached the age of twenty-five can adopt a child with the court's permission. Persons under the age of twenty-five can adopt if the adoption concerns their own child, a spouse's child or adopted child, or if particular reasons exist for doing so. Spouses are to jointly adopt children but one spouse may adopt the other spouse's child or adopted child with the other spouse's consent. One spouse may also adopt a child where the location of the other spouse is unknown, or the other spouse suffers from a serious psychiatric condition. Only spouses may adopt jointly, entailing that cohabitees may not jointly adopt a child.

A child under the age of eighteen years may not be adopted without the consent of the parents. Consent need not be obtained where the location of the parent is unknown, or if the parent suffers from a serious psychiatric condition. A mother's consent must be given after she has had time to physically recover from the birth. A child who has reached the age of twelve years may not be adopted without the child's consent. Consent is not necessary if the child is under sixteen years of age and the risk exists that it could be harmful to ask the child for consent, or if the child is not capable of giving consent because of a serious psychiatric condition or similar situation.

An adopted child is to be treated in the same manner as a biological child to the adoptive parent. The adoption severs the legal ties with the biological parent. If the child is adopted by one spouse, and is the biological child of the other spouse, the child is deemed to be their joint child.

216

Specific statutory provisions are applicable where the child and the party wishing to adopt do not reside in the same country. If they both reside in a Nordic country, a court in the country in which the person seeking to adopt resides has jurisdiction. If one of the parties lives outside the Nordic region, a Swedish court has jurisdiction if the party seeking to adopt is a Swedish citizen or permanently resides in Sweden, reflecting the requirements of the Hague Convention.[17]

According to Swedish law, an international adoption is to be carried out through an authorized adoption organization such as Swedish Friends of Children. Authorization is issued by the Swedish Intercountry Adoptions Authority (*Myndigheten för internationella adoptionsfrågor*), which also supervises adoption organizations with the objective of establishing and maintaining a high quality of intercountry adoption operations in Sweden. All adoption organizations in Sweden are to work in accordance with the terms of the Hague Convention and the United Nations Convention on the Rights of the Child.

Any parties petitioning for an international adoption must receive approval in advance from the social welfare committee in the municipality in which they live. The municipal social secretary conducts a home visit to make sure that the family is suitable to receive an adopted child. This home assessment is translated and sent together with the application to the child's country so that the authorities there have a description of the parents. The parents are also to attend compulsory parental education classes to receive information about the specific needs of adopted children. Adoptions from countries that have signed the Hague Convention are automatically valid in Sweden. Adoptions from other countries are to be completed by a Swedish court, after which the child becomes a Swedish citizen.

---

17 About 800 international adoptions take place annually in Sweden. Sweden signed the 1993 Hague Convention on Protection of Children and Co-operation in respect of Intercountry Adoption in 1993 and implemented the convention as Swedish legislation in 1997 (*lag 1997:191 med anledning av Sveriges tillträde till Haagkonventionen om skydd av barn och samarbete vid internationella adoptioner*) effective 1999. For more on the Swedish Intercountry Adoptions Authority in English, *see* its website at mia.eu.

7.3.3 THE CHILD'S NAME

A parent having custody of a child is to report the child's name in writing to the Tax Authority within three months of the birth of the child. If the child is christened in the Swedish Church, it is sufficient to report the name to the pastor at the baptism.

Rules exist with respect to both the last and first names of children. Reference is made in the Parental Code to "that legislated elsewhere," an oblique reference to the Name Act. Under the Name Act, if the parents have the same last name, the child is automatically to take that name. If the parents have different last names, the parents may choose one of their last names, or pre-marriage last names, as the child's last name if the first born. If the child already has siblings under the joint custody of the parents, the child's last name must be the same as the sibling nearest to the child in age. If a last name is not chosen within three months, the child will be given the last name of the mother. The rules concerning adopted children are the same, and the child's new name is part of the court judgment. Foster children have the right to take the name of a foster parent under certain circumstances, if the court finds it to be in the best interest of the child.

If the child receives a last name that only one of the parents has, the last name of the other parent can be given to the child as a middle name. The right to this middle name, however, is limited in that it cannot be passed on to a spouse or a child of that child.

A child can be given one or several first names. The Tax Authority makes an assessment as to whether the first name is appropriate. Names that are seen as controversial, assumed to be problematic for a person so named or for other reasons are apparently unsuitable are not to be approved.[18]

7.3.4 CUSTODY AND MAINTENANCE

Every child under the age of eighteen years is to be in the custody of at least one adult. Spouses receive both legal and physical custody automatically

---

18 The first names, Linus C:son Ferdinand, for example, were rejected because of the inclusion of "C:son" which the Tax Authority found to be a surname not suitable as a first name. The Supreme Administrative Court found it to be a suitable first name, *see* RÅ 2003 ref. 66.

with respect to any child born in the marriage. If the parents marry after the birth of the child, joint legal and physical custody automatically arises. If the parents are not married, the child is in the automatic legal and physical custody of the mother.

Under the sixth chapter of the Parental Code, those having custody of a child are charged with insuring that the child has the right to care, security and a good upbringing. Children are to be treated with respect and as individuals, and are not to be subject to corporal punishment or other violative acts. Children are also to receive supervision to the degree necessary taking into consideration their age, development and other circumstances, as well as sufficient support and education.

Parents are to financially contribute to the maintenance of the child to a reasonable extent taking into account the needs of the child and the financial circumstances of the parents. Parents are no longer financially responsible once the child turns eighteen years of age unless the child is still in primary or high school, then the obligation runs until the child is finished with school or becomes twenty-one years of age.

In addition, each child in Sweden receives a monthly state child subsidy (*barnbidrag*) paid to one of the parents regardless of the family's financial situation. The amount in 2012 is SEK 1 050 per month. If neither of the parents requests the subsidy, the monies go automatically to the mother.

The best interests of the child are to be decisive with respect to all decisions concerning custody, residence and visitation. The wishes of the child are to be considered in such decisions, taking into account the age and degree of maturity of the child. In assessing what is in the best interests of the child, particular weight is to be given to any risk that the child or another person in her family could be exposed to violence or that the child could be unlawfully taken or otherwise harmed, as well as the child's need for close and good contact with both parents.[19]

---

19 This provision did not refer to family violence until a 2006 amendment. Previously there were difficulties with the authorities and courts interpreting the best interest of the child simply to be good and close contact with both parents even in cases of domestic abuse. An abused spouse could receive a protective order mandating that the abusive spouse had to remain at a certain distance, or even receive a new identity, but still be forced to have contacts with the abusive spouse as the best interest of the child was deemed to be good and near contact with both parents. *See* Legislative Bill 2005/06:99 at 42.

If spouses divorce, or cohabitees separate, the main rule is that any joint physical and legal custody of the child is to continue. The parents are free to agree as to how custody is to be handled between them, and such an agreement is to be approved by the appropriate municipal social welfare committee. If the court is to decide custody, the court is to take into consideration the best interests of the child. The court can award joint or sole custody, but cannot award joint custody where both parents oppose it.

The parents can enter into an agreement as to the physical custody of the child, which also has to be approved by the municipal social welfare committee. A common solution nowadays is for parents to split physical custody in half, so that the child lives with one parent one week, and the other parent the next week. This also tends to reduce the need for financial support to be paid by one party, as both then theoretically share equally in the costs of food and housing. A parent who does not live with the child and does not have custody fulfills the support obligation by paying a monthly amount. Child support as awarded by court judgment is indexed to follow the changes in the statutory price base amount.

The parent not having physical custody of the child has the right to visitation. If that parent pays support, the parent has the right to deduct days the child spends with the non-custodial parent from the child support for any consecutive stay of at least five days, at that rate of 1/40 of the amount for each complete day. The custodial parent may also have to contribute to any costs, such as travel costs, incurred with the visitation.

7.3.5 THE LEGAL CAPACITY OF MINORS

A child under the age of eighteen years is not deemed to have the legal capacity (*rättshandlingsförmåga*) to dispose of property or enter into binding legal agreements with certain exceptions. Minors are seen under the Parental Code to successively acquire a limited legal capacity up to the age of eighteen years.

The employment of children is regulated partially in the Parental Code but also in the fifth chapter of the Work Environment Act (*arbetsmiljölag* 1977:1160). The latter act states that a child of thirteen years of age can be hired to perform lighter duties that cannot be deemed to negatively affect the health, development or schooling of the child. A minor that has reached the age of sixteen years can be employed if she has completed her mandatory primary education. A minor cannot be employed to perform work entailing risks for occupational accidents, overexertion or other harmful effects on the minor's health or development.

Under the Parental Code, a minor can accept a contract of employment but only with parental consent. The minor is free to terminate the employment, and after the age of sixteen, can enter into new employment without parental consent. Both the minor and the parents can terminate the employment contract immediately if deemed necessary, taking into account the child's health, development and education. If a parent has terminated the employment contract for these reasons, the minor may not enter into a new contract of employment without parental consent. A minor that has reached the age of sixteen years can dispose over funds received from her own employment including any interest accrued on such and any surrogate property. However, the parents still have the right to take the property away from the minor in light of considerations as to the child's upbringing or welfare if the municipal supervisor of guardians (överförmyndaren) consents.

A minor reaching the age of sixteen years can conduct her own business and take the legal actions necessary to conduct that business. If it is a business that has certain statutory bookkeeping requirements, a minor can only operate such a business with the consent of her parents as well as the consent of the municipal supervisor of guardians. Such consent is to be given only where it is suitable taking into account the minor's financial and personal circumstances and the nature of the business. A minor with her own household and/or child is considered regardless of age to have the legal capacity necessary to enter into legally binding agreements for the daily needs of the household.

The rules regarding gifts, inherited property and wills are more complicated. If a minor has received property either as a gift, through a will or as a beneficiary under a contract with the condition that the minor is to freely dispose over the property, the minor has the right to freely dispose over that property regardless of age. The property can be taken away by the parents, with the consent of the municipal supervisor of guardians, if the property is deemed to pose a threat to the child's upbringing or welfare. A minor is free to leave testamentary dispositions with respect to property under her control. If the minor has been or is married, the minor can draft a will with respect to all her property as stated in the Inheritance Code.

If a party has entered into a contract with a minor lacking the legal capacity to enter into such a contract, the minor is free to rescind the contract where it has not been ratified nor completely performed. If partial performances have been tendered, the parties are then to return any performances made, typically the seller monies and the minor goods. If the goods have been consumed or used, compensation is to be given for any deficiency in the goods to the extent the goods were of benefit to the minor. There is an element of subjectivity in this test, in that if the minor received no use, or a use not deemed to be beneficial but rather detrimental, there then is no requirement to pay compensation to the other party.

If the minor misled the other party by giving false information with respect to age, the minor is obligated to pay compensation for those damages arising from the invalid contract sufficient to place the other party in the same position as if the contract had never been reached (*negativa kontrakts-intresset*).

7.4 Guardianship

If a child has both parents, the parents act as guardians for the child. If neither of the parents can act as guardian, then a court is to appoint one. In certain cases, such as where a child has inherited significant property, the court can appoint a limited guardian (*god man*) to protect the interests of the child despite the presence of parents.

Limited and general guardians (*förvaltare*) can also be appointed with respect to adults. The objective with the rules in the eleventh chapter of the Parental Code is to minimize incursions in the liberty and dignity of adults found to be in need. If an individual, due to illness, psychiatric disorder, weakened health or similar situation needs assistance in order to protect her rights, manage property or take care of her person, the court can appoint a limited guardian to help with these needs. Such a decision is not to be taken without the consent of the individual unless the individual's condition prevents it. The limited guardian has limited legal authority and is more seen as support for the individual in need. If an individual cannot care for herself or her property, the court can order that a general guardianship be

created. A general guardianship is not to be created if a limited guardianship
is sufficient.

The guardianship is to be tailored in each individual case consistent
with the needs of the individual and can be limited, for example, to certain
types of property or certain types of decisions exceeding a stated value. The
court may leave it up to the municipal supervisor of guardians to determine
the extent of the guardianship. A delicate balance is to be reached between
allowing individuals in need of assistance to retain as much independence
and dignity as possible, while granting the guardian sufficient authority
to allow the guardian to assist in caring for the individual. Guardians are
under the supervision of the municipal supervisor of guardians. Acts taken
by guardians exceeding their authority do not bind their wards.

7.5 Inheritance Law

The regulations concerning inheritance are found in the Inheritance Code
(*ärvdabalk* 1958:637). When an individual dies, her assets and debts are to be
identified and an inventory of her estate taken. The inventory is to be prepared
by two executors within three months of the death and also include the assets
of any spouse or cohabitee. Any parties with interests in the estate are to be
summoned to a meeting. If the assets of the deceased are not sufficient to pay
for anything other than debts and funeral expenses, a notice can be given
instead of an inventory taken. An estate inventory must always be prepared
if real property or a site leasehold is included in the estate. If the decedent
had children under the age of eighteen years, a guardian *ad litem* is to be
appointed to represent the children in the proceedings.

If the decedent was married, the first act is to perform a division of the
marital estate in accordance with the regulations discussed above, with all
marital property after debts being divided equally between the spouses. If
the decedent was a cohabitee, a division of the mutual home and household
goods is to take place. If the surviving spouse or cohabitee wishes, a division
of the marital estate or mutual home need not take place and then each spouse
or cohabitee simply keeps his and her respective assets and debts. After the
division of property, the debts of the decedent are to be paid.

7.5.1 HEIRS

The assets remaining after the division of the marital estate, or division of the mutual home and household for cohabitees, become the estate of the decedent. Individuals with children, regardless of the age of the children, do not have complete testamentary freedom in Sweden.[20] If the decedent had any children, they are entitled to one-half of the decedent's estate, divided equally among the siblings regardless of whether they are whole or half-siblings (*laglott*). A child can choose to not exercise this right to a portion of the decedent's estate.

There are three classes of persons entitled to inherit in accordance with Swedish law. The first class comprises descendants, any children and grandchildren of the decedent, and they have a statutory right to a portion of the estate. If there are no descendants who can inherit in the first class, then those persons in the second class can inherit. The second class comprises of the deceased's parents and siblings (and the children of any sibling if the sibling is deceased). The persons in this class receive equal portions. The rights in the second class are not mandatory, in other words, the deceased can then will the entirety of her property away. If there are no survivors in the second class, then persons in the third class can inherit and again, there is complete testamentary freedom. The third class consists of grandparents and their children, but does not reach as far as cousins, who were removed from this class in 1928. If there are no living relatives in these three classes, and the decedent has left no will, the assets of the estate go to the National Inheritance Fund (*Allmänna arvsfonden*).[21]

Spouses could not inherit at all under the Code prior to 1988. Now the entirety of the decedent's estate goes to the other spouse unless the spouses were in the process of going through a marital divorce at the time of the death. If the decedent had no surviving children or grandchildren, the spouse receives the decedent's estate with a complete right of ownership and disposition. If the decedent had surviving children or grandchildren, the

---

20 This limitation in testamentary freedom dates back to the early Middle Ages in Sweden, when the limits were put in place so that wealthy persons could not leave their entire estates to the church and thus impoverish their families.

21 For more information on the National Inheritance Fund in English, *see* its website at arvsfonden.se.

spouse receives a life estate in the decedent's estate. The spouse may dispose of the property, but cannot leave it to another by will. After the surviving spouse dies, the heirs of the first spouse in the first and second classes are entitled to one-half of the estate of the second spouse.

Regardless of anything else, a surviving spouse is entitled to a portion of the decedent's estate equal to four times the statutory price base amount after the division of the marital estate. If a child with a statutory right to inherit is not the child of the surviving spouse, that child has the right to their portion of the estate immediately, but can defer taking out the portion.

7.5.2 WILLS

Many individuals in Sweden rely on the statutory rules of inheritance and do not write wills. If the decedent has children, she can only dispose over one-half of the estate through a will in the event the children choose to exercise their right to a portion of the estate. If there are no surviving children, the decedent can dispose over the entire estate in the will.

There are form requirements with respect to a will. The testator must be eighteen years of age, unless the will concerns property over which she can dispose, then she has to be at least sixteen years old. If the testator is or has been married, there is no age limit. The testator is to sign the will in the presence of two witnesses who must be at least fifteen years of age and not suffering from a mental disorder. In other words, the witnesses must be able to understand the significance of their witnessing the will, but they do not need to know the content of the will. Spouses, relatives or spouses to a relative of the testator cannot be witnesses. The witnesses are to sign the will and state their profession, place of residence, date of signature and any other circumstances that could be relevant to the validity of the will.

If a person is unable to draft a written will due to illness or other exigency, the testator can orally make a will before two witnesses, or have them write down the terms of the will and sign it. The testator must, however, draft a written will within three months of the date of the oral will or it will be deemed invalid. A will signed under duress, exploitation or deceit is not valid. Neither is a will valid that was signed under a psychiatric disturbance.

A number of interpretive rules are set out in the eleventh chapter of the Inheritance Code in unclear cases. The primary rule is that the will is to be given the interpretation that can be seen to be consistent with the intent of the testator. If the will has been given a content, which due to a mistake in writing or other mistake, deviates from the intent of the testator, the intent of the testator is to be given effect if it can be proven. Contracts entered into by beneficiaries regarding inheritances or testamentary bequests from persons not yet deceased are invalid.

CHAPTER 8

Agency

Every individual in Sweden is a legal subject, defined generally as having legal personhood, the ability to own property and be a party to a lawsuit.[1] Legal persons, in the form of corporations, partnerships, cooperative enterprises and foundations, gain legal personhood upon the fulfillment of all statutory requirements for that category of legal person. For example, a corporation becomes a legal person upon its rightful registration with the Swedish Companies Registration Office (*Bolagsverket*), entailing that the incorporators are no longer personally responsible for the corporation's obligations. Swedish law makes a distinction between legal personhood (*rättskapacitet*) and the right to enter into binding legal actions, legal capacity (*rättshandlingsförmåga* or *rättshabilitet*).

8.1 Legal Capacity

Individuals reach the age of legal majority in Sweden when they become eighteen years old as set out in Section 9:1 of the Parental Code as discussed in the preceding Chapter Seven. Before turning eighteen, the general rule is that parents, as the guardians of a minor, have the right to exercise legal authority on behalf of the minor. Contracts entered into with a minor are typically freely voidable to the extent any performances can be returned. Legal personhood, and consequently, legal capacity, expire upon the death of a person. For an individual, this means that upon death, any property, as well as certain legal rights and obligations, is transferred to the estate of the deceased and the administrator of the estate then makes the legal decisions concerning the

---

1   A child conceived but not yet born has the right to inherit under Section 1:1 of the Inheritance Code under certain circumstances.

property. For a legal person, upon either voluntary or involuntary liquidation, the assets as well as certain legal rights and obligations are also transferred to the trustee to be distributed to any creditors and shareholders.

Individuals who have reached the age of majority can still have their legal capacity limited by law. A contract entered into by a person under the influence of a psychological disturbance is voidable under the Act on the Validity of Contracts Entered into Under the Influence of a Psychological Disturbance (*lag 1924:323 om verkan av avtal, som slutits under påverkan av en psykisk störning*). A guardian (*förvaltare*) can be appointed for individuals under the eleventh chapter of the Parental Code. This occurs in cases where the individual no longer can take care of herself or her property due to sickness, mental disability or similar circumstances, as also discussed above in Section 7.4. A guardian can have varying degrees of authority depending on the individual case, from being granted the right to make all legal decisions for the individual, to only making more significant legal decisions, such as concerning the sale of real estate, with the individual retaining the right to make daily decisions.

The law can also impose restrictions on individuals who have taken voluntary actions with certain consequences. The legal capacity of either an individual or legal person who has been placed into bankruptcy is limited by Section 3:1 of the Bankruptcy Act (*konkurslag 1987:672*), discussed further below in Chapter Ten. A person placed into bankruptcy cannot as a general rule freely dispose of her property, the property instead becoming a part of the bankruptcy estate, nor can such a person enter into certain types of contracts. Certain personal property of the individual, however, remains outside of the bankruptcy estate.

A court can limit the legal capacity of certain individuals with respect to business transactions, placing them under a prohibition as to conducting business (*näringsförbud*) according to the Act on Prohibitions as to Conducting Business (*lag 1986:436 om näringsförbud*). This type of prohibition is judicially ordered taking into consideration public welfare concerns where an individual has grossly neglected certain obligations arising in business situations. Examples of such conduct include where an individual has grossly neglected business obligations to the degree of significant criminally liability, has failed to pay taxes, customs or other fees, or defrauded creditors in a bankruptcy. Exacerbating circumstances are where the conduct has been systematic or for the purpose of generating substantial profits, if the conduct has caused or was intended to cause considerable harm, or if the individual previously has been sentenced for economic crimes. A prohibition as to conducting business can be issued for a three-year minimum with a maximum of ten years against a person who is:

- A sole proprietor;
- A general partner in a limited partnership;
- A director or deputy director, chief executive officer or vice chief executive officer of a corporation or insurance company;
- A director or deputy director of a bank or commercial cooperative; or
- A member of corporate management of a European Economic Interest Group[2] located in Sweden under certain conditions.

A person subject to such a prohibition may not conduct business, be a partner in a partnership, act as an incorporator, director, vice or chief executive officer, signatory or shareholder of more than one-half of the shares of a corporation, or have a power of attorney to represent a sole proprietor or legal person in a business context.

The provision of professional advice by lawyers or accountants facilitating criminal acts is in itself criminal under the Act Prohibiting Legal or Financial Advice in Certain Cases (*lag 1985:354 om förbud mot juridiskt eller ekonomiskt biträde i vissa fall*). One of the sanctions that can be imposed is a prohibition as to providing legal or financial advice issued against such an individual for up to ten years with respect to more serious crimes. In the same manner, a real estate broker can have her license revoked for certain violations of the Act on Real Estate Brokers (*fastighetsmäklarlag* 2011:666).

---

2   A European Economic Interest Group is created under Council Regulation (EEC) No. 2137/85 on the European Economic Interest Grouping (EEIG). The purpose of this type of group is to facilitate or develop the economic activities of its members by a pooling of resources, activities or skills. It can be formed by companies, firms and other legal entities governed by public or private law which have been formed in accordance with the law of a Member State and which have their registered office in the Union. It can also be formed by individuals carrying on an industrial, commercial, craft or agricultural activity or providing professional or other services in the Union. An EEIG must have at least two members from different Member States.

8.2 Agency

A person with legal capacity can decide to voluntarily delegate legal authority to another party through a grant of authority (*fullmakt*) in order to enter into legally binding agreements on behalf of that person. Three parties are involved in such a legal relationship: the party granting the authority, the principal (*huvudmannen* or *fullmaktsgivaren*); the agent who is the party receiving the grant of authority (*fullmäktigen*); and the party with whom the agent forms an agreement, the third party (*tredje man*). By this, the principal consents to being bound to the third party by the acts of the agent acting within the scope of the authority as granted by the principal.

The general principles of agency law are contained in the second chapter of the Contracts Act (*lag 1915:218 om avtal och andra rättshandlingar på förmögenhetsrättens område* or in its simpler version, *avtalslagen*). Several categories of agents (*mellanmän*) exist under specific statutes enacted over a period spanning almost three hundred years, beginning with the 1734 Commerce Code. The discussion below first addresses the general provisions concerning the grant of authority under the second chapter of the Contracts Act, followed by brief descriptions of certain categories of agents as covered by specific laws, namely general agents, professional service providers, commercial agents and self-employed commercial agents. It should be mentioned here that there is no pervasive concept of fiduciary duties in Swedish law.

8.2.1 THE GRANT OF AUTHORITY

Sections 10–27 of the Contracts Act set out the principles for agencies established either by an express grant of authority (*fullmakt*), or by apparent authority based on status. A principal granting a person the power to bind the principal to a contract or legal action is bound to that contract or legal action according to Section 10 of the Contracts Act where the agent has acted within the scope of the authority as granted by the principal.

There is no general requirement of a writing to grant authority. Thus the grant of authority can be contained in a writing, such as a power of attorney, or it can be made orally to the third party. The writing can be general, giving a power of attorney that can be shown to any third party, or directed to a specific third party, for example, "to Johanna, Susan has the authority to purchase a car on my behalf." A grant of authority can also occur through the publication of a notice as to the agency. One exception to this lack of form requirements is that with respect to real estate transactions, such a grant of authority must be in writing.

The second category of agency recognized under the act does not require an explicit grant of authority, but rather is based on the apparent authority derived from the agent's status to the principal (*ställningsfullmakt*). This type of agency arises where an individual is either employed or has a contractual relationship with the principal that according to law or custom includes the authority to act on behalf of the principal. The principal is bound as long as the agent acts within the boundaries for such authority as set out by law or custom. The principal is not authorized to change the terms of such authority, the premise being that third parties need to be able to rely on the authority of the agent as typically existing in the industry or as holding that position.

An example of this status-based agency can be seen in relation to the role of an office manager in a corporation. The office manager has the authority to enter into contracts binding the principal, in this case the corporation, with respect to purchasing office supplies. However, if the office manager were to enter into a contract concerning a matter that must be decided by the board of directors or the shareholders, such as buying real estate for new corporate offices, the corporation is not bound by the contract as the office manager has acted outside the boundaries of her authority. In the same vein, a store cashier has the authority to accept monies for the payment of goods sold in the store, but does not have the authority to enter into a contract on behalf of the store for the purchase of a new computer system.[3]

These two types of agency, express agency and agency based on status, fall within the category of independent agencies (*självständiga fullmakter*).

---

3 A further distinction is made in Swedish law between agencies granted on the basis of status as discussed here, and the authority a party has as a representative for a legal person (*ställföreträdare*), such as a chief executive officer, which authority lies outside the Contracts Act. Another type of a more limited authority based on status is the right to sign contracts on behalf of a legal person (*teckna firma*) which authority is created by simply registering the right in the Companies Register or Trade Register kept by the Swedish Companies Registration Office. This limited authority does not include the right to take decisions, simply to carry them out.

Two additional types of independent agencies have been judicially recognized within this category, agency by estoppel (*toleransfullmakt*) and an agency based on a combination of status and estoppel (*kombinationsfullmakt*). With the first, the principal has repeatedly tolerated the individual acting as an agent despite a lack of authority, and has done nothing to prevent it. The courts have thus found that the principal is bound through its passivity. The second type of agency is a combination of the tolerated behavior, agency based on status and other factors as assessed judicially on a case-by-case basis.

Diametrically opposite to an independent agency is a dependent agency (*osjälvständig fullmakt*), which is referred to in Section 18 of the Contracts Act. This type of agency, also referred to as a Section 18 agency (*paragraf 18 fullmakt*) or commission agency (*uppdragsfullmakt*), exists where a principal grants authority directly to the agent but gives no notification of the grant of authority to any third parties. It is the agent who then informs any third party that she has the power to act as agent, while the third party has no information from the principal or evidence to confirm this. This type of agency is dependent solely on the representations from the principal to the agent with no outward manifestations to third parties. If the third party does not confirm the grant of the agency with the principal, the view in Swedish law is that the third party assumes the risks of the transaction and the risk that the agent has acted within the scope of the authority granted. The principal does not bear the risk in such situations as she has not demonstrated any outward intent to be bound by the actions of the agent. A principal naturally is free to ratify (*ratihibera*) any transaction entered into by the agent with a third party, but is not required to do so.

The principal is bound to a legal transaction in which the agent has acted within the boundaries of the authority granted. The scope of the authority as granted to an agent is categorized in Swedish law, based on Germanic law, into two types, the authority known to the third party (*behörighet*) and the limitations as to the authority as known between the principal and agent (*befogenhet*). If the agent acts outside the grant of authority known to the third party, the principal is not bound. If the agent acts outside the limitations in authority as known only by the agent and principal, the principal is bound according to Section 11 of the Contracts Act as long as the third party did not know, nor ought not to have known, that the agent was acting outside those limitations. Here the distinction between independent and dependent (paragraph 18) agencies can also be seen. If the paragraph 18 agent exceeds the limitations in authority, the principal as a rule is not bound to the agreement.

An example of this relationship between authority and limitations in authority can be seen in a case where the principal grants the agent the authority to purchase a corporation as explicitly set out in a written power of attorney. The third party knows that the agent has the authority to purchase a corporation on behalf of the principal. However, at the same time as issuing the written power of attorney, the principal informs the agent that the type of corporation must be a car manufacturing company and that the purchase price cannot exceed € 1 billion. If the agent enters into a contract to purchase a real estate company for € 2 billion, the principal is still bound by the transaction as the third party did not know of the limitations placed on the scope of the authority of the agent. The agent is then liable to the principal for any actual loss the principal has suffered due to the transaction as prescribed under Section 18:3 of the 1734 Commerce Code. The losses suffered have to be actual losses, which means that they are not necessarily the difference in price, € 1 million, but rather whether the corporation can be sold for the purchase price.

A question that can be raised is why would a principal grant authority to an agent and then limit it in this quasi-secretive manner. This is more a function of reality and the nature of negotiations than law. A principal can

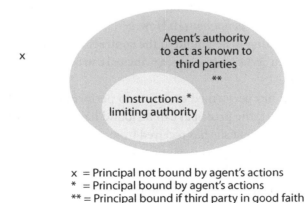

x = Principal not bound by agent's actions
* = Principal bound by agent's actions
** = Principal bound if third party in good faith

DIAGRAM 8.1 Agent's Authority to Act.

state that the agent has the authority to purchase shares, but perhaps the principal does not want to give her bargaining position away to the third party. The principal can then limit the authority of the agent to shares in the amount of € 1 million at a price of € 1 each so that the agent knows that the maximum is € 1 million, but the third party only knows that the agent is authorized to purchase shares. Otherwise the third party would know exactly how hard to drive the bargain.

The distinction between independent and dependent agencies is important from this aspect as stated briefly above. If an agent with authority as recognized by Section 18 of the Contracts Act acts outside the scope of the limitations in authority between the principal and agent, the principal is not bound according to the second paragraph of Section 11 even if the third party is in good faith. The distinction in the two types of authority is irrelevant with this type of agency, as the authority of the agent is known to the third party only through the representations of the agent, and not from the principal, and the legislator has chosen to place the risk on the third party instead of the principal.

An individual representing to a third party that she has a grant of authority is liable for any actions taken outside that scope of authority as against a third party in good faith under Section 25 of the Contracts Act. An agent who harms the principal by acting outside the limitations in authority as stated by the principal is liable under Section 18:3 of the 1734 Commerce Code for any actual damages caused to the principal.

In the event an agent has acted outside the scope of authority granted by the principal, the principal is not bound. However, the principal can ratify the contract by consenting to be bound to the contract afterwards despite the lack of authority. In certain situations, a principal can be bound through passivity (*passivitet*).

If the third party has performed or begun to perform in accordance with an invalid contract, the principal can be found liable to compensate the third party for any benefit she has received from the performance: This is arguably the case under the doctrine of unjust enrichment (*obehörig vinst*). This general principle of law, the existence of which is debated in Swedish academic circles, entails that the principal should not be allowed to benefit at the cost of the agent or any third party from the fact that a contract was not binding for the principal.

Another similar doctrine is that of *negotiorum gestio*, under which a person who is not authorized to act as an agent, but performs a service for another who is absent by protecting property in danger or another necessary action, has a right to be compensated for any costs incurred under Section 18:10 of the 1734 Commerce Code and general principles of private law.

8.2.2 REVOKING AN AGENCY

An agency can be limited in time as expressly stated by the principal and thus expires at the end of that period. A grant of authority can also be without any limitations in time, in essence, in perpetuity. The general rule as to revoking an agency is that it must be revoked in the same manner by which it was created. The rules as to revocation of an agency are set out in Sections 12–21 of the Contracts Act. If several of these rules are applicable to the revocation of an agency, all must be observed, with the exception that if the third party has been directly notified of the revocation by the principal, she cannot claim that another type of revocation is necessary.

If the grant of authority was created by a notification from the principal to a third party, the principal is to notify the third party that the agency is revoked and the revocation is effective when received. If the agency was created through a notice in a newspaper, another notice must be printed in the newspaper as to its revocation. If the agency was created by a writing not addressed to any one specific party, the agency is revoked by the principal regaining possession of the writing or destroying it. The agent has a duty to return any such writing to the principal. In the event the agent refuses to return the writing, or the writing cannot be returned as it has been lost or misplaced, the principal can request a court declare the writing void. If the court grants the petition, notice is to be published in *Post- och Inrikes Tidningar*[4] and the agency ceases to be valid two weeks from the date of publication. To revoke a Section 18 agency, the principal needs only notify the

---

4 This newspaper has the longest period of publication in Sweden, and perhaps one of the longest in the world, founded by Queen Kristina in 1645. It is used predominantly to publish legal notices. It is available at the website of the Companies Registration Office at poit.bolagsverket.se.

agent that the agency is revoked. The notification is effective when received by the agent.

To revoke an agency based on status, the principal has to remove the individual from the status giving rise to the agency. It generally is not sufficient to simply transfer the employee to another position or terminate her employment. The individual must be removed from the accoutrements of the position. For example, if a company has terminated an individual's employment as a cashier, but not ensured that the individual no longer has access to a cash register, the company can be bound by any transactions conducted by the individual standing behind the cash register even if no longer employed. The assessment here is based on a third party's understanding of the situation. A third party does not know that a person is no longer employed, but only sees that the same individual is standing behind the cash register as before. Naturally, if the third party has knowledge that the individual's employment has been terminated, the principal is not bound by the transaction.

If the principal has reason to anticipate that the agent, despite the revocation of the agency, will continue to enter into transactions with a specific third party based on the former agency, the principal has a duty to inform that third party as to the revocation of the agency. If the principal fails to do this, the principal can be bound by a contract entered into by that third party in good faith despite the revocation of the agency. Where a principal has instructed an agent not to use the grant of authority, but has not revoked it, the principal is not bound by the contract where the third party knew or ought to have known that the principal had so instructed the agent.

If the agent dies, the grant of authority expires upon the agent's death. An agency is still valid to a certain extent in the event the principal dies, unless specific circumstances exist entailing that it should expire. Even so, an estate of the deceased can be bound by legal actions as taken by an agent where the third party neither knew nor ought to have known of the death and its significance to the agent's authority to bind the principal. If a Section 18 agency, the agent cannot have known or ought not to have known of the death when taking the legal action for it to be binding upon the estate.

8.3 Specific Types of Agencies

Certain specific types of agencies are set out by statute, the main ones discussed below being general agents, professional service providers, commercial agents and self-employed commercial agents.

8.3.1 GENERAL AGENTS

General agents (*prokurist*) as defined under the Act on General Agents (*prokuralag* 1974:158) are individuals who have been given the authority to act as general agents (*prokura* or *handelsfullmakt*) for parties registered in accordance with the Act on the Trade Register (*handelsregisterlag* 1974:157). This means that a general agent can be authorized to act on behalf of a sole proprietorship or partnership, but not a corporation or cooperative enterprise. The agent is authorized to act on behalf of the principal in all aspects of the business. The only limitation is that the general agent is not allowed, in the absence of specific authority, to transfer real estate or site leaseholds, or register mortgages or user rights in such property. A written grant of authority gives the general agent the right to represent the principal before the courts and other public authorities. There is no requirement of a writing or registration, but typically a general agency is granted by a writing registered in the Trade Register (*handelsregister*).

A grant of this type of authority can be given to several persons to be exercised collectively. The grant of authority under this act is non-transferable and revocable at any time. The death of the principal does not automatically revoke a general agency. The statutory authority as set out for general agents cannot validly be restricted by the principal to a certain period of time or by any other manner as against any third party in good faith. The idea is that the authority of this type of agent, as defined by statute, is generally known to all third parties, and any restrictions as to this statutory agency would not be anticipated or known by third parties.

8.3.2 PROFESSIONAL SERVICE PROVIDERS

Another category of agency in Swedish law is granted to a group of persons comprising professionals providing services (*sysslomän*). This nebulous category has the common characteristic that each such individual, in the exercise of her profession, must have certain grants of authority. Examples here include lawyers, accountants, architects and real estate brokers. The agency itself is not the subject of the profession, as is the case, for example, with commercial agents. Instead, these professionals all need authority in certain aspects of their work. For example, a lawyer needs a power of attorney from a client to show the court that the lawyer is authorized to represent the client. An accountant needs a certain amount of authority in order to make certain decisions with respect to accounting and taxes. A real estate broker may be authorized to sell a property on behalf of a client. Each of these different professions has either specific statutory regulations, industry regulations or both that regulate their conduct and their relationship to their clients.[5]

The common denominator for all these professionals is that chapter eighteen of the 1734 Commerce Code regulates aspects of the internal relationship between the professional (*uppdragstagare* or *syssloman*) and the principal (*uppdragsgivare* or *huvudman*). In a claim for damages by a client as to work performed, the applicable provision is Section 18:3 of the 1734 Commerce Code. Section 18:3 states that the agent is to answer for all damages (and obligations after the circumstances), and indemnify the principal as to any harm, where the agent has acted disloyally or dishonestly (*oredligt*). Liability can also arise today based on negligence. An individual acting as an agent has the right under this chapter to reasonable pay for her efforts. If either the principal or the agent in such a relationship dies, this type of agency ceases according to Section 18:8. However, the validity of this provision with respect to the death of the principal is strongly questioned given that stated in Section 21 of the Contracts Act.

---

5   For example, the authority and actions of real estate brokers, also referred to as real estate agents, realtors or simply estate agents, are regulated in the Real Estate Agents Act (*fastighetsmäklarlag* 2011:666) and the Real Estate Agents Regulations (*fastighetsmäklarförordning* 2011:668).

8.3.3 COMMERCIAL AGENTS

A commercial agent (*kommissionär*)[6] is a type of agent who receives goods, negotiable instruments or chattels from the principal (*kommittent*) to sell in her own name, and is to receive compensation, a commission or provision, from the sale as regulated by the Commission Act (*kommissionslag* 2009:865). The commercial agent may also buy goods for her principal. As the commercial agent is acting in her own name, she is liable as against any third party instead of the principal. However, the ownership of the property transfers directly from the principal to the third party. This type of relationship is beneficial to the agent in that the agent need not take the economic risk of purchasing the property being sold. The principal is also protected in that the principal has the right to keep the property outside of the agent's bankruptcy (*separationsrätt*) and can remain anonymous with respect to the sale of the property.

A few of the provisions in the Commission Act are mandatory, such as those concerning the commencement of the grant of authority and the termination of the relationship, as well as in cases where the principal is a consumer. Otherwise, the rights and obligations of the parties are set out in detail in the act and two commercial parties are fairly free to contract out of these in a commission agreement (*kommissionsavtalet*). Under the act, the commercial agent is to take into consideration the interests of the principal. The commercial agent is to follow any written instructions of the principal, inform her of any contracts entered into and then submit monies received from the goods to the principal (*redovisningplikt*). The commercial agent is to first examine any goods received (*undersökningsplikt*) and then care for any goods in her possession (*vårdplikt*). If the goods are defective, the commercial agent must give notice of non-conformity (*reklamationsplikt*). The principal can set a limit for prices that the commercial agent is not to transgress, and if she does so, the principal can terminate the agreement and demand damages.

A commercial agent has the right to the agreed upon or a reasonable commission (*provision*) for contracts she has executed based on their amounts, as well as compensation for any direct costs. To insure payment, the commercial agent has the right to retain goods in her possession that are

---

6 Also referred to as commission merchants or factors.

owned by the principal, and eventually sell them if the principal has failed to pay. If the commercial agent has no goods in her possession, the act creates a comparable right of retention to any outstanding claims the principal has against third parties with which the commercial agent has entered into a contract. If either the principal or the commercial agent terminates the agreement prematurely without cause, that party can be liable to the other party for any damages caused. The principal has the right to terminate the relationship only if the commercial agent has materially neglected her duties.

The commercial agent enters into contracts in her own name with third parties. As a general rule, third parties must assert claims based upon the contract against the commercial agent, not the principal. However, consumers in certain cases, where the commercial agent is not available, may assert claims arising from the contract against the principal. The ownership of the goods transfers directly from the principal to the third party, so that the principal does not have any risks in case of an insolvency of the commercial agent. The principal always has the right to remove any goods from a bankruptcy or attachment proceeding as the commercial agent is not the owner. In addition, the principal has the right in bankruptcies and attachments to any monies arising under any contracts as entered into between the commercial agent and any third party.

8.3.4 SELF-EMPLOYED COMMERCIAL AGENTS

The Act on Self-Employed Commercial Agents (*lag 1991:351 om handelsagentur*) is based on Council Directive 86/653/EEC relating to self-employed commercial agents.[7] The directive was adopted on the European level to try to protect self-employed commercial agents, integral to the single market, assuring minimum wages and other rights. Certain provisions in the directive and the act are mandatory and cannot be contracted away by the parties.

A self-employed commercial agent (*handelsagent*) as defined under the act is a party that has agreed with the principal to continually and independently commercially sell or buy goods by submitting bids to the principal or negotiating and concluding such contracts on behalf of and

---

7 The Swedish act was passed in the period preceding Sweden's membership in the EU.

in the name of the principal in exchange for remuneration. The agent need not be a self-employed individual, but may be a legal person with several employees. Both the agent and principal have the right to request a written agency agreement (*agenturavtal*) containing all the terms and conditions and signed by both parties.

Obligations of the Agent

The agent is to take her principal's interests into consideration and act dutifully and in good faith as set out in the act. In particular, a commercial agent must:

a) Engage in serious efforts to obtain bids, and if included in the commission, conclude agreements if such fall under the agency agreement;

b) Communicate to her principal when a bid has been submitted and any contracts that have been executed as well as all necessary information known to her; and

c) Comply with reasonable instructions given by her principal.

The principal's goods are to be kept separately from those of the agent. The agent has a duty of care for any goods in her possession that are owned by the principal and is also to obtain any necessary insurance. In the event the agent has the right to receive monies on behalf of the principal, these monies are to be kept separate from those of the agent, and submitted to the principal.

Obligations of the Principal

This act differs from the Act on Commercial Agents in that the principal also has explicitly stated obligations in this legal relationship under the act. The principal is to act dutifully and in good faith in her relations with the agent. In particular, the principal is to provide the agent with:

a) Models, descriptions, price lists or other necessary materials concerning the goods at issue;

b) Necessary documentation relating to the goods concerned in order to perform the commission; and

c) Information without any undue delay as to whether the principal
   has accepted or rejected any offers that the agent has forwarded or
   that a contract brokered by the agent has not been fulfilled.

The principal is also to inform the agent within a reasonable time if the
principal anticipates that the volume of commercial transactions will be
significantly lower than that which the agent could normally anticipate.

Commissions

In the absence of any agreement as to the issue of remuneration between the
parties, an agent is entitled to the remuneration that agents appointed for the
goods forming the subject of her agency contract are customarily allowed
in the place where she carries on her activities. If there is no such customary
practice, an agent is entitled to reasonable remuneration taking into account
all the aspects of the transaction.

An agent is entitled to a commission on commercial transactions
concluded during the period covered by the agency contract:

a) Where the transaction has been concluded as a result
   of her action; or
b) Where the transaction is concluded with a third party
   whom she has previously acquired as a customer for
   transactions of the same kind.

Any commission is to be paid within one month after the expiration of the
annual quarter in which the commission was earned. An agent is also entitled
to a commission on commercial transactions concluded after the agency
contract has terminated generally if the transaction is mainly attributable
to the agent's efforts or if the order of the third party reached the principal
or agent before the agency contract terminated.

Termination of the Agency

An agency contract for a fixed period that continues to be performed by both
parties after that period has expired is deemed converted into an agency

contract for an indefinite period. Where an agency contract is concluded for an indefinite period, either party may terminate it by giving the appropriate notice. The period of notice is to be one month for the first year of the contract, and an additional month's notice for every additional year up to six months.

An agent or principal can immediately terminate the agreement where:

a) A party has failed to perform her obligations under the agreement or the law and the breach of contract is of material significance to the other party and the breaching party knew, or ought to have known this; or

b) Where an important reason for prematurely terminating the contract otherwise exists.

A party wishing to prematurely terminate the agreement is to do so without delay after gaining knowledge as to the circumstance being cited. A failure to do this can result in a forfeiture of the right to terminate. If either of the parties is placed into bankruptcy, the agency is terminated. The agent has the right to severance pay under certain conditions.

Any non-compete clause in an agency agreement is valid only if and to the extent that it is concluded in writing and relates to the geographical area or group of customers and geographical area entrusted to the commercial agent and to the kind of goods covered by her agency under the contract. A non-compete clause is not valid for more than two years after the termination of the agency contract. In this respect, the protection here mirrors quite well the protection seen in the case law applying Section 38 of the Contracts Act as discussed in the next chapter.

CHAPTER 9

Contract Law

General contract law has little statutory regulation in Sweden. The Contracts Act (*lag 1915:218 om avtal och andra rättshandlingar på förmögenhetsrättens område*), applicable to all contracts unless specific statutes state otherwise, is a relatively short statute. It comprises forty-one sections, of which almost one-half, those contained in Chapter Two Sections 10–22, concern agency as already presented above in Chapter Eight. The remaining chapters of the Contracts Act are discussed here, Chapter One concerning the execution of contracts, what constitutes an offer and an acceptance, and when a contract arises as set out in Sections 1–9, Chapter Three which sets out the principles concerning the invalidity of contracts in Sections 28–38, and Chapter Four which only has two substantive sections concerning knowledge and notice, Sections 39 and 40 respectively.

Given the brevity of the Contracts Act, other sources of law are often needed to resolve contractual issues. For example, the standard of performance under a contract, as well as any breach of contract, is not addressed at all in the act. Other sources of law invoked in contract law issues include the legislative preparatory works, case law, general principles of law, custom and usage generally, in the industry as well as between the parties, as well as the legal scholarship. The primary source when resolving contractual issues, however, is the contract itself, the terms and conditions as agreed upon by the parties to the contract. The parties are free to contract out of many of the provisions of the Contracts Act, particularly the first chapter concerning the execution of contract, and more sophisticated commercial actors do so routinely.

Certain general principles are considered central in Swedish contract law, the first of which is freedom of contract. Parties having legal capacity are free to enter into a contract regarding any subject matter with any party. There are naturally certain limitations as to this, the most evident in the consumer context. A party may also be forced by law to enter into a contract with a specific party (*kontraheringsplikt*). For example, insurance companies must by law provide certain types of policies to all consumers as normally provided by the company to the public in accordance with the Insurance Contracts Act (*försäkringsavtalslag* 2005:104). A commercial actor can also be found criminally liable for unlawful discrimination by refusing to contract with a party based on that person's race, color, nationality, ethnic origin or belief according to Section 16:9 of the Penal Code. Civil liability for discrimination can be imposed under the Discrimination Act (*diskrimineringslag* 2008:567). Other contracts can be found by the courts to be in violation of *pactum turpe* or *ordre public,* and consequently, the courts will not uphold them as they are in violation of fundamental principles of Swedish law. Case law examples here include tax evasion in a building contract (NJA 2002 p. 322), the signing of a non-negotiable promissory note in the amount of SEK 100,000 by a married man payable to his lover if he failed to divorce his wife within three months, which he failed to do (RH 1988:130) and another case involving the signing of a non-negotiable promissory note in the amount of SEK 25 million payable to a woman if she aborted her preganancy, which she did (RH 2004:41).

Another general principle permeating contract law is the sanctity of the contract, *pacta sunt servanda.* This is central to almost all Western legal systems, but assumes different guises in the different systems. Under Swedish law, the most evident effect of this principle is that specific performance, and not simply damages, is the primary remedy for breach of contract. Privity of contracts is also a central tenet in Swedish law. However, the courts in certain cases have found that a duty of loyalty between the parties exists even at the pre-contractual stage. Pre-contractual liability has been imposed by Swedish courts for negotiations carried out negligently, *culpa in contrahendo,*[1] or carried out in bad faith, *dolus in contrahendo.*

---

1 *See* NJA 1963 p. 105 and NJA 1990 p. 745, though damages were not awarded in the latter case and see also court of appeal cases, RH 2000:62 (damages awarded) and RH 1996:154 (damages not awarded, though acknowledging the possibility).

9.1 Offer and Acceptance

The basic model for the execution of a contract under the Contracts Act is that of offer and acceptance. An offer and mirroring acceptance are to be made expressing the intent of the parties to enter into a contract either orally or in writing. According to Section 1 of the Contracts Act, the general rule is that once an offer or an acceptance is made, it is irrevocable, binding (*löftesprincipen*) upon the party making it. Exceptions to this main rule can be made directly by statute, or voluntarily by the parties or custom and usage. For example, with respect to real estate transactions, the parties have no obligations until a contract exists (*kontraktsprincipen*) in accordance with the statutory requirements as set out in the Land Code.

The general irrevocability of offers can be negated by the offeror simply stating in the actual offer that the offer is not binding, as allowed under Section 9 of the Contracts Act. Another device used in Swedish contract negotiations is to term the offer something else, such as an inquiry (*offert*) or an invitation to tender (*förfrågan*). In such cases, when an offer is received

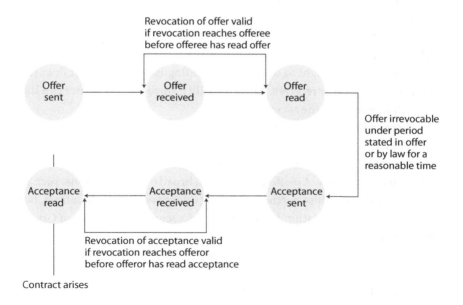

DIAGRAM 9.1 Offer and Acceptance under the Contracts Act.

in response to such an invitation and the offer materially corresponds to the original invitation, the original party has a duty to accept or reject the offer or otherwise risks being bound by a contract according to Section 9. This is the case if it is clear that the party submitting the true offer did so as a response.

The offer becomes irrevocable when the offeree has partaken of the offer as stated in Section 7. Although offers are irrevocable as a general rule, the offer can be withdrawn if a revocation reaches the offeree (*komma till handa*) before or at the same time as the offeree has partaken of the offer (*ta del av*).

The acceptance is to be received by the offeror within the period of time as stated in the offer (*acceptfristen*). If the offer does not state how long it is to be valid, the offer will be binding for a reasonable time (*den legala accept-fristen*), entailing that the acceptance has to be received by the offeror within that period. The assessment of a reasonable period is based on the subject matter of the contract and the opportunity to respond. If the offer concerns strawberries, a reasonable period would arguably be only a few days. If the offer concerns bicycles, a reasonable period might be as long as a week. The courts have stated that the assessment of reasonable must also include an appropriate time in which a response can be given. An exception here is that an oral offer must always be accepted immediately unless the offeror has consented to a longer period. By making offers binding, the view is that the offeree then has the time necessary for reflection as to whether to accept the offer. The counterweight to offers being binding is that a contract does not arise until the offeror receives, and in actuality, since the acceptance can still be withdrawn, reads the acceptance.

There are few requirements as to what constitutes an offer. There is no general requirement of a writing. Neither is there any requirement as to form nor any requirement of consideration as this is not a principle in Swedish contract law. An offer, if made to a broad circle of persons, such as an advertisement, is not deemed a binding offer to enter into a contract, but rather simply an invitation to do business. As seen from the Sale of Goods Act discussed below in Chapter Fourteen, the minimum requirement for what constitutes an offer of sale for goods can be seen as including the object of the contract and a quantity. All other terms and conditions can be supplemented by the courts through gap-filling legislation, the legislative preparatory works, custom and usage, general principles of law as well as the legal scholarship. However, too vague a description can be found by the courts to mean that no binding offer was intended.

The content of the acceptance must mirror the offer as set out in Section 6 of the Contracts Act. An acceptance that alters the terms of the offer does not function as an acceptance, but instead is considered a counteroffer. An acceptance given after the offer has explicitly expired, or in the absence of an expiry date, after a reasonable period as stated in Section 4, no longer functions as an acceptance but is also considered a counteroffer. The original offeror has no obligation to accept these counteroffers or even to respond to them. However, in certain situations, if the offeree believes that the acceptance was correct or in time, the offeror may have a duty to inform the offeree that the acceptance was not valid and that no contract exists or otherwise risk being bound. If an offer has been rejected prior to the expiration of the period of validity, the offer is no longer valid, despite the fact that the period has not yet expired.

An acceptance is binding but can be revoked if the revocation reaches the offeror prior to the offeror partaking of the acceptance as stated in Section 7. If an offer is originally made without requiring an explicit acceptance, the offeror has the right to request an explicit acceptance or otherwise the offer expires as prescribed in Section 8. In certain situations, the acceptance can be seen as being made by an action (*konkludent handlande*), by performing under the contract or taking property into possession. An example of this would be where a party has made an offer to sell something and the other party has picked up the goods offered for sale from the seller without verbally accepting the offer.

The fact that offers are binding has resulted in complicated implications for letters of intent and comfort letters. In legal systems where offers are not by rule binding, such as the Anglo-American systems, letters of intent are also not binding in the absence of consideration. As there is no requirement of consideration under Swedish contract law, this has resulted in Swedish courts at times finding that letters of intent or comfort letters are binding.[2]

As stated, there is no general requirement of a writing as to a contract under the Contracts Act. There are exceptions to this general rule, the most

---

2 *See, for example,* NJA 1994 p. 204 and NJA 1995 p. 586.

notable being contracts concerning the sale of real estate, which are discussed in Chapter Eleven below. A contract for the sale of real estate must include the actual purchase price, the names of the parties and the object of the sale, as well as an indication by the seller of a willingness to transfer the property. Other contracts that must be in writing as prescribed by statute are collective agreements.

9.2 Defenses to a Contract

Defenses to a contract (*ogiltighetsgrunder*) as set out in the third chapter of the Contracts Act are either defenses to assent or to performance. If a contract is found void under these provisions, there are no further obligations between the parties and any performances as made by a party are to be returned. There is no automatic right to damages under chapter three but rather follows from the doctrine of culpa and dolus i contrahendo.

9.2.1 DEFENSES TO ASSENT

The defenses that can be cited as to lack of consent include extreme duress (Section 28), lesser duress (Section 29), fraud (Section 30), usury (Section 31), and mistake (Section 32). The first four defenses have equivalents in the Penal Code, robbery (PC 8:5), extortion (PC 9:4), fraud (PC 9:1) and usury (PC 9:5).[3]

The requirements for successfully pleading the defense of extreme duress (*råntvång*) under Section 28 of the Contracts Act include: (1) A legal act (2) which a party was unlawfully (3) forced to take (4) through violence against the party or (5) threat which posed an imminent danger. This defense is only rarely successfully pled given this high threshold of proof. A fairly recent example was a case involving a disgruntled used-car customer. After the dealership attempted to repair his car numerous times, the customer went into the dealership and put a gun to the dealer's head, making him sign over and register a different used-car in the customer's name. Naturally, the customer was arrested and convicted and the contract was found to be void.

---

3   An English translation of the Swedish Penal Code is available at the website of the Government offices at sweden.gov.se.

If the violence or threat under Section 28 was by a third party to the contract and the counter-party was in good faith, the party forced to execute the contract has the duty to inform the counter-party as to the circumstances of the situation as soon as the threat or danger is no longer imminent. Otherwise, the person forced to sign the contract risks being bound.

Lesser duress (*lindrigt tvång*) arises according to Section 29 of the Contracts Act where a person is forced to take a legal act by unlawful means other than those encompassed by Section 28. The counter-party must have invoked the unlawful means or knew or ought to have known that the contract was executed due to unlawful means as invoked by a third party. Causality must exist between taking the legal action and the unlawful means. One case in which a court found lesser duress was where a municipality forced a party to become a surety for a contract under the threat of not granting a building permit.[4]

Fraud (*svek*) under Section 30 of the Contracts Act includes where a party directly intentionally uses incorrect information to mislead the other party into entering into a contract, or knows or ought to know that a third party has misled the party. The wrongful party must understand that the information is incorrect and that the other party does not know that the information is incorrect. Causality between the incorrect information and the legal action must be proven. A party can also be held accountable for an omission as to providing certain information of significance for the counter party.

Usury (*ocker*) is also a defense as to consent in Section 31 of the Contracts Act, further categorized as with respect to monies, chattels or services. Usury arises when a party unjustly exploits a contract situation, for example where the other party is in desperate straits, is in a dependent relationship or more vulnerable due to a lesser understanding. In addition, an obvious imbalance must exist between the performances under the contract, for example, that the services rendered are not worth the amount charged. Usury can be seen in contrast to duress and fraud, where the wrongful party created the situation. In the usurious context, the wrongful party exploits an already existing situation. A clear example of this is where a party lends monies at an interest rate of 2 000 % annually. Another example could be where

---

4   *See* NJA 1980 p. 1.

tow-truck operators demand extremely high fees for towing services in sparsely populated areas.

Mistake in general is not a defense to assent in Swedish contract law. However, according to Section 32 of the Contracts Act, a mistake can be cited as a ground for invalidity where a party, due to an error or other mistake, gives an offer or acceptance that then has a content deviating from that the party intended to give (*förklaringsmisstag*), and the counter-party knew, or ought to have known, that the offer or acceptance was incorrect.

Another exception to the general accountability with respect to mistakes is where a party sends a transmission by telegram or orally by messenger, which then in the recitation by telegram or messenger becomes incorrect when recounted to the receiving party (*befordringsfel*), even where the receiving party is in good faith. The sending party then is no longer accountable for the incorrectly recited offer or acceptance if the party, as soon as receiving knowledge of the mistake, notifies the counter-party of the mistake. If the sending party fails to do this, and the receiving party is in good faith, the offer or acceptance is valid.

9.2.2 DEFENSES TO PERFORMANCE

There are two general clauses (*generalklausuler*) with respect to defenses to performance, Section 33 of the Contracts Act which invalidates contracts that violate "faith and honor" (*tro och heder*) and Section 36, which allows for the invalidation or modification of a contract or term due to its being "unfair" (*oskälig*) or unconscionable. Of these two, Section 33 is the one invoked less often and less successfully.

According to Section 33, a party to an otherwise valid contract can be excused from performance if the party can show, based on the circumstances existing at the time of the execution of the contract, that requiring performance of the contract in light of these circumstances is in violation of faith and honor, and that the counter-party had such knowledge at the time of the execution of the contract. As apparent, this is a high evidentiary showing, as the party must not only prove that requiring the performance violates "faith and honor," a concept not defined in the statute, but that the counter-party also had knowledge of these circumstances. This general clause has seldom been invoked successfully.

Under Section 36, the party is to show that a contract term is unfair with respect to the content of the contract, circumstances existing at the time of the contract's execution as well as after, a considerably lower threshold than that required under Section 33. If such is proven, the contract term can be modified or voided: Circumstances arising both before and after the execution of the contract can be cited, entailing that the contract perhaps was fair at the time of its execution, but because of a later change in circumstances, it became unfair and consequently in need of modification. Another difference between Section 33 and Section 36 is that under Section 33 (as well as all the other defenses to assent), the entire contract is invalidated, while under Section 36, the court is empowered to invalidate the entire contract, or modify one or several terms of the contract, preserving the transaction between the parties. Last, the court is empowered under Section 36 to take into consideration the balance of power between the parties and the need of protection for a more vulnerable party, specifically consumers and employees.

9.2.3 OTHER CONTRACTUAL DEFENSES AND RIGHTS

There are several other miscellaneous defenses/rights to performance in the third chapter concerning sham transactions, pledges and non-compete clauses. If a negotiable instrument, contract or other written document has been drafted as a sham transaction, the general rule is that it is not valid. However, the document can be binding with respect to a third-party purchaser in good faith in accordance with Section 34 of the Contracts Act. In the same vein, any negotiable instrument or other document that is valid in the possession of a party, is still valid under Section 35 where the document has involuntarily left the party's possession if acquired by a party in good faith. The same is applicable where a receipt involuntarily leaves the possession of a creditor, the payment is still valid as with respect to a payment made by a debtor in good faith.

There is also a provision regarding pledges. Under Section 37 of the Contracts Act, any contract clause entailing that a pledge or other security is entirely forfeited in the event of only a partial lack of performance is void. This was a practice eventually seen as too unfair, for example, where a debtor had paid 99 % of a debt and the creditor took 100 % of the security for the outstanding 1 % of the debt. The creditor still has the right to sell the pledge, but may now only retain the amount still owing as opposed to the entire proceeds of any sale. In credit sales, the same result is insured by mandatory rules.

Section 38 serves as a protection for employees, vendors and independent contractors by prohibiting certain types of non-compete clauses. A non-compete clause is a contract term by which one party, typically an employer, requires the other party, again typically an employee, to not conduct a certain type of business, with certain customers, for a certain period of time, within a certain geographical area. The idea is that the employer is trying to protect its business or business secrets by binding the employee to such a clause. Under Section 38, a non-compete clause is void where it is too broad in contrast to that which can be seen as fair under the circumstances. The Swedish Labor Court has held that a non-compete clause simply for the purposes of retaining an employee by not allowing employment alternatives is not valid in general. However, geographically and time-limited clauses are generally accepted.

9.3 The Function and Interpretation of Contracts

The Contracts Act covers only the two broad areas presented above, execution of a contract and invalidity, as well as agency. Issues of interpretation are left to the courts. Given the lack of formalities with respect to entering into a contract in Swedish law, and the understanding of contract formation as based on the will of the parties (*viljeteorin*), the contract can be seen as having an evidentiary function rather than embodying the agreement between the parties.

Given this informality of contract formation under Swedish law, the rules of interpretation and the role of the judge become extremely important. Any evidence can be introduced to prove the intent of the parties under Swedish law, including evidence prior to, contemporaneous with or arising after the contract arose. There are no evidentiary exclusionary rules such as the parole evidence rule in Anglo-American law.

When interpreting a contract, a Swedish judge has the ability to interpret the contract extensively, in the spirit of *pacta sunt servanda*, as opposed to restrictively, the mandate of Anglo-American judges. The Swedish judge begins with the language of the contract. If this is not clear, there are several rules or canons of interpretation available. If a resolution still cannot be achieved by the terms of the contract, she then turns to the legislation. As discussed more extensively in Chapter Fourteen, the Sale of Goods Acts allows for extensive gap-filling, and can be applied by analogy to other types of contracts, such as the sale of services. If the legislation does not provide an answer, the Swedish judge then turns to the legislative preparatory works, case law, general principles of contract law, usage and custom as in the sector or between the parties, other standard contracts as well as the legal scholarship.

There are several different methods of contract interpretation applied by the Swedish courts. The first is based on interpreting the language of the contract (*språkinriktad metod*). Another method is a systemic interpretation (*systeminriktad metod*), by which the court interprets the term or condition at issue to be consistent within the structure of the entirety of the contract, the system as established by the parties to the contract. A systemic method can also be used by the courts in interpreting the contract to be consistent with usage within a certain sector (*branschinriktad metod*) or as between the custom and usage between the parties. The courts can also interpret the contract to be consistent with the intent as meant by the parties (*partsinriktad metod* or *subjektivistisk metod*). This requires the court to determine what the parties meant and understood when the contract was executed.

Statutory norms can also be used by the court to interpret a contract (*norminriktad metod*). An example of this can be where the provisions of the Sale of Goods Act are applied analogously by the court to a contract for the provision of services. Finally, the court can interpret a contract invoking a standard of fairness (*skälighetsinriktad metod*). Here a court would try to achieve a fair balance in the contractual relationship between the parties, much as discussed in Section 36 of the Contracts Act.

There are also several rules of contract interpretation that can be invoked by the courts. One is that any ambiguity in the contract is to be interpreted against the interests of the drafter (*oklarhetsregeln*). Another is that a writing will take precedence over print, meaning that anything in a contract written by hand will have higher precedence than pre-printed text.

9.4 Standard Agreements

Standard agreements (*standardavtal*) have a vital role in most legal systems as they generally are used to minimize transaction costs. There are two types of standard agreements, unilateral and bilateral standard agreements. Unilateral standard agreements are simply those that one of the parties typically uses, the most well-known example probably being the "I accept" window to a computer program.

Bilateral standard agreements, also referred to as agreed documents, are a fundamental part of the Swedish legal system. Bilateral agreements are entered between central organizations in a sector. One example is ABK 09 concerning the provision of engineering services. This twelve-page contract was negotiated between the central organizations representing architects and engineers as well as those organizations representing the purchasers of such services. There are myriads of standard agreements reached in this manner, another example is the General Conditions of the Nordic Freight Forwarders NSAB 2000.[5] These general conditions state that they are to be applied automatically to any contract entered into by a member of the Nordic Freight Forwarders and can also be contracted into by other parties.

The fact that a standard agreement has been negotiated by two central organizations is not, however, a guarantee that a good balance between the interests of buyers and sellers, rights and obligations has been reached. Certain of the standard agreements can be perceived as more seller or more buyer friendly. A typical seller friendly clause can be ceilings with respect to liability. A typical buyer friendly clause can include a right to damages beyond those defined as direct damages under the Sale of Goods Act discussed in Chapter Fourteen below.

Standard agreements can be applicable between parties to a contract in several ways, the first of which most obviously is that the parties simply sign under the contract itself. Another way can be seen from the general conditions for NSAB, which state that they are automatically applicable to all NSAB members.[6] Standard agreements are also sometimes seen as evidence

---

5   These general conditions are available in both English and Swedish at the website of the Swedish International Freight Association at swedfreight.se.

6   Whether such a clause would be binding is unclear, see for example RH 1990:7.

of custom and usage so that a rule contained therein can be seen as an expression of custom and usage. Finally, the parties to a contract can simply have a clause in their individual contract stating that a certain standard agreement is applicable to them, incorporating the standard agreement into their individual agreement.

The combination of the gap-filling function of the legislation, the evidence that can be presented to prove the agreement of the parties (basically everything), as well as the custom and usage as proven by standard contracts, and the incorporation of the latter actually into contracts, entails that Swedish contracts can appear deceptively short in contrast to contracts generated under other legal systems. Deceptive because if the content of all these periphery sources was actually included in the terms of the contract, as is mandated, for example, by Anglo-American law, the contracts would in all probability be longer, and perhaps as long as those contracts generated elsewhere. The contract regulation system as created in Sweden allows the parties to focus on key issues and leave the rest to gap-filling. However, the higher the stakes in the transaction, the greater the degree of individual negotiations, entailing more complex, detailed and longer contracts, regardless of legal system.

CHAPTER 10

Debtors and Creditors

This chapter is an assortment of several different areas of law with the common thread being debt (*skuld*).[1] First the creation of a claim to payment is addressed, then the perfection of security interests in chattels and real property, followed by payment, the execution of debts and the regulations concerning bankruptcy. The claim of a right to payment (*fordran*) by a creditor (*borgenär*) against a debtor (*gäldenär*) can arise in connection with several different types of situations, the most readily identifiable being with respect to contracts, tort damage liability and loans.[2] A party can also simply assume an obligation to pay.

If more than one debtor is liable for a debt, the primarily rule under the tenth chapter of the 1734 Commerce Code (*handelsbalk*) and Section 2(1) of the Act on Notes (*lag 1936:81 om skuldebrev*), is joint and several liability (*solidariskt ansvar*). Consequently, the creditor is free to assert the entire right as against any one of the debtors. The debtor who pays then has recourse against the other debtors for their shares of the debt. Joint and several liability is to be divided equally among the debtors absent an agreement otherwise.

---

1   For more information in English on Swedish commercial law, see Annina Persson, *Sweden – Commercial and Economic Law* in the series, Roger Blanpain, ed., INTERNATIONAL ENCYCLOPAEDIA OF LAWS (Kluwer International 2003).

2   A distinction is made in the Swedish legal system between a loan of specific goods (*lån*) where the intent of the lender is to receive the same goods back, and the loan of fungible goods (*försträckning*) where the purpose of the loan is to repay in comparable goods. The latter is the case, for example, when borrowing sugar from a neighbor. In the vast majority of cases, the same sugar is not returned, simply a comparable amount of sugar. Lending money falls into the second type of legal relationship as money is perceived of as fungible. No distinction is made, however, in the vernacular between these two types of loan.

Thus if three parties are jointly and severally liable, they are to pay one-third of the debt each between them.

If a creditor finds that the debtor is not sufficiently creditworthy, the creditor may require that the debtor provide a surety (*borgen*). The principle form of surety invoked is strict surety (*proprieborgen*), entailing that the surety is primarily liable for the debt to the same degree as the debtor. The inclusion of the words, "as for my own debt" (*såsom för egen skuld*) in the agreement is sufficient to create a strict suretyship. In the absence of this phrase, the person is a guarantor, secondarily liable for the debt. In both cases, if the surety or guarantor pays the debt, they have recourse against the debtor.

The statutes of limitations (*preskription*) with respect to claims for payment are set out in the Act Concerning Statutes of Limitations (*preskriptionslag* 1981:130). The main period for the statute of limitations is ten years from the date the claim arose, which period can be renewed for additional ten-year periods, for example, by the creditor sending a reminder of monies owed. There is no limit as to the number of extensions. A shorter statute of limitations is applicable with respect to consumers. If the debt concerns services, goods or other benefits as provided by a commercial seller (*näringsidkare*) to the debtor as a consumer, the statute of limitations is three-years. This shorter period can also be renewed innumerable times. In light of the technically possible perpetuity of a debt, it may be interesting to note here that the words for debt, guilt and virginity have the same root word in the Swedish language, *skuld*.

Once the statute of limitations has expired, the creditor no longer can receive a court judgment or assert the claim in a bankruptcy. The creditor still has a right of set-off as discussed below and can also invoke a right of retention or claim against any pledged property held. If the debtor voluntarily pays a prescribed claim, the payment is not treated as a gift. A partial payment of a prescribed debt by a non-consumer can generally be enough to revive the entire debt.

Another way by which a creditor can lose the right to assert a claim is by being barred from asserting the claim (*preklusion*) after certain proceedings, a type of estoppel. This can happen, for example, where a meeting is called of all creditors, known and unknown, with respect to distributing the assets of a debtor. If the creditor fails to attend such a meeting, the claim can be barred.

Finally, if the whereabouts of a negotiable instrument or other legal instrument bearing rights is not known, the party that has misplaced the negotiable note or instrument can invoke a judicial process to declare it null and void (*mortification*), "killing" it under the Act on Declaring Lost Legal Instruments Null and Void (*lag 2011:900 om dödande av förkommen handling*). Notice is to be placed in the *Post- och Inrikes Tidningar* calling all unknown creditors to a hearing. There is also a one-year waiting period to insure that any party actually holding the instrument has a chance to assert it. After a judicial decree that the instrument is null and void, the party that lost it can assert the rights under the instrument against the party issuing it. The party can also request the issuance of a new instrument.

Several provisions of the Contracts Act concerning negotiable instruments can also be mentioned here, particularly Section 34 which states that the general rule, that an instrument executed as a sham is not a valid contract, is not applicable if the instrument is acquired by a third-party purchaser in good faith. Section 35 mandates that any negotiable instrument valid in the possession of party is still valid where the document has involuntarily left the party's possession if acquired by a party in good faith.

10.1 Payment and Debt Instruments

Several different types of debt and payment instruments exist under Swedish law, both negotiable and non-negotiable. This presentation is not exhaustive, but takes up some of the major types of instruments as set out by law. Trade in negotiable instruments (*värdepapper*) is, and always has been, extremely international, with those laws forming the foundation based on the law merchant, *lex mercatoria*, which began to be established already during the late Middle Ages.

10.1.1 NOTES

Notes (*skuldebrev*), also referred to as promissory notes, are regulated in the Act on Notes (*lag 1936:81 om skuldebrev*).[3] The requirements for the

---

3 The act is a product of the Nordic Council. The Act on Notes is fairly central not only with respect to notes, but also with respect to claims for payment of monies (*fordringar*) generally, with the intent that the act serve in a gap-filling function for all types of payment claims.

actual note are not set out in the Act, simply their regulation. A note is a written unilateral undertaking to pay a certain amount of money. There are no additional form requirements other than that the note be a (1) written (2) unilateral (3) undertaking to pay monies. The act makes a distinction, however, between non-negotiable notes (*enkla skuldebrev*) and negotiable notes (*löpande skuldebrev*), the latter having requirements as to the wording used to create negotiability.

Non-negotiable Notes

Non-negotiable notes are not, as seen from the term, negotiable instruments. They instead are simply promises to pay a certain amount to a certain person. If a non-negotiable note is destroyed, the debt still remains as the note simply serves as evidence of the debt, but does not embody it (*bevispapper*).

The fact that the note is non-negotiable does not mean that it cannot be assigned. Non-negotiable notes can be assigned freely unless doing so is to the detriment of the debtor in certain cases. The new holder takes the note with any objections or defenses that the debtor can raise against the original holder. For example, where the original non-negotiable note was issued in conjunction with a sales contract, the debtor can refuse to pay the note where the debtor has not received the goods, if the goods have been delayed, or if they are non-conforming. The same objections can be raised against a new holder.

In the case of an assignment, either the original holder or the assignee needs to notify the debtor as to the new party to be paid with respect to the note (*denuntiation*). Otherwise, if the debtor pays the original creditor in good faith without such notice, the payment is seen as discharging the debt even if to the wrong party.

Negotiable Notes

If a note is negotiable, it is acquired by any new holders free of any objections or defenses that could have been raised under the original contract. For example, if a negotiable note is issued in connection with a sales contract, and the goods are not delivered, the buyer can refuse to pay the seller under the note for the failure to deliver the goods. However, if the seller has transferred the negotiable note to a bona fide purchaser, *i.e.* a purchaser in good faith, the buyer will have to pay the note when it becomes due regardless of whether the buyer has received the goods. The buyer still has rights as against the seller, but instead of refusing to pay, the buyer will now have to get compensation from the seller, placing the buyer in a more precarious position with respect to remedies. Because the note is negotiable, it is easier to sell than a note that is non-negotiable, as the non-negotiable note takes all defenses and objections to the original contract with it. This in turn means that a negotiable note can generally be capitalized at a higher price than a non-negotiable note.

Although defenses to the contract cannot be raised against a holder in due course of a negotiable instrument, certain general defenses (*starka ogiltighetsgrunder*) can be raised. These include extreme duress as set out under Section 28 of the Contracts Act or that the document being asserted is a forgery.

The holder of a negotiable note must present the note for payment (*presentationspapper*). Upon payment, the debtor is to insure that verification of payment is written on the note, or that the note is taken into possession by the debtor or voided (*makulerad*). If the payment is not noted on the note, and the note comes into the hands of a *bona fide* purchaser, the debtor may be required to pay again. In the event a negotiable instrument is destroyed, the obligations under the instrument can no longer be asserted. The obverse of this is that if the debtor pays a party other than the holder of the negotiable note, that payment will not discharge the debt as embodied by the note.

Negotiable notes are further divided under the act into those notes that are payable to bearer (or holder), and those notes payable to order.

Negotiable Notes Payable to Bearer

Negotiable notes payable to bearer (*innehavarskuldebrev*) are identified simply by the language used in the note, pay to bearer (or holder). Possession of a note payable to bearer is sufficient evidence that the party is a holder in due course and has the right to the payment (*aktiv legitimation*), and that the debtor can pay that party and be discharged from the debt (*passiv legitimation*).

Negotiable Notes Payable to Order

Negotiable notes payable to order (*orderskuldebrev*) can also be identified by the language used, which typically is "pay to Johanna or order." A valid chain of endorsements (*indossament*) must be shown for the party in possession of a note payable to order to be seen as a holder in due course authorized to receive payment. Forgery of a signature here is a real defense that can be asserted against the holder unless there was no apparent defect in the chain of signatures and the holder had no reason for suspecting such.

10.1.2 BILLS OF EXCHANGE AND CHECKS

Bills of exchange (*växel*), also referred to as drafts, are another type of negotiable instrument and are regulated by the Act on Bills of Exchange (*växellag* 1932:130). A bill of exchange or draft differs from a note in that instead of two parties to the instrument, there are three. A bill of exchange is a written order by the drawer (*trassenten*) to the drawee (*trassaten*) to pay a specific sum of money to the payee (*remittenten*). The drawer validates this order to pay by signing the bill of exchange on its face. Bills of exchange can be assigned by the payee's endorsement. The endorsement, however, does not simply assign the bill, it is also an admission by the payee to act as a guarantor for payment on the bill. The last holder of the bill must first demand payment from the drawee, but if the drawee refuses to pay, the holder can seek payment from any party endorsing the bill. That party then has a right of regress as to any parties that endorsed the bill previous to her.

Checks are treated distinctly from bills of exchange in the Swedish system, and regulated under the Check Act (*checklag* 1932:131). A major distinction between a bill of exchange and a check is that the drawee with respect to a check is always a bank. In addition, a check can be made out simply to bearer or holder. A check must be deposited for payment within twenty (20) days of its date under Swedish law. Issuing a check without funds to cover the amount is a criminal offense under the Penal Code. Checks never were as widely used in Swedish society as, for example, in the United States.

10.1.3 THE GIRO SYSTEM

The system of payment that can be seen to have gained the greatest acceptance in Sweden is the giro system as available at banks and also formerly from the Swedish Post Office. This is also a three party system in that a person makes a request, fills in a giro ordering a bank to pay a certain amount of money to a certain party's account. The difference, however, between the giro system and bills of exchange is that the payee does not present a bill or a check for payment, but rather, payment is deposited directly into the payee's account based on the giro without the payee having to do anything. The bank will not make the payment unless the funds are available, also removing the risk, as with checks, of overdrafts. Payments can still be requested on paper giro forms, but the majority of giros today are done simply over the Internet. Paypal is an international example of a giro system.

10.2 Perfecting Security Interests

The basic type of perfected security interest generally granted in Sweden is a pledge, entailing that the creditor must have physical possession of the security in order to perfect the security interest. The law regarding security interests is mostly regulated by the principles developed in the case law, with little statutory regulation. This area of law falls within the broader area of property rights (*sakrätt*) encompassing both an owner's rights, for example, to yields from the property (*statisk sakrätt*) as well as third-party interests in property (*dynamisk sakrätt*). A sharp distinction is maintained in Swedish law, based on Roman law, between the obligations arising between the parties to a contract (*obligationsrätt*), and any claims that can be made by third parties as to ownership rights or security interests. The focus in this section is on perfecting security interests.

A pledge (*panträtt*) is created when the debtor, pledgor (*pantsättare*) pledges property (*pant*) to the pledgee (*panthavare*), who then takes it into her possession (*tradition*). If this is a voluntary pledge (*konventionell panträtt*), there is also a requirement of a pledge agreement (*pantavtal*). If the pledge arises by operation of law (*legal panträtt*), no agreement is necessary. For example, commercial agents as discussed above in Chapter Eight have a right to keep property purchased on behalf of the principal in their possession as a pledge for payment under the Commission Act.

10.2.1 SECURITY INTERESTS IN CHATTELS

The main form of pledge in chattels is referred to as a "hand pledge" (*handpant*) in that the object is surrendered into the hands of the creditor. This procedure is set out Section 10:1 of the 1736 Commerce Code: "If a man pledges gold, silver or any chattels whatsoever, does this with two witnesses,

or signs a handwritten agreement, in the other's hands it becomes a pledge."
This section is clearly dated, with the parties to such a transaction typically
regulating it instead in their agreement.

There is a duty of care for the pledgee to take care of the property while
in her possession under liability of paying for any damages. If the day of
payment arrives and the pledge has not been reclaimed (and payment not
made), the pledgee can either sue for payment in court or eventually sell
the pledged property. Under Section 37 of the Contracts Act, any contract
clause entailing that a pledge or other security is entirely forfeited in the
event of only a partial performance is void. The creditor has the right to sell
the property, but cannot keep 100 % of the proceeds for debt of a lesser value.

There is a limited ability to perfect a security interest under the Sale of
Chattels Act (*lag 1845:50 p. 1 om handel med lösören, som köparen låter i
säljarens vård kvarbliva*) through registration. This act originally provided
a way by which a purchaser could allow property to remain in the hands
of a seller but receive an ownership interest despite the lack of possession
(*besittning*). A purchaser can obtain a perfected interest by observing certain
formalities and publishing the right in a newspaper and then recording the
agreement with a court. This right is seldom used.

The disadvantage with a pledge system is that the debtor cannot use the
property while it is in the possession of the creditor. This has given rise to
a quasi-pledge system (*hypotekarisk pantsättning*) with respect to certain
types of property. These are security interests perfected through the creation
of a deed and the registration of the possession of the deed. The deed acts as
a proxy for the property. Such security interests can only be created by way
of statute in Swedish law, and to date only with respect to ships, airplanes,
floating charges , certain types of secured obligations, and real estate.[4]

With each of these specific types of property, the debtor applies to the
court or appropriate public authority to receive a deed for a certain amount.
There is a stamp duty governed by Section 21 of the Stamp Duty Act (*lag
1984:404 om stämpelskatt vid inskrivningsmyndigheter*) on the face amount
of a deed certificate for real estate, ships, aircrafts or floating charges. The

---

4   There is no general lien system in Sweden, for example, tying liens to automobiles in
    the national automobile register or as with the uniform commercial code security
    interest filing system in most states in the United States.

amount of the stamp duty on deed certificates varies between 1 and 2 % depending on the type of property.[5] Because of the stamp duty, the system has been structured so that the deeds can be reused, thus avoiding new stamp duties.

This deed system works as follows. If the owner of the property receives a mortgage deed in the amount of SEK 1 million, she can then turn the mortgage deed over to a creditor (either physically or digitally). The creditor then has the deed in its possession (physically or digitally through registration) until the debt is paid, when the property owner receives the mortgage deed back. In the event the face value of a pledged mortgage deed exceeds the claim for which it was pledged, the property owner is entitled to that excess amount. The holder of the deed is usually given leeway for a supplemental amount (*tillägg*) based on the face amount of the deed, for example 15 %, depending on the type of property. This allows the deed holder to be protected for 115 % of the face value. After making payment and receiving the deed back, the property owner can re-use the deed for a different loan.

The list of property in which this type of security interest can be granted may appear somewhat haphazard, but at least land and ships (and by way of extension through modern technology, aircraft) have a strong historical connection. The Torrens system, a title by registration land system developed by Sir Robert Torrens in Australia in 1858, was based in part on the system for registering ships used in the United Kingdom at that time. Two specific statutes regulate the creation of perfected security interests in ships (*skeppshypotek*) and aircraft (*luftfartygsinteckning*), the Maritime Act (*sjölag* 1994:1009) and the Act on Security Interests in Aircraft (*lag 1955:227 om inskrivning av rätt till luftfartyg*), respectively. Only floating charges and security interests in cooperative apartments are discussed further below in this section, with security interests in real property discussed in the subsequent section.

---

5   The total revenues received from stamp duties in Sweden in 2009 were SEK 8.1 billion. For this and more information on the Swedish tax system in English, *see* the report, 2011 Taxes in Sweden, An English Summary of Tax Statistical Yearbook of Sweden report available at the website of the Swedish National Tax Authority (*Skatteverket*) at skatteverket.se.

Floating Charges

In order to allow businesses to retain possession of assets but still use them as collateral, a system of floating charges (*företagshypotek*) was established and is now regulated under the Floating Charges Act (*lag 2008:990 om företagshypotek*).[6] In order to be able to provide a floating charge, the business must apply for a floating charge certificate for a specified amount, *e.g.* SEK 1 million with the Swedish Companies Registration Office. No floating charge is valid unless the Companies Registration Office has issued the certificate.

The certificate does not provide any collateral until it is transferred, either physically or digitally, to the creditor (or if a third party has the certificate in her possession, until she is notified that the certificate has been used as collateral). If the debt is paid, the certificate may be used again as collateral with the same or other creditors. It is also possible to use any portion of the floating charge represented by paid capital as collateral for another debt. For example, if the floating charge has a face value of SEK 1 million and the debtor has paid SEK 400 000, the debtor can use the amount that has been amortized, SEK 400 000, as collateral for a different loan. Consequently, two creditors can have interests in the same floating charge certificate.

A company can apply for more than one floating charge certificate. There is no requirement that the face amount of the certificate be covered by assets in the company. This issue tends to be self-regulating though, as creditors have no use for amounts in the floating charges not covered, and companies are not likely to pay stamp duties on amounts they cannot use. The floating charge covers most personal property, movables, in the company. Specifically exempted from the floating charge are monies and bank accounts, shares and other financial instruments intended for public sale, property that can be the object of a perfected security interest and property that cannot be attached or included in a bankruptcy.

---

6   This is the third generation of floating charges in Swedish law. The first was under the Floating Charges Act of 1984 (*lag 1984:649 om företagshypotek*) and required courts to issue the charges. The second was the Floating Charges Act of 2003 (*lag 2003:528 om företagsinteckning*) and required the Companies Registration Office to issue charges which then were considered as general statutorily protected security interest, had a ceiling of 55 % of the assets in the company, and could only be asserted in bankruptcy.

If a company has more than one floating charge certificate, the certificates will have different priorities based on the date of application for the certificate, not based on when the creditor received the certificate or when the debt was incurred. Thus the first certificate issued always has priority over later certificates. If the amount stated on the certificate is insufficient to satisfy the claim, the creditor who has the first pledge in a certificate is entitled to the supplement. The supplement may not exceed 15 % and interest thereon. The interest rate is the Swedish reference interest rate (*referensränta*) as determined by the Swedish National Bank (*Riksbanken*)[7] with an additional four percentage points.

The floating charge is treated as a perfected security interest in specific property and can be asserted in either an attachment proceeding or a bankruptcy. The stamp duty on floating charges is currently 1 %.

Housing Cooperatives
Other types of security that can be created in personal property include the pledging of shares and user rights. The only ones addressed here are shares in housing cooperatives, rental tenancies and land leases. Such security interests are perfected by notification of the security interest to the housing cooperative, landlord or lessor by the creditor or debtor. There is no national register for security interests in housing cooperatives, but the board of each housing cooperative is to keep a register of the pledges made with respect to each apartment owned by the housing cooperative association. The other rights are to be registered in the Land Register (*fastighetsregistret*).

10.2.2 RIGHT OF RETENTION

A general right of retention, of holding another's property until payment is received, can be loosely seen as regulated in Section 11:3 of the 1736 Commerce Code, in that a party who has another's property in their possession need not return that property until any necessary costs for the property have been paid by the property owner.

---

7   For the reference interest rate, and more on the Swedish National Bank, *see* its website at riksbank.se.

There are several different specific statutory rights of retention granted. The Consumer Sale of Services Act (*konsumentjänstlag* 1985:716) gives commercial providers of services the right to withhold property in their possession in connection with the provision of services until payment is made or security for payment provided, unless credit was given. There is also a right for hotel owners to retain the property of guests for unpaid bills under the Act on Retention Rights for Claims against Hotel Guests (*lag 1970:980 om retentionsrätt för fordran hos hotellgäst*). Another example is with commercial agents as discussed above in Chapter Eight who are permitted by statute to retain the principal's goods until the principal has paid any monies owed.

10.2.3 SECURITY INTERESTS IN REAL PROPERTY

A perfected security interest in real estate, or more specifically, a property unit, can be created and registered in accordance with the provisions of chapters six and twenty-two, respectively, of the Land Code. The owner of a property unit as defined under the Land Code sets in motion a process that generates a mortgage deed.[8] The owner applies for the issuance and registration of a mortgage deed (*inteckning*) of a certain face value, and when the application is granted, the land registration authority issues the mortgage deed (*pantbrev*).[9] The mortgage deed can be either physical or digital and is registered in the Mortgage Deed Register (*pantbrevsregistret*), which is a national, but not public, register. Information in this register can be obtained by certain parties, for example, a property unit owner, as to which party holds

---

8   The use of the term "mortgage" here is somewhat of a misnomer. Mortgages in Anglo-American legal systems are private legal institutions requiring no action by the state in general. The mortgage is perfected in most of these systems when registered by the mortgagee. However, a failure to register a mortgage in the Anglo-American systems in no way invalidates the mortgage itself. The security interest is simply not perfected as against third parties. In contrast, that which is referred to here as a mortgage in the Swedish system, *inteckning*, requires state registration to be created and then the issuance of a mortgage deed by the state and registration in the state register.

9   Also referred to as a "mortgage certificate." For a more in-depth work in English as to the Swedish mortgage system, *see* Jonny Flodin, SECURITY IN REAL PROPERTY – AN INTRODUCTION TO THE SWEDISH SYSTEM (Jure 2007).

a deed, or a bank. At the time of this printing, there were almost 11.3 million outstanding mortgage deeds in Sweden worth approximately SEK 3.5 trillion. Approximately ten million mortgage deeds are now digital. Stamp duty is paid on the face amount of the deed when issued at the rate of 2 %.

After its issuance, the mortgage deed can then be used as security for a loan. The loan does not have to be in connection with the purchase of the real estate. However, it is common in the Swedish real estate market for a residential property owner to have two mortgage deeds. A property unit owner can obtain a mortgage deed, for example in the amount of SEK 1 million, for her primary mortgage (*bottenlån*). The owner then often takes out a second mortgage deed used as security for the secondary mortgage (*topplån*).

As example, a property owner can take out a first mortgage deed in the amount of SEK 1 million in 2000 and use it for a loan taken out in 2000. She then can take out a second mortgage deed in 2004, using the second mortgage deed as security for the second mortgage in 2004. She pays off the first mortgage in 2006 and receives the first deed back. She decides to take out a third mortgage in 2007, and then can re-use the first mortgage deed as security. The third mortgage taken in 2007 then has a better right of priority than the mortgage taken in 2004 as the first registered mortgage deed is used to secure it. If the third mortgage was for SEK 500 000, the third mortgagee would have a perfected security interest for SEK 500 000, and the remainder of the first mortgage deed, SEK 500 000, would fall to the owner.

One reason for creating this ability to re-use mortgage deeds is to avoid stamp duty. When financing a new real estate acquisition, potential acquisition costs can include the purchase price, the stamp duty on the purchase price as well as the stamp duty on the face value of any mortgage deed taken out by the new owner. Stamp duty is paid on the purchase price of the property unit at the rate of either 1.5 or 4.25 %, depending on the type of purchase. Another stamp duty is paid on the face amount of the mortgage deed of 2 %. This can entail an additional cost of 3.5–6.25 % to the purchase price. By reusing mortgage deeds, owners can in certain situations avoid "double" stamp duty. New owners can use mortgage deeds as taken out by previous owners, as the deeds run with the property unit and not the persons.

10.3 Payment and Discharge

The rules regarding the payment (*betalning*) and discharge of debts (*betala med befriande verkan*) are set out in the Act on Notes with respect to notes, but are applied generally to all types of payments, with certain exceptions in consumer relationships. The debtor has the obligation to insure that any payment of the debt is made to the correct party. Where the parties have remained the same throughout the life of the debt, this is not problematic. As concerns the assignment of a claim to another party (*cession*), the main rule is that creditors can assign their rights freely, while debtors must have the consent of the creditor for the assignment to be valid. If the creditor has assigned a non-negotiable instrument, either the creditor or the new assignee must inform the debtor of the assignment, otherwise payment by the debtor to the original creditor in good faith is seen as discharging the debt. There is no requirement of notice of assignment with a negotiable note as the note must be presented for payment. However, payment of an installment to the latest known holder of the negotiable instrument absent any notification as to assignment will discharge the debtor as to that amount, but only if the note includes an installment payment schedule. There is also no requirement that the debtor personally pay the debt, any party can pay the debt on behalf of the debtor.

The second requirement for a payment to discharge a debt is that the correct amount must be paid. A partial payment reduces the debt, but does not discharge it. The currency in which payment is to be made is the currency of the place of payment. There is no automatic right to interest, if interest is to accrue on the debt, such a provision must be included in the agreement. There is a statutory right to late payment interest (*dröjsmålsränta*) in accordance with the Interest Act (*räntelag* 1975:635). The interest rates set out in that act are at either two or eight points over the reference interest rate (*referensränta*) as determined by the Swedish National Bank (*Riksbanken*).

The third requirement is that the payment must be on time. If no payment date has been agreed upon, payment is to be tendered when the creditor requests it. The payment must also be made to the right place. The main rule has been the residence of the creditor, but if the creditor is a business, then the place of payment is the place of business of the creditor. Today payment occurs often electronically between accounts as designated by the creditor.

If all these requisites are fulfilled, the payment when made in full discharges the debt.

In certain situations, a payment can be made incorrectly, either the payment is for too much or to the wrong party. In such cases, according to the general principle of *condictio indebiti*, the party making the wrong payment has the right to repayment. In one case, a woman had sent her granddaughter money through a bank giro several Christmases and never received any thanks. After several years, she finally asked the granddaughter about the money and discovered that she had paid to the wrong account. The person holding the account argued that since the money came every year at Christmas, he thought it was from Santa Claus. The court ordered him to repay the monies. In NJA 2011 p. 739, the Supreme Court found that the Swedish Tax Agency was obligated to repay monies sent by a taxpayer's accountant to the wrong account. However, in a situation where an employee receives too much in wages, the employer often does not have an automatic right to demand the monies back unless the employee knew or ought to have known that she was paid too much.

10.4 Set-Off

In a situation where the debtor and creditor have mutual claims against each other, a set-off (*kvittning*) is allowed under certain conditions to discharge the debts instead of payment. This can be a voluntary set-off as between the parties and then there are no further legal requirements, the agreement between the parties is sufficient.

In certain cases, one party may be able to invoke a set-off against another party's will and then certain requirements as set out by general (not statutory) principles of law have to be fulfilled. First, there must be two claims, the primary set-off claim (*huvudfordran*) and the counter set-off claim (*genfordran* or *motfordran*). Both claims have to be for monies, and both must be due for payment unless it is in a bankruptcy situation. If these conditions are fulfilled, the debtor can notify the creditor of the set-off (*kvittningsförklaring*) by citing the counter set-off claim. Set-off is particularly important in a bankruptcy. If a bankruptcy creditor has the right to a set-off, that creditor has the right to do so, meaning that its claims, to the extent they are covered by the set-off, are paid and do not become unsecured debt. Another important general feature is that set-off is allowed even when the counterclaim is prescribed.

10.5 Enforcing Debts

In the event a debtor fails to pay a debt when due, the creditor can refer the debt to a debt collection agency (*inkassofirma*) which can send a demand letter (*inkassobrev*) to the debtor demanding payment. This procedure is regulated by the Act on Debt Collection (*inkassolag* 1974:182), which imposes requirements on debt collection agencies and creditors. A demand letter is to be in writing, state the original amount of the debt, the amount of interest and the costs for collecting the debt. The last date of payment before further action is to be taken is also to be specifically stated in the letter. The amounts that can be recovered from a debtor for certain debt collection actions are set out in the Regulation on Compensation for Debt Collection Costs (*förordning 1981:1057 om ersättning för inkassokostnader*) unless compelling reasons exist otherwise: a creditor can charge SEK 50 for sending a reminder letter, SEK 160 can be charged for a demand letter if it fulfills the requirements set by statute. The creditor can charge SEK 150 for drawing up a debt repayment plan.

If the debtor still has not paid the debt after a demand, the creditor can send the claim to the Enforcement Authority (*Kronofogden*) for an enforcement title (*betalningsföreläggande*).[10] There were 980 000 applications for the enforcement of payments submitted to the Enforcement Authority in 2008.[11] This is a summary procedure, which means that unless the debtor actively contests the debt claim as submitted by the creditor, the failure to act is seen as an admission of the debt and the Enforcement Authority then issues a summary judgment as to an enforcement title (*utslag*) that has the same effect as a court judgment and can be enforced. To issue such a decision and enforcement title, the application by the creditor has to include a claim for a certain amount of money, the basis of the claim, the amount of the original claim, the due date, and the interest that is being claimed as well as any other

---

10 An English translation of the Enforcement Code (*utsökningsbalk* 1981:774) can be found at the website of the Government Offices.

11 Over 2 000 minors under the age of seventeen years had debts registered with the Enforcement Authority in 2007.

costs. The application is served on the debtor and the debtor has ten days to object to the application in writing. If the debtor contests the application, the creditor has four weeks to request that the case be transferred to a general district court for trial. If the creditor does not request this, the application is dismissed. However, the creditor still has the claim, simply a summary judgment is not issued.

If a summary judgment is issued, the Enforcement Authority automatically executes the enforcement title without any further action being required by the creditor. The different types of executive measures that can be taken include the attachment and levying (*utmätning*) of personal and real property for sale at auction and garnishing wages (*utmätning av lön*). Property sold at auction must be sold at a public auction held by the Enforcement Authority. The monies received from the auction are to go towards the amount of debt as determined in the summary judgment and the costs for the attachment, levying and auction.

The property levied must be the debtor's, have an economic value and be transferable. The main rule is that in situations of attachment and levying, all property in the debtor's possession can be assumed by the authority to belong to the debtor unless the true property owner can prove ownership. The property should have an economic value in that monies will be paid for the property. If the property is not transferable, it cannot be levied as it cannot be sold.

The debtor is allowed to exempt certain property seen to be necessary for a minimum existence (*gäldenärens existensminimum*) even if it has economic value. Items that can be exempted on behalf of the debtor from being levied (*beneficium*) include: clothes and other items exclusively used by the debtor unless they are too valuable, furniture and household goods necessary for a home and its care. Analogue televisions are excluded almost as a rule, but a different assessment is made with respect to more expensive flat screen televisions. Work tools and other equipment, livestock and feed necessary for the debtor to make a living can be exempted unless of a high value. Items of great personal value can also be exempted, such as gifts. The right to live in a cooperative apartment in some cases has been exempted if the value of the share in the housing cooperative is not worth too much. Wages, pensions and similar income can be garnished after the debtor is insured a certain minimum standard of living (*förbehållsbelopp*). For a person living alone, this amount in 2009 was SEK 4 549 per month to include all living costs except the costs of a residence. Higher amounts can be exempted upon a showing of need by the debtor, for example, for dental or medical costs.

The debtor's real property can be levied and auctioned if the sale would generate sufficient proceeds to pay all debts with a higher priority than the debt being enforced as well as the costs of the execution (*täckningsprincipen*). A certain amount, referred to as the protected amount (*skyddsbeloppet*), must be reached through the sale. This protected amount is the sum of all debts with better rights than the debt at hand and the costs of levying and for the auction. In most cases, the protected amount is the lowest bid the Enforcement Authority can accept at an auction with respect to real property. The creditor requesting the sale has a veto right as to the sale if she will not get paid. Another rule applied in the execution of real estate is the assumption principle (*övertagandeprincipen*). This principle means that all claims having mortgage deeds in the property unit and falling within the protected amount, with the exception of the costs of levying and of the auction and certain interest, are to be assumed by the purchaser of the real estate at the auction as part of the payment price. The general order of interests protected is that as set out for perfected security interests in specific property under the Act on the Rights of Secured Creditors (*förmånsrättslag* 1970:979): certain types of obligations and derivative instruments, mortgage deeds in ships and aircraft, hand pledges, certain rights under insurance policies, floating charges, mortgage deeds in real estate and site leaseholds, generally addressed in that order.

The sale of the property does not discharge the debtor from the total debt to the extent any debts are not covered by the proceeds from the auction or garnishment of wages. As stated, the statute of limitations for debts typically is a renewable ten-year period.

10.6 Bankruptcy

An alternative to an enforcement title and the attachment and levying procedure above is for the creditor to place the debtor into bankruptcy under the Bankruptcy Act (*konkurslag* 1987:672). This is seen as a more drastic measure than levying as the legal capacity of the debtor is limited in a bankruptcy, the debtor is neither allowed to dispose over the majority of her property, enter into certain contracts nor administer her affairs. The bankruptcy trustee does these things instead. The debtor needs to be insolvent (*på obestånd*) to be placed into bankruptcy, meaning that she is unable to pay her debts when due for more than a temporary period. All of her assets, with the exceptions as stated above for personal use and household, are to be used to pay her debts.

A creditor or the debtor can petition the district court to place the debtor in bankruptcy. The majority of bankruptcies in Sweden are initiated by the state or the debtor. A creditor with a perfected security interest in specific property cannot request that a debtor be placed into bankruptcy, but can seek an action to attach and levy the property as discussed above instead.

Evidence needs to be presented to the court that the debtor is unable to pay her debts. Typically a creditor proves this by demonstrating that the debtor has not paid a claim for more than six months. If the debtor is a legal person with statutory bookkeeping requirements, the creditor can request that the debtor pay a debt due, and if the debtor does not do so within one week, the creditor can request that the debtor be placed into bankruptcy within three weeks if the debt is still not then paid. If the court finds the debtor to be insolvent, the court will place the debtor into bankruptcy.

The district court appoints a bankruptcy trustee (*konkursförvaltare*) to administer the bankruptcy estate (*konkursboet*) and dispose of its assets and pay the debts. Generally, only members of the Swedish Bar Association can be selected as trustees. Any payments or gifts made by the debtor within a certain period prior to the bankruptcy can be reclaimed by the bankruptcy trustee (*återvinning*) under certain conditions as set out by law. If an individual has been placed in bankruptcy, that individual is still responsible for any debts not paid after the assets are sold. If a legal person is placed into bankruptcy, the legal person is dissolved when the bankruptcy estate is distributed.

The payment of creditors by the bankruptcy estate is to follow the rules set out in the Act on the Rights of Secured Creditors. The first division made is that between secured (*prioriterade*) and unsecured (*oprioriterade*) creditors, with the latter receiving payment on a *pro rata* basis from that which is left in the estate after the secured creditors are paid. Secured creditors are divided into two categories: those holding perfected security interests in specific property (*särskilda förmånsrätter*) and those holding statutorily protected security interests (*allmänna förmånsrätter*), the latter category only applicable in bankruptcies and not in the attachment and levying of property.

Perfected security interests in specific property include certain types of obligations and derivative instruments, mortgage deeds in ships and aircraft, hand pledges, certain rights under insurance policies, floating charges, mortgage deeds in real estate and site leaseholds, generally addressed in that order. General statutorily protected security interests include the costs for the creditor in placing the debtor in bankruptcy, payment to accountants for the work in the bankruptcy, outstanding employee wages and future employee pensions. The general statutorily protected security rights are to be paid in the order as stated in the act, and for those rights arising under the same section of the act, they are to have the same rights as between them, in other words, paid on a *pro rata* basis.

The first party to receive payment is the bankruptcy trustee for her fees and the costs of the bankruptcy. The perfected security interests in specific property as a class are then paid in the order generally as set out above. One exception is that the general statutorily protected security interests given to the creditor for the costs incurred in the bankruptcy or to the administrator of a debt structuring, as well as the security interest given to accountants, have precedence over the perfected security interests in floating charges as well as personal property that has been attached other than site leaseholds.

The general statutorily protected security interests are then paid from that which remains. If anything is left after the general statutorily protected security interests are paid, the unsecured creditors are paid on a *pro rata* basis. After the unsecured creditors have been paid, any unpaid criminal fines or claims based on criminal acts are to be paid as well as any claims by donees based on enforceable promises of gifts that have not been fulfilled.

An alternative to bankruptcy for private individuals is debt restructuring (*skuldsanering*). An individual can voluntarily agree to live at a minimum existence for a period of up to five years, which will result in the majority of cases in the discharge of all the debts included in the restructuring plan under the Act on Personal Debt Restructuring (*skuldsaneringslag* 2006:584). This is in contrast to a bankruptcy in which all of an individual's debts are not discharged in all cases. The individual must be residing in Sweden and cannot conduct business to a significant extent. An application for this type of debt restructuring is to be made to the Enforcement Authority. The Enforcement

Authority assists the debtor in renegotiating her debts, which means that all the creditors (except those with perfected security interests in property) agree to be paid a certain *pro rata* amount, for example SEK 50 for every SEK 100 of debt. The debtor also agrees to live a minimum existence for a certain period of time, at the most five years, after which the debts included in the plan will be paid at the agreed upon levels.

Debt restructuring is also available for legal persons or private persons conducting business (*företagsrekonstruktion*) under the Act on Corporate Debt Restructuring (*lag 1996:764 om företagsrekonstruktion*). Both the debtor and creditors can apply for debt restructuring at a district court. A stay of execution is put in place until a debt restructuring plan can be drafted. The debtor and creditors can also agree to debt restructuring without the assistance of a court (*underhandsackord*).

CHAPTER 11

Property Law

As with most property systems in the world, property in Sweden is divided between real property/immovables (*fast egendom*) and personal property/movables (*lös egendom*). The presentation in this chapter begins with the general rules as to property, and then more specifically examines the rules concerning real property.

Ownership in both real and personal property is nowadays viewed as acquired in one of three ways: By being the original owner (*originära fång*), by obtaining derived ownership (*derivativa fång*) or by adverse possession (*exstinktiva fång*). Ownership can be acquired with respect to specifically identifiable assets (*singulära fång*) or to the entirety of an estate (*universiella fång*), for example, belonging to an individual, legal person or bankruptcy.

With original ownership, the owner in question is the first ever to own the property, a feat not so common in reality. Examples of original ownership can most easily be found with respect to intangible rights such as intellectual property. The inventor of a patented object is the first owner of the patent. Derivative ownership is where the current right of ownership has been acquired from a previous owner, either through purchase, barter, inheritance or gift. A derivative owner is not the first owner of the property, as they have acquired the property from the previous owner. Ownership based on adverse possession is where a party has acquired ownership rights by law despite the ownership rights of the true owner, for example, as a bona fide purchaser or through adverse possession.

Ownership can either be in the form of individual ownership or co-ownership as tenants in common (*samäganderätt*) under the Act on Tenants in Common (*lag 1904:48 s. 1 om samäganderätt*). As tenants in common, each co-owner has an equal right to the entirety of the property if nothing otherwise has been agreed. Such ownership interests are freely transferable by will or statute to the parties' respective heirs and there is no right of survivorship between tenants in common. There is no other type of shared ownership in Swedish law, such as joint tenancy under Anglo-American law with a right of survivorship. Any type of shared ownership other than tenants in common is prohibited by law. Trusts[1] are also not recognized in Swedish law.

Private ownership of property is a fundamental premise in the Swedish legal system, but there are certain statutory incursions as seen in this chapter as well as in Chapters Seventeen (land leases) and Eighteen (landlord/tenant law) below. Property owners are not free to do anything they wish in all circumstances. Owners have the right to transfer ownership (*överlåtelse*) fairly freely and also the right to grant user rights (*upplåtelse*) while retaining ownership. Possession (*besittning*) of personal property creates a presumption of ownership as discussed above in Chapter Ten.

11.1 Personal Property

Personal property is a default category. Everything that is not real property as defined by Section 1:1 of the Land Code (*jordabalk* 1970:994)[2] is personal property. Personal property then is divided implicitly into two categories: tangible personal property or chattels (*lösa saker*) and intangible personal property.

---

1 Briefly, a trust is a fiduciary relationship in which one person, the trustee, holds the legal title to a property for the benefit of another, the beneficiary or equitable owner. There is a type of Swedish legal person for the purpose of receiving property to be administered for the benefit of another person or a purpose, a foundation (*stiftelse*) that is the nearest equivalent to a trust and discussed further in Chapter Thirteen below. However, a foundation is a legal person and not a type of property ownership.

2 An English translation of the Land Code, as well as of other real property legislation is available at the website of the Department of Real Estate and Construction Management, at the School of Architect and Built Environment at the Swedish Royal Institute of Technology ("KTH"), www.kth.se/en/abe/inst/fob. A complete listing of all the statutes in English as well as an English/Swedish, Swedish/English glossary concerning real estate terms can be found there under Swedish Land and Cadastral Legislation, www.kth.se/abe/om_skolan/organisation/inst/fob/avd/fastighets-vetenskap/publikationer/slcl/swedish-land-and-cadastral-legislation-1.33609. These English translations are also available in Hans Mattson & Tommy Österberg, ed., Roger Tanner, transl., SWEDISH LAND AND CADASTRAL LEGISLATION (3rd ed. Jure 2007).

11.1.1 CHATTELS

The sale or barter of personal property is regulated by the Sale of Goods Act (*köplag* 1990:931). The sale of goods to consumers is regulated in the Consumer Sale of Goods Act (*konsumentköplag* 1990:932) and the international sale of commercial goods is regulated in a third act, the International Sale of Goods Act (*lag 1987:822 om internationella köp*), all of which are discussed in Chapter Fourteen below. The creation of security interests in chattels was already discussed above in Chapter Ten. The primary manner by which creditors perfect security interests in personal property is through pledges, entailing that the creditor must have possession of the property used as security in order to perfect her security interest as against third parties.

11.1.2 INTANGIBLES

Intangible personal property can be further divided into shares, rights, negotiable instruments (*värdepapper*) and intellectual property (*immateriella rättigheter*) in the form of copyrights (*upphovsrätt*), patents (*patent*), trademarks (*varumärke*) and trade secrets (*företagshemligheter*). Intellectual property rights are addressed in Chapter Fifteen below. Certain types of negotiable interests, particularly negotiable notes, were also discussed above in Chapter Ten. Shares in business organizations are discussed cursorily in Chapter Thirteen. Housing cooperatives are discussed below in more depth given their significance as a residential form of living.

11.1.3 HOUSING COOPERATIVES

Almost twenty percent of the Swedish population lives in housing cooperatives (*bostadsrätt*). Rights in housing cooperatives[3] are regulated in the

---

3 Also referred to as "tenant ownership." Sveriges Bostadsrättsföreningars Central-organization ("SBC"), founded in 1921, is an umbrella organization representing five thousand housing cooperatives. Information in Swedish about the organization and housing cooperatives in general is available at its website at sbc.se. Two other central organizations representing (and sometimes actually building the premises of) housing cooperatives are HSB and Riksbyggen. Information about these organizations is available in English at their websites, hsb.se and riksbyggen.se respectively. Riksbyggen was created in the 1940's for the purpose of building and financing housing for construction workers during the then acute housing shortage.

Act on Housing Cooperative Rights (*bostadsrättslag* 1991:614).[4] Housing cooperatives (*bostadsrättsföreningar*) as legal persons are regulated by this act and the Act on Commercial Cooperatives (*lag 1987:667 om ekonomiska föreningar*) discussed more generally in Chapter Thirteen.[5]

The rights with respect to shares in housing cooperatives are not governed by the Land Code, as are the rights of tenants, for example, because the rights created with this legal institution are not rights in real property, but rather intangible personal property rights, shares in a cooperative tied to a right to use a specific cooperative apartment. The rights of a member ("co-op owner") in a housing cooperative that owns real estate are invoked when the member has the right, through her membership in the cooperative, to live in an apartment in a building owned by the cooperative. There is no national public register as to housing cooperatives with respect to the ownership or pledging of shares. Housing cooperatives have individual registers as to their members and any pledges. There is no statutory public right to information with respect to the security interests, but the register of shareowners is available to the public.

A co-op owner pays for the share in the cooperative including the right to use a specific apartment. The price of this share is evaluated based on a combination of the attractiveness of the apartment and the economic stability of the housing cooperative, for example, its debt/equity ratio. For most co-op owners, the monthly payment for living in the cooperative apartment consists of repaying the debt taken to purchase the share in the cooperative, and the monthly fees as charged by the cooperative for the maintenance of the building as well as to repay any debts the cooperative may have. Co-op owners, as members of a housing cooperative, are not responsible for the cooperative's debts as the cooperative is a separate legal person. However, if the building owned by the cooperative is destroyed and not rebuilt, the housing cooperative is liquidated and the members share in the assets according to their shares.

The statute regulating rights in housing cooperatives is fairly extensive, consisting of eleven chapters. The first chapter concerns the general

---

4   The first act on housing cooperatives was enacted in 1930, replaced in 1971 and finally replaced by the current 1991 act.

5   This act is also referred to as the "Act on Economic Associations."

definitions and provisions with respect to housing cooperatives. According to its Section 1:1, a housing cooperative is a cooperative enterprise that has the objective of conveying apartments in a building owned by the cooperative to co-op owners. Housing cooperatives must have at least three members, be registered, have bylaws, a board of directors and at least one auditor.

The conveyance of a cooperative apartment can only be made as prescribed by statute to a member in the cooperative in exchange for payment and for an indefinite term. Only a housing cooperative can convey the original rights to a cooperative apartment. The member can then sell her share and rights later. The conveyance is to be with respect to a building or part thereof, but may include land connected to the building.

Under the Property Acquisition Rights (Conversion to Housing Cooperatives or Cooperative Rentals) Act (*lag 1982:352 om rätt till fastighetsförvärv för ombildning till bostadsrätt eller kooperativ hyresrätt*), both housing cooperatives and cooperative rentals[6] have the right to request that a rental unit[7] be converted to either cooperative apartments or cooperative rentals, respectively. If at least two-thirds of the tenants in the building are interested in converting the premises, notice is to be given to the owner of the building as to this interest to convert by either a housing cooperative or cooperative rental association.

This right to convert is enforced by the requirement that the owner must in most cases first offer any such housing unit to sale to any association giving notice of an interest to convert prior to selling or exchanging the unit to a third party. This right of first refusal needs not be recognized by the owner if an acquisition of the building by an association would be unfair taking into account the relationship between the owner and the third party or the terms and conditions of the transfer. A proposed purchase agreement is to be submitted by the owner to a Regional Rent Tribunal (*hyresnämnden*), which is to ensure that the cooperative has received the offer. These actions are to

---

6 Cooperative rentals are discussed below in Chapter Eighteen.
7 According to Section 1 of the act, the rental unit must be taxed as a rental unit, or if the building is leased for purposes other than recreation, as a single-family house, but is not applicable to property with less than three apartments. The act is also applicable to site leaseholds.

be registered in the Land Register Section of the Real Property Register and the notification is valid for a period of two years.

11.2 Real Property Legislation

Real property law in the Swedish legal system is divided into general real property law, as governed by the Land Code ("LC")[8] and specialized real property law as found in specific statutes. Specialized real property law is further categorized into environmental law as set out in the Environmental Code; and land use law as governed by specific acts, such as the Real Property Formation Act (*fastighetsbildningslag* 1970:988). The total number of acts concerning real property in Sweden reaches well over twenty, so that a presentation of all of these is well beyond the scope of this chapter.[9] The focus here instead is on general real estate law as set out in the Land Code.

The Land Code comprises twenty-four chapters divided into two main sections. The first section concerns rights with respect to real property, the second the registration of these rights. The chapters follow a certain transactional structure.

---

8   Two statutes are also typically considered a part of general real property law, the Housing Cooperative Rights Act as discussed in the previous section, and the Cooperative Rental Rights Act (*lag 2002:93 om kooperativ hyresrätt*) as discussed further in Chapter Eighteen below.

9   For a more detailed description of Swedish real estate law, *see* Laura Carlson, AN INTRODUCTION TO SWEDISH REAL PROPERTY LAW (Jure 2008).

TABLE 11.1 The Land Code.

Part One: Real Property	
The Property Unit and Ownership	
Chap. 1 The Property Unit	Chap. 4 Purchase, Exchange or Gift
Chap. 2 Fixtures	Chap. 5 Repossession by a Rightful Owner
Chap. 3 Relations to Neighbors	Chap. 6 Mortgage Deeds
User Rights	
Chap. 7 User Rights Generally	Chap. 12 Landlord Tenant Law
Chap. 8 Land Leases Generally	Chap. 13 Site Leaseholds
Chap. 9 Agricultural Land Leases	Chap. 14 Easements
Chap. 10 Residential Land Leases	Chap. 15 Easements for Electrical Power
Chap. 11 Commercial Land Leases	
Claims as to Better Ownership or User Rights	
Chap. 16 Adverse Possession	Chap. 18 Acquisitions in Good Faith
Chap. 17 Rights Based on Registration	
Part Two: Registration of Real Property Rights	
Chap. 19 Registration Proceedings	Chap. 22 Registration of Mortgage Deeds
Chap. 20 Registration of Ownership	Chap. 23 Registration of User Rights
Chap. 21 Registration of Site Leaseholds	Chap. 24 Registration of Fixtures

Land leases are treated separately in Chapter Seventeen and landlord tenant law in Chapter Eighteen below. Security interests in real property were addressed above in Chapter Ten.

Despite the fact that the Land Code primarily regulates voluntary agreements between two private parties, it must be kept in mind that its provisions also dovetail decisions as issued in cadastral procedures by the cadastral authority, the National Land Survey (*Lantmäteriet*).[10] The formation of property units and any changes thereto are governed by the Real Property Formation Act. Any subdivision of a property unit must occur in accordance with the procedures as set out in that act, otherwise it is void. In other words, parties cannot privately validly agree as to the formation, subdivision or merger of property. Once the boundaries to a property unit

---

10 For more information on this Swedish government authority, *see* its website at lantmateriet.se.

are lawfully determined, these boundaries are to be marked on the property and become the boundaries for the property unit.

A party desiring modifications or clarifications with respect to a property unit, or certain user rights to another property unit, can obtain such through a cadastral procedure as regulated primarily by the Real Property Formation Act. A short list of cadastral procedures that can be requested includes: Subdivision, reallotment, boundary demarcation, transfer of fixtures, mergers of properties, establishment of joint facilities or common grounds, partitioning for tenants in common, utility easements, ownership determinations and the legalization of private subdivisions carried out before 1972.

11.3 Property Units

Real property is defined in Section 1:1 of the Land Code as "land" (*jord*). Real estate parcels, or property units (*fastigheter*), are the sum of the land, fixtures and any appurtenances, such as easements. Property units are registered in the Real Property Register (*fastighetsregistret*), under the auspices of National Land Survey, and given a unique registration designation. There are over three million objects registered in the Real Property Register.

Both two and three dimensionally delimited properties can be created according to the Land Code, but the latter are still rare in Sweden as this possibility was only fairly recently introduced in 2004. Only sixty-five 3-d properties had been created as of 2007.[11] A 2-d property unit is delineated on the ground by width and length, while a 3-d property unit adds the dimension of height. The requirements for forming a 3-d property unit are not found in the Land Code but rather in Section 3:1a of the Real Property Formation Act: A 3-d property unit or space may only be formed if it is clear that such a measure is more appropriate than any other measure for achieving the purpose intended and may take place only if:

---

11 For an in-depth analysis of the history and present adoption of 3D property, *see* Jenny Paulsson, 3-D PROPERTY RIGHTS – AN ANALYSIS OF KEY FACTORS BASED ON INTERNATIONAL EXPERIENCE, Report 4:99 (Section of Real Estate Planning and Land Law, Royal Institute of Technology. Stockholm 2007). Paulsson's thesis is available on-line at the KTH website portal at diva-portal.org.

1   The 3-d property unit is to contain a building or other facility or part of the same;

2   The 3-d property unit is assured those rights necessary in order for it to be used in an appropriate manner;

3   It is clear that the measure:

   a) Is justified, taking into consideration the construction and use of the facility; and

   b) Is calculated to lead to a more appropriate management of the facility or to secure financing or construction of the facility; and

4   The property unit, if intended for residential housing purposes, is calculated to comprise at least three dwelling units.

The question of allowing residential 3-d property units, condominiums (*ägarlägenheter*), has been a highly debated political issue in Sweden. It was not possible to create single residential condominiums in the first trial with respect to 3-d property and this became possible only after 1 May 2009. The preference politically and historically has been for cooperative apartments (*bostadsrätt*) as discussed in the previous section.

11.3.1 FIXTURES

The property unit consists of the sum of the land, fixtures and easements. A fixture (*tillbehör*) is personal property that has become attached (either physically or functionally) to the land and the property unit. Fixtures can be either physical, in the case of chattels that have become attached to a property unit, or legal, in which case a right such as an easement has become attached to the property unit. The second chapter of the Land Code addresses only physical fixtures, further categorizing them into property fixtures, building fixtures and industrial fixtures.

Unity of ownership is required for personal property to become a fixture. Consequently, a fixture cannot be created where there is different ownership, for example, where the party owning and affixing the personal property and the one owning the property unit are not the same. The same is true of personal property that a property unit owner has affixed to the property unit but does not yet own. If the personal property was transferred with a retention of title provision,[12] *i.e.* an industrial fixture, the property does not become a fixture as long as the provision is in force and the creditor's right has been registered in the property register. An exception is made to this latter rule, however, for personal property that by statute is designated as either a general or building fixture. Such property always remains a fixture despite any retention of title provision.

An assignment of an object deemed to be a fixture is not valid against third parties until the object is removed from the property unit in a way clearly indicating that it no longer belongs to the property unit, or in the alternative, a decision has been registered in the Land Register Section determining that the object is no longer a fixture.

Property Fixtures

A property unit includes general property fixtures in the form of any buildings, utility conduits, fences or other constructions for permanent use in or above the ground; trees rooted in the ground as well as other vegetation; and any natural manure (the latter clearly evidencing the origins of Swedish society in agriculture).

The key to becoming a property fixture is that the personal property is to be present and connected to the property unit functionally in some fashion. The requirement that the property actually be attached or connected to the ground has been diluted in recent years. An example here could be a fuel tank that has been placed on a property to store oil for fuel. It is not affixed in a manner making removal from the property difficult, but functionally it can be seen as fulfilling a task necessary for the use of the property unit in general. The second element for a property fixture is that the personal property be intended for permanent use.

---

12   A retention of title clause (*äganderättförbehåll*) is typical in a purchase agreement whereby the seller retains title, ownership, to the property until the purchase price has been paid in full.

Building Fixtures

Building fixtures are defined as any property provided for the permanent use of a building (which in its turn is to be a property fixture in the property unit). The two elements here for building fixtures are that the property be placed in a building for permanent use. The latter is assessed on an objective basis, that necessary for a typical user, and not for any specific individual. Examples named in the Land Code are: permanent partitions, elevators, handrails, water pipes, heating or lighting, faucets, outlets and similar equipment, hot water heaters, radiators, boilers, inner windows, awnings, emergency equipment and keys. The list is not meant to be exhaustive but rather to serve by way of example.

As a rule, however, the following personal property is almost always deemed a building fixture in accordance with section 2:2 of the Land Code:

- For residences: bathtubs and other sanitation equipment, stoves, ovens and refrigerators as well as washing machines and mangles;
- For commercial land leases: shelves, counters and window display devices;
- For auditoriums: stages and seating;
- For agricultural outbuildings: livestock feeding and milking machines; and
- For manufacturing plants: cooling and ventilation systems.

The courts have found that a built-in dishwasher, the motor to a central vacuuming system and a parabola antenna can be building fixtures.[13] If different parts of a building belong to different property units, the personal property as listed above is to be a building fixture for the property unit in which that part of the building is located.

Industrial Fixtures

The third category of industrial fixtures consists of machines and other personal property used for an industrial purpose. The first requirement here is that some type of production of goods necessitating the use of machinery is

---

13 *See* NJA 1996 p. 130 and NJA 1997 p. 699, respectively.

or has been conducted on the property unit, and that leasehold improvements were made to the building tailored after those operations. The second requirement is that the object has a functional connection to the operations, not necessarily a physical connection to the property. Last, the object is to be used primarily on the property unit. There are no requirements as to the extent or size of the operations. Personal property specifically exempted from being industrial fixtures include vehicles, office equipment and hand tools.[14]

Chattels do not become industrial fixtures if the owner of the property makes a declaration as to that effect in accordance with chapter twenty-four of the Land Code. The idea behind allowing such declarations, that certain chattels remain personal property, and do not become industrial fixtures, is to facilitate the financing of purchases of larger machinery through, for example, leasing. A seller can have a retention of title provision in the sale agreement valid against third parties only with industrial fixtures, and no other type of fixture. This creates a tension in the system, for an object can only be one type of fixture at a time, but most creditors desire that the property they sell be classified as industrial fixtures and not property or building fixtures as they can obtain a more secure interest with industrial fixtures. The owner of the property unit has the right to apply for registration of a declaration as to industrial fixtures in the Land Register Section.

11.3.2 EASEMENTS

Easements are the third component of a property unit after land and fixtures. Easements can be voluntary or involuntary. Voluntary easements are governed

---

14 These different items are not defined in the Land Code, but rather in the legislative bill to the Land Code, Legislative Bill 1966:24 at 94–95. This illustrates an important aspect of Swedish legislative technique. Swedish statutes are often purposefully drafted in broad terms. The legislative preparatory works provide the detail. Thus a court, when interpreting legislation, is to first turn to the legislative preparatory works to divine the intent of the legislator. For example, the legislative bill to the Land Code names "office equipment" as an exception to personal property that can become an industrial fixture. "Office equipment" according to the legislative bill includes all inventory that has its use in an office environment. Consequently, a computer used in an office and not in production would not be an industrial fixture according to the legislative history.

by chapter fourteen of the Land Code, entered into through agreement voluntarily by the parties. Involuntary easements are determined through a land surveying procedure governed by the Real Property Formation Act. The provisions in chapter fourteen are not applicable to easements created through the latter procedure or by expropriation or other similar compulsory acquisition.

An easement is a right for one property unit, the dominant property unit, to use another property unit, the servient property unit, for a specific purpose. A servitude is that right as it encumbers the servient property unit. The requirements for easements in Swedish law are derived from Roman law: Proximity (*vicinitas*), utility (*utilitas fundo*) and duration of need (*perpetua causa*). The requirement of proximity with respect to certain categories, such as access to electrical power, has become rather diluted over time.

An easement can be characterized as either positive or negative. A positive easement is where the owner of the servient property is to permit or suffer some act to be done on her property. A negative easement restrains the property unit owner from using the property in a way that could impair the easement. The Roman legal principle that the owner of the servient estate should not be forced to take actions except by way of exception, *servitus in faciendo consistere nequit,* has been followed in Swedish law.

Involuntary Easements

Involuntary easements, those imposed upon a property unit owner by the state, for the benefit of the state or another property owner, are governed by several different acts, of which the Utility Easements Act (*ledningsrättslag* 1973:1144) is of primary interest here by way of example. Under the Utility Easements Act, a party can receive the right to run cable or lines through another property unit. This right can be granted to a party or run with the property unit. Approval of such a right is to be issued by the cadastral authority in a cadastral procedure. A utility easement is not to be granted where the objective of the easement can be achieved in another manner, or where the inconvenience resulting from the easement to the public or private property unit outweighs the advantages gained. Neither can an easement be granted that violates any safety measures necessary with respect to the lines or cable, or is in violation of a detailed plan.

The party desiring the easement is to file an application with the appropriate cadastral authority having jurisdiction over the area in which the servient property unit is located. The cadastral authority provides the technical work and evaluation necessary to determine whether the utility easement should be granted. The decision by the land surveyor as to the easement can be appealed. Compensation, if mandated, is to be paid to the owner of the servient property unit for the involuntary easement in accordance with the Expropriation Act (*expropriationslag* 1972:719) discussed below.

Voluntary Easements

An easement[15] may be privately conveyed by agreement within the parameters set out in chapter fourteen of the Land Code if it promotes better land use by allowing the dominant property unit to use, build or dispose over the servient property unit with regard to a particular aspect. The easement may only concern a purpose that is of enduring significance to the dominant property unit and may not be combined with an obligation of the servient unit to do other than maintain roads, buildings or other facilities encompassed by the easement. The easement is united with the ownership right to the dominant property unit and may not be independently transferred.

An easement is to be granted in writing by the owner of the servient unit. The writing must reflect the identities of the dominant and servient units and the purpose of the grant of the easement. A grant failing to do this is invalid as an easement.

The owner of the dominant unit is to act in a manner that does not unnecessarily burden the servient unit when exercising the right. Where the dominant unit owner has a road, building or other facility on the servient unit, that owner is to keep it in such a condition that harm or inconvenience to the servient unit is not caused unnecessarily. In the event the dominant property unit owner has exceeded the rights under the easement, or the owner of either property unit has neglected any obligations connected to the

---

15 Easements concerning the right to electrical power are addressed in the few provisions of Chapter Fifteen of the Land Code and also under other specific acts, such as the Utility Easements Act.

easement, that owner is to restore that which has been disturbed or to fulfill that which is due and compensate for any damage. If such an act or failure to act is of material significance to the other owner, and corrective action is not taken within a reasonable time after a request to do so, the other owner has the right to terminate the easement and receive compensation for damages.

Registration is required to completely protect user rights granted by a voluntary easement. Chapter twenty-three of the Land Code governs the registration of voluntary, contractual user rights, easements and electrical utilities in the Land Register. Such an application for registration is to be made by the right holder or property unit owner and submitted with documentation evidencing the right.

11.3.3 JOINT FACILITIES

Joint facilities (*gemensamhetsanläggningar*) are an additional type of property arrangement in Swedish law, basically entailing the grant of one easement jointly to several property units. Joint facilities are defined in the Joint Facilities Act (*anläggningslag* 1973:1149) as facilities common to several property units, fulfilling a purpose of continual significance to the property units, a type of shared easement. Typical examples of joint facilities are private roads, sewage pipes, parks, parking lots and garages, central antennas, lighting, water, telephone and electrical lines, bridges, harbors and grain elevators. The requirements for establishing a joint facility are that the facility has a specific purpose, that this purpose is significant for the property units involved, and that the economic or other advantages outweigh the costs and inconveniences of the joint facility.

A joint facility is established through a specific cadastral procedure (*anläggningsförrättning*). It is to be created in a manner causing the least amount of inconvenience and trespass at a cost reasonable for achieving the objective. A joint facility is not to be established where the owners of the participating property units and any lessees thereto oppose its creation for significant reasons. Land or other space for the joint facility may be expropriated from a property unit involved in the joint facility.

The costs for creating and maintaining a joint facility are to be borne proportionally by the property units benefiting from the joint facility, taking into account that which is fair with respect to the benefit received. A joint facility management association is often formed, which then is registered in the Joint Property Management Association Register as maintained by the National Land Survey.

11.4 Ownership and its Limits

Ownership of a property unit can be in the form of either individual ownership or as tenants in common. A transfer of ownership to a property unit cannot be limited in time. Entailed estates, *i.e.* estates for life with a perpetual right of survivorship within a family (*fideikomiss*) could previously be granted, whereby an individual received the right to use a property unit for the term of her life. Entailed estates were outlawed in 1810, but as of 2006, twenty-four such land grants were still in existence, constituting many of the largest estates owned by individuals presently in Sweden.

Ownership rights in a property unit have several other limitations that are not self-evident from the Land Code. The ownership of land does not:

- Include mineral rights *per se*;[16]
- Extend to the center of the earth, but simply to a certain level below the ground surface;
- Extend infinitely up in space; nor
- Include a right to control air space above a certain height.

Certain restrictions as to exercising ownership rights are found in the third chapter of the Land Code, addressing the use of the property unit with respect to neighbors. However, these provisions are only a small part of the restrictions that exist with respect to ownership rights under Swedish law, as set out, for example, in the Environmental Code. The restrictions in

---

16 For an in-depth analysis of the history and current treatment of the Swedish legislation regarding mineral rights, see Eva Liedholm Johnson, MINERAL RIGHTS – LEGAL SYSTEMS GOVERNING EXPLORATION AND EXPLOITATION, Report 4:112 (Section of Real Estate Planning and Land Law, Royal Institute of Technology, Stockholm 2010). Liedholm Johnson's thesis is available on-line at the KTH website portal at diva-portal.org.

ownership rights discussed below include the right of public access, nuisance laws, expropriation and preemption.

11.4.1 THE RIGHT OF PUBLIC ACCESS

A fairly extensive restriction in an owner's right to exert exclusive control over a property unit is the right of public access (*allemansrätten*). The right of public access was first established by medieval custom and as of 1974, is now constitutionally protected in the last paragraph of Article 15 of the second chapter of the Instrument of Government, which states that "[e]very individual is to have access to nature in accordance with the right of public access."

The right of public access is not more explicitly defined by law other than a right to have access to nature. This right has been deemed to include the right to walk, bicycle, ride a horse and ski on another person's land without that owner's permission. The physical extent of this right of access does not extend to private gardens, the immediate vicinity of a dwelling (within one hundred meters) or land under cultivation, and has certain restrictions with respect to nature reserves and other protected areas.

This right of public access also includes the right to pick wildflowers, wild mushrooms and wild berries that are not protected as endangered, if picked in a manner that does not destroy any roots. Cultivated plants cannot be picked. Every person also has the right to camp with a tent for one night without permission on certain lands. The right of public access also includes the right to visit beaches, swim in any lake and put a non-motorized boat on any water unless the beach is close to a residential dwelling. Restrictions exist as to fires and dogs in nature during certain times of the year.

Private bridges are not publicly accessible for boats or bathing. Fishing also remains essentially private, apart from certain public lakes and the coasts of the Baltic Sea, Öresund, Kattegatt and Skagerrak. Access to land by means of motor vehicles can be limited or restricted. The right of public access does not include the right to drive a car on a private road, nor to camp in a trailer on such roads or on private parking places. A divide in the right of access can be identified in that as long as the access consists of a person physically taking herself over the land, it is permitted. Once any type of motorized vehicle is used, the right is limited or non-existent. The exercise and protection of the right of public access is overseen by the Swedish National Environmental Protection Agency (*Naturvårdsverket*).[17]

11.4.2 CHANGES IN THE PROPERTY UNIT OR USE

A property owner is entitled to enjoy her property within the bounds of the defined current use of the property unit. There are several public documents regulating land use: the two primary ones are the comprehensive plan (*översiktsplan*) for an entire area setting out basic features such as land and water use as well as development, and the detailed plan (*detaljplan*), which as the name implies, sets out the details as to zoning issues, building restrictions, and other infrastructure information. The comprehensive plan is not legally binding for subsequent land use decisions, but rather is viewed as advisory. However, the detailed plan is binding. Building permits issued for individual properties also define the use of a specific property unit in addition to these two general documents.

Any significant change in a property unit requires a building permit. A change can be new construction, modification of the property unit or its use, or demolition. In certain cases, simply the intended new use of a building can require a new permit (and often a change in the detailed plan) even where no changes are made to the actual physical structure of the building, depending on that stated in the detailed plan and prior permits with respect to the permitted use of the building.

Municipalities grant building permits for construction, land use modifications and demolitions. The procedure for obtaining a building permit gives neighbors a chance to state their opinions as to the project prior to its commencement. Neighbors are to be given notice of the work before it is begun as well as the opportunity to contest the project. The right for concerned neighbors and other parties to appeal a building permit begins three weeks after service of process. If a neighbor has not been served process as to the application for a building permit, she may have a right to appeal the permit long after the modification or change in use has been put into place.

---

17 For more information on the National Environmental Protection Agency and the right of public access in English, *see* its website at naturvardsverket.se.

If the permit is in violation of a detailed plan, the permit may be revoked upon appeal.

Another limitation as to the exercise of ownership rights is that an owner cannot freely use a property unit for any purpose whatsoever, but only for those purposes permitted by the detailed plan and building permit encompassing the property unit. In addition, an owner can use the property unit only for those purposes not in conflict with certain interests of neighbors. Every individual is to show reasonable consideration for the neighbors of a property unit in her use of the property as prescribed by LC 3:1. The obverse of this limitation is that each property unit owner has an implicit right to quiet enjoyment of her property.

If the owner of a property unit is planning excavation or similar work on the property unit, that owner is to take all measures necessary as set out in the third chapter of the Land Code to prevent damage to other adjacent property units. If the protective measures cost more than the potential harm resulting from the work, the property unit owner can refuse to take such measures and risk paying damages instead.

The assessment of any damages caused by one property owner stemming from work on that property unit to another property unit is regulated by chapter thirty-two of the Environmental Code as discussed below. A security for damage liability can be requested according to the second chapter of the Enforcement Code (*utsökningsbalk* 1981:774),[18] to be deposited with the appropriate county administrative board prior to the commencement of the work.

11.4.3 LIABILITY UNDER THE ENVIRONMENTAL CODE

Chapter thirty-two of the Environmental Code (*miljöbalk* 1998:808)[19] governs damage claims for certain environmental harms and nuisances, as well as other claims by individuals. According to Section 32:1 of the Environmental Code, damages are to be paid for injuries caused by operations on a property

---

18 An English translation of the Enforcement Code is available from the Government Offices of Sweden at sweden.gov.se.

19 An English translation of sections of the Environmental Code is available from the Government Offices of Sweden at sweden.gov.se.

unit to its surroundings, persons or property as well as "pure" economic losses, *i.e.,* damages not directly related to an injury to person or property. Pure economic losses not caused by a criminal act, however, are only to be compensated if the damage is of some significance. Damage caused unintentionally or through negligence is to be compensated only to the extent that the disruption was beyond that which reasonably ought to be tolerated, taking into consideration the circumstances in the area or its existence in general under comparable circumstances.

Damages are to be paid generally in accordance with Section 32:3 of the Environmental Code for harm caused by:

1 Pollution of water areas;
2 Pollution of ground water;
3 Changes in ground water levels;
4 Air pollution;
5 Land pollution;
6 Noise;
7 Vibrations; or
8 Other similar disturbances.

A harm will be deemed to have been caused by one of these disturbances if there is a greater probability, when taking into account the type of disturbance and harm, other possible causes as well as the circumstances in general, that such a causality between the disturbance and the harm exists.

The party liable to pay damages is the party performing the work or allowing it to be performed as owner of the property unit or site leaseholder. If the party is simply a user of the property unit, the user is liable for damages only if the injury was caused intentionally or negligently. In the event that the property unit affected has become completely or partially unusable, the party causing the harm has a right to buy the property unit instead of paying damages.

A party has the right to sue for an injunction against continued work or as to forcing the other party to take precautionary measures in addition to damages. There is also a right to sue as a class action, a fairly recent innovation in Swedish procedural law in general. An additional procedural innovation in this chapter in the Environmental Code has been allowing standing for interests groups in such actions.

11.4.4 EXPROPRIATION

The ultimate restriction in relation to real property ownership is expropriation. Expropriations, takings or eminent domain, are also regulated outside of the Land Code, by both the Instrument of Government and the Expropriation Act (*expropriationslag* 1972:719). The right to compensation in cases of expropriation is guaranteed by Article 15 of second chapter of the Instrument of Government:

> The property of every person is to be secured so that no person can be compelled to surrender his or her property through expropriation or other procedures to the state or a private person, or to tolerate restrictions by the state as to the use of land or buildings, other than those necessary to satisfy compelling public interests.
>
> A person compelled to surrender property by expropriation or other such procedure is to be guaranteed compensation for his or her loss. Such compensation is also to be guaranteed to any person whose use of land or buildings is restricted by the state in such a manner that continued land use in part of the property affected is substantially impaired, or harm results that is significant in relation to the value of that part of the property. The amount of compensation is to be determined based on grounds as stated by law.

Only a brief presentation of the regulations concerning expropriation is given here to supplement the depiction of the system as set out in the Land Code.

Expropriation under the act can be with respect to ownership, user rights or easements. Specific rights to a property unit can also be terminated or limited if the rights are possessed by a party other than the state, with the exception of rights as to reindeer grazing or access to roads. The decision as to whether property is to be expropriated is to be made by the Government. This authority can be delegated to a county administrative board or other authority to decide where the application is not contested or the decision is of minor importance with respect to public and private interests.

An application for expropriating property is to be submitted in writing, stating the matter and circumstances upon which the decision is to be based, identifying the property units concerned as well as the names and addresses of all concerned property unit holders. The decision granting the expropriation is to state the extent of the expropriation as well as the rights thereto granted.

If the right of ownership is expropriated, any voluntarily granted rights in the property unit are also extinguished unless otherwise determined by the expropriation decision or by a court. Involuntary rights in the property, such as involuntary easements, remain with the property unless the expropriation decision states otherwise. Most mortgages and claims cease to be valid with an expropriation. A user right or easement created through expropriation in the majority of cases has a better right than those already existing in the property unit.

Compensation is to be paid in most expropriation cases. If the entire property unit is expropriated, the governing rule is compensation at the fair market value of the property unit. If only a part of the property unit is expropriated, compensation is to be paid for the decrease in the value of the property unit suffered as a result of the expropriation. If the owner of the property unit is caused other harm by the expropriation, this can also be compensated in certain cases.

In the event that the underlying reason for the expropriation has affected the value of the property unit, compensation is to be based on the market value that the property unit would have had if not for the reason, but only to the extent that such is fair taking into consideration the circumstances in the area or the general effect of such actions in similar situations. In addition, any increases in the market value of the property unit in the most recent ten to fifteen years attributable to the expectation of the project that is the basis for the expropriation, as a rule, are not to be included in the compensation. An expropriation decision becomes void if not brought to a land and environment court for a determination of compensation within one year. This was a legislative amendment due to criticism by the European Court of

Human Rights[20] for the delays in payment, which could be years, previously typical in expropriation cases.

11.4.5 PREEMPTION RIGHTS

Another limitation in exercising ownership rights to property units in Sweden occurs with respect to preemption rights, which can be seen as the obverse of expropriation. With expropriation, the state takes property from the owner for compensation. With preemption rights, certain groups are entitled to purchase a property unit instead of an intended buyer. Different categories of groups have had this statutory preemption right under Swedish law: the municipalities, lessees under an agricultural land lease combined with a residence or a residential land lease, and housing cooperatives and cooperative rental associations as discussed above. However, the preemption rights of municipalities were abolished with the repeal of the Preemption Act (*förköpslag* 1967:868) in 2010.

Preemption rights, or a right of first refusal, is prescribed by law with respect to purchasing certain types of property. The general procedure is that the preemption right allows the right holder to generally acquire the property unit on the same terms and conditions as agreed upon between the seller and a buyer. In most cases, the right must be exercised within a certain time from the buyer's application as to ownership registration, or notice is to be put in the real estate register. Certain restrictions exist typically with respect

---

20 Sweden has been brought to the European Court of Human Rights for violations of the European Convention with respect to several issues concerning real property law. One of the first of these cases is *Sporrong and Lönnroth v. Sweden*, judgment dated 23 September 1982, Series A No. 52, where the Court first formulated a fair balance test in issues of expropriation, holding that an idea of proportionality was inherent in the Convention. *Sporrong* involved leave to expropriate property that was in effect for 23 and 8 years respectively, prohibiting construction by the owner on the properties in question during those periods. The Court held that there had been a violation of Article 1 of Protocol No. 1 due to the long duration in which the property was under the threat of expropriation, even though an expropriation never took place.

to when the right cannot be exercised as being too unfair, for example, to the seller or buyer. Preemption rights with respect to tenants are discussed in more detail in Chapter Eighteen below.

11.5 Conveying Property Units

Chapter Four of the Land Code governs derivative ownership, the conveyance of a property unit by purchase (LC 4:1–27), exchange (LC 4:28) or gift (LC 4:29–31). It should be noted that in addition to the provisions in the Land Code regarding the validity of a transfer of real estate, certain general principles of contract law may have a bearing on the validity of real estate contracts, including Sections 28–33 and 36 of the Contracts Act (*lag 1915:218 om avtal och andra rättshandlingar på förmögenhetsrättens område*) as discussed in Chapter Nine.

11.5.1 DOCUMENTATION REGARDING A TRANSFER BY SALE

General Swedish contract law is characterized by its lack of requirements with respect to formalities. The parties to a contract are free to enter into oral or written agreements with little required other than their names, the object of the contract identified and the quantity of goods or services. The other terms and conditions of the contract can be derived from gap-filling legislation, custom or usage. Real estate purchase agreements are one of the few exceptions to this contractual freedom from form, with the legislation imposing a requirement of a writing as well as rather rigorous form requirements. The other deviation from general contract law with respect to real estate transactions is that an offer to sell, or an option to purchase, real estate in the future is not binding on the parties. This is in contrast to the main rule in general Swedish contract law that an offer is binding unless stated otherwise.

The sale of real estate often involves two documents, a purchase agreement and purchase deed. However, there is no legal requirement of two documents, the transaction can be validly performed with only one, typically the purchase agreement. The purchase agreement usually includes the terms of the purchase, meeting the requirements as stated below. The second document, the purchase deed, is usually drafted by the seller when the requirements of the purchase agreement have been fulfilled, typically upon payment of the purchase price. If the purchase agreement fulfills the form requirements below, the sale is valid. If the subsequent purchase deed is defective with respect to these requirements, the sale is still valid according to the purchase agreement, and the deed then functions more as a receipt rather than an admission of performance.

Mandatory Form Requirements

A real estate purchase agreement, deed or other documentation for the purchase of real estate must be evidenced by a writing and signed by the seller and buyer. The writing is to identify both the parties to and the object of the sale, and include the actual purchase price. The inclusion of the requirement as to the actual purchase price is for tax purposes. Stamp duty is imposed on the purchase price. In addition, real property is subject to property taxes. A tax value is ascribed most property units, targeted at approximately three-fourths of the actual value of the property.

Any agreement as to price not reflected in the purchase agreement is invalid as far as the relationship between the parties is concerned. The reason for parties falsifying the purchase price in this manner is usually tax evasion, avoiding either stamp duties, capital gains taxes or real estate taxes. However, if the invalidity of a side agreement becomes too onerous for one of the parties, the price in the document may be adjusted taking into consideration the circumstances at the time of the agreement and the circumstances subsequently in general.

The document must also contain a declaration by the seller of the intent to transfer the property. Usually simply one of the terms "sale," "give" or "exchange" is seen as sufficient by the courts to designate such an intent. As long as any of the form requirements under LC 4:1 are not fulfilled, the parties are not bound to sell nor buy the property unit, nor are they liable for damages.

There is no explicit requirement in chapter four in the Land Code as to witnesses with respect to a purchase agreement. A new owner of a property unit is to register new ownership within three months of the conveyance of ownership. The absence of witness signatures can be a basis for declaring the registration application inactive according to chapter twenty of the Land

Code. Another requirement not included in chapter four but which can also come into play when registering new ownership is the need for consent by a spouse or cohabitee. Spouses and cohabitees have certain rights with respect to the couples' mutual residence that are protected in other legislation, specifically Section 7:5 of the Marriage Code (*äktenskapsbalk* 1987:230) and Section 22 of the Cohabitees Act (*sambolag* 2003:376). These statutes mandate the consent of the other spouse or cohabitee as to any transfer of real property that constitutes the couple's mutual home.

Mandatory Inclusion for Validity

Certain terms with respect to the purchase of real estate are not valid unless they are specifically included in the purchase agreement. The following terms do not have to be included in an agreement, but if they are to be a valid part of the transaction, they must be included in the agreement:

1 Conditions for the execution or completion of the acquisition;
2 A condition that the seller has no further obligations with respect to any repossession by a third party from the buyer; or
3 Restrictions in the buyer's right to transfer the property unit or register a mortgage or in another way dispose over the property.

A term entailing that the purchase will not be completed within two years from the date of the agreement is not valid. If the fulfillment of the term is for a period longer than two years, the purchase (not only the provision) is void. However, a condition based on the payment of the purchase price, subdivision of the property or other legal requirement is permissible if for longer than two years. If the period within which any of the above conditions must be performed is not specified, it is deemed to be two years.

If the purchase agreement prescribes that a purchase deed is to be drafted, this is deemed to mean that the execution or performance of the acquisition is conditioned upon the payment of the purchase price. If the performance or execution of the real estate purchase is conditioned upon certain terms in the real estate purchase agreement, these terms are no longer deemed a condition for the acquisition in the event a purchase deed is drafted not including the term. In other words, the drafting of a purchase deed without the term is an implicit affirmation by the seller that all the necessary conditions for the purchase as stated in the purchase agreement have been fulfilled.

11.5.2 TRANSFERS REGARDING PART OF A PROPERTY UNIT

Private agreements as to subdividing (*avstyckning*) or merging (*samman-läggning*) property units are invalid. Section 4:7 of the Land Code reaffirms this, stating that a purchase concerning only a part of a property unit is valid only if the partitioning of the property unit is done in accordance with law. An application for partitioning the property unit must be made within six months from the date of the purchase agreement. In the event an application for partitioning is not submitted during this period, partitioning proceedings are to be commenced based on the terms and conditions in the purchase agreement. A party purchasing a part of a property unit without the condition that the part is to be partitioned from the property unit in accordance with the law will be deemed a tenant in common with the seller for the entire property unit.

11.6 The Rights and Obligations of Sellers and Buyers

The bulk of the provisions in chapter four of the Land Code concern the rights and obligations of sellers and buyers, and the allocation of the risk as to defects. The basic rule is that the risk for defects in the property unit passes to the buyer when the buyer assumes possession of the property unit. Sections 4:11–19c concerning defects are mandatory in that they cannot be contracted away by the parties where the seller is a business entity and the buyer a consumer purchasing the property for private use.

11.6.1 ALLOCATION OF RISK

Any yields, leasing or rental fees or any other revenues derived from the property unit before the agreed upon date of possession accrue to the seller unless otherwise agreed by the parties. In addition, the seller may only cut wood for household purposes and reap crops in a customary manner. The buyer is to pay any fees levied on the property unit after the closing date. The buyer is also responsible for the payment of stamp duties with respect to the acquisition as far as the relationship between the parties is concerned.[21] Stamp duties are assessed on the highest of either the purchase price or tax value at a rate of 1.5% for private persons and certain legal persons, such as housing cooperatives and the estates of decedents, and generally 4.25 % for most legal persons.

The seller bears the risk for the property unit while the property unit is in the seller's possession. As a rule, the risk passes to the buyer upon the buyer's possession of the property unit. However, the risk can also pass to the buyer where the property unit is not in the possession of the buyer, despite the agreed upon date of possession having passed, if the failure to take possession is due to a delay by the buyer. In such cases, the seller still has a duty of care with respect to the property unit.

If the seller fails to vacate the property unit in due time, the buyer is entitled to compensation and can even cancel the purchase[22] if the delay is of material significance. The seller is to provide the buyer with any related surveys or other documentation with respect to the property unit that can be of significance to the buyer. If the documentation also concerns another property unit, it is to be submitted upon request by the buyer.

In the event the property unit is accidentally damaged or is in a worsened condition due to an event for which the seller has the risk, the buyer has the right to a price reduction. If the damage is of material significance, the buyer has the right to terminate the purchase agreement. If the property

---

21 According to Section 27 of the Stamp Duty Act (*lag 1984:404 om stämpelskatt vid inskrivningsmyndigheter*), both parties are jointly and severally liable for any stamp duties due on the purchase price. If the seller has to pay the stamp duties to the state, she can demand compensation from the buyer pursuant to LC 4:10 unless otherwise agreed.

22 If the buyer has registered or conveyed a mortgage in the property unit, the buyer can only cancel the purchase if she has paid so much of the purchase price that the seller can retain an amount equal to that for which the property unit has become encumbered. If this amount is not sufficient, the buyer cannot cancel the purchase unless she pays the difference. If more than one property unit is encumbered, the amount has to be sufficient for the joint liability. Where the buyer has granted rights to a third party that have materially reduced the value or use of the property unit for the seller, or if the property unit has materially deteriorated due to another act of the buyer, the buyer may only cancel if the seller receives compensation for the reduction in value.

unit is damaged or its condition deteriorates after the purchase due to the seller's negligence or intent, the buyer also has the right to damages. In both cases, there is a one-year statute of limitations with respect to terminating the purchase agreement, commencing on the date of possession. This statute of limitations is not applicable where the seller has been grossly negligent or acted in violation of faith and honor.

11.6.2 PHYSICAL DEFECTS

In addition to the defects as stated above, a seller can be liable for certain other defects arising after the risk has passed to the buyer. Two such categories of defects with a property unit can be identified, the first defects having to do with the physical condition of the property unit, tangible defects. The second is a catch-all category where the defects tend to be intangible. These include defects in the chain of ownership with respect to the property unit, impediments caused by the seller with respect to registration of ownership, and limitations as to use of the property unit due to governmental or private action.

Before the 1970 Land Code, the seller generally was liable only for defects falling within those warranties explicitly stated in the purchase agreement, with the general principle *caveat emptor* applicable to the highest degree. This has successively given way to a more nuanced allocation of risk between the seller and buyer, with the seller now liable for certain latent defects as seen in Sections 4:19–19d. However, the buyer still has a far-reaching duty to inspect the premises, the failure of which can act as a bar to asserting certain claims for defects.

Where the property unit is not in the condition that can be assumed from the purchase agreement, or otherwise deviates from that which the buyer could reasonably assume at the time of the purchase, the buyer has the right to a price reduction. Defects can be measured as against contracted terms, or certain universal standards, much as an implied warranty of habitability. Defects can also be based on statements made by the seller other than in the contract, but a line is drawn in the Swedish case law between statements meant as warranties with resulting legal rights and obligations, and those statements that must be seen as simply marketing , puffery or hyperbole.

If the defect is of material significance, the buyer can cancel the purchase. There is a one-year statute of limitation with respect to any lawsuit concerning the cancellation of the purchase, commencing on the date of possession. In addition, the buyer has the right to compensation for damages, if the defect or loss depends on negligence by the seller or where the property unit deviated from that which the seller had represented. There is a ten-year statute of limitation with respect to monetary damages for latent defects.

A buyer is barred from alleging any defects the buyer ought to have discovered upon an inspection of the property unit, taking into account the property unit's condition, the normal condition of comparable property units as well as the circumstances with respect to the purchase.

11.6.3 INTANGIBLE DEFECTS

Three categories of intangible defects arising with respect to the transfer of ownership to a property unit are addressed in chapter four of the Land Code: impediments to registration due to a failure by the seller, third-party claims to the property unit; and limitations that can arise due to governmental or third-party actions.

Impediments to Registration

If the seller fails without cause to execute a purchase deed or any other obligation as required by the purchase agreement so that the buyer can lawfully be registered as owner, the buyer is entitled to compensation or to cancel the purchase if the impediment is of material significance.

If the buyer is unable to register ownership in cases other than those as stated above, and the failure is not due to the buyer or a reason known to her at the time of the purchase, she has the right to cancel the purchase and claim damages if the harm is of material significance. The statute of limitations, which despite its apparent wording only applies to the right to terminate the agreement and not to the right to damages, is one-year from the day when the time for application of ownership has expired, or a negative decision as to such has been issued, unless the seller has acted with gross negligence or in violation of faith and honor.

Third-Party Rights

A seller in certain cases has a duty to protect user rights, and in a parallel manner, a buyer cannot terminate certain user rights that are statutorily protected. The rules can generally be considered as follows:

1 Registered rights always prevail against any new owner;
2 The seller has a duty to preserve any unregistered rights of third parties in the purchase agreement with the buyer. If the seller fails to do this, she can be liable for damages as to the third party;
3 Certain rights are protected even if not registered or included in the purchase agreement as against the new owner. Included here are tenancies in which the agreement is evidenced by a writing and the tenant has assumed possession of the premises; and
4 The rights of the third party in certain cases will be protected as against a new owner if the new owner is in bad faith, either the new owner knew about the right or had reason to know about the right despite the fact it was not registered, included in the purchase agreement, or protected by statute.

In the event the property unit is encumbered by mortgages or rights exceeding those assumed at the time of the purchase, the buyer has the right to retain a part of the purchase price equivalent to the difference between the amount paid and the value of the property unit with the right. If little of the purchase price remains and the seller does not pay the difference within one month of being requested to do so, the buyer has the right to cancel the purchase and receive compensation for damages.

If a third party successfully claims a better right to the property unit as against the buyer, the buyer has the right to a return of the purchase price, and if the buyer was in good faith, also a right to compensation for damages. If the third party successfully claims a better right to only a part of the property unit, the buyer has the right, if in good faith, to cancel the purchase of the entire property unit and receive compensation for damages. The statute of limitations is then to run from the date upon which the right of the third party prevailed with respect to that part of the property unit unless the seller has been grossly negligent or acted in violation of faith and honor. If the seller is unable to comply with the provisions above, the buyer has the right to demand repayment from any third party receiving proceeds to the extent that that party is not freed from liability. To the extent the buyer has not paid the full purchase price when a claim of ownership is made by a third party, the buyer has the right to retain a part of the purchase price as security for the performance of the seller in the event the suit is successful.

The same rights and obligations as in the preceding paragraph are to be applicable where the purchase agreement cannot be fulfilled due to the property unit being assigned to a third party, and that assignment has precedence. The statute of limitations in such a case is one-year from the day when the time for application of ownership has expired or a negative decision as to such has been issued, unless the seller has been grossly negligent or acted in violation of faith and honor. When a lawsuit as to competing claims has been filed, the buyer has the right to retain a part of the purchase price as security for the performance of the seller in the event the suit is successful.

Limitations in Use

If a government authority issues a decision negative to the buyer's ownership rights that the buyer did not have reason to foresee at the time of the purchase, the buyer may cancel the purchase and claim damages if the consequences of the decision are of material significance. The decision must be in effect as of the date of the execution of the contract.

11.6.4 NOTICE AS TO DEFECT

The buyer forfeits the right to claim that the property unit has a defect that arose when the seller bore the risk for the property unit due to the seller's negligent or intentional act (LC 4:12), due to third-party rights (LC 4:17) or to a failure to conform to the contract or express or implied warranties (LC 4:19) where the buyer does not notify the seller as to the defect within a reasonable time after noting or ought to having noted the defect. However, if the seller has been grossly negligent or has acted in violation of faith and honor, the buyer still has a right despite any failure to notify. If the buyer has sent notification in an appropriate manner, the notification can be cited even if it is delayed, incorrectly reworded or not received. The statute of limitations for a claim of defect in a property unit is ten years from the date of possession, if not tolled before then.

Any reduction in the purchase price is to be calculated so that the relationship between the reduced and contracted purchase price is proportionate to the relationship between the property unit's non-conforming and contracted conditions at the point of time of the possession of the property unit.

11.6.5 BUYER'S FAILURE TO PAY

The purchase may be cancelled by the seller due to a failure by the buyer to pay the purchase price where such a provision has been included in the purchase agreement. The buyer is to compensate the seller for any damages. In the event the seller has the right to interest with respect to the purchase price, the Interest Act (*räntelagen* 1975:635) is applicable. There otherwise is no statutory right for repossession.

The seller has the right to cancel the purchase and claim damages in accordance with Section 4:26 only if such a provision has been made in the purchase agreement in the event the buyer is placed into bankruptcy, debt renegotiations, execution, stops payments or in other cases can be considered insolvent so as to be unable to make the payment.

11.7 Registration of Ownership

National land registration systems typically fall into one of two categories with respect to registration of ownership and other rights, a deed registration system that historically has been predominant in common law countries, and an ownership (title) registration system, such as the Torrens system. The deed registration system incurs very low costs for the state. The state makes no affirmative statements as to the ownership of a property, but simply records any documents filed related to that property. It is the task of the individual (whether purchaser or creditor) to determine, at their own cost and risk, who has the best ownership rights in the property based on the documents in the file. Under the ownership registration system, the state makes an affirmative statement, to a greater or lesser extent, as to who the owner of the property is. The disadvantage with this system is the greater cost incurred by the state in comparison to a deed registration system. The advantage naturally is the degree of greater certainty with respect to land ownership and rights.

The Swedish land register falls within the ownership registration category. The National Land Survey (*Lantmäteriet*) manages and develops the Real Property Register (*fastighetsregistret*), the Mortgage Deeds Register (*pantbrevsregistret*) and the Joint Facility Property Management Association Register (*samfällighetsföreningsregistret*). These are updated primarily by the cadastral and land registration authorities with the cadastral authorities providing the cadastral information, while the land registration authorities provide registration information such as to ownership, mortgages and rights. The interests that can be registered are ownership, user rights, easements and mortgages. The public had free access to the register prior to 2000 based on the constitutional principle of public access to official documents. After 2000, access to the register has been restricted in order to comply with the requirements of EU law as to privacy and electronic communications to basically parties that can demonstrate a need for having the information, such as banks or potential purchasers.[23]

Once ownership is registered, this means that the person named as owner of the property unit is the owner of that property as backed by a certain liability for damages by the state. The state does not fully guarantee that the registered owner is the owner, making Sweden less than a complete ownership registration system. A party who has suffered harm due to a technical mistake in the Land Register Section or another system connected to it at a land registration authority, by a registration authority, cadastral authority or other authority as encompassed by Section 4:34a of the Real Property Formation Act, has the right to damages. The right to damages for human mistakes is not regulated by the Land Code, but rather by third chapter of the Tort Liability Act (*skadeståndslag* 1972:207), which governs state tort liability. In the event of an unlawful disclosure of private information, damages are regulated by

---

23 Directive 95/46/EC of the European Parliament and of the Council on the protection of individuals with regard to the processing of personal data and on the free movement of such data and later Directive 2002/58/EC of the European Parliament and of the Council concerning the processing of personal data and the protection of privacy in the electronic communications sector.

the Personal Data Privacy Act (*personuppgiftslag* 1998:204).[24] The amount of compensation for any technical error can be reduced or entirely nullified if deemed fair where the injured party has contributed to the harm by failing to take action without good cause to protect her rights, or where the injured party has been contributorily negligent.

The issue of whether a conveyance is valid or for any other reason cannot be asserted may be tried even if the conveyance has been registered. Registration does not impede an assessment of whether the registration conflicts with the rights of another party. However, where specific regulations prescribe the legal effects of a registration or that a complaint is to be filed within a certain time, those regulations are applicable. This provision is what demarcates the Swedish land registration system from a pure title registration system in that registration as such is not complete and exclusive evidence of ownership.

In the event the party claiming ownership cannot submit documentation evidencing ownership, or the documentation is deficient, the land registration authority is to set up a meeting upon the request of the applicant of all interested parties to investigate the ownership of the property unit (*lagfartssammanträde*). The land registration authority is to summon the applicant and other interested parties, or their representatives, to a meeting at which a decision is to be made as to who the rightful owner is.

There has been a problem with the registration procedures in that it has been possible for a party to register a falsified document referring either to a sale or gift, and based on that falsified document, become the registered owner of a property unit (colloquially referred to as ownership hijacking or *lagfartskapning*). The purpose of such fraud is either to sell the property unit later or, which is more likely, to obtain loans using the property unit as collateral. The former is more difficult to achieve in actuality as the buyer in most cases should want to inspect the premises, and the true owner would most likely still be in possession of the premises. However, if the property is a recreational cabin or other property vacant at certain times during the year, such fraud is fairly simple. If the fraudulent party succeeds in obtaining a mortgage deed on the property unit, and uses the deed as collateral for a loan, the deed runs with the property unit, not the person, entailing that the

---

24 An English translation of this act is available from the Swedish Data Inspection Board at www.datainspektionen.se/in-english/legislation/the-personal-data-act.

true property owner has liability for the monies lent based on the mortgage deed. The state has accepted liability to pay damages in cases where true owners are harmed by this type of registration by a fraudulent party. The National Land Survey also now has a service whereby property unit owners can check the information as to their property unit on the National Land Survey's website for any inaccuracies.

11.8 Competing Ownership or Rights Claims

Competing ownership or user claims in general can be seen to arise in three different types of situations, adverse possession of a property unit by a party other than the true owner, double conveyances of a property unit by the true owner, and the transfer to a bona fide purchaser by a party other than the true owner, as regulated by chapters sixteen, seventeen and eighteen of the Land Code, respectively. This section ends with the provisions regarding the legal ramifications of being dispossessed by the rightful owner.

11.8.1 ADVERSE POSSESSION

Chapter sixteen of the Land Code addresses ownership claims based on adverse possession. If a party has obtained ownership registration to a property unit that has passed out of the hands of the rightful owner, and thereafter for a period of twenty consecutive years possesses the property without any claim of a better ownership right being asserted, that party has the best claim to the property under LC 16:1 due to her adverse possession. Where the possession was based on a transfer, and the possessor neither knew nor ought to have known that the transferor was not the true owner, the same is true except that the period is shortened to ten years instead of twenty. These provisions are also applicable where a property has been held by several consecutive parties. The requirement as to being a registered owner or executing a transfer in good faith is then applicable only to the first possessor.

11.8.2 PRIORITY OF COMPETING RIGHTS BASED ON REGISTRATION

Chapter seventeen of the Land Code contains the regulations applicable as to the precedence between competing rights based on conveyances by the true owner of the property unit or grants of user rights, easements or rights to electrical power based on registration. The general rule is that where a property unit has been transferred, or a user right, easement or electrical power right in the property unit has been granted to several parties, the first party to register the right in good faith has the best right with certain exceptions.

11.8.3 BONA FIDE PURCHASERS

Chapter eighteen addresses bona fide purchasers. If a property unit has been acquired by transfer and the transferor was not the rightful owner of the property due to her or a previous party's unlawful possession, the acquisition is valid if the transferor's application for ownership registration has been approved and the transferee, at the time of the transfer, was in good faith, in other words neither knew nor ought to have known that the transferor was not the rightful owner.[25] The same is applicable to grants of user rights, easements or a right to electrical power made by a party not the rightful owner of the property due to her or a previous party's unlawful possession, if the right holder at the time of the grant was in good faith.

If a security interest in a property unit has been conveyed, and the assignor was not the true owner of the property unit due to her or a predecessor's unlawful possession, where the assignor's interest in the property was registered and the creditor was in good faith at the time of the assignment, the security interest is valid.

However, the above provisions are not applicable where:

1   The documents upon which the ownership rights are based are forged or issued by a party lacking such legal authority or are invalid due to such duress as encompassed by Section 28 of the Contracts Act;
2   The rightful owner, when executing the documents upon which the right of ownership is based, was in bankruptcy, lacked legal capacity, was under the influence of a psychological disturbance, or had been appointed a guardian in accordance with the Parental Code (*föräldrabalk* 1949:381); or

---

25   Executive auctions are exempted from this provision as stated in LC 18:1.

3   The acquisition is invalid under the law, as it was not taken in the
    prescribed form or by observing other legal requirements or with the
    consent of another whose right was affected or with the permission or
    other act by a court or authority.

In the event the acquisition is found to be valid against the rightful owner, the
rightful owner has a right to compensation from the state for her loss. Where
the rightful owner has contributed to the loss by a failure to take measures
to protect her rights without good reason, or in another manner contributed
to the loss through her own fault, the compensation can be reduced or set at
null based on that which is found to be reasonable. A party whose acquisition
is found not enforceable against a rightful owner also has a right to compensation if she at the time of the acquisition was in good faith as to that the
transferor or grantor was not the rightful owner.

11.8.4 DISPOSSESSION BY A BETTER RIGHT

The rights and obligations between a party found to be in wrongful possession
of a property unit and a rightful owner are governed in the fifth chapter of
the Land Code. The dispossessed party is to compensate the true owner for
any yields that the property generated during a certain period. The period
commences on the date upon which the better claim was made known, or
service of process completed, until the dispossessed party no longer is in
possession of the property unit.

Compensation is also to be paid for any leasing fees, rents or other
revenues derived from the property unit during this period. However, the
dispossessed party may deduct any reasonable compensation for those
costs that have arisen in generating the yields and revenues as well as for
maintaining the property during this period. If the yields or income have
been less than that which reasonably could be generated due to the negligence
of the party possessing the property unit, that party is to compensate the true
owner for the difference.

Where the property unit has been damaged or in another manner reduced
in value due to a measure or other circumstance attributable to the party
possessing the property unit, that party is to pay the true owner compen-

sation for the decrease in value to the extent this is not unfair, taking into consideration the party's actions and circumstances in general.

The prevailing party is to compensate the dispossessed party for any necessary costs that the dispossessed party has had for the maintenance of the property during the period in which that party held the property and for expenditures regarding improvements where such were not made after the party wrongfully possessing the property unit knew of the better claim. Compensation for improvements is to be paid only for the amount by which the property unit has increased in value. If the dispossessed party has incurred expenses for measures other than those necessary for the property unit, and these measures can be removed from the property unit, she may do so unless the party having the better claim wishes to buy that property out.

Any property not removed within three months after the buyout offer was refused or from its expiry becomes the property of the prevailing party without any obligation to pay for it. The party vacating the property unit may not remove any property from the premises without the consent of the true owner before providing a security for any liability or paying such liability. The property is to be restored to its former state after any removal by the dispossessed party.

11.9 Dispute Resolution

The alternatives to litigation encouraged as means for resolving legal issues are set out in the Land Code and other legislation. These include giving land surveyors legal authority to decide certain legal issues as seen above, for example, with respect to determining property boundaries or ownership of a property unit. In addition, alternative courts have been established, such as the land and environment courts (*mark- och miljödomstolar*) and the Land and Environment Court of Appeal (*Mark- och miljööverdomstolen*) discussed in this section, and the tribunals, the Regional Tenancies Tribunals (*Arrendenämnden*) addressed in Chapter Seventeen and the Regional Rent Tribunals (*Hyresnämnden*) in Chapter Eighteen below.

Certain property issues and appeals concerning real property decisions are to be brought to one of the five land and environment courts. According to the Regulation on the Scope of Competence for Land and Environment

Courts (*förordning 2010:984 om mark-och miljödomstolarnas domsområden*), the general courts in Umeå, Östersund, Nacka, Växjö and Vänersborg are to have land and environment courts, which are to hear those cases as referred to it by specific statutes. The land and environment courts are housed in the same buildings as the general courts. A panel for a land and environment court consists of legally trained judges, and can include technical advisors who are employees of the court as well as other experts. One of the legally trained members is to chair the judging panel. The legally trained members are to be selected from the judges sitting in the general courts. Any technical member are to have technical training and experience in land formation or valuation, and often are land surveyors. The expert lay members are to have good knowledge of the conditions of their geographic areas and are appointed by the county administrative board. The chair of the judging panel can order that one or more of the members of the panel physically inspect a site. Typical cases taken to the land and environment courts include issues concerning:

- permits for waterworks operations as well as environmentally harmful operations;
- protection of the public health, environmental protection, sanitation, contaminated areas and toxic waste;
- damages and compensation with environmental aspects;
- building, demolition and site improvements in accordance with planning and building laws;
- site leasehold rights;
- appeals of planning matters;
- property registration, construction and utility easements; and
- expropriation.

Appeals of the decisions by any of the five land and environment courts are to be filed with the Land and Environment Court of Appeal (*Mark- och miljööverdomstolen*). This court was established in 2011 as a unit within the Svea Court of Appeal. The mandate of this court is to assess these cases "against the background of the overarching objective of promoting a sustainable societal development entailing an appropriate use of land and that present and future generations will be ensured a healthy and good environment."[26] The court of appeal is also to have a technical advisor sit on the panel hearing these appeals, unless this is found evidently unnecessary. Two technical advisors can sit on the panel if needed. The chair of the panel in the court of appeal also has the authority to order a site inspection.

---

26 Taken from the Court's website at www.svea.se/Svea-hovratt/Miljooverdomstolen/.

CHAPTER 12

Tort and Insurance Law

Placing both tort and insurance law within the same chapter may be an unusual structure, but to understand either system within Swedish law, they must be understood together. During the 1970's, the emphasis in both criminal law and tort law was intentionally redirected from punitive objectives to reparation and rehabilitation, with deterrence also naturally attributed a lesser role. A system was created with the objective of harms being compensated, not through tort litigation, but through insurance. To such an end, an extensive insurance system was created that included many types of no-fault insurance. Losses were to be distributed over as wide a spectrum (or group) as possible. The stance was that tortfeasors should not be bankrupted by liability for large amounts simply for making mistakes. This approach still very much affects assessments of liability and damages as made by the courts today. There was no statutory tort law to speak of until the Tort Liability Act (*skadeståndslag* 1972:207) was enacted in the early 1970's. Prior to that, tort claims were based on the 1864 Penal Punishment Act (*strafflag*).[1]

12.1 Torts

Torts, civil wrongs not arising out of contractual duties, are typically classified as intentional and unintentional, the latter including negligence and strict liability. Intentional torts are not explicitly defined in Swedish civil law, but rather, the criminal code is still indirectly used as the basis. This is not to say that certain types of intentional torts do not exist in the Swedish legal

---

1   The 1864 Act was in effect until 1965 when the present Penal Code came into effect. During the seven-year period between 1965 and the passage of the Tort Liability Act in 1972, claims could be based on the new Penal Code. The 1864 Act had in its turn replaced the 1734 Penal Punishment Codes (*straffbalken* and *missgärningsbalken*).

system, such as defamation or battery, but that the legal basis for such are mostly defined in the Penal Code and other criminal statutes.

The Tort Liability Act is a framework statute, entailing that it sets out broad principles, leaving it to the courts to determine their application and establish further principles. The courts can impose strict liability, but do this rarely in the absence of a statute imposing strict liability.

There are three stages with respect to an assessment of damages under the Tort Liability Act:

1   The assessment of liability;
2   Determining the amount of compensation; and
3   Assessing whether there should be any reductions in the compensation awarded.

12.1.1 THE ASSESSMENT OF LIABILITY

Liability is imposed under Section 2:1 of the Tort Liability Act: "A party who has intentionally or negligently caused injury to a person or property is to compensate for the injury." The courts have found this sentence to contain several requisites that need to be proven in order to hold a party liable in tort under the act:

1   There must be an act or omission;
2   A person or property must have suffered a compensable harm;
3   The act or omission is not excused;
4   Adequate causality must exist between the act and the harm; and
5   The party causing the injury must have acted either intentionally or negligently.

If all these requisites are proven, tort liability can be imposed. The first four of these requisites are objective, in that they are assessed against objective standards, while the fifth is subjective, assessed against the state of mind of the tortfeasor.

Act or Omission

That an act has been committed is an objective assessment not too difficult to prove. There is a general duty under Swedish law to act in a manner that does not harm others. An omission, however, is a different assessment. There is no general duty under Swedish law for a person to act. In other words, if a person is in need of assistance, there is no duty to assist. Tort liability based on an omission to act is imposed only if there is a specific duty to act. An example here would be the omission of a parent as to supervising a child as set out in the Parental Code or preventing a child from committing a crime where no danger existed to the parent in doing so. Another failure to act would be where a real estate owner fails to keep rooftops and eaves free from ice as required by law.

Injury

Third-party injuries are not recoverable as a rule except when allowed by statute in the Swedish system. There are four types of injuries for which liability can be imposed, the first two being as stated in the Tort Liability Act, injury caused to person or property. Injuries to persons are either physical or psychological as can be medically proven, as well as loss of income. Injury to property includes both physical injury to the property itself, as well as loss of use of the property.

"Pure" economic loss (*ren förmögenhetsskada*) is the third category of injuries and is not recoverable in most cases unless by statute or where the tortfeasor has acted criminally. Pure economic loss is defined in Section 1:2 of the Tort Liability Act as such losses arising that do not have a connection with an injury to a person or property. This is an intentional limitation in damage liability, the premise being that pure economic losses are not in the same need of protection as injuries to persons or property. According to Section 2:2 of the Tort Liability Act, if the act causing the harm is criminal, pure economic losses are to be compensated. An example of a pure economic loss could be seen as defamation of a legal person that leads to loss of business for a firm. Such a loss is a pure economic loss under Swedish law as it does not fall within the definitions of compensable harms to persons or property as a legal person cannot be defamed under Swedish law.

The limitations in the Tort Liability Act with respect to compensation for pure economic losses are not to be seen as a total prohibition as to damages for such harms in cases where no crime has been committed. The legislative history makes it clear that the courts may expand the area in which damages are given for pure economic losses, and that the act is not to be construed restrictively.[2] The courts have cautiously begun to find liability for pure economic losses in contexts other than criminal acts. Two cases that can be mentioned is where the Supreme Court imposed liability for pure economic losses arising from an incorrect real estate valuation (NJA 1987 p. 692) and from a third party's fraudulent acts in collusion with a contracting party taken to harm the other contracting party (NJA 2005 p. 608).

The fourth type of injury consists of acts often falling within a category similar to the common law idea of trespass to persons, non-physical harms caused by acts violative of the rights of that person (*kränkning*). Examples here are harms caused by unlawful discrimination, invasion of privacy or sexual harassment. These intangible harms occur where the privacy, liberty or integrity of a person is violated or harmed. This has been a problematic category for the courts to work with in actuality for several reasons. The consensus is that such harms cannot be measured in economic terms, resulting in the courts being loathe to award damages to any marked extent in civil cases. Another difficulty is that the purpose of this type of damage award is partially compensatory but also deterring, for example with respect to businesses that discriminate. This leaves the courts in the complicated position of perhaps being seen as giving higher damages for such harms than for example, the death of a spouse due to negligence. A recent Supreme Court case found that damages of SEK 5 000 for each plaintiff resulting from unlawful discrimination were sufficient to compensate for the harm caused.[3]

---

2   *See* Legislative Bill 1972:5 at 568.

3   *See* NJA 2008 p. 915. The case concerned unlawful discrimination by a restaurant owner. There was no question that the discrimination had occurred or that it was unlawful. The Supreme Court lowered the trial court's damage award of SEK 20 000 per plaintiff to SEK 5 000 per plaintiff. In addition, the Supreme Court ordered the parties to bear their own legal costs and fees as opposed to the main rule that the losing party, here the restaurant owner, pays the prevailing party's costs and fees. By deviating from the main rule, the Court negated any gains with respect to damages for the plaintiffs as well as reduced the amount of losses for the defendant.

Absence of a Lawful Defense

Defenses that can be asserted as against the imposition of tort liability are the same as those that can be asserted as defenses to criminal acts, specifically those found in chapter twenty-four of the Penal Code. These criminal defenses include self-defense and defense of others, necessity, consent and the duty to obey orders.

Sufficient Causality

To impose tort liability, the act of the tortfeasor must have caused the injury and this causality (*kausalitet* or *orsakssamband*) must be deemed to be sufficient (*adekvat*) and not too remote. The first part of this assessment is a cause-in-fact inquiry, an objective assessment of whether the act was necessary to the inception of the injury (*betingelseläran*) or *conditio sine qua non*. If the injury would have arisen despite the absence of the act, it was not necessary to the injury and thus no liability will be imposed. In a landmark case by the Supreme Court as to this issue, a dog had been chasing a moose.[4] The moose ran out onto the road and caused a traffic accident. The persons injured in the traffic accident sued the owner of the dog. The Supreme Court found that it was not proven that the moose would not have run out onto the road if the dog had not been chasing the moose. The Court dismissed the complaint as it did not find it proven that the chasing by the dog was a cause-in-fact.

The next step with respect to causality is assessing whether the causality can be seen as being sufficient enough in causing the injury to impose liability. This is also an objective assessment that has been summarized as that the injury must lie within the zone of danger (*skadan måste ligga i farans riktning*). If the injury was foreseeable or probable, the tortfeasor will be held liable for damages, as there is a causal relationship between the act and injury, and that relationship is deemed to be sufficiently adequate to impose liability. Another example from the case law is where a train had departed from a station early because the departure signal had been incorrectly given. A woman was in the process of lifting her baby carriage off the train, and upon

---

4 *See* NJA 1983 p. 606.

seeing this, one of the conductors tried to get the attention of the engineer to stop the train. The conductor slipped on some snow, fell under the train and was killed. The Supreme Court found that sufficient causality had not been proven between giving an incorrect departure signal and slipping on snow and being killed by the train in order for tort liability to be imposed.[5]

Intent or Negligence

The subjective requisite is determining whether the tortfeasor has acted in a manner that can be seen as culpable, either through acting intentionally to cause harm or acting in a negligent manner. An intentional act requires simply proof of an intent to harm.

In contrast, negligence must be assessed against a standard of care. There is no tort liability for pure accidents. The standard of care in assessing whether an act has been negligent can be based on statutory requirements imposing duties. In the absence of any such statutory guidance, the late Professor Jan Hellner adopted a standard of care test in negligence based on the American Justice Learned Hand's formula. Learned Hand's formula was that an assessment of negligence should be based on three factors:[6]

- The probability that the harm would occur;
- The cost of the harm; and
- The defendant's cost to avoid the harm.

If the cost to avoid the harm was less than the cost of the harm within a certain degree of probability, then negligence can be found. Professor Hellner added another prong to this test:

- The defendant's ability to foresee the harm.

This fourth prong in essence narrows the scope of liability in certain cases considerably. All four requisites must be proven in order for the tortfeasor to have liability for damages based on negligence. A recent example of

---

5   *See* NJA 1944 p. 164.
6   This standard of care test was articulated by Justice Learned Hand in *United States v. Carroll Towing Co.*, 159 F.2d 169 (2d Cir. 1947).

this can be found in the Supreme Court case, NJA 2011 p. 454, in which an apartment tenant had failed to turn off the water to a counter top dishwasher. The landlord alleged that the tenant should be held liable for the damages resulting from the breaking of the hose running from the countertop dishwasher to the faucet. The Court found that the probability of the hose breaking was not great but that the harm at risk, damage from the water, could be seen as significant. The cost for shutting off the water, avoiding the harm, was nil. However, the tenant did not have the possibility of foreseeing the harm as there were no visible defects in the hose. Consequently, the Court found that she could not be held liable for the damages.

Another standard that can be invoked in the absence of statutory guidance is that of *bonus pater familias,* the good family father. The assessment under that standard is that which a good family father would do in the situation at hand. After a finding of intent or negligence, the next step is to determine the amount of the compensation.

12.1.2 COMPENSATION

The basic rule is that the injured party is to be completely compensated for the injury arising. Punitive damages do not exist under Swedish tort law and hence only general damages can be awarded. No specific guidelines as to damage awards are set out in the Tort Liability Act with respect to the categories of intangible harms and pure economic losses.

The injured party has a duty to take reasonable measures to mitigate any damages under the Tort Liability Act. This issue can arise, for example, with a claim for lost income where the injured party has not made any attempt to find suitable employment if capable of work.

Injuries to Persons

Under the fifth chapter of the Tort Liability Act, compensation for injuries to persons is to include compensation for medical and other costs, for both temporary and permanent physical and psychological suffering, and for loss of income. It should be kept in mind that medical care in Sweden has been socialized. Consequently, the compensation for medical costs is only for those costs that the injured person is required to pay. Certain costs incurred by family members in connection with the injury can also be compensated including the costs of hospital visits.

Loss of income from employment or business covers all income that would have been generated during the period the person is unable to work due to the injury, including revenues from hobbies or costs to replace work typically done in the home. If the personal injury resulted in death, compensation is to be paid for funeral costs, loss of support or maintenance, and any injury to a person near to the deceased.

Injuries to Property

Compensation for injuries to property includes compensation for the value of the property at the time of the damage, the cost of repairs and any reduction in value, other costs arising in connection with the injury, and loss of income from employment or business due to the injury to the property.

Pecuniary and Non-Pecuniary Damages

With respect to general damages as discussed above, a distinction is made between those damages that can be measured in economic terms, pecuniary damages (*ekonomisk skada*), and those damages that cannot be measured in economic terms, non-pecuniary damages (*ideell skada*). Certain types of damages as listed above can obviously be measured in economic terms; medical costs, loss of income, the value of an object, the costs of repair, and naturally pure economic losses.

Non-pecuniary damages arise only with injuries to persons. These are assumed by Swedish law not to be measurable in economic terms, but rather to be of an entirely subjective nature. These posts include pain and suffering, and the injuries termed above as intangible harms. As no objective measurements have been determined within the legal system, the general rule with respect to non-pecuniary is that they only can be awarded when authority to do so is set out by statute. Certain types of injuries, such as to affection or grief, are not compensable.

Different types of non-pecuniary damages can be awarded according to guidelines (*schablonersättning*). For example, the table created by the Swedish

Road Traffic Injuries Commission (*Trafikskadenämnden*)[7] is used by parties and the courts to assess pain and suffering in a range of cases involving traffic accidents. The Labor Court has historically awarded damages for sex discrimination in the range from SEK 15 000 to SEK 50 000. Compensation for intangible harm in criminal cases can vary greatly, from about SEK 5 000 for simple battery to SEK 500 000 for criminal sexual conduct involving children, in addition to any compensation for the physical harm suffered.[8]

12.1.3 REDUCTIONS IN COMPENSATION

In assessing whether the entire amount of compensation is to be paid by the tortfeasor, the court can look at several different factors. If the person causing the harm was suffering from a mental disorder that was not self-induced or temporary at the time of the act, the amount of damages awarded can be reduced or nullified under Section 2:5 of the Tort Liability Act. If the amount of damages is unreasonably burdensome for the defendant in light of her financial circumstances, the amount of the damages can also be reduced or nullified under Section 6:2. The amount of damages can also be reduced in light of any insurance proceeds received by the injured party.

If the tortfeasor is a minor, the standard of care applied in tort is still that of an adult. However, the amount of damages can be reduced, or nullified, under Section 2:4 if such a reduction is considered fair taking into account the age and level of development of the child, the nature of the act, whether liability insurance exists, as well as economic and other circumstances.

The amount of damages awarded can also be reduced (*jämkas*) under Section 6:1 of the Tort Liability Act due to the contributory negligence of the person harmed (*medvållande*) if that person "intentionally or through gross recklessness has contributed to the harm." Compensation for damage to property or pure economic losses can also be reduced if the property owner has contributed to the harm.

---

7   For more information on these compensation tables and the Commission in English, *see* it website at www.trafikskadenamnden.se.

8   *See* Marcus Radetzki, PRAKTISK SKADESTÅNDSBEDÖMNING (Studentlitteratur 2010) at 68.

Another ground for a reduction in the amount of compensation awarded is where the injured party has received a benefit from the harmful act under the principle *compensation lucri cum damno*. The amount of any benefit is to be deducted from the compensation received. One example of such a benefit is where the value of property that has been harmed actually increases due to the repairs. The application of this principle is limited to benefits of an economic nature and applied restrictively.

12.2 Respondeat Superior

Vicarious liability is imposed on private employers and the state as a public employer in the form of *respondeat superior* under the third chapter of the Tort Liability Act. Section 3:1 states that an employer having an employee in its service is to compensate for any:

1 Injuries to persons or property that the employee causes through mistake or negligence in employment;
2 Pure economic losses that the employee causes in employment through a criminal act; and
3 Injuries resulting from the fact that the employee [seriously violated another person through a crime that constituted an attack on that individual's person, liberty, peace or privacy] through mistake or negligence in employment.

Section 3:2 imposes a corresponding liability on public employers, whether state, municipal or regional, for:

4 Injuries to persons or property, or pure economic losses, that are caused by mistake or negligence in the exercise of public authority over an individual in those operations for which the state and municipalities are responsible; and
5 Injuries resulting from the fact that the employee [seriously violated another person through a crime that constituted an attack on that individual's person, liberty, peace or privacy] through mistake or negligence in the exercise of such public authority against an individual.

The state and municipalities are also to compensate for pure economic losses caused by a public authority providing incorrect information by mistake or through negligence if the court finds reason to award such damages taking into consideration all the circumstances.

12.3 Employee Liability

According to Section 4:1 of the Tort Liability Act, an employee can be held liable for injuries caused by mistake or negligence in employment only if there are particularly compelling reasons for doing so taking into account the nature of the act, the position of the employee and the interests of the injured party and other circumstances. The court can also find that the employer should pay, for example, two-thirds of the compensation, and the employee one-third. It is rare, however, for the court to find an employee liable for any damages under this provision.[9]

12.4 Strict Liability

Strict liability (*strikt ansvar*) can be imposed by a court for dangerous activities, but the majority of the cases concern strict liability as imposed by statute. Examples of areas in which strict liability has been legislated include injuries arising in connection with road traffic accidents, electrical power plants, power stations and power lines, air traffic, nuclear power facilities, oil spills, train traffic and consumer product liability. While strict liability is imposed in these areas by different statutes, the statutes can also include ceilings as to the amounts of liability.

One example of strict liability as imposed by statute is that found in the Motor Traffic Liability Act (*trafikskadelag* 1975:1410) which imposes strict liability on car owners with respect to damages to third parties. This system is discussed further below in section 12.6.3.

An example of strict liability with restrictions as to damage amounts can be found in the Train Traffic Act (*järnvägstrafiklag* 1985:192). Compensation for damage to property borne by passengers on a train is limited in Section

---

9   *See* Radetzki at 83.

2:5 of the act to an amount for each journey that is one-half the statutory base amount for the year in which the damage arose. In addition, liability is imposed on the railways only for certain injuries, for example there is no strict liability for injuries to passengers under Section 2:2 not related to the maintenance of the railways and which the railway could not avoid or prevent even if it had taken all possible measures that could be required.

The Act on the Supervision of Dogs and Cats (*lag 2007:1150 om tillsyn över hundar och katter*) imposes strict liability on the owners of dogs in Section 19: "An injury caused by a dog is to be compensated for by its owner or the party in possession of the dog, even if he or she did not cause the injury." A right of regress is created in the same paragraph, in that the owner or party in possession has the right to receive that paid out in compensation from the person causing the injury. The imposition of strict liability on the owners and parties in possession of dogs can be interpreted to mean that negligence or intent is required with respect to holding the owners of cats, horses and rabbits liable for damages caused by such animals.[10]

12.5 Products Liability

The Products Liability Act (*produktansvarslag* 1992:18) imposes strict liability on product manufacturers for consumer personal injuries caused by a product due a safety defect. Prior to this 1992 act, there was no products liability in Swedish law, simply liability as imposed under the Tort Liability Act, entailing the necessity of proving either intent or negligence. The act was passed in 1992 to harmonize Directive 85/374/EEC.[11]

Strict liability under the act is imposed for injuries to property only if the product was not safe, was typically for personal use, and was being used for personal use when the injuries arose. In other words, only consumers are protected under this act with respect to injuries to property. Another

---

10 This manner of reasoning is referred to in the Swedish legal literature as *e contrario* reasoning, in other words, that which is not prohibited is permitted.

11 The Products Liability Act is the Swedish implementation of the EU products liability directive, Council Directive 85/374/EEC on the approximation of the laws, regulations and administrative provisions of the Member States concerning liability for defective products.

limitation under the act is that any injuries to the product itself are not compensated under the act. This limitation to products for personal use while being used as such entails that plaintiffs harmed by unsafe products used commercially must demonstrate either the intent or the negligence of the manufacturer under the Tort Liability Act, or sue for breach of contract.

Liability under the Products Liability Act is imposed on manufacturers of the finished product, as well as manufacturers of component parts that have caused the harm, any party importing the product into the European Economic Area, the European Trade Association or the EU, as well as any party affixing its trademark on the product. If these parties cannot be identified with respect to the product, the party selling the product is to be held liable under the act. The latter can be released from liability if the selling party can identify any of the previous parties in the chain of sale and manufacture.

Strict liability under the act is imposed for those damages caused by a product not being safe. A safety defect as stated in Section 3 is seen to exist where the product is "not as safe as reasonably can be expected." Safety is to be assessed taking into consideration not only how the product could be foreseen to be used, but also how it was marketed, the product instructions included, the point of time at which the product was released into the market and other circumstances.

A party liable under the act can be released from liability if the party can show:

- That the party did not put the product into circulation;
- That it is probable that the defect causing the damage did not exist at the time when the product was put into circulation by the party;
- That the defect was due to the compliance of the product with mandatory regulations issued by public authorities; or
- That the state of scientific and technical knowledge at the time when the party put the product into circulation was not such as to enable the existence of the defect to be discovered.

A deductible (*självrisk*) of SEK 3 500 is to be subtracted from any property damage award. In addition, the court can decrease the damage award if deemed fair by taking into account any contributory negligence of the person suffering the harm. A party paying damages under the act has a certain right of regress against other responsible parties. The statute of limitations for a product liability claim under the act is three years from the date the individual knew or ought to have known that a claim could be made. However, any claim must be made at the latest within ten years of the date when the party allegedly liable under the act put the product into circulation.

12.6 Insurance Law

An extensive insurance system, both public and private, has been created in Sweden, with roots going back to the beginning of the twentieth century. No fault insurance with respect to motor vehicles was established already in 1916. The system was significantly expanded in the 1970's with the objective of reparation for most injuries. This extensive system has affected the development of the tort law as discussed above, with insurance solutions sought for many types of injuries.

12.6.1 PUBLIC INSURANCE

The public social insurance system in principle covers the entire population. The scope of coverage afforded under Social Insurance Code (*socialförsäkringsbalk* 2010:110) is very broad. Coverage exists for general social insurance comprising family benefits, health and occupational insurance, disability benefits, pensions, survivors' benefits and housing benefits. The comprehensive scope of the Social Insurance Code can be seen as one of the main reasons why Swedish tort law can be so circumscribed and damages so modest.

Certain of the public benefits offered are tied to employment, particularly sick leave and rehabilitation pay, occupational insurance, parental leave pay,[12] retirement pensions and survivor benefits. The sick leave and parental leave systems are described more fully below in Section 16.4.3. The Code also

---

12 For the history of the parental leave benefit, *see* Laura Carlson, SEARCHING FOR EQUALITY, SEX DISCRIMINATION, PARENTAL LEAVE AND THE SWEDISH MODEL WITH COMPARISONS TO EU, UK AND US LAW (Iustus 2007) at 85 and the treatment in the collective agreements as to parental leave benefits at 205.

provides insurance coverage for persons injured at work. The employment aspects of the system are primarily financed through employer contributions as supplemented by social security contributions from self-employed persons, employees and the state. Employer contributions (*arbetsgivaravgifter*) in 2012 amounted to approximately 31.42 % of any wages paid. The insurance as provided under these acts is administered by the Swedish National Insurance Office (*Försäkringskassan*).[13]

12.6.2 PRIVATE INSURANCE

In addition to public insurance, private insurance covering certain types of injuries is mandatory by law. For example, mandatory liability insurance for health care providers with respect to patients is prescribed under the Act on Patient Injuries (*patientskadelag* 1996:799). This is compulsory patient insurance which must be taken out by health care providers and basically has ultimately eliminated litigation concerning medical malpractice claims. The insurers in these types of insurance policies as a general rule have no right of regress against the person causing the harm. The person receiving compensation under these types of systems usually has to waive the right to litigate the issue further in order to receive compensation.

Another example of a sector wide insurance solution can be seen with the insurance for pharmaceuticals. This insurance is available for persons who have suffered adverse effects from prescribed pharmaceutical products or pharmaceuticals purchased at a Swedish pharmacy (*apotek*), or have received pharmaceuticals at a hospital or are suffering adverse reactions or effects due

---

13 For more information in English on the Swedish Social Insurance Agency (Försäkringskassan) and the social security system, *see* its website at forsakringskassan.se. An individual without means and not eligible for financial support from any of the insurance systems, whether state or private, can apply for financial social assistance from the municipality in which she resides. The municipality is obliged by statute to provide such assistance. The Government annually recommends standard levels for financial social assistance (*försörjningsstöd*) as guidelines for the municipalities. For a single individual, the social security benefit in 2012 was approximately SEK 3 900 per month, which amount is to cover normal living expenses, excluding housing and medical costs.

to participation in clinical trials covered by the insurance.[14] Coverage is not available for homeopathic or natural medicines. If an individual accepts compensation from this insurance, she must waive any rights to litigate the issue. These two examples serve as illustration not only on the focus of the law as to insurance rather than tort solutions, but also the high degree of self-regulation existing in these insurance areas.[15]

Several of the central organizations in the different sectors have also created insurance funds, for example with respect to employment rehabilitation compensation (*trygghetsförsäkring vid arbetsskada*). This insurance fund was created by employers and labor unions to assist employees injured at work, with the employers bearing the costs. This insurance is secondary to that provided by the public insurance system, supplementing those benefits.

It is fairly common in general for employment benefits, particularly in the white-collar sector, to include insurance supplementing public insurance benefits. For example, the public insurance benefits with respect to sick leave cover approximately eighty percent (2012) of a person's income up to a certain ceiling tied to the statutory price base amount, currently 7.5 times that amount. The employment insurance can then in certain cases supplement the difference with up to one hundred percent of any income lost due to the limited public benefit coverage.[16]

---

14 Information about this insurance is available in English at lakemedelsforsakringen.se. A claim made to this insurance takes about four months to process. For more on the legal regulation of the pharmaceutical industry in general, *see* the Medical Products Agency's (*Läkemedelsverket*) website at lakemedelsverket.se. Given the international character of the pharmaceutical industry, many of the agency's regulations have been translated into English.

15 For more information in English as to this constellation of self-regulation, soft law as well as pre-set damages, *see* Jessika van der Sluijs, *The Soft Law Regulation of Insurance Contracts* in Scandinavian Studies in Law – Soft Law, Vol. 58 (Stockholm 2012).

16 For a report in English on these supplemental insurances as provided in employment, *see* Gabriella Sjögren Lindquist and Eskil Wadensjö, The Swedish Welfare State: The Role of Supplementary Compensations (SOFI 2006) available at the website of the Swedish Institute for Social Research (SOFI) at www.sofi.su.se/polopoly_fs/1.65007.1323949614!/WP06n01.pdf. *See* also by the same authors, Gabriella Sjögren Lindquist and Eskil Wadensjö, National Social Insurance: Not The Whole Picture, Supplementary Compensation in Case of Income Loss (ESS 2006:5) available at the Offices of the Government of Sweden at www.regeringen.se/sb/d/6189/a/72834.

12.6.3 AN EXAMPLE OF NO-FAULT PRIVATE INSURANCE

An example of how the no-fault private insurance system works can be seen with respect to injuries caused in traffic. The Motor Traffic Liability Act (*trafikskadelag* 1975:1410) creates a mandatory private insurance system for all motor vehicles (not drivers) encompassed by the act. If an injury arises as a result of motor traffic, the Tort Liability Act is not applicable. The injuries are instead compensated under the Motor Traffic Liability Act. The objective is that all injuries arising in road traffic are to be compensated by motor vehicle insurance. Motor vehicle insurance is mandatory for motor vehicle owners. Even in those cases in which there is no motor vehicle insurance, compensation for injuries is awarded. It is paid by the association of motor vehicle insurance companies (*trafikförsäkringsföreningen*), which in its turn receives a fee from the owner of the uninsured motor vehicle.

A condition for compensation for an injury under the motor vehicle's insurance is that the injury is caused as a "consequence of road traffic." That meant by an injury caused as a consequence of road traffic is not entirely clear. An accident in which someone opened a car door in a parking lot and thereby injured a pedestrian has been considered to be an injury as a consequence of traffic.

If an injury has occurred in traffic, the injured party does not need to prove that any party has been negligent or acted intentionally in order to receive compensation from the insurance. Motor vehicle insurance is based on strict liability for any injuries to persons or property occurring in traffic. Exceptions exist with respect to a collision between two insured motor vehicles. In such cases, the following is applicable:

- Any personal injury to a driver and any passengers is compensated by the insurance for the motor vehicle in which those persons were traveling;
- Property injury to the actual motor vehicle and any other property included (for example, baggage) is to be compensated by the motor vehicle insurance of the other car if it can be proven that the driver of the other car drove in a manner intentionally or negligently causing the damage. *Culpa* (intent or negligence) is required in such cases. If *culpa* cannot be proven, the body insurance for the motor vehicle (*vagnskadeförsäkring*) damaged is to compensate for the injuries;

- Injuries to property other than the motor vehicle, for example, to a mailbox or a bicycle, is to be compensated by the motor vehicle insurance belonging to the motor vehicle that caused the damage, regardless of whether this occurred intentionally or negligently.

According to Section 9 of the Road Traffic Injuries Act, the amount of the compensation is to be determined based on the fifth chapter of the Tort Liability Act. The injured party can thus receive an amount comparable to a tort injury award from the motor vehicle insurance. There are also rules in the Road Traffic Injuries Act regarding reducing or nullifying the amount of damages comparable to those in the Tort Liability Act. If the injured party has significantly contributed to her own bodily injuries, the traffic injury compensation can be reduced. If the injured party, or a party close to her, has contributed to property damage, the compensation can be reduced to null.

12.6.4 THE LEGAL REGULATION OF PRIVATE INSURANCE

The total of insurance premiums paid in Sweden in 2010 amounted to SEK 270 billion, making the insurance industry one of the largest in the country.[17] Swedish insurance legislation was adapted to the European Parliament and Council Directive 95/26/EC, the Third Non-Life and Life Insurance Directive, and the EU regulations for annual and consolidated accounts in insurance undertakings have been part of Swedish law since 1996. Two statutes now form the cornerstones of the legal regulation of the private insurance industry in Sweden. The Insurance Contracts Act regulates the relationship between the insurer and the insured, and the Insurance Business Act establishes regulations for insurance operations.

The Insurance Contracts Act (*försäkringsavtalslag* 2005:104) replaced both the Insurance Contracts Act of 1927 and the Consumer Insurance Act of 1980. The Insurance Contracts Act applies to both consumer and commercial policyholders, and both with respect to property and personal insurance. The

---

17 This and much of the following information is taken from the website of Insurance Sweden, the Swedish insurance federation, with more information available in English at svenskforsakring.se. The insurer members of this federation account for ninety percent of the insurance business in Sweden.

act regulates the legal relationship between the insurer and the insured as well as others covered by the policy. The law applies to consumer insurance (such as homeowners, car and travel insurance), business insurance and personal insurance (such as life, accident and sickness insurance). The act also applies to both individual and group insurance and to collectively agreed insurances. The act is mandatory unless stated otherwise, which means that any insurance clauses less favorable to the policyholder than those mandatory rights as set forth in the Act are not valid.

The Insurance Contracts Act regulates:

- Customer information both prior to the policy subscription and during the life of the policy;
- The right to obtain insurance coverage, which is mandatory to the benefit of consumers in most cases;
- Termination of the agreement by either the insured or the insurer;
- The limitations in coverage the insurer can make;
- Premiums and payments; and
- Insurance settlements.

The act places duties on insurers to provide information to both companies and consumers. The insurer is obliged to provide customers with specific information both before the policy is taken and during the insurance period. The insurer is to send the policyholder a written confirmation of the agreement in which the essential terms of the policy are pointed out as soon as possible after the policy has been subscribed. If the insurer fails to do this with respect to a consumer, the insurer is prohibited from citing terms in the policy negative to the consumer. However, the insurer does not have to provide information to a company if such is deemed unnecessary. An insurer making this decision must prove to the supervisory authority that there was no need to disclose the information, for example if the same insurance had been taken out previously by the company.

The previous act did not regulate cancellation of an agreement during the insurance period. Now the policyholder has the right to cancel, unless otherwise agreed, if the insurer has committed a significant breach of the agreement or law, if the insured no longer needs the insurance or if the insurer has amended the terms of the policy during the insurance period.

The insurer's right to cancel or amend the terms of the policy during the insurance period under the act is more restricted. It is limited by a mandatory rule to situations where the insured has committed a significant breach of the agreement or there has been a change in circumstance significant enough to alter the calculation of risk.

Swedish law historically has applied the principle of privity of contract strictly. Under the old act, an injured party could make a claim against the insured's insurance directly if the insured were in bankruptcy. Under the new act, third parties have a somewhat expanded right to file a claim for compensation directly against the insurer when it comes to third-party liability insurance. This right is restricted, however, to compulsory third-party insurance or to certain cases where the insured is unable to pay compensation for the damages caused, for example again when the insured is in bankruptcy. Otherwise, the third party must still first present the claim to the party causing the damage.

The other major regulatory act with respect to private insurance is the Insurance Companies Act (*försäkringsrörelselag* 2010:2043) which sets out the company law rules applicable to insurance companies. The Insurance Companies Act contains regulations specific to insurance companies as well as regulations that in essence correspond to those found in the Companies Act as applicable to corporations.

The requirements for establishing insurance companies, as well as the rules pertaining to their operations and overall supervision, are set out in the Act. An authorization from the Financial Supervisory Authority (*Finansinspektionen*)[18] is necessary in order to become an insurance company or to expand a company's existing product portfolio. The application is to be granted if the insurance company is deemed able to satisfy the requirements for sound insurance operations. Supervision by the Financial Inspection Authority is to have the objectives of maintaining stability and transparency in the insurance industry.

---

18 For more on the Financial Supervisory Authority in English, *see* its website at fi.se.

The Insurance Brokers Act (*lag 2005:405 om försäkringsförmedling*)[19] sets out the rules applicable to insurance brokers and intermediaries, registration and licensing requirements as well as supervision by the Financial Supervisory Authority. The act also sets out good insurance practices to be observed by insurance companies with appropriate care, taking also into consideration the interests of the insured.

12.6.5 CONSUMER RECOURSE

The Consumers Insurance Bureau (*Konsumenternas försäkringsbyrå*)[20] is a tri-partite foundation created in 1979 by the Consumer Agency, the Financial Supervisory Authority and the Insurance Federation. The bureau gives guidance free of charge to consumers making insurance purchasing decisions. The Bureau can also act as a mediator in insurance disputes.

There is also a National Board for Consumer Complaints (*Allmänna reklamationsnämnden*), a state authority that has the task of providing a forum for settling consumer claims. The Board has an insurance department that handles consumer insurance issues, which have amounted to approximately 800 annually for the past three years, with consumers successful in about 15 cases annually.[21]

---

19 The EU Commission is currently carrying out a review of the Insurance Intermediaries Directive 2002/92/EC which may ultimately lead to a new Insurance Intermediaries Act in Sweden.

20 For more information in English on the Consumers Insurance Bureau, *see* its website at konsumenternasforsakringsbyra.se.

21 For more information in English on the National Board for Consumer Complaints, *see* its website at arn.se.

Specific Topics in Contract and Commercial Law

This last part of the book addresses several specific areas of contract and commercial law, namely the law of business organizations, sales, intellectual property and unfair trade law, labor and employment law, land leasing and landlord tenant law. Though disparate by topic, these areas share aspects common to the Swedish legal model, of large central organizations as well as self-regulation to the extent that quasi-legislative authority has been granted to certain of these organizations. This delegation has in its turn produced a code of corporate governance, standard agreements, national labor agreements and rent negotiations for tenants on a national level. Any understanding of the Swedish legal system is incomplete without knowledge of the integral role played by these organizations.

On a final note, several major areas of law have not been addressed in chapters of their own in this work, those coming most readily to mind being tax and environmental law. These are in themselves extensive and important areas of law, and much information is available in English on the regulations in these areas, mostly from the government authorities charged with their care. For tax law there is the National Tax Authority (*Skatteverket*), mentioned several times already in this work, with information as to the tax system in English available at skatteverket.se. In environmental law, there is the Environmental Protection Agency (*Naturvårdsverket*), which also has information available in English at its website at naturvardsverket.se.

Now onto the final topics.

CHAPTER 13

The Law of Business Organizations

The law governing business organizations is found in several different statutes depending upon the business form in question. Four major categories of business forms are defined under Swedish law, sole proprietorships (*enskild firma*), companies (*bolag*) including joint ventures (*enkla bolag*), partnerships (*handelsbolag*) and corporations (*aktiebolag*), cooperatives (*föreningar*) including both commercial (*ekonomiska föreningar*) and non-profit cooperatives (*ideella föreningar*), and foundations (*stiftelser*).

The National Tax Authority (*Skatteverket*) estimates that there were about one million businesses declaring income in 2010, approximately a little over one-half of which were sole proprietorships. The statistics for the different business forms in 2009 were as follows:

TABLE 13.1 No. of Organizations Registered and No. of Employees in Sweden (2010).[1]

2010	No. of Organizations	No. of Employees
Sole Proprietorships	552 504	59 564
General Partnerships	67 078	46 708
Corporations	289 385	2 518 726
Cooperatives – Commercial	22 437	47 616
Cooperatives – Non Profit	28 600	97 836
Foundations	4 238	23 871
Other Organizations	11 793	28 818
Total:	976 035	2 823 139

The total tax bill of legal entities in 2010 was SEK 140 billion, with corporations accounting for 72 % of those taxes.

---

1   Taxes in Sweden 2011. A Summary of the Tax Statistical Yearbook of Sweden 2011, table 26.

13.1 Sole Proprietorships

Sole proprietorships, sole traders or private firms (*enskild firma*) are not defined in Swedish law. A sole proprietorship is where an individual simply conducts business. A sole proprietorship is not a legal person, but can hire employees and enter into contracts, but does so with unlimited personal liability. This form of doing business is fairly common in Sweden, historically due to the high share capital and auditing requirements that have been in place for corporations.

There are only two legal requirements with respect to sole proprietorships, aside from the ubiquitous tax requirements. The first is that any firm name has to be registered in the Trade Register (*handelsregister*) maintained by the Companies Registration Office as mandated by the Act on the Trade Register (*handelsregisterlag* 1974:157). In addition, certain minimal bookkeeping records have to be kept. If the sole proprietorship conducts business to the extent it has to keep annual reports, it has to be registered with the Companies Registration Office. The sole proprietor is taxed on income, entailing that the revenues generated in this business form are added to other earned income by the proprietor from employment or business.

With respect to taxes, a sole proprietor first has to pay any net value added taxes.[2] Then she has to pay social security contributions (*egenavgifter*) of approximately 29 % on the income after expenses.[3] After social security contributions are deducted, net income is taxed. Income taxes are at three basic levels. Up to approximately SEK 401 100 (2013) annually is taxed at the rate of 32 %. Any income over that breaking point (*brytpunkt*) is taxed at the rate of 52 % up to SEK 574 300. Any income exceeding SEK 574 300 is then taxed at the rate of 57 %.[4]

---

2   Value-added tax is at the rate of 25 % with certain exceptions, for example books are taxed at 6 %.

3   More information on the Swedish tax system is available in English at the website of the National Tax Authority at skatteverket.se.

4   These rates are based on 2010 and include an estimated 32 % for municipal taxes.

13.2 Companies

The category of companies (*bolag*) is defined by several factors that each of the following, joint ventures, partnerships and corporations, have in common. These include a contractual legal relationship between the owners, a common purpose, and a duty for the owners to work towards that purpose.

13.2.1 JOINT VENTURES

Joint ventures (*enkla bolag*) are agreements by two or more individuals or legal persons to engage in a defined activity that is not a partnership. A joint venture is not a legal person. The parties individually own any assets contributed to the joint venture. The parties to the joint venture cannot bind each other legally with respect to third parties nor are they responsible for any obligations assumed by the other party with respect to any third parties.

Joint ventures, together with partnerships, are regulated under the Act on Partnerships and Joint Ventures (*lag 1980:1102 om handelsbolag och enkla bolag*). The rights and obligations relating to the parties are defined by their joint venture agreement. Any revenues derived from the joint venture are taxed for each party if an individual in the same manner as described in the previous section for sole proprietors, as part of "income from employment and business." If the party is a legal person, the party is taxed in their own business.

Joint ventures can be very simple, such as buying a lottery ticket together, or very complex, such as developing a new cancer treatment. The parties are free to define their relationship to a large extent in their agreement. The joint venture ends when the purpose of the agreement has been achieved, the agreement has expired, or alternatively, when one of the parties has terminated the agreement, with the joint venture liquidated six months after that date. If a termination date has been included in the contract, and the parties continue operations past that date, the joint venture is deemed to be in place until further notice. If one of the parties dies or is placed into bankruptcy, the joint venture is immediately terminated.

13.2.2 GENERAL PARTNERSHIPS

General partnerships (*handelsbolag*) are created by an agreement between two or more individuals or legal persons. General partnerships are legal persons but the partners still have unlimited liability. There are statutory requirements that must be fulfilled before gaining this legal status. First, there must be a partnership agreement between two or more parties to conduct business. The second is that the partnership must be registered in the Trade Register. If this last requirement is not fulfilled, the partnership is treated as a joint venture.

A general partnership as a legal person can own property, assume legal obligations and sue in court. The partners are free to decide the allocation of profits and debts between them in the partnership agreement. In the absence of such an agreement, the parties are to split any profits or debts evenly. Thus if the partnership has four partners, they are each entitled to one-fourth of the profits and liable for one-fourth of the debts. As against third parties, however, they are jointly and severally liable with a right of regress against each other. Each partner can bind the partnership unless otherwise agreed, and has the right to be compensated for any efforts expended in managing the partnership. Each partner also has a right to interest with respect to any contributions made to the partnership.

The partners are taxed in the same manner as the parties to a joint venture as revenue attributable to the tax category of "income from business." The partnership is to be dissolved in accordance with the partnership agreement. If the agreement is until further notice, it is to be dissolved six months after one of the parties has terminated the agreement. If a termination date has been included in the partnership agreement, and the partners continue operations past that date, the partnership is deemed to be in place until further notice. A partnership is to be immediately dissolved if one of the partners dies or is placed in bankruptcy.

A new partner joining an existing partnership is jointly and severally liable for all the debts of the partnership, even those existing before becoming a partner. Where a partner harms the partnership intentionally or negligently, she can be liable to the partnership for damages. If a partner leaves the partnership, the partner is responsible for all debts of the partnership up to the date of leaving, and can also be liable for any debts entered into by the partnership after that date with respect to a third party in good faith. In other words, the partner that has left is liable if the third party did not know or ought not to have known that the party no longer was a partner. If a partnership is placed into bankruptcy, a claim against the partnership can be asserted immediately as against the partners even if the claim is not yet due for payment.

13.2.3 LIMITED PARTNERSHIPS

Limited partnerships (*kommanditbolag*) are a hybrid between general partnerships and corporations, allowing for limited liability with respect to certain of the partners, but single taxation[5] as with a general partnership. Limited partnerships are governed by the same statute as general partnerships, the Act on Partnerships and Joint Ventures. A limited partnership is a legal person, and thus can acquire rights, assume obligations and sue in court. Certain statutory requirements have to be fulfilled, such as the existence of an agreement between the partners, registration of the partnership, but also most importantly, there must be two classes of partners. There must always be a general partner (*komplementär*), with the same rights and unlimited liability as in a general partnership described above. The other class of partners is the limited partners (*kommanditdelägare*). These partners have liability limited to the amount paid for their shares in the limited partnership.

The general partner is the only partner authorized to bind the partnership. The general partner can be an individual or legal person, but cannot be a foundation (*stiftelse*) or non-profit cooperative (*ideell förening*). Limited partners have the right to share in the profits in accordance with the partnership agreement, but are not to be involved in the management of the limited partnership. Limited partners are typically free to sell their shares in the partnership, and if a limited partner dies, the partnership is not dissolved. However, if the general partner dies or is placed into bankruptcy, the limited partnership is to be dissolved.

---

5   Single taxation here refers to the fact that the income is taxed in the tax category of "business" for the partners, while a corporation is first taxed as a legal person and then the shareholders are taxed as to any dividends, resulting in "double" taxation.

13.2.4 CORPORATIONS

Corporations or limited liability companies[6] (*aktiebolag*) are regulated in the Companies Act (*aktiebolagslag* 2005:551) which is a detailed, modern statute replacing the 1975 act of the same name. Both public (*publikt aktiebolag*) and private corporations (*privat aktiebolag*) are regulated under the act. The 2005 Companies Act has several innovations both materially and from the perspective of legislative technique. The first example of the latter is that a table of contents is given in the first chapter and in addition, definitions for certain terms of art are explicitly listed in the statute, as opposed to simply relying on that stated in the legislative preparatory works. The Companies Act consists of thirty-two chapters with the following basic structure:

TABLE 13.2 The Companies Act.

General Provisions	
Chap. 1 General Provisions	Chap. 6 Share Certificates
Chap. 2 Incorporation and	Chap. 7 Meetings of the Shareholders
Articles of Incorporation	Chap. 8 Corporate Management
Chap. 3 Bylaws	Chap. 9 Auditors
Chap. 4 Shares	Chap. 10 General and Specific Audits
Chap. 5 Share Register	
Corporate Financing	
Chap. 11 Increases in Share Capital,	Chap. 17 Protection of Equity
New Shares, Loans	and Value Transfers
Chap. 12 Bonus Issues	Chap. 18 Dividends
Chap. 13 New Issues	Chap. 19 Acquisition of Treasury Shares
Chap. 14 Warrants	Chap. 20 Decreases in Share Capital
Chap. 15 Convertible Debentures	or Reserves
Chap. 16 Directed Issues	Chap. 21 Loans to Shareholders
	Chap. 22 Compulsory Share Purchases
Changing Corporate Form	
Chap. 23 Corporate Mergers	Chap. 25 Liquidation and Bankruptcy
Chap. 24 Corporate Splits	Chap. 26 Changes in Corporate Category

---

6 Corporation is the American term and limited liability company the British. It should be noted, however, that certain states in the United States also have limited liability companies that are not corporations, but a legal person closer in form to a limited partnership.

Miscellaneous Provisions	
Chap. 27 Registration	Chap. 30 Criminal Acts and Sanctions
Chap. 28 Corporate Names	Chap. 31 Appeals
and Authorized Signatures	Chap. 32 Corporations
Chap. 29 Liability for damages	with Dividend Restrictions

The discussion below provides an overview as to the basic regulations under the act. As a corporation is a legal person, the general rule is that shareholders are liable only to the amount they have already paid for their shares, in other words, they have limited liability and are not responsible for the debts of the corporation. There are specific exceptions to this rule in certain cases of insolvency caused by the acts of a shareholder, and also with respect to certain environmental crimes. A public corporation is not by definition listed on a public stock market, but only a public corporation can eventually be publicly listed.

There are not many differences in the regulations with respect to private and public corporations. One of the major differences is that the minimum share capital for a private corporation is SEK 50 000 and for a public corporation is SEK 500 000. The share capital requirements are seen as creditor protection. There is a requirement that the share capital be always intact, in other words, dividends cannot be issued leading to a decrease of equity below these thresholds. If losses result in a situation in which the equity is less than one-half of the registered share capital, board members and/or shareholders may face personal liability for debts assumed by the corporation thereafter if steps are not taken to restore the equity or liquidate the corporation.

Another restriction is that a corporation as a main rule may not lend monies to shareholders, board members, a chief executive officer or any party closely related to these persons. A violation of this prohibition is a criminal offence. A corporation may also not provide loans for the purchase of its own shares, or the shares of a parent corporation (*moderbolag*). However, such a loan is allowed for the purchase of shares in a subsidiary (*dotterbolag*). Loans are such a significant issue as such loans can be used as devices for evading or perpetually postponing taxes.

A corporation can be incorporated by one or more persons referred to as incorporators (*stiftare*).[7] The incorporators are personally liable for any debts incurred until all the legal requirements for incorporating the corporation are fulfilled. To incorporate, the incorporators must draft and sign a document (*stiftelseurkund*) referred to either as articles of incorporation (American) or a memorandum of association (British). In addition, all shares must be subscribed to and paid. Different series of shares can be created, but the corporation is not allowed to hold them for future issues. It was illegal in general for a corporation to subscribe to or own its own shares at all until 2000, and now there is a 10 % ceiling as to the amount of its own shares a public company can possess.

The articles of incorporation are to include the amount to be paid for each share, information as to the board members and auditors, the assets in the company and the costs of incorporation. The board is to register the corporation with the Swedish Companies Registration Office (*Bolags-verket*) within six months of the date of the articles of incorporation. Bylaws (*bolagsordning*) are also to be adopted by the shareholders. The bylaws are to include the name of the corporation, the registered office of the board, the corporate purpose, the amount of share capital, the number of shares issued as well as their rights and any restrictions, the number of board members, board deputy members and auditors and the process by which shareholders are to be duly convened.

As a main rule, all the shares in a corporation are to have equal voting and dividend rights. However, different share series can be created with rights that can differ, for example A series shares and B series shares, with the latter typically being preferential shares. With respect to voting rights, there is a maximum ceiling in that one series of shares cannot have voting rights greater than ten times that of any other series. The sale of shares can be restricted in certain ways if all the statutory requirements for such restrictions are fulfilled. One restriction is by placing a right of first refusal to the benefit of the other shareholders (*förköpsklausul*) on the shares. Another right is for existing shareholders to be able to demand to buy shares as acquired by a new owner (*hembudsförbehåll*). The corporation is to keep a share register

---

7   There are rules under the Companies Act that certain actors, such as incorporators, have to be Swedish legal persons or individuals residing in the EEA.

containing information as to the shares and their owners. The failure to maintain a share register or refusing access to a share register is a criminal offence. Shares can be issued digitally, but otherwise shareholders in certain companies have the right to demand physical share certificates.

Corporate governance in the Swedish system is based on a division of power and responsibilities between the shareholders (as exercised through the shareholder meetings), the board of directors, corporate management and the auditors. The shareholders, however, hold the ultimate power in the corporation.

The basic structure of the Swedish system can be illustrated as follows:

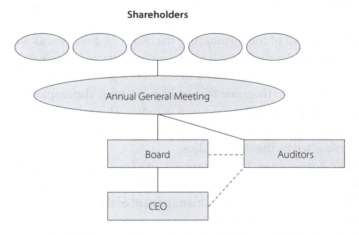

DIAGRAM 13.1 Swedish Corporate Governance System (this diagram is taken from the website of the Swedish Corporate Governance Board at www.corporategovernanceboard.se).

Four organs consequently control a corporation. The first three are internal, the meetings of the shareholders, the board of directors and corporate management as headed by a chief executive officer ("CEO") (American) or managing director (British). The fourth is to be external, the auditors are to check the actions of the other three organs. There are two types of shareholders meetings (*bolagsstämma*), the general annual meeting of the shareholders, which is mandated by law (additional meetings can be required in the bylaws), and extraordinary meetings as called by the board of directors. Certain decisions must be taken at the general annual meeting of the shareholders by statute, including approving the corporate income statement and balance sheet, any dividends or distribution of losses, the release of the board and the chief executive officer from liability and any other matters duly addressed. It is permissible in Sweden for a corporation to have only one shareholder.

The board of directors (*styrelse*) is to be elected by the shareholders. The board is responsible for the organization and administration of the corporation. A public corporation is to have at least three board members, a private corporation is allowed to have one or two if a deputy is also appointed. If the board has more than one member, a chairperson has to be appointed. If the corporation has at least twenty-five employees, the employees have the right to appoint two of the members of the board of directors, as well as a deputy for each, under the Board Representation (Private Sector Employees) Act (*lag 1987:1245 om styrelserepresentation för de privatanställda*).[8] If the corporation has more than one thousand employees, the employees have the right to appoint three directors and deputies. However, the number of directors as appointed by the employees is not to outnumber the number of directors as elected by the shareholders.

A public corporation has to have a CEO (*verkställande direktör*) as appointed by the board. A private corporation does not have to have a CEO. The CEO is to take care of the daily management of the corporation and has the authority to sign on behalf of the corporation for such purposes. If the board for some reason cannot meet to make a more significant decision, the CEO is authorized to do so if necessary to corporate operations. A CEO may not be a minor, under guardianship, be in bankruptcy or under a prohibition as to conducting business. As discussed in Chapter Eight, there are no overarching principles of fiduciary duties in Swedish law. The Companies Act does state, however, specific obligations of the CEO, the board and shareholders. For example, the CEO may not decide as to a contract between the corporation and the CEO, a legal person owned by the CEO or a third party in which the CEO has a significant interest.

---

8   An English translation of this act can be found at the website of the Government Offices of Sweden at sweden.gov.se.

At least one auditor is to be appointed for a public corporation. The auditor is to be elected by the shareholders and is to audit the corporate books and submit an auditor's statement at year-end as to the state of the corporate books. The requirement of an auditor for private corporations was removed in 2010.

Issues concerning corporate financing, such as increases and decreases in share capital, the issuance of new shares, bonus shares, warrants, convertible debentures and private placements, are addressed separately in individual chapters of the Companies Act. One type of minority shareholder protection given under the act is in the form of a compulsory purchase of a minority shareholder's shares by a majority shareholder controlling more than 90 % of the shares in the corporation (*tvångsinlösen*). The corporation itself does not redeem the shares, as is the case with compulsory redemption, in part because historically corporations were not allowed to own their own shares in Sweden. Instead, the majority shareholder is to buy the minority shareholder's shares in a procedure that begins as arbitration but can be appealed to the courts on its merits.[9] This legal institution can also act to the majority shareholder's advantage by facilitating mergers.

Two corporations can merge into one (*fusion av aktiebolag*), or a corporation can split its assets and debts as between two separate legal persons (*delning av aktiebolag*) in a spin-off. The shareholders of a corporation can also decide on a voluntary liquidation or be placed into involuntary liquidation in the form, for example, of bankruptcy as discussed above in Chapter Ten, or for failure to observe the statutory corporate form. A corporation can also change from a private to a public corporation, and vice versa.

Chapter twenty-nine in the Companies Act sets out liability for different corporate actors. An incorporator, director or CEO is liable to the corporation or the shareholders for causing damages intentionally or negligently when

---

9   This minority shareholder buyout process was formerly purely an arbitration procedure with no recourse available to the courts other than for procedural issues. This has been changed to include the right to a judicial trial to be in compliance with Article 6 of the European Court of Human Rights. This process of minority shareholder buyouts has been brought to the European Court of Human Rights, and the Court found that Article 1 of the European Convention applied to the ownership of shares in a company in *Bramelid and Malmström v. Sweden,* European Court of Human Rights, judgment dated 12 October 1982, App. Nos. 8588/79 and 8589/79.

performing her duties. An auditor can also be liable for such damages, as well as for any losses caused by an assistant. A shareholder is liable for any damages caused intentionally or by gross negligence to the corporation, a shareholder or another party by any violation of the Companies Act, the statutory provisions with respect to annual accounting reports or the bylaws. In such a case, the shareholder can also be forced to purchase the shares of the shareholder injured.

Certain criminal liability is imposed in chapter thirty. Examples of such are when a party intentionally markets the sale of shares, notes or options in a private corporation to more than two hundred persons, or for the failure either intentionally or negligently to maintain the share register or keep it accessible to whosoever requests access. Such offenses can be sentenced to criminal fines or maximum one-year imprisonment.

The Swedish corporate governance model is defined in part by the Companies Act, but also by other legislation and self-regulation. The other two main statutes are the Accounting Act (*bokföringslag* 1999:1078) and the Annual Accounts Act (*årsredovisningslag* 1995:1554). There are also self-regulating frameworks, such as the Code of Corporate Governance (*kod för bolagsstyrning*), first drafted by the Corporate Governance Board (*Kollegiet för bolagsstyrning*)[10] in 2004, with the third version issued in 2010. The Code was adopted as the market organizations considered self-regulation to be preferable to legislation.

The Corporate Governance Board is responsible for the management and administration of the Code. The Board monitors and analyzes how the Code is applied in practice and the development of corporate governance in Sweden and internationally. The Board can also amend the Code. The members on the Board are appointed by the Association for Generally Accepted Principles in the Securities Market (*Föreningen för god sed på värdepappersmarknaden*).[11] Members in this latter association include:

---

10   For more information in English on the Corporate Governance Board and an English translation of the 2010 Code of Corporate Governance, *see* its website at corporategovernanceboard.se.

11   For more information on the Association of Good Principles in the Securities Market in English, *see* its website at godsedpavpmarknaden.se.

- The Association of Publicly Traded Companies (*Aktiemarknadsbolagens Förening*);
- The Institute for Authorized Public Accountants, FAR SRS;[12]
- The Swedish Investment Fund Association (*Fondbolagens Förening*);[13]
- Institutional Owners Association for Regulatory Issues in the Stock Market (*Institutionella ägares förening för regleringsfrågor på aktiemarknaden*);
- NASDAQ OMX Stockholm AB;[14]
- The Stockholm Chamber of Commerce (*Stockholms Handelskammare*);[15]
- The Swedish Bankers' Association (*Svenska Bankföreningen*);[16]
- The Swedish Securities Dealers Association (*Svenska Fondhandlare-föreningen*);[17]
- The Confederation of Swedish Enterprise (*Svenskt Näringsliv*);[18] and
- The Insurance Sweden (*Sveriges Försäkringsförbund*).[19]

The Stockholm Stock Exchange began applying the Code in 2005 to all its listed corporations with a market capitalization exceeding SEK 3 billion. Approximately one hundred corporations applied the Code by 2008. The Code is not legislation, but rather meant as a supplement to the existing statutory provisions applicable to publicly listed corporations. However, deviations from the Code are to be "openly" reported as well as the reasons

12 For more on the Institute for Authorized Public Accountants in English, *see* its website at farsrs.se.
13 For more on the Swedish Investment Fund Association in English, *see* its website at fondbolagen.se.
14 For information in English on the Nordic NASDAQ OMX, *see* its website at nasdaqomxnordic.com.
15 For more information in English on the Stockholm Chamber of Commerce, *see* its website at chamber.se.
16 For more information in English on the Swedish Bankers' Association, *see* its website at bankforeningen.se.
17 For more information in English on the Swedish Securities Dealers Association, *see* its website at fondhandlarna.se.
18 For more information in English on the Confederation of Swedish Enterprise, *see* its website at svensktnaringsliv.se.
19 For more information in English on the Swedish Insurance Federation, *see* its website at svenskforsakring.se.

PART III   SPECIFIC TOPICS IN CONTRACT AND COMMERCIAL LAW

for such deviations given. This is to give the actors in the market the opportunity to individually assess the solutions the corporation has chosen in the alternative to the Code.

13.2.5 EUROPEAN COMPANIES

Council Regulation (EC) No. 2157/2001(4) establishes rules for European Companies, referred to as a *Societas Europaea* ("SE"). The regulation aims at creating a uniform legal framework within which companies from different Member States should be able to plan and carry out the reorganization of businesses on a EU scale. The Swedish implementation of the regulation has been through the Act on European Companies (*lag 2004:575 om europabolag*), applicable only to European Companies with their registered offices (seats) in Sweden. Council Directive 2001/86/EC supplementing the Statute for a European Company with regard to the involvement of employees has been implemented in Sweden by the Act on Employee Influence in European Companies (*lag 2004:559 om arbetstagarinflytande i europabolag*).

A European Company is to be designated as such with the use of SE in its name. For example, a Swedish corporation can be designated as such with AB (*aktiebolag*), so a name for a Swedish corporation could be AmSvensk AB. If a European Company, the name would then be AmSvensk SE. European Companies are to be registered in Sweden with the Companies Registration Office.

A European Company can be registered in any Member State, and the registration can be easily transferred to another Member State. A European Company can be created by the:

1 Merger of national companies from different Member States;
2 Creation of a joint venture between companies (or other entities) in different Member States;
3 Creation of a European Company subsidiary of a national company; or the
4 Conversion of a national company into a European Company.

There is a requirement of a minimum of € 120 000 of subscribed capital to start a European Company. The objective for creating a European Company

© THE AUTHOR AND STUDENTLITTERATUR

form is to allow for greater freedom of movement of companies within the European Union.

13.3 Cooperative Enterprises

Cooperative enterprises (*föreningar*) are another attractive alternative to corporations in Sweden due to the absence of any share capital requirements for Swedish cooperatives, as well as the potential for greater owner participation. There are three categories of cooperative enterprises, commercial cooperatives, non-profit cooperatives and European Cooperative Societies.

13.3.1 COMMERCIAL COOPERATIVES

Commercial cooperatives are regulated by the Act on Commercial Cooperatives (*lag 1987:667 om ekonomiska föreningar*). Under the act, a commercial cooperative can be created in order to promote the financial interests of its members through financial operations in which the members participate as consumers or other users, as vendors, with their own work, by using the cooperative's services or in another similar manner. In addition, commercial cooperatives are to have the objective of promoting their members' financial interests through member participation. Both the interests and the operations have to be financially tinged to be a commercial cooperative.

Commercial cooperatives are legal persons once they are registered with the Companies Registration Office, which must be done within six months of being formed. A commercial cooperative is to have at least three members, and is to adopt bylaws and elect a board with at least three directors, as well as an auditor. A chief executive officer is to be appointed if the commercial cooperative has had an average of two hundred employees or more for two years. Board members, chief executive officers and auditors can be liable to the cooperative for injury caused intentionally or negligently.

A commercial cooperative cannot deny a person membership unless a specific reason exists with respect to the nature, extent or object of the cooperative's operations. Each member has one right to vote, and member meetings (*föreningsstämma*) are to be held annually. The members are to approve the income statement and balance sheet, any dispositions of profits or losses, release of liability for the board and chief executive officer and any other matter duly taken up at the meeting.

There are statutory requirements with respect to accounting and audits that vary depending upon the number of members and the financial revenues of the cooperative. Any profits are to be distributed among the members (*överskottsutdelning*) based on their contributions to the cooperative or based on the number of shares held by each member. A cooperative can decide to voluntarily dissolve itself, or be involuntarily dissolved if the number of members is less than three or another triggering event as set out in the bylaws for the cooperative occurs.

Residential cooperatives are a specific variation of commercial cooperatives that have two forms, providing housing for the members of the cooperative (*bostadsrättsförening*) as further discussed in section 11.1.3 above, or providing rental housing units for members of the cooperative (*kooperativ hyresrättsförening*) as discussed below in section 18.2.

13.3.2 NON-PROFIT COOPERATIVES

The other type of Swedish cooperative enterprise is non-profit cooperatives (*ideell förening*). Such cooperatives do not have both a financial objective and financial operations. Instead, the cooperatives falling within this category can have, for example, both a non-profit objective and non-profit operations, such as a cooperative created for bird watchers. Another can have a financial objective but non-financial operations, such as a labor union, or still yet, a non-profit objective but financial operations, such as a charity soup kitchen. There is no general statutory regulation as to these types of cooperatives. However, if the non-profit cooperative conducts financial operations, it needs to be registered in the Trade Register with the Companies Registration Office.

Non-profit cooperatives are treated in the case law as legal persons despite this absence of statutory regulation as soon as bylaws are adopted and a board elected. A non-profit cooperative can own property, acquire debts and sue in court. The members are not personally liable for the cooperative's debts.

Non-profit cooperatives have been a part of Swedish society for centuries. One of the oldest ones, the Royal Society Pro Patria (*Kungliga Sällskapet Pro*

Patria), is considered to have been founded in the 15th century by King Karl VIII Knutsson Bonde and Engelbrekt. Pro Patria currently has the objective of supporting children in need. Several of the organizations that are part of the Corporate Governance Board discussed above fall into this category of cooperative, as well as certain political parties and labor unions.

13.3.3 EUROPEAN COOPERATIVE SOCIETIES

Council Regulation (EC) No. 1435/2003 on the Statute for a European Cooperative Society (SCE) allows for the creation of European Cooperative Societies, *Societas Cooperativa Europeae* ("SCE"). The Swedish implementation of this regulation is through the Act on European Cooperative Societies (*lag 2006:595 om europakooperativ*). The Swedish Act is only applicable to those European Cooperative Societies based in Sweden. Council Directive 2003/72/EC supplementing the Statute for a European Cooperative Society with regard to the involvement of employees sets out rules about employee representation and involvement and has been implemented in Sweden through the Act on Employee Influence in European Cooperatives (*lag 2006:477 om arbetstagarinflytande i europakooperativ*).

Article 2(1) of the SCE Regulation provides for European Cooperative Societies to be formed in five ways, by:

- At least five natural persons resident in at least two Member States;
- At least five natural and legal persons resident in, or governed by the law of, at least two Member States;
- Two or more legal persons governed by the law of at least two Member States;
- A merger between at least two cooperatives governed by the law of at least two different Member States; or by the
- Conversion of a single cooperative formed under the law of a Member State, if it has had an establishment or subsidiary in a different Member State for at least two years.

The minimum capital requirement for a European Cooperative Society is € 30 000. Registration is to occur with the Companies Registration Office.

13.4 Foundations

A foundation (*stiftelse*) is a legal person created to manage assets for a certain objective, regulated under the Act on Foundations (*stiftelselag* 1994:1220). The requirements under the act are property, a written agreement (*stiftelseurkund*), management and a defined objective. The property, which in accordance with a provision in a written signed agreement (*förordnande*) is to be the object of the foundation, must be separated from the donor's other property and permanently managed independently for a defined objective. A foundation is not, however, a trust. The property is considered separated when a party that has assumed responsibility for managing the property takes it into their possession. Foundations are generally used today for non-profit purposes. Historically they were also used as a means for avoiding inheritance tax between generational shifts. Many of the central organizations participating in the self-regulation of certain sectors as discussed throughout this book take this form. Other uses include, for example, municipal housing foundations. By forming a foundation, it may be difficult for a new political majority to make changes.

A foundation as a legal person can acquire rights, assume obligations and sue. The extent of the legal liability of a foundation is its assets. Parent and subsidiary foundations can be created. Management of the foundation can either be internal if by individuals (*egen förvaltning*) or external (*anknuten förvaltning*) if the foundation is managed by a legal person. If the foundation is run by individuals, they are members of a board that manages the foundation. If the foundation is managed by a legal person, that legal person becomes the administrator (*förvaltare*) of the foundation. The Act on Foundations sets out rules with respect to the foundation's bookkeeping with the requirement of at least one auditor for each foundation. Board members and administrators can be liable for damages to the foundation caused intentionally or by negligence. If the assets in the foundation are worth more than SEK 1.5 million, the foundation must keep certain financial records as well as issue an annual report.

Foundations generally are to be registered in the foundation register in kept by the county administrative board (*länsstyrelse*) in the county in which the foundation has its registered offices. The county administrative board has oversight authority with respect to the actions of the foundation. Foundations can be liquidated under the act in certain cases, such as when the capital dissipates. If the purpose for which the foundation was created no longer is relevant, in certain cases the objective can be modified (*permutation*). In such cases, permission for the modification by the Legal, Financial and Administrative Services Agency (*Kammarkollegiet*) is required.[20]

---

20 This agency was founded in 1539 by King Gustav Vasa for managing the tax monies. Today it has a rather eclectic range of over thirty tasks, including authorizing translators and interpreters. For more on this agency in English, *see* its website at kammarkollegiet.se.

CHAPTER 14

Sales

Sales law involves the sale of either goods or services. The sale of goods can be governed by one of several different acts in Sweden. There is no statute regarding the sale of services generally in Sweden except for the one applicable to consumers, the Consumer Sale of Services Act (*konsument-tjänstlag* 1985:716). This chapter first addresses the Sale of Goods Act (*köplag* 1990:931), the Consumer Sale of Goods Act (*konsumentköplag* 1990:932), the Consumer Sale of Services Act, and then the International Sale of Goods Act (*lag 1987:822 om internationella köp*).

14.1 The Sale of Goods Act

The Sale of Goods Act, a product of Nordic legislative cooperation, has been enacted in all the Nordic countries with the exception of Denmark. The Sale of Goods Act does not address issues such as the offer and acceptance to the contract, nor the contract's validity. These issues are instead governed by the Contracts Act as discussed in Chapter Nine. The Sale of Goods Act begins with the premise that a contract has duly been executed.

The Sale of Goods Act is based on freedom of contract between the parties, and the parties consequently can contract out of the act. The act functions as a gap-filler to the extent the contract, binding custom and usage between the parties, in the industry or generally, do not address a specific issue. For example, if the parties forget to include the price of the goods in the contract, the price then will be a fair price according to the Sale of Goods Act.

There are several prongs with respect to determining whether the Sale of Goods Act is applicable to a sales transaction. The first assessment that must be made is with respect to the object of the contract. The act is applicable to the sale or exchange of personal property, not only chattels, but to both tangibles and intangibles. The act is not applicable to services or to transactions concerning site leaseholds. If the contract contains a combination of the purchase of goods and services, the portion concerning the sale of goods is to be greater in order for the act to be applicable.

The second assessment is with respect to the parties to the contract. Generally, the Sale of Goods Act is applicable between merchants, when a consumer sells to a merchant, or between two private parties. The act is not applicable to the sale of goods to a consumer, which instead is covered by the Consumer Sale of Goods Act discussed in the next section. The latter act, however, only covers the sale of chattels, so in certain situations the Sale of Goods Act can be applicable to a consumer as a buyer.

Last, the act needs to be assessed from an international perspective. Naturally, unless the parties have contracted out of the act, the act is applicable to two Swedish parties where the buyer is not a consumer. The Sale of Goods Act is not applicable to international sales falling within CISG, unless the parties are Nordic. If the parties are Nordic, the Sale of Goods Act as applicable in the Nordic country in which the Seller conducts business becomes applicable under the default rule due to the Nordic cooperation and the Naboland (neighbor) clause as seen from Article 2 of CISG as discussed below in section 14.4.

14.1.1 THE TRANSFER OF RISK

The main type of sale (*köp*) in the act is where the buyer picks up the goods at the seller's premises (*hämtningsköp*), "ex-works" in Incoterms.[1] The other type of sale addressed in the act is a delivery sale (*transportköp*) where the goods are delivered to the buyer's premises. Delivery sales are categorized under the act as either local, those delivered by the seller within a certain local geographic area (*platsköp*) or those delivered by a carrier (*distansköp*).

The risk for the goods is transferred to the buyer in the first type of sale when the buyer either collects the goods or is to have done so in accordance

---

1   Incoterms, international commerce terms, are a set of trade definitions drafted by the International Chamber of Commerce, the most recent version being Incoterms 2010. For more information on these trade terms, *see* the International Chamber of Commerce's website at iccwbo.org.

with the terms of the contract between the parties. Where the goods are transported, the risk is transferred to the buyer when the seller hands the goods over to the buyer if the seller is delivering the goods. If the goods are being transported by carrier, the risk for the goods is transferred to the buyer when the seller hands the goods over to the carrier, the incoterm "free carrier".

After the risk is transferred to the buyer, the buyer must pay for the goods regardless of whether the goods are destroyed, lost, deteriorated or diminished as a consequence of an event not attributable to the seller. The point of time at which the risk passes to the buyer is also important in that if the buyer wishes to assert a defect in the goods, she must prove that the goods were non-conforming prior to the transfer of the risk. Up to the time of the transfer of risk, the seller is liable for any costs incurred connected to the goods. After that time, the buyer is liable for such costs. If the goods were sold on a trial basis, the buyer has the risk for the goods until they are returned to the seller.

14.1.2 THE GOODS

The goods are to be in conformance with the contract. As discussed in Chapter Nine, there is no requirement as to any degree of specificity with respect to contracts generally under Swedish law. The seller has the right to demand that the buyer provide specifications as to the goods, and in the event the buyer fails to do this, the seller is allowed to act in accordance with that which can be presumed to be in the buyer's best interests. If the buyer fails to provide specifications, it naturally becomes more difficult for the buyer to prove that the goods are non-conforming.

The four categories of defects in the Sale of Goods Act mirror those as seen in the Land Code in Chapter Eleven above: concrete defects (*konkreta fel*), abstract defects (*abstrakta fel*), defects in ownership (*rättsliga fel*) and defects in the right of use (*rådighetsfel*).

Section 17 of the Sale of Goods Act concerns concrete and abstract defects. A concrete defect exists where the goods do not conform to the contract with respect to type, quantity, quality, other characteristic or packaging. An abstract defect exists where the goods are not in conformance with certain abstract standards as set out in Section 17. The goods are to be:

- Fit for the purpose for which goods of a similar type are generally used;
- Fit for a particular purpose for which the goods are intended to be used, however, the seller at the time of the sale must have known about this specific purpose;
- Consistent with the characteristics the seller has referred to through samples, models or marketing materials as provided by the seller or manufacturer; and
- Packaged in a suitable and appropriate manner.

An abstract defect can also be found in other cases where the goods deviate from the buyer's reasonable expectations. This is also the standard with respect to goods sold "as is." The seller is not released from all liability with respect to such goods, but rather the buyer can claim defect based upon certain circumstances, including the omission of relevant information by the seller, or that the condition of the goods was significantly worse than the buyer, with regard to the price and other circumstances, reasonably could have expected.

The two categories of intangible defects are more technical, the first having to do with defects in ownership, that the buyer has not received ownership to the goods because of a third-party interest. The second category has to do with the buyer not being able to use the goods for the purpose intended because of legislation or other government decisions.

As to physical defects, the buyer must inspect the goods upon their receipt (or prior to) and give the seller notice of non-conformity as soon as possible in order to preserve the buyer's rights. A failure to inspect the goods in a timely manner can lead to a forfeiture of further rights. A latent defect must be cited as soon as detected but at the latest within two years of the delivery of the goods. Where the seller has acted grossly negligent or in bad faith, the two-year limitation is not applicable.

14.1.3 PERFORMANCE BY THE PARTIES

The seller is to deliver conforming goods in time. If the delivery date is not set out in the contract, it is to be a reasonable time from the date of the sale. If no manner of delivery is set out in the contract, the seller can choose an appropriate means of transportation upon customary terms and conditions.

The buyer is to pay for the goods, facilitate the transaction and receive the goods. If the price is not set out in the contract, it is to be a reasonable price.

Payment is to occur at the premises of the seller, and if no payment date is set out in the contract, payment is to be made when the seller demands it. If the buyer receives an invoice from the seller, the buyer is bound by the price in the invoice unless the buyer notifies the seller within a reasonable time that she does not agree to the price, or that a lower price is stated in the contract or the price stated in the invoice is not reasonable.

The seller has no obligation to deliver the goods until payment is received, and the buyer has no obligation to pay for the goods until they are delivered. The parties are free, however, to agree to a different arrangement.

The mutual duty of loyalty the parties have towards each other is seen as the sum of several different duties. Both parties have a duty to care for goods in their possession belonging to the other party. They have a duty to mitigate any losses that may arise due to a breach of contract. They also have a duty to inform each other as to any impediments to contractual performance, as well as to any deficiencies in performance, and as to the intention to terminate the agreement.

14.1.4 REMEDIES

Remedies are available for the seller's delay in delivery (*dröjsmål*), for non-conforming goods (*fel i godset*), for the buyer's late payment and the buyer's failure to facilitate the transaction (*medverkan till köpet*). If the goods are non-conforming for a reason not attributable to the buyer, the buyer may demand that the seller cure the goods (*avhjälpande*), delivery substitute goods (*omleverans*), agree to a reduction in price (*prisavdrag*) or withhold payment. The buyer is also entitled to damages with any of these options. The primary remedy is specific performance. However, if the defect is a material breach of contract, and the seller knew or ought to have known this, the buyer can terminate the contract and request damages. The remedies available for delay by the seller not due to the buyer are specific performance, contract termination and damages. The remedies available to the seller for the buyer's breach of contract are specific performance (payment, accepting the goods or facilitating the transaction), termination and damages.

An interesting mechanism exists in the Sale of Goods Act by which one of the parties can grant an extension of time (*tilläggstid*) in which the other party is to perform under the contract. For example, if the goods are non-conforming, the buyer can request that the seller cure the goods within two weeks. If the seller then has not cured the goods within these two weeks, the buyer is entitled to terminate the contract without having to prove a material breach or the other party's knowledge. The only caveat is that the extension of time must be reasonable, in other words, the party should be able to cure their performance within the extended time granted.

Losses resulting from breach of contract are categorized as either direct losses (*direkta förluster*) or indirect losses (*indirekta förluster*). There is no clear definition set out in the Sale of Goods Act of either of these categories. Section 67 states that indirect losses include those losses resulting from loss of production, loss of use, loss of profits and similar losses. A party is entitled to receive damages for indirect losses only if the seller has been negligent or in breach of a warranty. There is a force majeure exception to damage liability generally in that a party is not liable to pay damages for losses arising from acts that were a consequence of an impediment beyond the control of the party, which that party could not reasonably have anticipated at the time of the contract, nor reasonably avoided or overcome.

Both parties also have the right to terminate the contract for an anticipated breach of contract where the conduct of the other party, or its financial circumstances, can lead to the presumption that the party will not be able to perform under the contract. If this assumption of breach turns out to be incorrect, the party terminating the contract for anticipated breach will itself have breached the contract. A buyer also has the right under certain circumstances to terminate successive deliveries if one of the deliveries is non-conforming. If a seller has already sent goods to be delivered, and circumstances exist giving rise to an anticipated breach, the seller has the right to stop the goods in transit (*stoppningsrätt*). The seller must give notice of this to the buyer, and if the buyer provides acceptable security, the seller must perform under the contract.

If the contract is terminated, all obligations of the parties as to performance cease, and any partial performances are to be returned to the parties making them. If goods cannot be returned in the same condition as delivered, damages are to be paid for the difference in value.

14.2 The Consumer Sale of Goods Act

Swedish contract law historically was based on freedom of contract, relying on the assumption that the parties to the contract had equal bargaining power. However, in certain areas this assumption began to be modified, particularly in the consumer context, in the 1970's. There presently are four acts that govern consumer sale transactions:

- The Consumer Sale of Goods Act (*konsumentköplag* 1990:932);
- The Consumer Sale of Services Act (*konsumenttjänstlag* 1985:716);
- The Consumer Credit Act (*konsumentkreditlag* 2010:1846); and
- The Act on Consumer Protections with Mail Order and Door-to-Door Sales (*distans- och hemförsäljningslag* 2005:59).

There is no one universal definition of consumer applicable to all these acts, but a general definition of consumer can be seen as an individual who purchases goods, services or credit for private use from a commercial actor selling the goods, services or credit as a part of its business activities. The boundary between private and commercial use is not specifically defined, but is significant. For example, as seen in Chapter Twelve on tort law, only goods purchased for private use fall within the scope of the Swedish Products Liability Act.

The consumer protection act with respect to mail order and door-to-door selling was originally enacted in 1971. It has since been amended to be in conformance with Council Directive 85/577/EEC to protect consumers in respect of contracts negotiated away from business premises and Directive 97/7/EC of the Council and European Parliament on the Protection of Consumers in respect of Distance Contracts. According to the present Swedish act, a consumer has the right to certain information, as well as the right to cancel a purchase made via telephone sales, door-to-door sales, over the internet and through mail order, within fourteen days of receiving the goods or services. The goods or services have to be offered by a business offering such for delivery to the consumer (*distansavtal*) or a contract that has been entered into by a representative going door-to-door or at a place other than the business's permanent location (*hemförsäljningsavtal*). The fourteen-day period does not run until the consumer has received the requisite information. The goods or services need to be returned in an unaltered state.

The Consumer Sale of Goods Act is based on the Sale of Goods Act with certain exceptions to give consumers a higher level of protection than commercial actors due to their perceived more vulnerable status in relation to commercial actors. The Consumer Sale of Goods Act is applicable to a purchase or barter by a consumer of chattels for personal use as sold by a business. The act also covers custom ordered goods, but not services.

14.2.1 THE TRANSFER OF RISK

The main type of sale in the Consumer Sale of Goods Act is where the buyer picks up the goods at the seller's premises, again ex-works. If the delivery date is not contracted, it is to be a reasonable time from the date of purchase. However, the seller has no obligation to deliver the goods until payment is received. The seller is to bear any delivery costs unless the parties have agreed otherwise, and the goods are considered delivered when in the possession of the consumer.

The risk for the goods is transferred when the consumer has the goods in her possession. The seller is liable for any costs incurred connected to the goods until in the possession of the consumer, after that time, the consumer is liable for such costs. After the risk is transferred to the consumer, she must pay for the goods regardless of whether the goods are destroyed, lost, deteriorated or diminished as a consequence of an event not attributable to the seller. Any defect the consumer wishes to cite must also lie before the transfer of the risk. If the goods were sold on a trial basis, the consumer bears the risk for the goods until they are returned to the seller.

14.2.2 THE GOODS

The standard of performance with respect to the quality of the goods under the Consumer Sale of Goods Act is the same as for the Sale of Goods Act, with concrete defects existing where the goods are not in conformance with the contract. An abstract defect exists where the goods are not in conformance with a certain standard. The goods are to be:

- Fit for the purpose for which goods of a similar type are generally used;
- Fit for a particular purpose for which the goods are intended to be used, however, the seller at the time of the sale must have known about this specific purpose;
- Consistent with the characteristics the seller has referred to through samples, models or marketing materials as provided by the seller or manufacturer; and
- Packaged in a suitable and appropriate manner.

An abstract defect also exists where the seller has failed to inform the consumer of a circumstance that the consumer would have wished to be informed of, if this would have affected the purchase. If the goods deviate from the buyer's reasonable expectations, they are deemed non-conforming, as is also the case with respect to goods sold "as is." Where the seller has assumed responsibility for installing the goods, and the installation is faulty, the goods are also non-conforming.

Goods can also be non-conforming where they are in violation of the Products Liability Act, the Marketing Act (*marknadsföringslag* 2008:486) or other statutory provisions, or where the product is so defective that its use poses a danger to life or health. Goods deviating from the marketing materials of the seller or manufacturer can also be found defective. Defects can also exist with respect to situations in which a third party has ownership rights or security interests in the goods.

The buyer is to inspect the goods upon their receipt. If a defect arises within six months after receipt of the goods, the defect is presumed to have existed at the time of the transfer of the risk, unless the defect is related to the nature of the goods. For example, bananas may not last six months. The consumer has to give notice of non-conformity as soon as the defect becomes known, but if notice is given within two months of the defect being detected, this is deemed in due time. The statute of limitations for latent defects is three years for consumers. If the seller has been grossly negligent or acted in violation of faith and honor, or the defect was in violation of the Products Liability Act or the Marketing Act or its use posed a danger to life or health, the three-year limit is not applicable.

14.2.3 PERFORMANCE AND REMEDIES

The seller is to deliver conforming goods in time. The buyer is to pay for and receive the goods. If the price is not set out in the contract, it is to be a reasonable price. Remedies available for the seller's delay in delivery or non-conforming goods include specific performance, curing the goods, redelivery, withholding payment, price abatement or compensation for curing the goods or terminating the contract, and in addition, damages.

The right to damages is broader under the Consumer Sale of Goods Act than the Sale of Goods Act, as damages also include any losses arising due to the defect with respect to other property belonging to the consumer or someone in her household. Liability for damages due to late delivery or defect includes any costs or loss of income or price differences caused by the delay. The parties also have a duty to take reasonable measures to mitigate any losses.

The amount of damages to be paid by the seller can be decreased or nullified if unreasonably onerous taking into consideration the seller's financial situation, any insurance held by the consumer, and the seller's ability to foresee and prevent the losses or other particular circumstances. In any event, a party is not liable to pay damages under force majeure, for losses arising from acts that were a consequence of an impediment beyond the control of the party which that party could not reasonably have anticipated at the time of the contract, nor reasonably avoided or overcome. The consumer may terminate the contract due to a delay or defect that is of material significance. There is no requirement that the seller knew that the delay or defect was material, as required under the Sale of Goods Act.

The remedies available to the seller for the buyer's breach of contract include withholding the goods, requesting payment (specific performance), termination and damages. The parties can grant each other an extension of time in which to perform under the contract as discussed in the preceding section under the Sale of Goods Act. If performance is not completed within this extension of time, the party can then terminate the contract automatically.

If the contract is terminated, all obligations of the parties as to performance cease, and any partial performances are to be returned. If goods cannot be returned in the same condition as delivered, damages are to be paid for the difference in value.

14.2.4 PRIVITY OF CONTRACT

Privity of contract is still a strong doctrine in Swedish contract law, as seen in the slow progression in insurance law that injured parties in certain cases can now go directly against the insurance company of the tortfeasor. A similar development has occurred with the Consumer Sale of Goods Act. If the seller is insolvent, no longer in business or otherwise not available, the consumer has the right to make a claim with respect to a defect in the goods against a party higher up in the sales chain, for example a distributor or manufacturer.

A consumer can only go against a previous party in the chain of sale to the extent the defect could have been alleged against that party by the next party in the chain. In other words, only if the seller could have made the claim against the distributor, or the distributor could have made the claim against the manufacturer, can the consumer make the claim. A notice of non-conformity has to be given within a reasonable time by the consumer to either the seller or the party against whom the defect is being claimed, or else the consumer forfeits the right to make the claim.

14.3 The Consumer Sale of Services Act

The Consumer Sale of Services Act has no equivalent on the commercial side and is loosely based on the Consumer Sale of Goods Act. The Consumer Sale of Services Act is applicable to an agreement by a commercial service provider to provide services to a consumer including work on chattels (but not live animals), work on real property or buildings or other facilities on land or in water, or the storage of chattels (but again not live animals). Particular statutory provisions are applicable with respect to building residential houses. Agreements containing provisions less favorable than those provided in the act are not valid as against the consumer as a general rule.

14.3.1 THE DUTIES OF THE SERVICE PROVIDER

A service provider is to perform services in accordance with professional standards. In addition, she is to take into account the interests of the consumer and consult with the consumer to the extent necessary if possible. Unless otherwise agreed, the service provider is to provide any necessary materials.

The service provider is to insure that the services are in compliance with any regulations or government authority decisions that have the objective of insuring that the object of the services is reliable from a safety perspective. Neither can the service be in conflict with the Products Liability Act or the Marketing Act.

The service provider also has a duty to advise the consumer not to purchase services that cannot be seen to be of a reasonable benefit to the consumer taking into consideration the price, value of the object or other circumstances. The same is true if work is commenced and it appears that the cost for the services is going to be considerably higher than originally planned. If the service provider cannot reach the consumer to inform her of this, the service provider is to stop the work unless there is reason to believe that the consumer would have wished the work to continue despite the costs.

If a service provider fails to advise the consumer as to the absence of a reasonable benefit or as to the higher costs, and there is strong reason to believe that the consumer would have discontinued the services, the service provider does not have a right to compensation greater than that she would have had if the consumer would have cancelled or not ordered the services. However, the service provider has the right to costs to the extent the consumer otherwise would receive an unfair benefit.

14.3.2 NON-CONFORMING SERVICES

The services are to be deemed non-conforming if the results of the services deviate from that stated in the contract. An abstract defect exists where the results deviate from that which the consumer has the right to demand with respect to professional standards, even if the deviation is due to an accident or similar circumstance. An abstract defect also exists where the result of the services deviates from any government regulations or government authority decision as to safety, or the Products Liability Act or the Marketing Act. The services are also non-conforming where they deviate from material information as supplied by the service provider, another commercial actor, a sector organization, or a supplier of materials used in the services. Finally, services are deemed to be non-conforming where the service provider has failed to provide the consumer with material information, and this omission has affected the agreement.

The assessment of whether the services are non-conforming is to be made when the services are completed, or if the services concern a chattel, when the chattel is again in the possession of the consumer. If the completed services deteriorate after this point of time, the services are to be deemed defective where the deterioration is due to the service provider. Notice of non-conformity must be made by the consumer to the seller within a reasonable time after the consumer knows, or ought to have known, of the defect. The statute of limitations is three years, but for buildings or other facilities on land or water, the statute of limitations is ten years. In the event the service provider has been grossly negligent or acted in violation of faith and honor, notice can always be given for latent defects within ten years of the services being completed.

14.3.3 PAYMENT BY THE CONSUMER

If the price is not stated in the agreement, the consumer is to pay that which is reasonable taking into account the type of service, the extent and performance, standard price or price calculations for comparable services as well as the circumstances in general. If the service provider has given an estimated price, the final price may not exceed that price by more than 15 % unless otherwise agreed, or if the service provider has the right to an additional price amount and the services cost more due to circumstances attributable to the consumer that the service provider could not foresee. The service provider is also to submit a detailed invoice as to the services if so requested by the consumer. The consumer is obligated to pay for the services when completed if the parties have not agreed otherwise. In the event the consumer has requested a detailed invoice, the consumer is not obligated to pay for the services prior to receiving the invoice.

The consumer is not obligated to pay for work that the service provider has performed or materials that have been provided to the extent the services or materials have been lost or deteriorated due to an accident. If the consumer cancels the agreement prior to the services being completed, the service provider has the right to compensation for that portion of the services performed or that must be performed despite the cancellation. The price is to be comparable to the price that would have been applicable if the agreement had only concerned the services performed. In addition, the service provider has the right to compensation for any losses in the form of costs for the remaining portion of the services and losses in general due to refusal of other work in order to be able to perform the contract. The service provider does not have this right, however, if the consumer no longer has a reason for the work to be performed. This can be where the object of the work has been damaged or lost not due to the consumer, or where the consumer has been prevented from benefiting from the services due to government regulations.

14.3.4 REMEDIES

In the event the services are non-conforming, the consumer has the right to withhold payment, request a cure of the services, a price reduction, terminate the contract, and/or claim damages as well. If the services are delayed, the consumer has the right to withhold payment, require specific performance or terminate the agreement, and request damages.

The right to damages under the Consumer Sale of Services Act due to non-conforming services includes compensation for any losses arising due to the defect with respect to the property or other property belonging to the consumer or someone in her household. The service provider is also liable to pay for losses caused the consumer due to the service provider's negligence. If a party other than the service provider, for example another commercial actor, sector organization or vendor of materials, has intentionally or negligently provided misleading information of significance for the consumer's assessment of the services, and the resulting services are non-conforming due to the misleading information, that party can also be liable to the consumer for damages. The same is true if such a party fails to provide safety information as required under the Products Liability Act or Marketing Act and the failure can be seen to have negatively affected the outcome of the services.

The amount of damages to be paid by the service provider can be decreased or nullified if unreasonably onerous taking into consideration the service provider's financial situation, any insurance held by the consumer, and the service provider's ability to foresee and prevent the losses or other particular circumstances. In any event, a party is not liable to pay damages for losses arising from acts that were a consequence of an impediment beyond the control of the party, which that party could not reasonably have anticipated at the time of the contract, nor reasonably avoided or overcome. These rules are not applicable with respect to compensatory damages for injuries to persons.

The remedies available to the service provider for the consumer's breach of contract due to failure to pay include withholding any goods in the service provider's possession, withholding services, requesting payment (specific performance), termination and damages.

14.4 International Sale of Goods – CISG

The Swedish Sale of Goods Act, though a product of Nordic legislative collaboration, is based on the 1980 United Nations Convention on Contracts for the International Sale of Goods ("CISG"), also known as the Vienna Convention.[2] Sweden signed and enacted CISG in 1987 as Swedish law effective 1989 through the Act on the International Sale of Goods (*lag 1987:822 om internationella köp*) originally with the exception of CISG's Part II, Articles 14–24.[3] This was amended in 2012, and now the entirety of CISG will be applicable as Swedish law on the date as decided by the Swedish Government. Sweden and the other Nordic countries signing CISG had opted out of part two of the convention dealing with the execution of a contract. CISG in this part is based on the contract principle (*kontraktsprincipen*) while the Contracts Act, as discussed already in Chapter Nine, is based on the principle that offers are binding as the general rule (*löftesprincipen*). Another exception made by Sweden and the Nordic countries when enacting CISG was under the Naboland Clause (*Nabolands-klausulen*), that CISG would not be applicable to transactions where both the seller and buyer had their places of business in Denmark, Finland, Iceland, Norway or Sweden.

---

2 For an extensive electronic database concerning CISG, *see* the Pace Law School Institute of International Commercial Law website at cisg.law.pace.edu. Seventy-seven countries have signed CISG as of August 2011. Another good source for information concerning CISG can be found at the website for the CISG Advisory Council at cisgac.com.

3 As discussed in Chapter Two, the dualism practiced in Sweden allows for international agreements to become Swedish law through either incorporation or transformation. CISG was incorporated into Swedish law through the act in the six official languages, which have according to the incorporating act a higher dignity than the Swedish translation.

CISG is divided into four parts as seen from the table:

TABLE 14.1 Convention on the International Sale of Goods.

Part I Sphere of Application and General Provisions, Art. 1–13
• Chap. 1 Sphere of Application, Art. 1–6 • Chap. 2 General Provisions, Art. 7–13
Part II Formation of the Contract, Art. 14–24
Part III Sale of Goods, Art. 25–88

• Chap. 1 General Provisions, Art. 25–29
• Chap. 2 Obligations of the Seller, Art. 30–52
  – Sec. 1 Delivery of the Goods
  – Sec. 2 Conformity of the Goods
  – Sec. 3 Remedies for Breach of Contract by Seller
• Chap. 3 Obligations of the Buyer, Art. 53–65
  – Sec. 1 Payment of the Price
  – Sec. 2 Taking Delivery
  – Sec. 3 Remedies for Breach of Contract by Buyer
• Chap. 4 Passing of Risk, Art. 66–70
• Chap. 5 Provisions Common to the Obligations of the Seller and of the Buyer, Art. 71–88
  – Sec. 1 Anticipatory Breach and Installment Contracts
  – Sec. 2 Damages
  – Sec. 3 Interest
  – Sec. 4 Exemptions
  – Sec. 5 Effects of Avoidance

Part IV Final Provisions, Art. 89–101

The application of CISG depends upon the subject matter of the contract, the specific issue at dispute, the domicile of the parties to the contract as well as the actual contract provisions. CISG is based on freedom of contract, and the parties are free to contract out of CISG as seen from Article 6. CISG does not cover all issues that can arise with respect to a transaction concerning the international sale of goods. For example, the validity of contracts is outside the scope of CISG as expressly stated in Article 4. A seller's liability for death or personal injury also falls outside the scope of CISG as stated in Article 5.

According to its Article 1, CISG is applicable to the sale of goods between "parties whose places of business are in different states," when those countries are contracting states to CISG or are obliged to follow CISG under rules of private international law. CISG does not apply to the sale of goods for personal use or to contracts for services or labor.

CISG consequently has a narrower scope than the Swedish Sale of Goods Act. CISG also does not cover all disputes that could arise under the contract. For example, as stated above, CISG does not govern the validity of contracts. If the transaction falls within CISG or the parties choose CISG as the applicable law, the parties also ought to choose a national law as a secondary legal system. If the parties do not choose a national law, the main rule according to the Convention on the Law Applicable to International Sale of Goods, the Hague Convention of 1955, enacted as Swedish law in 1964 (*lag 1964:528 om tillämplig lag beträffande internationella köp av lösa saker*) is that the applicable law will be the law of the seller's place of business.

14.4.1 THE OFFER, ACCEPTANCE AND CONTRACT

Article 14(1) states that "[a] proposal for concluding a contract addressed to one or more specific persons constitutes an offer if it is sufficiently definite and indicates the intention of the offeror to be bound in case of acceptance." An offer under CISG must indicate the goods, and expressly or implicitly fix or make provisions for determining the quantities and the price. Offers as a rule are not binding under CISG, but there is no requirement as to rendering an offer irrevocable other than by simply stating it is so. This is in direct contrast to the Nordic main rule of binding offers, but is also in contrast to the Anglo-American requirement of consideration in order to make an offer binding. If the offer does not designate a period of time during which it is valid, it is to be valid for a reasonable period. Offers are terminated by a rejection, a counter-offer, a revocation or its expiration.

The mirror image rule is applied to the acceptance. Article 19(1) views any acceptance containing material additions, limitations or other modifications as a rejection and thus a counter-offer. Material additions are defined as those concerning price, payment, quality and quantity of the goods, place and time of delivery, liability and the settlement of disputes. CISG does not address the manner of acceptance, only that the acceptance must be made within the period as designated by the seller. In addition, there is no requirement of consideration under CISG, nor any requirement of a writing. However, if the parties include a term in a written contract stating that modifications to the contract have to be in writing, such must be in writing to be valid under CISG.

According to Article 18(2), an acceptance becomes effective the moment the indication of assent reaches the offeror. This combination of revocable offers and acceptances effective upon receipt within CISG mirrors the compromises reached between the common law and the civil law countries in the convention. Though offers are revocable under CISG in accordance with the common law view, the counterbalance offered in the common law of acceptances effective upon dispatch under the mailbox rule is missing. Instead, the civil law approach of acceptances effective upon receipt was adopted.

14.4.2 CONTRACT INTERPRETATION

Consistent with the view in many civil law countries, the verbal contract is seen in CISG as simply a part of the entire agreement between the parties, not necessarily its entirety, with the rules concerning contract interpretation in CISG reflecting this. Article 8(3) states that all relevant circumstances, including negotiations, any practices the parties have established between themselves, usages and subsequent conduct of the parties can be taken into consideration when assessing the intent of the parties. National custom and usage does not bind the parties unless they expressly agree to such. CISG provides gap-fillers for price [Article 55, *compare* Article 14(1)], place of payment [Article 57(1)], place of delivery (Article 31), delivery date (Article 33) and payment date (Article 58).

14.4.3 THE TRANSFER OF RISK

Under CISG, the seller is to deliver the goods as well as any necessary documents. If no specific delivery place is stated in the agreement, the seller's typical obligation is to deliver the goods to the first carrier with respect to the carriage of goods. The risk for the goods transfers to the buyer at this point of time. If the parties have agreed to a date or period, the seller is to deliver the goods on that date or within that period. Otherwise, the seller is to deliver the goods within a reasonable time after the conclusion of the contract.

14.4.4 THE GOODS

Historically, the sale of goods traditionally was in accordance with *caveat emptor*, "buyer beware." CISG is more based on *caveat venditor*, "seller beware." Article 35 addresses the conformity of goods, with the same two categories of defects as found under the Swedish Sale of Goods Act: concrete defects where the goods are not of the quantity, quality, description or packaging as required by the contract. The second category of abstract defects invokes as standards that the goods are to be fit for ordinary purposes, fit for any particular purpose expressly or implicitly known to the seller, possess the quality of goods consistent with any samples or models, as well as be adequately contained and packaged.

Article 30 sets forth the obligation of the seller to deliver the goods as required by the contract. This means that title to the goods in the majority of cases must be free from any third-party ownership claims. Article 41 mandates that the goods be free from any infringement as to any industrial or other intellectual property.

14.4.5 PERFORMANCE BY THE PARTIES

Article 30 states that the seller is to deliver the goods as well as any documents relating to them, and transfer the ownership in the goods. Under Article 53, the buyer is to pay the price for the goods and take delivery of them as required by the contract and CISG.

A material breach under CISG is defined in Article 25 as "fundamental if it results in such detriment to the other party as substantially to deprive him of what he is entitled to expect under the contract." In addition, there is a good faith exception in Article 25, "unless the party in breach did not foresee and a reasonable person of the same kind in the same circumstances would not have foreseen such a result."

The breaching party has the opportunity to cure the delivery in the case of an early delivery in accordance with Article 37. Article 39 establishes a statute of limitations as to the right to rely on a lack of conformity of the goods if the buyer does not give notice within two years after the delivery. Article 40 creates an exception to this two-year period for defects of which the seller was aware or could not have been unaware of and which were not disclosed to the buyer.

Article 79 of CISG excuses a failure to perform due to an impediment outside of the control of the party that could not reasonably be expected at the time of the contract. Under CISG, the legal effect is an exemption from liability for damages. If the risk is foreseeable, the performance of a party cannot be excused. Complete performance of the duties under the contract discharges the contract in full. Substantial performance, less than complete performance, entitles the party performing to a right of discharge under the contract despite minor deviations in performance. The performing party must have acted in good faith and the other party must still receive the important and essential benefits under the contract. The party failing to perform perfectly is still liable for any damages caused by the breach.

14.4.6 REMEDIES

Both parties have a duty to mitigate any losses caused by the other party's breach of contract as stated in Article 77. The primary remedy of the buyer under Article 46 is specific performance,[4] that the buyer may require performance by the seller of the obligations, unless the buyer has resorted to a remedy inconsistent with this requirement. An election of remedies lurks in the article. The buyer may also require the delivery of substitute goods in the case of a material breach. The buyer may also request that the seller remedy a lack of conformity. The buyer under Article 47 can grant an extension of the period of performance, during which the buyer cannot resort to any other remedy. If the seller after this extension has expired still has not performed, or if there is a material breach of the contract, the buyer in accordance with Article 49 may terminate (avoid) the contract. In addition, according to Article 50, the buyer may reduce the price paid under the contract in proportion to any nonconformity of the goods.

---

4   Specific performance as the primary remedy is very much opposite to the Anglo-American view of damages as the primary contractual remedy. A resolution as to this conflict was reached in Article 28, which states that a claim for specific performance does not have to be enforced by a court unless it would be enforced by the law of the country in which the court is sitting.

In cases of breach by the buyer, the seller has the right under Article 62 to demand that the buyer pay the price or take delivery, seen as specific performance, terminate the contract for a material breach, or grant an extension of time for performance and then terminate the contract under Articles 63 and 64. In the event the buyer has failed to provide specifications as under the contract, the seller has the right to make them herself under Article 65.

Both the seller and buyer have the right to compensatory damages in accordance with Article 74 for all losses incurred due to the breach that were foreseeable, explicitly including loss of profit. This scope of damages is much broader than that available under the Swedish Sale of Goods Act. Both parties have a right to damages consisting of the difference between the market and contract price under Article 76. The buyer also has a right to cover damages according to Article 75. Interest can be recovered under Article 78.

CHAPTER 15

Intellectual Property Rights and Unfair Trade Practices

This chapter consists again of the marriage of two fields of law, intellectual property rights and unfair trade practices. The latter category is referred to in the Swedish system as market law (*marknadsrätt*), comprising trade secrets (*företagshemligheter*), marketing law (*marknadsföringsrätt*) and competition (anti-trust) law (*konkurrensrätt*). These two areas of law are often addressed together, a treatment rationalized by the reality that intellectual property rights, exclusive rights for the holder, taken to their extreme can become competition law issues with respect to abuse of market dominance and anti-competitive agreements. Intellectual property rights, particularly trademarks, can be abused in certain types of marketing practices. As abuse of intellectual property rights can be seen as the theme, this chapter begins with intellectual property rights, copyrights and industrial property. Aspects of unfair trade practices, trade secrets, marketing law and competition law, are treated in their own separate sections afterwards.

15.1 Intellectual Property Rights

The development of intellectual property rights in Sweden has followed not only internationalization and Europeanization, but also the transition from an industrial economy to one of services and then knowledge. According to the Confederation of Swedish Enterprises, eighty percent of the assets in the 500 largest Swedish companies in 1975 comprised real estate, machinery and other comparable hard assets. By 2005, eighty percent of their assets were based instead on intellectual property rights.

Intellectual property rights as granted in Sweden to a high degree have become Europeanized and internationally standardized. Intellectual property rights in Europe are divided into two categories, the first being industrial property, encompassing inventions (patents), trademarks and industrial designs. This chapter begins with the second category, copyright. In each of these areas there is a convergence of systems on the Swedish, European and/or international levels. On the European level, patents are handled by the European Patent Office ("EPO"), which decides whether a patent can be registered in the designated countries. This patent right, however, is a national patent right enforceable under national law.[1] Trademarks and designs are administered within the EU by the Office of the Harmonization in the Internal Market ("OHIM"), which grants the community trademark and design.[2] On the international level, the most important agreement for all intellectual property rights today is the Agreement on Trade-Related Aspects of Intellectual Property Rights ("TRIPS Agreement") of 1994, administrated by the World Trade Organization ("WTO").[3] Further, the International Bureau of the World Intellectual Property Organization ("WIPO") coordinates certain issues with respect to national copyrights, trademarks and design rights.[4] The focus of the following presentation naturally is on the Swedish rules as against this background.

15.1.1 COPYRIGHTS

The Act on Copyrights to Literary and Artistic Works (*lagen 1960:729 om upphovsrätt till litterära och konstnärliga verk*),[5] the Copyright Regulation (*upphovsrättsförordning* 1993:1212) and the International Copyright Regulation (*internationell upphovsrättsförordning* 1994:193) form the gist of the Swedish copyright system. As with patents, Sweden has signed several international agreements in this area, several of which are addressed in the latter regulation: The Berne Convention for the Protection of Literary

---

1   For more information about EPO, *see* its website at epo.org.
2   For more information about OHIM, *see* its website at oami.europa.eu.
3   For an example of the international debate, *see* the discussions at the EU and WTO levels concerning the Anti-Counterfeiting Trade Agreement ("ACTA") of 2011, and the negations of the ACTA-agreement.
4   For more information about WIPO, *see* its website at wipo.int.
5   An English translation of the Act on Copyright in Literary and Artistic Works (1960:729) can be found at the Government Offices of Sweden's website at sweden.gov.se.

and Artistic Works of 1886, the Universal Copyright Convention of 1952, the European Agreement as to Broadcasting of 1960 with protocols, the International Convention for the Protection of Performers, Producers of Phonograms and Broadcasting Organization of 1961, the WIPO Copyright Treaty of 1996 and the WTO Performances and Phonographs Treaty of 1996.

On the European level, several directives can be seen to constitute the backbone of Union law in the area of copyright:

- Satellite and cable transmissions of copyrighted materials (Directive 93/83/EEC);
- Legal protection of databases (Directive 96/9/EC);
- Conditional access (Directive 98/84/EC);
- Copyright/information society (Directive 2001/29/EC);
- Resale rights of artists (Directive 2001/84/EC);
- Civil enforcement of intellectual property protections (Directive 2004/48/EC);
- Rentals and loans and intellectual property rights (Directive 2006/115/EC);
- Copyright Term (Directive 2006/116/EC); and
- Legal protections for computer programs (Directive 2009/24/EC).

Though copyright law is being harmonized on the EU level, the power of granting and protecting copyrights remains with the Member States.

To obtain a copyright in Sweden, the requirements as set out under the Copyright Act must be met. Under the first section of the first chapter of the Swedish Copyright Act, the physical person(s) who has created the work is to be granted the copyright to the work. Works that are protected under the act include fictional or descriptive presentations in print or orally, computer programs, musical or dramatic works, films, photographs or other pictorial art, architecture and applied art or other similar works that have come to fruition in another manner. The work needs to have a degree of originality (*verkshöjd*). The copyright comes into existence when the work is created, consequently there is no registration of such rights in Sweden. Therefore, it is sufficient, but not necessary, for the author/artist to affix a copyright sign © in order for the copyright to be proven to exist. A copyright is valid for the lifetime of the individual artist, and for an additional period of seventy years after the artist's death.

The copyright gives the author the exclusive economic right to dispose over the work by making copies or making it available to the public. The author also has moral rights to the work. The moral rights are twofold: the work cannot be used in a way seen as denigrating to the copyright holder, and the creator has the right to be indicated as such on the work. A famous example of this occurred in connection to the beloved Swedish children's author, Astrid Lindgren. An adult film was made, loosely based on one of her books, Pippi Longstocking. She received damages for this infringement of her *droit moral*.

There are certain limitations in the copyright holder's economic exclusivity, but moral rights always have to be respected. These limitations include making a work accessible to disabled persons, citing a work with proper citations, depicting buildings or works in public places, or in the retelling of current events. Every individual has the right to cite a work. Government authorities also have the right to cite works in different contexts, such as in legislative preparatory works or in court judgments. An exception that has given rise to a heated debate is that of copies made for personal use. Before digitalization, this was not such a significant issue as the copying process in itself was time consuming, for example, with photocopying or recording to a cassette tape. However, now specific exemptions exist to this exception, particularly with respect to computer programs. This is a pertinent example of the law not quite keeping pace with technology.

15.1.2 PATENTS

The Swedish patent system revolves around the Patent Act (*patentlagen* 1967:837). The international character of this field of law can be seen already with the Paris Convention for the Protection of Industrial Property of 1883, which Sweden signed in 1885.

Under the current Swedish Patent Act, the invention must be novel (*nyhetskrav*), non-obvious (*uppfinningshöjd*) and have an industrial application (*industriellt tillämpbar*). The requirement of novelty is based on the current state of the art internationally. The Patent Act was amended in 2011 to facilitate the patenting of new uses for already-known pharmaceuticals, syncing the Swedish act with the comparable rights in the European Patent Convention of 1973. The difference between novelty and non-obviousness is that an invention is not novel if it has previously been made or described in the state of the art. In accordance with the principle of equivalence, it has to be found to be non-obvious. Non-obviousness goes to the fact that even if the invention has never been made, persons of an average skill in the craft might be able to deduce how to make it quite readily should the need arise. In that case, the invention is "obvious" and not patentable. The third requirement of an industrial application in the majority of cases is not difficult to fulfill.

A Swedish patent (as well as trademark and design protection) is granted by the Swedish Patent and Registration Office ("PRV").[6] The applicant is to submit a complete application form, description of the invention and patent claims, an abstract, drawings if any, and the filing fee. The filing fee for a Swedish patent is SEK 3 000 (2012). The patent has a life of twenty years (twenty-five years for certain medical inventions given extra protection by statute) as long as the annual fees for the patent are paid to the PRV. A decision of the PRV can be appealed to the Court of Patent Appeals (*Patentbesvärsrätten,* "PBR").[7] For the period from 1991–2011, almost eleven thousand cases were brought to this court, and of these, 1 799 concerned patents. The decisions of the Court of Patent Appeals can be appealed to the Supreme Administrative Court subject to a grant of leave to appeal. Cases concerning the validity or infringement of a patent are brought to the general courts. Patents historically have not been litigated to a great degree in Sweden. Another example of this can be seen from the fact that there were only two published judgments by the Swedish Supreme Court for the period from 1948 to 2000 concerning patent infringement, NJA 1972 p. 462 and NJA 2000 p. 497.

Parties contemplating applying for patent protection need to decide whether they wish to apply for Swedish patent rights through the Swedish government authority, the PRV, or through the European Patent Office ("EPO"). Statistics demonstrate the competition the Swedish patent faces internationally. In 2010, 2 549 applications for a Swedish patent and 2 050 international applications were submitted to the PRV.[8] According to PRV's

---

6   For more information in English on this authority, *see* its website at prv.se.

7   For more information in English on the Court of Patent Appeals, *see* its website at pbr.se.

8   The PRV is one of only five authorities globally competent to handle international applications.

statistics, Swedes submitted 3 147 application to the EPO and 3 840 to the Unites States Patent and Trademark Office. Within Sweden, 15 994 Swedish patents and 80 097 EPO patents were in effect in 2011, with an average life of 12.17 and 13.23 years respectively. To date there is no European Union law generally addressing the patent law in the Member States with the exception of Directive 98/44/EC on the legal protection of biotechnological inventions. This directive has given the EU Court the opportunity to harmonize certain aspects of the national patent laws in the EU Member States, which opportunity was taken, for example, in a 2011 case, *Brüstle v. Greenpeace*, with respect to the patenting of the results of stem-cell research.[9]

15.1.3 TRADEMARKS

The Swedish Trademark Act (*varumärkeslag* 2010:1877) governs trademarks, collective marks, guarantee or certification marks, as well as community trade marks ("CTM") in accordance with the Community Trade Mark Regulation 207/2009/EC. Under the Swedish act, a trademark can consist of any sign that can be reproduced graphically. The trademark can contain specific words, including personal names, as well as figures, letters, numbers and forms or trade dress. In addition to the requirement of an object falling within this list, the trademark must also be distinguishable. The trademark must have a distinctive character. It is distinctive if it allows the products or services of one provider to be distinguished from those products or services of another provider. Marks that are not inherently distinctive can be protected if they are found to have acquired secondary meaning through use.

Trademark rights entail exclusive use for a period of ten years, which can be renewed unlimited times. If the trademark is registered, but not used within a period of five years, the right to the trademark can be revoked if challenged.

Given the functions of trademarks, identifying the origins of goods and services, acting as a guarantor of quality in certain cases, and as a form of communication to the public, trademarks often reflect the goodwill value of a firm. This importance can be seen as reflected in the statistics before the

---

9   Case C-34/10 *Brüstle v. Greenpeace* [2011] ECR --, celex no. 62010CJ0034.

Court of Patent Appeals, of the eleven thousand cases before that court in the past twenty years, over seven thousand concerned trademarks.

Swedish trademark protection is granted by the PRV. The application is to include the name and information about the party wishing to receive the rights, a clear rendition of the trademark, a listing of the goods or services the trademark is intended to be used for as well as their class designation, and the filing fee of SEK 1 500 (2012). Almost ten thousand applications for trademark protection were submitted to the PRV in 2011. Once a trademark right is granted, the holder can have the right in perpetuity as long as the legal requirements, for example as to fees and of use, are met.

Here again potential intellectual property right holders need to decide whether to apply for a trademark through the Swedish, European or international WIPO system. On the European level, the Office for Harmonization in the Internal Market (Trade Marks and Designs) can grant a Community Trade Mark for the entirety of the European Union. The Union law applicable here is the Community Trade Mark Regulation, 207/2009/EC. A CTM is valid for a period of ten years through all twenty-seven member states. The filing fee is € 900 online, € 1 050 if submitted in paper form.

On the international level, in 2011 Sweden signed the Singapore Treaty on the Law of Trademarks of 2006. The international system of applications for national trademark rights is administered by the International Bureau of the World Intellectual Property Organization in Geneva according to the Madrid Protocol. An application for trademark protection can be submitted either directly to the WIPO or through the Swedish PRV. In an application submitted to the WIPO, the applicant can designate the European Union and be granted protection equivalent to the CTM.

15.1.4 DESIGN RIGHTS

Design rights are granted under the Design Protection Act (*mönsterskyddslag* 1970:485) which has been amended to be in conformance with the Design Protection Directive 98/71/EC. A design under the act is the appearance of a product or portion thereof, which is determined by the actual product's details or by details in the product's formation, particularly with respect to lines, contours, colors, forms, outer structures or materials. The design must be novel (*nytt*) and unique (*särpräglat*). A design is novel if no other identical design has been publically available before the registration date. Designs can be considered identical even if minor differences exist. Designs are to be considered unique if an informed user's impression of the design is that it differs from all other designs publicly known prior to the registration date. In the assessment as to uniqueness, consideration is to be taken of the amount of variation possible for the designer when creating the design.

Design rights, in contrast to copyrights, must be registered. The application to the PRV for a design right is to include the name of the applicant, any assignment of rights, product information and class, whether the design is to be registered in color, attached photographs, models, information as to priority and confidentiality and a filing fee of SEK 1 900 (2012). After registration, Swedish design rights are granted for a period of five years, which can be renewed five times for a total of twenty-five years.

There is a design protection on the EU level through the Community Design Regulation 6/2002/EC for both registered and unregistered community designs. The registered Community Design is administered by OHIM. A Community design can be protected through use of the design in at least one Member State for three years. Otherwise, the same rules regarding registration apply to the Community design as for the national design rights. The OHIM has registered approximately 460 000 designs to date covering the period from 2003–2012. The registered Community Design has a protection period first of five years, which can be renewed for a maximum of twenty-five years. The unregistered Community Design has a maximum protection of three years. During the first year that the design is made available to the public, it can be registered and gain a longer protection of twenty-five years.

15.1.5 INFRINGEMENT OF INTELLECTUAL PROPERTY RIGHTS

The holders of intellectual property rights are granted an exclusive use of the right for a certain period that can vary depending on the right, three years initially for design rights, five years initially for patent rights, seventy years after death for copyrights, and for trademarks, in perpetuity as long as all the requirements are met. The unauthorized use of the intellectual property right is an infringement of the right holder's exclusivity. Such an infringement can be a crime in Sweden, entailing that the prosecutor would file the case. However, the right holder has the right to sue under private law for unauthorized use. Specific procedural rules can also be applicable, for example, patent, community trademark and community design infringement cases are to be brought to the Stockholm District Court, and if appealed, to the Svea Court of Appeal and ultimately, the Supreme Court. Criminal sanctions include fines, imprisonment, damages, seizures and destruction of infringing goods, as well as prohibitions as to future acts. If a civil lawsuit, the main remedy is damages.

15.2 Trade Secrets

Trade secrets (*företagshemligheter*) are protected in Sweden by the Trade Secret Protection Act (*lag 1990:409 om skydd för företagshemligheter*). Trade secrets naturally do not go through any type of registration process, as the objective is that they are not to become a part of the public domain but have to remain confidential.

The act defines "trade secret" as "such information concerning the business or operational relations of a party conducting business activities that the party wishes to keep confidential and the disclosure of which would likely cause damage to the party from a competitive perspective." Information is defined in the act as "both information documented in some form, including drawings, models and other similar technical prototypes, and the knowledge of individual persons about specific circumstances even where it has not been documented in some form." The act only addresses unauthorized disclosures of trade secrets. Neither does the act prescribe what must be done for the party to be seen as having kept the information confidential.

An individual found to have unlawfully disclosed a trade secret can be convicted of the crime of corporate espionage, with criminal sanctions of fines and/or imprisonment up to two years, or if the crime is aggravated, up to six years. A party knowingly acquiring a trade secret can be sentenced to unlawful possession of a trade secret, with criminal sanctions of fines and/ or imprisonment up to two years, if aggravated, up to four years. In both cases, the individual can be liable to pay damages for any harm resulting from the unlawful acts. If a party having authorized access to a trade secret unlawfully discloses it, the party can be liable for any damages resulting from the disclosure.

15.3 Marketing Law

Marketing law in the Swedish system is not focused on protecting only consumers against deceptive trade practices, but is targeted at protecting both consumers and commercial actors from such practices. The main statute is the Marketing Act (*marknadsföringslag* 2008:486),[10] which has implemented Directive 2005/29/EC concerning unfair business to consumer commercial practices.

The Marketing Act, however, is not the only statutory regulation in this field, as can be seen from its first paragraph listing the specific statutes that also address marketing issues:

- The Package Vacation Tours Act (1992:1672);
- The Tobacco Act (1993:581);
- The Deposit Guarantee Act (1995:1571)
- The Act on the Obligation to Give Notice of Certain Financial Operations (1996:1006);
- The Marketing of Crystal Glass Act (1996:1118);
- The Act on Cross-Border Payments within the European Economic Area (1999:268);
- The Investor Compensation Act (1999:158)
- The Act on Electronic Commerce and other Information Society Services (2002:562);
- The Deposits Business Act (2004:299);
- The Price Information Act (2004:347);
- The Distance and Door-to-Door Selling Act (2005:59);
- The Insurance Contracts Act (2005:104);
- The Insurance Mediation Act (2005:405);
- The Franchise Disclosure Act (2006:484);
- The Aviation Transportation Act (2010:510);
- The Radio and Television Act (2010:696);
- The Alcohol Act (2010:1622);
- The Consumer Credit Act (2010:1846); and
- The Act on Consumer Protection in Timeshare Contracts (2011:915).

---

10 An English translation of this act is available from the WIPO website at wipo.int.

The Marketing Act is applicable in four situations: when commercial actors either advertise or demand products in their commercial operations, to televised broadcasts, when the Consumer Ombudsman is exercising its authority as set out in Regulation 2006/2004/EC on cooperation between national authorities responsible for the enforcement of consumer protection laws, or when an authorized agency is exercising its authority as set out in Directive 2006/123/EC concerning services in the inner market.

The act sets out requirements as to identifying advertising as such. All advertising is to be formulated and presented in such a way that it is clear that it is a matter of marketing, and the party responsible for the advertisement is to always be clearly indicated.

Under the Act, advertising or marketing is to be in accordance with good marketing practices. Good marketing practices entail a significant reliance on soft law, i.e., the recommendations by the International Chamber of Commerce ("ICC"). Notably, certain commercial communications not in accordance with good marketing practices escape sanctions under the Marketing Act. For instance, discriminatory advertising and libel in media are subject to self-regulation and the sanction is negative publicity by the Consumer Ombudsman. Marketing that contravenes good marketing practices is to be regarded as unfair if it appreciably or potentially affects the recipient's ability to make a well-founded transaction decision. Aggressive marketing is also prohibited under the act, defined as aggressive if involving harassment, coercion, physical violence, threats or other aggressive ways of bringing pressure to bear. Aggressive marketing is to be regarded as unfair if it appreciably affects or probably affects the recipient's ability to make a well-founded transaction decision.

Misleading marketing is also prohibited under the act where it affects or probably affects the recipient's ability to make a well-founded transaction decision. Traders are not to make incorrect statements or other representations that are misleading with respect to the trader's own or another person's business activity. This is true in particular to representations concerning:

1 The product's existence, nature, quantity, quality and other distinguishing characteristics;
2 The product's origin, uses and risks such as impact on health or environment;

3   Customer service, processing of complaints and method and date
    of manufacture or supply;
4   The product's price, basis for calculating the price, special price
    advantages and payment terms;
5   The qualifications, position on the market, commitments,
    trademarks, trade names, distinctive symbols or other rights
    of the trader or of another trader;
6   Awards or distinctions awarded to the trader;
7   Terms of delivery for the product;
8   Service needs, spare parts, exchanges or repairs;
9   The trader's commitment to comply with codes of conduct; and
10 The consumer's rights under law or other regulation.

Further, a trader may not omit material information when marketing its own
or another person's business activity. Misleading omissions also refer to cases
where the material information is provided in an unclear, incomprehensible,
ambiguous or other inappropriate manner as communicated in the public
media. Misleading advertisement can also exist with respect to sales, price
reductions or special offers, product comparisons, product specifications
and depictions. Aggressive and misleading marketing as specified in points
1–31 of Annex I to Directive 2005/29/EC is always to be regarded as unfair
under the Swedish act and include not only public communications, but also
direct communications in situations such as when a commercial actor and
consumer meet face to face.

Sanctions available under the act include injunctions as to future conduct,
penalty fines, fines for market distortion and damages. Cases seeking the
remedies of injunctions or fines are to be brought to the Market Court by
either commercial actors, the Consumer Ombudsman or an association
representing consumers. Decisions by the Consumer Ombudsman can be
appealed to the Market Court.

15.4 Competition Law

Competition regulation can be seen as a relative newcomer to the fields of
law governed within the Swedish legal system. Prior to the 1983 Act, there
was a 1931 act on disloyal competition (*lagen 1931:452 med vissa bestämmelser*

mot illojal konkurrens) and a subsequent act in 1953 as to combating certain types of anti-competitive behavior in the private sector (*lagen 1953:603 om motverkande i vissa fall av konkurrensbegränsning inom näringslivet*). Both were replaced by the first Competition Act in 1983, which was replaced in 1993 and again in 2008.

The Swedish state historically has had state monopolies in several markets. This has been the case, for example, with respect to tobacco retail sales (*Svenska Tobaks AB* from 1915 until 1961), radio broadcasting (from 1924 until 1962), television broadcasting (from 1956 until 1987), train traffic (from 1856 until 1988), mail delivery (from 1636 until 1993), electricity (deregulated in 1996 except for the electrical grid), pharmaceuticals (from 1970 until 2009) and telephone services (*Telia AB* from 1853 to 1993). State monopolies still exist with respect to retail alcohol sales (*Systembolaget AB* from 1955 until now with respect to retail, wholesale ended in the 1990's due to EU membership) and gambling. Healthcare as well as education on the preschool, primary, secondary and post-graduate levels and job placement services have been socialized, also entailing little or no private competition in certain of these areas historically. There is a current movement towards both privately-run schools and healthcare. Elderly care was deregulated in 1991, private schools and work agencies allowed in 1992. Consequently, the combination of state monopolies, socialization, the relative geographical isolation of Sweden, its large land mass as well as small population base, have resulted that in many areas, the Swedish markets historically have not been exposed to strong competition.

15.4.1 THE REGULATION OF COMPETITION

The current Swedish Competition Act (*konkurrenslagen* 2008:579)[11] is mainly the implementation of the EU Merger Regulation 139/2004/EC and Regulation 1/2003/EC concerning the enforcement of Articles 81 and 82 of the EC Treaty (now Articles 101 and 102 TFEU). Two prohibitions form the framework for the act, the prohibition against agreements between undertakings limiting competition, and the prohibition against a company abusing a dominant

---

11 An English translation of the 2008 Competition Act is available at http://www.kkv.se/upload/Filer/ENG/Publications/The_Swedish_Competition_Act.pdf.

position. Outside the presentation here, but pertinent to this field, are the rules on both the EU and Swedish levels regarding state aid and public procurement, ensuring level playing fields for the actors in the market.

With respect to competition (antitrust) regulation, agreements that have as their object or effect the prevention, restriction or distortion of competition in a market are prohibited under the Competition Act and can be declared void. Included in the explicit prohibitions are agreements that directly or indirectly fix prices, control production, divide markets, create competitive disadvantage through applying different conditions, or invoke tie-in agreements. Certain agreements despite this are permissible, where they contribute to improving production or distribution, promote technical or economic programs, or allow consumers a fair share of resulting benefits. Such agreements are permissible only if limitations imposed are necessary to reach such benefits, and the agreements do not give the concerned undertakings the possibility to distort competition to an extent that outweighs the benefits. Certain specific exemptions to the prohibition against such agreements are given in the act, such as with respect to certain taxi operations.

An abuse of a dominant position by one or more undertakings is also prohibited. Specific prohibitions are stated in the act mirroring those with respect to agreements: abuse that directly or indirectly imposes unfair prices, limits production, creates competitive disadvantage through applying different conditions or tie-in agreements. These different aspects all merged in a case submitted by the Market Court to the Court of Justice for a preliminary rule concerning the royalty determinations made by STIM, a Swedish copyright management organization. STIM charged different royalty fees for public and private television, which practice the Court found to be an abuse of a dominant position in violation of Article 82 EC (now 102 TFEU).[12]

Concentrations of undertakings, often in the form of mergers, are also to be assessed under the act to insure competition if they together have in Sweden over SEK 1 billion in turnover, with at least one of them having turnover exceeding SEK 200 million. The Swedish Competition Authority's

---

12 Case C-52/07, *Kanal 5 Ltd and TV 4 AB v. Föreningen Svenska Tonsättares Internationella Musikbyrå (STIM)*[2008] ECR I-9275. For more information about STIM in English, *see* its website at stim.se.

decision that a proposed merger limits competition to an unlawful degree can be appealed to the Market Court.

15.4.2 THE SWEDISH COMPETITION AUTHORITY

The Swedish Competition Authority (*Konkurrensverket*) is charged with enforcing the Competition Act.[13] This authority is active in competition areas, and by way of extension, public procurement issues. One hundred and sixty-two decisions have made by this authority to date under the Competition Act and Articles 101 and 102 TFEU, fifty-eight concerning mergers and concentrations and thirty-two concerning anti-competitive activities by public entities. The sanctions available to the Swedish Competition Authority include requiring the termination of such agreements or abuse, administrative fines, trading prohibitions and compensatory damages.

The Swedish Competition Authority cooperates with the European Commission as well as the competition authorities from other Member States. There is also a Nordic cooperation in this area, as well as with the Competition Committee of the Organisation for Economic Cooperation and Development ("OECD").

15.5 The Market Court

Certain issues as raised under the Marketing Act and the Competition Act are taken to the Market Court (*Marknadsdomstolen*).[14] This Court was established in the early 1970's and has jurisdiction in competition, marketing and certain consumer cases as brought by the Consumer Ombudsman (*Konsumentombudsmannen*) and by the Consumer Agency (*Konsument-verket*). However, individual consumers do not have standing before this Court. The decisions of this court under the Marketing and Competition Acts cannot be appealed.

---

13 For more information about this authority in English, *see* its website at konkurrensverket.se.

14 For more information about this court in English, *see* its website at marknadsdomstolen.se.

A judging panel for the Market Court consists of seven members, a chair, vice-chair and five other members. The chair, vice-chair and one member have to be legally-trained and experienced judges. The other four members are experts in economics. Of the forty-two cases filed with the Market Court in 2011, eight were brought under the Competition Act (a doubling in numbers since 2009 when four cases were filed), thirty-three under the Marketing Act and one under the Act on Consumer Contract Terms (*lagen 1994:1512 om avtalsvillkor i konsumentförhållanden*).

CHAPTER 16

Labor and Employment Law

As seen in the preceding chapters with respect to insurance law and corporate governance, self-regulation is an integral component in the Swedish legal system. This aspect of self-regulation is perhaps strongest and most institutionalized within labor law, with both employers and employees often organized on several levels. The Swedish model of industrial relations (*den svenska arbetsrättsmodellen*) falls within the "Nordic model," perceived here again as a third alternative to the more liberal, deregulated models found in countries such as the United Kingdom, and the more regulated models such as in Germany.[1]

There are 4.2 million employees in Sweden, which has a population of almost 9.5 million as of 2012. A little over one-third of all employees work in the public sector, while two-thirds work in the private sector. Approximately two million women actively work, of which one-half work full-time defined as 35 hours or more per week. One-half of all women work in the public sector, one-half in the private sector. Two-thirds of the employees in the public sector are women while one-third in the private sector is women.[2] The public and private sectors can be further divided, the private sector between white and blue-collar workers, and the public sector between state, municipal and county council employees.

---

1 For a further presentation of the Swedish labor model, labor law and employment law, *see* Ronnie Eklund, Tore Sigeman and Laura Carlson, SWEDISH LABOR AND EMPLOYMENT LAW: CASES AND MATERIALS (Iustus Förlag 2008).
2 These statistics are taken from, Women and Men in Sweden – Facts and Figures 2010 (*På tal om kvinnor och män*) generated by Statistics Sweden and available in English at their website at scb.se.

16.1   The Stages of Labor and Employment Law

The development of labor and employment law[3] in Sweden can be seen as comprising four stages. The first stage began with the transition in Sweden from a rural (and guild-based) economy to an industrialization that occurred relatively late on the European timeline, the latter half of the nineteenth century. This was a fairly lawless period from a labor and employment law perspective.[4] The second stage involves the creation and establishment of the Swedish model, which began to be put into place already with the December Compromise (*decemberkompromissen*) of 1906 between SAF[5] and LO.[6] With this compromise, the social partners agreed that the employer would have the prerogative/right to freely hire, fire, direct and allocate work. In return, employers would recognize labor unions and the right of employees to join labor unions. By resolving these problems internally within the labor market, the social partners kept the state at bay. The 1928 Collective Agreements Act was passed (*lag 1928:253 om kollektivavtal*) and the Labor Court was established in 1929. These state acts were countered by one of the largest strikes in Swedish history, involving almost a quarter of a million workers. An act banning for-profit employment agencies was passed in 1935,[7] and an act recognizing the right to join labor unions was legislated in 1936. The

---

3   The terms "labor law" and "employment law" fall within the same Swedish term, *arbetsrätt*. This Swedish term is sometimes categorized as collective labor law (*kollektiv arbetsrätt*) and individual labor law (*individuell arbetsrätt*), referred to in this chapter as labor law and employment law, respectively.

4   However, an act on worker safety was enacted already in 1889, the Occupational Hazards Act (*lag 1889:19 om yrkesfara*) and eventually ultimately replaced by the 1977 Work Environment Act (*arbetsmiljölag 1977:1160*).

5   The Swedish Employers' Confederation (*Svenska Arbetsgivareföreningen*) ("SAF"). SAF joined the Federation of Swedish Industries (*Industriförbundet*) in 2001 to become the Confederation of Swedish Enterprise (*Svenskt Näringsliv*). For more information on this latter organization in English, *see* its website at svensktnaringsliv.se.

6   LO (*Landsorganisationen i Sverige*) currently covers 1.5 million of the 4.2 million employees in the Swedish labor market. For more information in English on this central employee organization, *see* its website at lo.se.

7   This ban as to private employment offices, staffing agencies, was in place for almost sixty years until 1993. There is still a ban on charging a job applicant or an employee a fee for services rendered by a staffing agency. A public employment office is available in Sweden free of charge.

Swedish model was further cemented by the Basic Agreement (*Saltsjöbad-savtalet*) in 1938, which agreement is still valid today. This agreement signaled the beginning of a turning point during which the Swedish labor market enjoyed several decades of industrial peace.

One of the most significant features of the Swedish model is the underlying premise that the state should be neutral with respect to the social partners, the employer and employee organizations, the perception being that legislation is an unwanted intrusion in the labor market. Legislation historically was (and still often is) quasi-mandatory, giving the social partners the opportunity to opt out of statutory requirements through collective agreements usually at the central levels.

This second phase in Swedish labor law, characterized by this absence of legislation and an emphasis on self-regulation, lasted until the 1970's. The balance of power in the labor market shifted during this decade in favor of the labor unions, as there was a shortage of workers. At that time, Sweden had one of the highest gross national products per capita in the world, a result of a combination of Sweden's neutrality during WWII and the fact that it had the raw materials, expertise and industries needed for rebuilding Europe. A plethora of legislation was enacted during that decade, marking the commencement of the third stage, both with respect to labor and employment law. Many of these acts are still in place, some amended due to requirements of EU law:

- The 1972 Private Board Representation Act (*lag 1972:829 om styrelse-representation*);
- The 1974 Employment Protection Act (*lag 1974:12 om anställningsskydd*);
- The 1974 Labor Union Representative (Status at the Workplace) Act (*lag 1974:358 om facklig förtroendemans ställning på arbetsplatsen*);[8]
- The 1974 Labor Disputes (Judicial Procedure) Act (*lag 1974:371 om rättegången i arbetstvister*);[9]

---

8 For an English translation of the Labor Union Representative (Status at the Workplace) Act, *see* the website of the Government Offices at sweden.gov.se.
9 For an English translation of the Labor Disputes (Judicial Procedure) Act, *see* the website of the Government Offices at sweden.gov.se.

- The 1974 Employee's Right to Educational Leave Act (*lag 1974:981 om arbetstagares rätt till ledighet för utbildning*);[10]
- The 1976 Employment (Co-Determination in the Workplace) Act (*lag 1976:580 om medbestämmande i arbetslivet*);[11]
- The 1976 Act on the Right to Parental Leave (*lag 1976:280 om rätt till föräldraledighet*);[12]
- The 1977 Annual Leave Act (*semesterlag 1977:480*);[13]
- The 1977 Work Environment Act (*arbetsmiljölag 1977:1160*); and
- The 1979 Equal Treatment between Women and Men in Employment Act (*lag 1979:503 om jämställdhet mellan kvinnor och män i arbetslivet*).

A second Employment Protection Act was adopted in 1982.[14] An act prohibiting discrimination on the basis of race was first passed in 1986. A new Act on Board Representation (Private Sector Employees) Act (*lag 1987:1245 om styrelserepresentation för de privatanställda*) was passed in 1987.[15]

The fourth phase in labor and employment law began in the 1990's with Sweden's membership in the European Union in 1995 and the need to harmonize legislation to Community demands as well as to be in compliance with the European Convention. The Swedish industrial relations model has had to make certain adjustments with respect to the requirements under EU law and the European Convention. One aspect has been that the social partners no longer have complete freedom to contract out of statutory requirements, particularly those as mandated by EU law. The parties can

10 For an English translation of the Employee's Right to Education Leave Act, *see* the website of the Government Offices at sweden.gov.se.
11 For an English translation of the Employment (Co-Determination in the Workplace) Act, *see* the website of the Government Offices at sweden.gov.se.
12 This act was already replaced in 1978 and again in 1995 by the current Parental Leave Act (*föräldraledighetslag 1995:584*). An English translation of the current act is available at website of the Government Offices at sweden.gov.se.
13 For an English translation of the Annual Leave Act, *see* the website of the Government Offices at sweden.gov.se.
14 The 1974 act was replaced by a 1982 act of the same name (*lag 1982:80 om anställningsskydd*). An English translation of the current Employment Protection Act can be found at the website of the Government Offices at sweden.gov.se.
15 For an English translation of the Board Representation (Private Sector Employee) Act *see* the website of the Government offices at sweden.gov.se.

derogate from such statutory provisions, but only if the terms of the collective agreement are more favorable to the employees than the statutory provisions.

The greatest area of change in this fourth stage has been regarding unlawful employment discrimination, and this also due to EU law requirements. The Discrimination Act of 2008 (*diskrimineringslag* 2008:567) came into effect 1 January 2009 and forbids unlawful discrimination on the basis of sex, transgender identity or expression, ethnicity, religion or other belief, disability, sexual orientation or age with respect to employment, education, labor market policy, starting a business and professional recognition, membership in organizations such as labor unions, housing, providing goods and services, both as the provider and customer, social benefits, social insurance, military service and public employment. Exceptions to certain of these protections in certain areas are set out in the statute. For example, age is not a protect basis in every context. The 2008 Discrimination Act prohibits unlawful discrimination, defined as direct and indirect discrimination, harassment, sexual harassment and instructions to discriminate.

16.2 The Social Partners

As seen from the historical overview above, the social partners (*arbetsmarknadsparterna*) in effect have been regulating the labor market for over one hundred years. The major employer's organization, the Confederation of Swedish Enterprise, can be traced back to 1902, and the major private worker organization, LO, was founded in 1898. The organizations in the private professional sectors, as well as the public sector, developed at later stages in the 1930's as public employment legally became more and more comparable to private employment.

Both the employer and employee sides are highly organized. Swedish employees historically have had high union membership rates, today approximately 70 %.[16] Union membership exists even at professional levels, such as for professors, judges and physicians. A contributing factor to the historically

---

16 *See* Reinhold Fahlbeck and Bernard Johann Mulder, LABOUR AND EMPLOYMENT LAW IN SWEDEN (Lund 2009) at 16, *citing* The National Mediation Office Annual Report (2008) at 30. A summary of the 2008 Annual Report is available in English at the website of the National Mediation Office at mi.se.

very high degree of organization, when compared internationally, can be seen as the fact that certain social benefits, such as unemployment benefits, have been administered by the unions instead of the state almost since the turn of the twentieth century. However, unemployment benefits, though still heavily subsidized by the state to the unions, are not currently subsidized to the same degree, which has entailed a recent drop in union membership as the unions have had to charge their members more for unemployment insurance.

The social partners are represented by strong centralized organizations, each having a hierarchy comprising umbrella organizations, national labor or employee organizations belonging to the umbrella organizations, then local and club organizations belonging to the national organizations. Central collective agreements, referred to as recommended agreements, can be entered into between the umbrella organizations, but such agreements must be adopted on the member level within these organizations to have effect.

Under the umbrella organizations, the national organizations (*förbund*) can be based on sectors, for example, there is a national construction workers' union and a national construction employers' organization. Under these national organizations, there can also be local units for particular workplaces. There are no direct statutory regulations with respect to forming any of these organizations, for example, there is no legal requirement that a labor union be registered, approved or recognized through a certain state process to be able to exercise rights.

16.2.1 THE EMPLOYER CENTRAL ORGANIZATIONS

Within the public sector, the umbrella employer organizations include the Swedish Agency for Government Employers[17] for the state, covering 250 employer members having 250 000 employees. SALAR[18] represents the municipalities and county councils as employers, covering employer members with nearly 1.2 million employees. Collective agreements in the

---

17   For more information in English on the Swedish Agency for Government Employers (*Arbetsgivarverket*), *see* its website at arbetsgivarverket.se.

18   For more information in English on the Swedish Association of Local Authorities and Regions (*Svenska Kommunförbundet och Landstingsförbundet i Samverkan*) ("SALAR"), *see* its website at skl.se.

public sector are negotiated by these organizations. As a result of several reforms introduced successively in 1965, 1976 and 1994, wages and other terms and conditions of employment for state and municipal employees are now mainly regulated by collective agreements through the same system and procedures as for private employees with only certain limited exceptions.

On the private employer side, the main umbrella organization is the Confederation of Swedish Enterprise, with 50 sectoral and employer associations encompassing over 60 000 member companies covering almost 1.7 million employees.[19] In addition, there are also several smaller private employer organizations. One is the Banking Sector Employers Organization (*Bankinstitutens arbetsgivarorganisation*) with 150 member banks having 47 000 employees.[20] Another is KFO with commercial cooperatives as members, including 3 700 such organizations with 87 000 employees having over 400 collective agreements.[21]

16.2.2 THE EMPLOYEE CENTRAL ORGANIZATIONS

LO, TCO and SACO are the major umbrella organizations on the employee side. LO is the largest employee umbrella organization covering mainly blue-collar workers, with 15 unions and nearly 1.5 million members. LO historically has had close ties with the Social Democratic Party.

The Swedish Confederation for Professional Employees ("TCO") is the largest organization in the salaried employee sector, with 15 affiliated national unions and 1.2 million members.[22] The Swedish Confederation of Professional Associations ("SACO") organizes primarily university-educated employees, having 22 unions and slightly more than 600 000 members.[23] There are only a few smaller central organizations aside from these three umbrella organizations. Even though national unions can belong to different umbrella

---

19 For more information in English on the Confederation of Swedish Enterprise (*Svenskt Näringsliv*), *see* its website at svensktnaringsliv.se.
20 Information about BAO is available in Swedish at its website at bao.se.
21 Information about KFO is available in Swedish at its website at kfo.se.
22 For more information in English on the Swedish Confederation for Professional Employees (*Tjänstemännens Centralorganisation*), *see* its website at tco.se.
23 For more information in English on the Swedish Confederation of Professional Associations (*Sveriges Akademikers Centralorganisation*), *see* its website at saco.se.

organizations, they can still enter into negotiating cartels or coalitions on certain issues with each other. One example of this in the private sector is the Council for Negotiation and Co-operation ("PTK"),[24] comprising a number of national unions from TCO and SACO, negotiating with the Confederation of Swedish Enterprise as to pensions and insurance issues. A similar coalition exists on the public employment side between fifteen national labor unions, the Public Employees' Negotiation Council.[25] These coalitions strengthen the bargaining positions of the national unions. Outside of these more institutionally established employee organizations is the Swedish Workers Central Organization – Syndicalists (*Sveriges arbetares centralorganisation - Syndikalisterna*), which perceives its role as a counterpoint to the more traditional, and in their view, stagnified worker's movement.

The charters of these organizations define the mutual rights and duties between the members and the employee organizations. There is no Swedish legislation explicitly regulating the internal affairs of labor market organizations. However, the 2008 Discrimination Act expressly prohibits unlawful discrimination by employee and employer organizations on the basis of sex, transgender identity or expression, ethnicity, religion or other belief, disability, sexual orientation or age with respect to employment, labor market policy, professional recognition and membership in organizations. There is no general duty of representation by labor unions as to its members other than as set out in the union's charter and in contract law under the rules governing principals and agents.

16.3 Labor Law

Labor law, the law governing the legal relationship between the social partners, has historically been emphasized over employment law, the law governing the relationship between the employer and employee. This

---

24 The Council for Negotiation and Co-operation (*Privattjänstemannakartellen*, "PTK"), is a joint organization of 25 member unions, representing 700 000 salaried employees in the private sector. For more information on this organization in English, *see* its website at ptk.se.

25 For more on the Public Employees' Negotiation Council (*Offentliganställdas Förhandlingsråd*), *see* its website with information available in English at ofr.se.

focus on labor law is a natural extension of the Swedish labor law model, leaving it to the social partners to regulate employment issues through collective agreements. Many employees historically have had only collective agreements regulating the terms of their employment, with few or no terms in the individual employment agreement. A trend towards a greater emphasis on employment law can be detected, however, mostly as a result of EU law.

The main statutory labor law provisions are set out in the Employment (Co-Determination in the Workplace) Act (*lag 1976:580 om medbestämmande i arbetslivet*). When originally enacted in the 1970's, it replaced the 1928 Act on Collective Agreements and the 1936 Act on the Right to Organize and Negotiate. Four main themes can be seen as addressed in the act, freedom of association, collective agreements, the duty of industrial peace, and the system of joint regulation (co-determination) created at the work place between the social partners. The social partners have been given the power to self-regulate the administration of the collective agreements and legislation, and they generally have the right to institute proceedings on behalf of their members in labor disputes. This is the system in place in Sweden as opposed to a Works Council.

Under the collective agreements entered into at the turn of the twentieth century, arbitration was the resolution mechanism of choice for the social partners, particularly given their skepticism and desire to keep the state out of all labor market issues. The state supported this by passing the first labor mediation act in 1906[26] and later by setting up a central labor mediation institution[27] as well as a central labor arbitration institution in 1920.[28] By then, over 400 000 Swedish workers were covered by collective agreements,

---

26 The 1906 Act on Mediation in Labor Disputes (*lag 1906:113 om medling i arbetstvister*). The Mediation Institution was replaced in 2000 by the National Mediation Office, with the same general jurisdiction as to resolving labor conflicts, but with the addition of two new mandates, promoting efficient wage formation and overseeing the statistics governing such. For more information in English on the National Mediation Office, *see* its website at mi.se.

27 *See* The 1920 Act on Mediation in Labor Disputes (*lag 1920:245 om medling i arbetstvister*).

28 *See* The 1928 Act on the Labor Court (*lag 1928:254 om arbetsdomstol*) and the 1920 Act on a Central Arbitration Board for Certain Labour Disputes (*lag 1920:246 om central skiljenämnd för vissa arbetstvister*).

many of which had arbitration clauses. The Labor Court came into existence in 1929, established in line with the 1928 Collective Agreements Act, replacing the arbitration institution set up in 1920. The Labor Court's primary task was to resolve labor law issues, disputes regarding the interpretation and application of collective agreements and the non-strike regulations of the Collective Agreements Act.

The present expanded jurisdiction of the Labor Court to all issues between the social partners has had several causes: Collective agreements are now applied to the entire labor market, extended to include salaried private employees and the public sector. Through the expansion of employment legislation reaching a peak in the 1970's and the new Labor Disputes (Judicial Procedure) Act in 1974, the Labor Court's jurisdiction was broadened to include employment law, basically to all employment issues.

The composition, as well as the procedure before the Court, is regulated in the Labor Disputes (Judicial Procedure) Act and to the extent a specific issue is not regulated there, the procedural rules as found in the Code of Judicial Procedure are applicable.[29] A judging panel for the Labor Court consists of at most seven members total. Three typically are non-partisan members, a chair and vice-chair trained in law, with the third member an expert in the labor market. Four are then partisan members, two appointed by the employer organizations and two by the employee organizations. The composition of the Labor Court had until 2008 remained unchanged since its inception in 1929 as traceable back to the central arbitration panel established in 1920. Now in cases concerning claims of unlawful discrimination, a judging panel can consist of only five members, three non-partisan members as described above, and only two partisan members, unless the social partners request otherwise.[30]

---

29 The objectivity of the composition of the Swedish Labor Court was addressed by the European Court of Human Rights in 2004, which found that the composition of Labor Court in the case at hand was not in violation of the requirements of objectivity or independence as set out in Article 6. *See AB Kurt Kellermann v. Sweden*, European Court of Human Rights, judgment dated 26 October 2004, App. No. 41579/98.

30 For more information in English on the judgments of the Labor Court with respect to discrimination cases, *see* Laura Carlson, SEARCHING FOR EQUALITY, SEX DISCRIMI-NATION, PARENTAL LEAVE AND THE SWEDISH MODEL WITH COMPARISONS TO EU, UK AND US LAW (Iustus 2007).

The social partners are under a statutory obligation to negotiate most issues, almost always at the local and often also at the central levels, after which they can bring a case to Labor Court. Cases involving only the social partners are always brought directly to Labor Court as it has exclusive jurisdiction in such issues. Other cases, such as when a labor union or the Equality Ombudsman (*Diskrimineringsombudsmannen*) prosecutes a discrimination claim on behalf of an employee, are also brought directly to the Labour Court. However if a private person prosecutes a claim under the employment legislation, such as with respect to discrimination, the case is first brought to the general district courts. Appeals of decisions by the general district courts then are made to the Labor Court. In either case, the judgment of the Labor Court is the final judgment.

The Labor Court is limited in the relief it can grant. It can grant a motion for a declaratory judgment (*fastställelsetalan*), such as whether an employment relationship exists, order performance based on a legal obligation (*fullgörelsetalan*), or declare certain acts by the social partners invalid, as well as collective agreements or clauses therein contained (*ogiltigförklaring*). The other primary remedy that the Labor Court can award is damages to either the individual employer or employee, the organization, or both. Damages can be either compensatory damages (*ekonomiskt skadestånd*) or general damages (*allmänt skadestånd*) falling within the category of intangible harms (*kränkning*) discussed in Chapter Twelve above on torts. The first category of compensatory damages is based on any actual economic losses suffered and proven by the party. The second category of general damages is awarded by the Court typically within a range of amounts. The amount decided by the Court here is determined with regard, *inter alia*, to the extent of any economic loss suffered by the injured party, but can also be imposed even if no economic loss has occurred or, if such loss has occurred, the award may be higher than the loss. The Court is free to make adjustments downwards to null. For example, damages for unlawful discrimination had historically have been in the range between SEK 15 000 to SEK 40 000. With the 2008 Act, the Labour Court now has the possibility to award discrimination damages (*diskrimineringsersättning*) that are to be in an amount that is deterring, not simply compensatory. The Court under this new category has now awarded such damages on several occasions to date, with respect to age discrimination in the amount of SEK 125 000 to each employee (AD 2011 no. 37) and SEK 75 000 to a job applicant (AD 2009 no. 91), as well as unlawful sex discrimination in the amount of SEK 30 000 (AD 2011 no. 2), and unlawful pregnancy discrimination in the amount of SEK 50 000 (AD 2011 no. 23).

16.3.1 FREEDOM OF ASSOCIATION

Protection of the freedom of association (*föreningsrätt*) was first explicitly recognized in the private sector by the 1906 December Compromise and later incorporated in the 1936 Act on the Right to Organize and Negotiate. This right was also retained in the 1976 Employment (Co-Determination in the Workplace) Act. Article 1(5) of the 1974 Instrument of Government also protects freedom of association generally.

Section 7 of the Employment (Co-Determination in the Workplace) Act defines freedom of association as the right for both employers and employees to belong to an organization and exercise such membership rights, giving protection to the positive right of association. Any party violating the right of association can be liable for damages for losses arising to the organization as well as to its members. If the violation consists of the dismissal of an employee, the dismissal is to be declared invalid.

Freedom of association, however, has two faces, the positive freedom of association that entails the right to join an association, and the negative freedom of association, which entails the right to be able to refrain from joining an association. The negative freedom of association, the right to not be compelled to belong to an association, historically has not been protected under Swedish law. However, according to the Employment Protection Act, an employee cannot be dismissed from employment for refusing to join a labor union.

The negative right of freedom of association has begun to be given greater recognition in Swedish law due to the case law of the European Court of Human Rights with respect to the protections under the European Convention.[31] Article 11 of the European Convention provides for the right to freedom of peaceful assembly and to freedom of association with others,

---

31 For a discussion of this issue, *see, for example, Evaldsson and others v. Sweden*, European Court of Human Rights, judgment dated 13 February 2007, App. No. 75252/01.

including the right to form and to join labor unions for the protection of an individual's interests. The European Court of Human Rights has interpreted Article 11 to include protection for both the positive and to a lesser extent negative rights of association.

16.3.2 THE GENERAL RIGHT TO NEGOTIATE AND THE RIGHT TO TAKE INDUSTRIAL ACTION

A general right to negotiate (*allmän förhandlingsrätt*) was recognized at the turn of the twentieth century in the collective agreements, and first explicitly recognized by statute in the 1936 Act on the Right to Organize and Negotiate. This protection was retained in the Employment (Co-Determination in the Workplace) Act. Section 10 of the act defines the right as belonging to an employee organization "to negotiate with an employer on any matter relating to the relationship between the employer and any member of the organization who is, or has been, employed by that employer."

If an employee organization approaches an employer with the objective of reaching a collective agreement, the employer must attend the negotiations and discuss the demands presented, a duty sanctioned under the act by damages. Such an obligation to negotiate exists even if the union only has one member at the workplace. The general right to negotiate as granted by Section 10 of the Employment (Co-Determination in the Workplace) Act does not create any obligation on the part of either party to reach an agreement.

If the parties cannot come to an agreement, and there is no collective agreement already in place between the parties, the social partners are normally free to take industrial action (*stridsåtgärder*), a right protected by Article 14 of chapter two of the Instrument of Government. Such conflicts are termed "interest disputes" for which industrial action is an appropriate resolution mechanism. Industrial action can take the form of a strike, lockout or boycott or any similar measure against the other party, failing any provision to the contrary by law. Industrial action is not defined by statute, but rather purposively untouched to allow for greater flexibility and protection of rights. The National Mediation Office is currently empowered under the Act to attempt to resolve industrial disputes through mediation. Other restrictions as regards the right to industrial action exist in certain basic agreements concluded centrally. The Parliament is empowered under the Instrument of Government to intervene statutorily in certain cases. The Government, however, cannot act solely in such issues.

As soon as a collective agreement is reached, the right of the parties to take industrial action in principle ceases according to Sections 41–42 of the Employment (Co-Determination in the Workplace) Act. Industrial action may not be taken in order to bring about changes in a collective agreement. Such a conflict with respect to amending a collective agreement is termed a "rights dispute" and must first be negotiated and failing a resolution by the parties, ultimately taken to the Labor Court instead. Settlements in such cases are quite common, as the social partners prefer to resolve their disputes internally rather than judicially. A party to a collective agreement, however, is generally entitled to take secondary actions (*sympatiåtgärder*) without restrictions in order to assist another party in an ongoing lawful labor conflict.

A social partner that has taken an unlawful industrial action can be sanctioned by the Labor Court in the form of damages. On the labor side, only the labor unions can exercise the right to take industrial action. An employee may not take industrial action without the sanction of the respective labor union. If unlawful, liability for damages caused by the action may be imposed on individual employees, though normally not in an amount exceeding SEK 2 000 per employee. In the event an organization has organized the unlawful action, individual employees cannot be sanctioned by damages for participation in the action.

16.3.3 COLLECTIVE AGREEMENTS

There is no statutory requirement that an employer has to have a collective agreement. In addition, there is no mechanism in Swedish law by which collective agreements are declared to be universally applicable, *ergo omnes,* in a sector. At work places where an employer is not bound by a collective agreement, the terms of employment in practice often conform to the terms of the major collective agreement within that sector. Because of this, even though only 70 % of the workforce is unionized, the collective agreements in practice are applied to 90 % of the workforce.

If there is a collective agreement at the work place, the parties bound to the collective agreement are deemed to have waived their right to take industrial action and are deemed to be under a duty of peace (*fredsplikt*). This gives rise to the function of collective agreements as peace instruments. This obligation to not take industrial action in the presence of the existence of a collective agreement acts as an inducement for employers to sign collective agreements.

Collective agreements fall into four main categories by sector: public sector state, public sector municipalities and county councils, private sector salaried employees and private sector blue-collar workers. One employer can be bound by several collective agreements regarding its workforce, for example, with respect to salaried employees and blue-collar workers. Collective agreements can also exist on three levels, local, national and central. The agreements can overlap both horizontally and vertically. Certain central agreements as adopted by the umbrella organizations, such as LO, PTK, SACO or the Confederation of Swedish Enterprise, recommended agreements, must be adopted by the national organizations to be applicable. Local agreements can also be entered into between local labor unions and employers, but these are effective only at that work place. Employers not already members of an employer organization can be given the option of signing an already existing collective agreement, an accessory or tie-in agreement (*hängavtal*), usually containing a minimum of terms and conditions mirroring those found in the collective agreement for the sector.

Collective agreements are legally binding both in terms of the parties to the agreement as well as their members. The law does not regulate the legal effects of collective agreements with regard to employees who are not union members nor are members of a different union. In practice, the collective agreement is usually also applied to employees who are not union members. The collective agreement can also be applied in practice to employees of other unions who do not have an applicable collective agreement at that workplace. This can follow explicitly from the collective agreement, or implicitly under the case law of the Labor Court, which often finds that collective agreements contain implied (in the absence of explicit) commitments by employers to not apply other terms of employment to those employees outside the collective agreement. This insures that the terms of the collective agreement are not circumvented, for example, by employers hiring employees not covered by the agreement at lower costs.

The social partners have fairly extensive freedom with respect to the content of collective agreements. According to the Employment (Co-Determination in the Workplace) Act, collective agreements are to be in writing and concern employment terms and conditions or the relationship in general between employees and employers. This is the extent of the statutory regulation. The primary issues addressed in collective agreements tend to be wages and employment terms and conditions.[32] No minimum wage legislation exists in Sweden, with the social partners instead regulating wage setting through collective agreements, often centrally for entire business sectors for the entire country. A national agreement can be reached for an entire business sector, and thereafter supplemented by local agreements. The white-collar agreements tend to contain the principles by which to set wages, while the blue-collar agreements tend to have actual figures at the local levels.

This lack of regulations as to the content of collective agreements is seen as one of the strengths of the Swedish model. Collective agreements allow the social partners to adapt the terms and conditions of employment to each trade/sector. The parties to the agreement are free to negotiate the terms affecting employees and employers within the specific sector and at a specific workplace. For example, issues with respect to employee compensation costs for travel expenses might be regulated in great detail in a collective agreement concerning construction workers who must travel to different jobsites, while this issue may not be regulated in as much detail for the collective agreement covering day care providers. There is, however, one legal limit as to the content of collective agreements, and that is that they cannot deviate to the detriment of employees from statutory rights as required by EU law.

---

32 The 1997 Agreement on Industrial Development and Wage Formation ("Industry Agreement") in private manufacturing can be mentioned here. This agreement was concluded in 1997 by twelve SAF employer associations and eight labor unions from LO, TCO and SACO and created a bipartite Industry Committee (*industrikommitté*) which is now named Industry Council (Industrirådet). An English translation of this Agreement is available at the website of the Council at industriradet.se under the heading industriavtalet. The objective of the agreement is to create conditions conducive to constructive wage negotiations.

Because of the duty to keep the industrial peace while a collective agreement is in place, collective agreements are typically re-negotiated prior to their expiration. Over 500 collective agreements were renegotiated in 2007, 85 % of all agreements covering approximately 2.8 million employees. The year 2011 was a relatively calm year with only 150 collective agreements renegotiated. In 2012, 500 collective agreements will expire covering approximately 2.2 of the total 4.2 million employees.

Individual terms in the employment contracts can be entered into between employers and individual employees in addition to collective agreements. An individual employment contract may not be in conflict with the applicable collective agreement.

The principle of free movement of services established under EU law has raised issues with respect to collective agreements and different standards of employment benefits and wages. One specific issue raised has been the use of collective agreements as a regulatory instrument for implementing directives. Directive 96/71/EC of the European Parliament and of the Council concerning the posting of workers in the framework of the provision of services was implemented in Sweden through the 1999 Foreign Posting of Employees Act (*lag 1999:678 om utstationering av arbetstagare*).[33] The Swedish act sets out the list of Swedish statutory provisions with respect to employment that must be observed by all employers (Swedish or foreign). This list corresponds to the one contained in the Posting of Employees Directive except with respect to minimum wages established by law or collective agreements with *erga omnes* effect, since as discussed above, Sweden has neither of these mechanisms with respect to wages. An additional problem that has been raised under the right to free movement has been where a foreign provider is already bound by a collective agreement reached in the home country on terms less favorable to the employees than those of the comparable Swedish agreement.

Both of these issues came to a head in the Swedish context in the *Laval* case referred by the Labor Court to the Court of Justice.[34] The Court of

---

33 An English translation of the Foreign Posting of Employees Act is available at the website of the Government Offices at sweden.gov.se.

34 Case C-341/05, *Laval un Partneri Ltd v. Svenska Byggnadsarbetareförbundet and Others* [2007] ECR-11767.

Justice found that the industrial actions taken by the Swedish labor union were in violation of the freedom of movement. Section 41c was added to the Employment (Co-Determination in the Workplace) Act to clarify the unlawfulness of industrial actions taken in conflict with Section 5a of the Posting of Workers Act.[35] That section states that an industrial action against an employer in order to bring about a collective agreement governing posted workers may only be taken if the terms in the collective agreement correspond to terms in a central agreement, only concerns minimum wages or working conditions, and the terms in the collective agreements are more advantageous than certain specific provisions in the employment legislation. If the employer can demonstrate that the employees already have comparable employment terms, the industrial action is not lawful.

16.3.4 JOINT REGULATION/CO-DETERMINATION

One of the most significant aspects of the labor law legislation adopted in the 1970's was the statutory establishment of joint regulation, co-determination, between the employer and the employee with respect to issues in the work place. Joint regulation had existed between the social partners through agreement before the enactment of this legislation, but now was affixed by statute. The Swedish model of joint regulation differs from the German model of works councils. However, in line with the requirements of Union law, Sweden has adopted the necessary legislation with respect to works councils for European companies.[36]

Historically, it was the prerogative of the employer to hire, fire, direct and allocate work, basically manage the business without interference as affirmed by the December Compromise in 1906. This was reaffirmed by the Labor Court in 1929, with this right to freely lead and direct work referred to as the

---

35 Information is available in English as to posting of workers in Sweden at the website of the Work Environment Authority at av.se.

36 Act on European Works Councils (lag 2011:427 om europeiska företagsråd) in accordance with Directive 2009/38/EC on the establishment of a European Works Council.

"29/29 principle."[37] This complete freedom of employers was slowly eroded during the following decades with the expansion of employee influence, arguably beginning with the Basic Agreement in 1938 limiting the right of employers to freely terminate employment. The right to freely hire employees has also again been circumscribed now by the discrimination legislation.

The employer has the right to freely direct and allocate work unless otherwise provided by statute or relevant agreement. As the employers' freedoms with respect to employment were curtailed, the rights of employees through labor unions to influence the employer's decision-making processes at different levels were expanded. All labor market organizations have the rights concerning freedom of association and the general right to negotiate as discussed above. However, special rights are granted to the labor union that has succeeded first in reaching a collective agreement with an employer. This union is then deemed the "established" or signatory union. The Employment (Co-Determination in the Workplace) Act guarantees special rights to established unions in that they become representatives of the interests of the entire workforce at a given work place in all significant matters concerning joint regulation.

The current statutory regulations concerning joint regulation are primarily those as set out in the Employment (Co-Determination in the Workplace) Act and other acts as discussed below. The structure of joint regulation and labor union influence can be seen to comprise the following:

- Statutory rights for labor union representatives including paid time-off to conduct union activities;
- The primary right to negotiate and the employer's duty to consult with the labor unions;
- The labor union's right to information;
- The union's right to veto certain employer decisions;
- The right of interpretation by the union with respect to certain issues under the collective agreements such as the employee's duty to perform work;

---

37 The 29/29 principle acquired this name because the judgment confirming the right of employers to lead and allocate work was issued in 1929 and was the 29th judgment issued by the Labor Court that year, consequently, AD 1929 no. 29.

- The establishment and rights of employee safety delegates at the work place; and
- Mandatory representation of employees on the board of directors for private corporations and public entities.

Many of these statutory provisions concerning joint regulation are quasi-mandatory, entailing that the social partners are free to contract out of them with the exception of those rights provided to employees under EU law. Section 32 of the Employment (Co-Determination in the Workplace) Act under the collective agreements the parties to a collective agreement regulating wages and similar matters to enter into an agreement about entering into agreements. Upon the request of the employee party, the parties are also to negotiate a collective agreement concerning the employees' right to joint regulation. Such joint regulation agreements have been reached in the most important sectors of the labor market. One example is the 1982 "Agreement on Efficiency and Participation between the Swedish Employers' Confederation (SAF), the Swedish Labor Union Confederation (LO), and the Federation of Salaried Employees in Industry and Services (PTK) Development Agreement" (*utvecklingsavtalet*).[38]

Labor Union Representatives
The 1974 Labor Union Representative (Status at the Workplace) Act (*lag 1974:358 om facklig förtroendemans ställning på arbetsplatsen*)[39] grants the representative of an established labor union the right to perform work on behalf of the union during work hours, and still receive pay from the employer. These rights are technically not deemed part of the joint regulation structure between the social partners, but have greatly facilitated joint regulation by

---

38 An English translation of the "Agreement on Efficiency and Participation between the Swedish Employers' Confederation (SAF), the Swedish Labor Union Confederation (LO), and the Federation of Salaried Employees in Industry and Services (PTK)" can be found at the website of the PTK at www.ptk.se/Global/Material/Avtal/PTK_agreement.pdf.

39 For an English translation of the Labor Union Representative (Status at the Workplace) Act, *see* the website of the Government Offices at sweden.gov.se.

allowing labor union representatives to perform certain tasks without being forced to make economic sacrifices, for example, in the form of lost wages.

The Primary Right to Negotiate and the Employer's Duty to Consult
The primary right to negotiate (*primär förhandlingsrätt*) as granted in Section 11 of the Employment (Co-Determination in the Workplace) Act is distinct from the general right to negotiate as discussed above. The primary right to negotiate entails that an employer, before deciding on any important alterations to its activities, must initiate negotiations with the established labor union to which it is bound by collective agreement. The objective of this right is to compel employers to receive input from the employees as to certain decisions. The rule is also applicable where an employer wishes to make major alterations to the terms of employment or conditions of work in relation to an employee. In certain cases, an employer may make and effect a decision prior to fulfilling its duty to negotiate. However, the Labor Court has interpreted "important alterations" fairly broadly and has also required not only formal compliance, but substantive compliance, with the duty to consult, finding in several cases that the employer acted too late as the decision had already informally been made prior to the consultation with the labor union. This right to negotiate, however, is limited simply to that, once the negotiations are concluded, the employer is free to make any decision it considers best for the company.

An employer is obliged to negotiate even with respect to matters not involving major alterations, if a labor union party to a collective agreement with the employer, but not the established union, so requests under Section 12 of the same act. In certain cases, a labor union not bound by a collective agreement has a right to negotiate under Section 13, namely where a matter specifically concerns the work or employment conditions of an employee belonging to that union. The employer may also be requested to negotiate in these types of matters by a central organization of employees under Section 14 of the Employment (Co-Determination in the Workplace) Act. An employer not bound by any collective agreement must negotiate with all the labor unions involved, *i.e.* all unions having at least one member employee affected by the measure under consideration, before a decision on collective dismissals or transfer of an undertaking can be made.

The Labor Union's Right to Information
The primary right to negotiate includes an obligation for the employer to provide detailed information on the subject-matter of the negotiations. Sections 19–20 of the Employment (Co-Determination in the Workplace) Act contain in addition provisions regulating a right to information with the more general objective of providing employees with a certain amount of insight into company affairs. The employer is to keep the labor unions to which it is bound by collective agreement continuously informed about the development of the employer's operations as well as any personnel policies. In addition, the employer is to allow the unions the right to inspect any accounting and financial documents to the extent the union needs to do so to guard the interests of its members in relationship to the employer. The employer can also be requested to provide copies of certain documents. If either party cites a document during negotiations, the other party has a right to access the document. Employers of work places without collective agreements are also to provide the same information to any labor unions having members employed at the work place. The latter acts as an incentive to have a collective agreement as the number of unions having the right to information can in such a manner be drastically reduced.

The Labor Union's Right to Veto Certain Employer Decisions
A labor union that is party to a collective agreement has a right of veto with respect to certain staffing decisions taken by an employer. This veto right gives labor unions leverage in situations in which the employer wishes to assign work to consultants or temporary workers, instead of having the work performed by its regular workforce.[40] If the employer wishes to take such a decision, the employer must in the majority of cases then notify the union to which it is bound by collective agreement and negotiate according to Section 38 of the Employment (Co-Determination in the Workplace) Act.

---

40 The Swedish labor law model created at the turn of the twentieth century was based in part on the premise that the labor unions were to have a monopoly with respect to the supply of labor, comprising part of the motivation for the general statutory ban on for-profit employment agencies in Sweden in place from 1935 until 1993. The right of veto is seen as a counterbalance to allowing alternative labor sources.

The central labor union involved then has the right to veto the planned measure according to Sections 39–40 of the act if the measure is in violation of the law or of a collective agreement applicable to the work in question, or if the decision otherwise is in conflict with the practices generally accepted by the parties concerned within their bargaining sector. This veto right has been a politically sensitive issue. It was abolished in 1994 and then reintroduced already in 1995 after a change of Government. The reintroduction contained, however, restrictions of the right to insure that it would not be used in contravention of EU law concerning public procurement.

The Labor Union's Right of Interpretation
Another facet of the joint regulation between the social partners is the union's right of interpretation as set out in Sections 33–37 of the Employment (Co-Determination in the Workplace) Act. Historically, under the 29/29 principle and the case law of the Labor Court,[41] the employee had a duty to obey the orders of the employer, which entailed that any orders that were in violation of an employee's rights still had to be followed and then the employee or her union could make a claim for damages after the fact. Under the union's right of interpretation as set out in the act, an employee may be released from the obligation to follow the employer's orders if the labor union party to a collective agreement finds that there is no duty to perform the work. The union's view then normally prevails until the dispute is settled. If the employer wishes to maintain its position, the employer then is forced to bring the issue to the Labor Court for its judgment. Comparable provisions exist in Section 33 with respect to interpretations of joint regulation agreements and cases of disputes relating to the application of such provisions.

A similar mechanism is also in place with respect to any rights dispute regarding wages. Sections 35–37 of the act prescribe that it is the employer's responsibility to request negotiations and, if necessary, commence legal proceedings in case of a legal dispute over wages arising between an employer and a labor union party to the collective agreement. If the employer fails to comply with these provisions, the employer is forced to pay the sum

---

41 In AD 1934 no. 179, the Labor Court found that an employer's refusal to rehire an employee, Zachrisson, who refused to perform overtime work in violation of the collective agreement, was lawful.

demanded by the union as long as the amount is not unreasonable or completely lacking any basis.

Employee Safety Delegates

Another aspect of employee influence, established already in 1912 and strengthened during the 1970's, was the reform relating to safety delegates (*skyddsombud*) and the rights granted them by the 1977 Work Environment Act (*arbetsmiljölag 1977:1160*).[42] A safety delegate is to be appointed from among the workers at a given work place, first usually by the local union that has a collective agreement with the employer. The safety delegate is to monitor the safety at a work place as well as any occupational hazards. Under Section 6:6 of the Work Environment Act, the safety delegate can even suspend work "[i]f a particular job involves immediate and serious danger to the life or health of an employee and if no immediate remedy can be obtained through representations to the employer." The suspension will be in place until the Work Environment Authority (*Arbetsmiljöverket*) issues a decision.[43]

The safety delegate is not personally liable for production losses or other damages that may be caused by a decision to stop work. If a safety delegate abuses this power, the union may remove the delegate from office. However, if the safety delegate orders a suspension of work without reason, the employees may have to forfeit wages for the time not worked.

Board Representation

The Act on Board Representation (Private Sector Employees) (*lag 1987:1245 om styrelserepresentation för de privatanställda*)[44] mandates employee representation within boards of directors for corporations, commercial cooperatives and other types of organizations such as banks and insurance companies. Under this Act, two members of the board of directors in such organizations

---

42 For more information on safety delegates, *see* Maria Steinberg, SKYDDSOMBUD I ALLAS INTRESSE (Stockholm 2004) with a summary chapter in English, *Safety delegates – a historical and empirical legal study.*

43 For more information in English on the Work Environment Agency, as well as an English translation of the Work Environment Act, *see* its website at av.se.

44 An English translation of the Board Representation (Private Sector Employee) Act is available at the website of the Government offices at sweden.gov.se.

are to be representatives of the employees if the organization has at least 25 employees. Three members may be appointed in certain organizations having at least 1 000 employees. The local labor unions bound by the applicable collective agreement are to appoint the employee directors. However, the number of employee members is never to exceed the number of other board members, so that employee members are always to be at the most one-half, more likely, in the minority. The employee directors are to have the same rights and obligations, including a duty of confidentiality in certain areas, as regular board members. A similar right to representation on boards of directors of public entities in the public sector is set out in the Personnel Representation Regulation (*personalföreträdarförordning* 1987:1101).

The above sets out the general allocation of obligations and rights between the social partners with respect to joint regulation. Employment law as addressed in the next section concerns the allocation of rights and obligations as between employers and employees.

16.4 Employment Law

The Employment Protection Act is the main statutory framework of rights and obligations between employers and employees, supplemented by acts on specific topics, such as the Discrimination Act. Historically, the social partners were free to contract out of certain of these statutory provisions, but now any rights as accruing under EU law cannot be contracted away by the individual employee or the social partners. The Employment Protection Act applies only to employees and not to independent contractors. In addition, certain categories of persons are exempted under the Act, such as corporate management, employees belonging to the employer's family or household, and individuals in certain state assistance programs.

There is no statutory definition of an employee in the Act, with the courts often turning to the legislative preparatory works for guidance. There are three types of employment under the Act, employment until further notice (*tillsvidareanställning*), fixed-term employment (*tidsbegränsad anställning*) and trial employment (*provanställning*). Fixed-term employment can include general fixed-term employment, substitute employment, seasonal work and employees who are 67 years or older. Trial employment is only to be for a maximum of six months. The primary type of employment under the legislation is to be permanent employment, in other words, until further notice, with fixed-term and trial employment to be the exceptions.

The employer is to provide written information as to all the material conditions of the employment within one month of the commencement of employment, unless the employment is for a period of less than three weeks. Additional specific information is to be provided to workers posted abroad.

16.4.1 EMPLOYMENT PROTECTION

Employment, or as referred to in the Employment Protection Act, a contract of employment (*anställningsavtal*), is normally to apply until further notice and may be terminated by the employer only when objective grounds for termination can be cited. These objective grounds (*sakliga grunder*) are further categorized as due to either personal reasons or redundancy. The former is based on the employee's performance or other personal circumstances, while the latter is based on the employer's needs. If a contract of employment until further notice is terminated without objective grounds, the termination can be declared invalid by the Labor Court and/or damages awarded. The employee is normally allowed to remain in employment during the interim until the Court issues a judgment as to the lawfulness of the termination.

Termination for Personal Reasons

The standard to be applied for objective grounds for personal reasons is fairly high. A three-step procedure has been established under Section 7 of the Employment Protection Act and the case law. The employer must assess first whether it has objective grounds to terminate the employment. The employer must then assess whether the employee can be transferred to other work within the work place. If the termination is due to personal reasons relating to the neglect of employment duties, the duty to transfer is negligible. Third, the employer is to assess whether the employee has sufficient qualifications for the other work. Consequently, an employer must seriously consider alternative employment for the employee. In addition, the employer may not generally terminate employment for reasons known to the employer for more than two months before the notice of employment termination was given.

Termination for personal reasons can either be effective after a certain period of notice (*uppsägning*) or effective immediately (*avskedande*). If the former, the act sets out certain notice periods from one to six months that are based on length of service. If the latter, the employer is to give a one week notice before the immediate termination is seen to be effective, entailing in essence that the employee is relieved of duties with pay for that week in the majority of cases.

For the employer to immediately terminate an employee without any notice period, the employee must have grossly neglected obligations to the employer. The legislative preparatory works state that for a summary dismissal, it is necessary that the employee be guilty of "such intentional or grossly negligent actions that [such] reasonably need not be tolerated in any legal relationship."[45] The employer in both cases is to give the employee a written notice of termination and include information on how to appeal the termination and/or request damages, and if the employee so requests, the reasons for the termination. The employee has a right to wages and benefits during the notice period. Any income derived from other sources can, however, be deducted from the wages during this period, and the employee cannot be relocated if doing so would make finding new employment more difficult.

Termination Due to Redundancy

An employer can give notice of termination of employment based on redundancy. There is no requirement that an actual lack of work exists, simply that the employer has business reasons for the redundancies. When determining the order of redundancy, the employer is to observe certain statutory rules concerning seniority: 1) the length of employment, 2) the age of the employee and 3) whether an employee who can be transferred to another

---

45 Legislative Bill 1973:129 at 149.

job due to seniority has sufficient qualifications to perform the new work. The local parties, the employer and the local union, are free to derogate from these rules by means of a collective agreement where a national agreement is already applicable. The social partners are still always bound, however, by that perceived to be good practice on the labor market. An employer with ten or fewer employees may exempt two "key" employees from the seniority lists in order to protect the retention of skills necessary in the business. An employment termination based on redundancy in violation of the rules as to seniority lists cannot be declared invalid due to the impact the invalidity would have on the other employees on the same list. Liability for monetary damages, however, still exists.

The same rights as to wages, notice and written requirements are applicable here as for termination of employment based on personal reasons. A person employed for more than twelve months normally has a right of priority to re-employment with the same employer within a period of nine months after the former employment ceased to have effect.

Certain institutional structures have been set up by the social partners for events such as redundancy. The 1998 Agreement on Transition between SAF and PTK (*omställningsavtal*) sets out benefits for redundant salaried employees. A similar agreement on transition was entered into between LO and SAF in 2004 with respect to blue-collar workers. Only the municipal sector currently lacks such a structure. These structures create support in addition to that provided by the state programs to those who are eligible.[46]

16.4.2   EMPLOYMENT CONDITIONS

Employment conditions are generally not regulated by statute in Sweden. Wages as discussed above are typically set in collective agreements and there is no minimum wage legislation. There are, on the other hand, protections for employees with respect to wages in cases of employer insolvency under the

---

46   *See* Gabriella Sebardt, REDUNDANCY AND THE SWEDISH MODEL IN AN INTERNATIONAL CONTEXT (Kluwer 2006) for a detailed account in English of the system created with respect to redundancy and the benefits granted in the Swedish collective agreements.

Wage Guarantee Act (*lönegarantilag* 1992:497), giving employees the status of statutorily protected creditors.[47]

Other statutes address specific issues such as working hours and vacations. Working hours are usually set by collective agreement with regard to both number and scheduling within the framework as set out in the Working Hours Act (*arbetstidslag* 1982:673).[48] This act stipulates that regular working hours are not to exceed 40 hours per week. Overtime is permitted under the act to a limited extent, normally not exceeding 48 hours during a four-week period and 200 hours annually. Certain derogations to this Act may be made in a collective agreement reached at the national level, but not with respect to EU law protections to the detriment of the employee.

As already touched upon with safety delegates, the Work Environment Act prescribes the conditions for a work place with the objectives of preventing occupational injuries and creating good work environments. Monitoring compliance with the act falls within the duties of the safety delegate, but is also enforced by the Work Environment Authority with sanctions in the form of penalties. At work places with fifty or more employees, a safety committee is to be appointed, consisting of the representatives of the employer as well as of the employees, whose tasks include planning and monitoring activities concerning work environment safety.

16.4.3 EMPLOYMENT LEAVE

Employees are guaranteed certain types of leave from employment by statute. The three main forms, vacation, sick and parental leave, are discussed below. In addition to these three, there are several other specific acts granting employees the right to take leave from employment. One is the right to take leave to study as granted in the Employee's Right to Educational Leave Act

---

47 An English translation of the Wage Guarantee Act is available at the website of the Government Offices at. This act replaced a previous Swedish act and is the implementation of Council Directive 80/987/EEC on the approximation of the laws of the Member States relating to the protection of employees in the event of the insolvency of their employer as amended by Directive 2002/74/EC of the European Parliament and of the Council.

48 For an English translation of the Working Hours Act, *see* the website of the Government Offices at sweden.gov.se.

(*lag 1974:981 om arbetstagares rätt till ledighet för utbildning*).[49] Another is the right to take leave to conduct a business operation according to the Right to Leave to Conduct a Business Operation Act (*lag 1997:1293 om rätt till ledighet för att bedriva näringsverksamhet*) under which an employee may take a leave of up to six months with the right to return to her job.[50]

Employees are also entitled to take leave to care for a spouse, child or close friend who is seriously ill at a maximum of 100 days per person cared for under the Leave Compensation and Leave for Care of Relatives Act (*lag 1988:1465 om ledighet för närståendevård*). The employer is not obliged by law to pay employees during this leave, but the employee is entitled to a state benefit, set at around 80% of normal pay up to the sick pay ceiling discussed below. Employees have the right to take "family emergency" leave without pay in the event of a family member's illness, accident or death requiring the employee's immediate presence. There is no statutory limit on the number of days of such leave under the Right to Leave for Urgent Family Reasons Act (*lag 1998:209 om rätt till ledighet av trängande familjskäl*).

Newly arrived immigrants have the right to take leave under the Swedish Language Education Act (*lag 1986:163 om rätt till ledighet för utbildning i svenska för invandrare*) in order to attend Swedish-language courses provided by the municipal authorities. There is no statutory limit on the duration of the leave. The employer is not obliged by law to pay employees during this leave. Employees are entitled to return to their former job following this leave.

Employees who have had a health condition that has reduced their work capacity for more than 90 days are entitled to unpaid leave from their current employment to try out a new job with a different employer. Under the Act on the Right to Leave to Try a Different Work (*lag 2008:565 om rätt till ledighet för att på grund av sjukdom prova annat arbete*), the employee has the right to return to her former job after the leave, if they wish.

---

49 An English translation of the Employee's Right to Educational Leave Act is available at the website of the Government Offices at sweden.gov.se.

50 An English translation of this act is available at the website of the Government Offices at sweden.gov.se.

Vacation Leave

Annual leave in the form of vacation with pay has been protected by statute in Sweden since 1938. The present protections are now found in the Annual Leave Act (*semesterlag* 1977:480),[51] which stipulates that an employee is entitled to a minimum of five weeks of leave annually. A system of annual leave pay (*semesterlön*) is also set up under the act, giving a vacation wage supplement. Collective agreements may provide better vacation benefits.

Sick Leave

Leave is also available for health reasons. The right to take sick leave is not guaranteed by law, but the right to compensation for sick leave is guaranteed under both the Social Insurance Code and the Sick Pay Act (*lag 1991:1047 om sjuklön*). The first day of any sick leave is without any compensation resulting in a wage loss for the employee. After that, the first two weeks of the sick leave are to be paid by the employer under the Sick Pay Act at the rate of 80 %. After these two weeks, the national insurance compensates employees on sick leave at approximately 80 % of the employee's wage up to a certain income ceiling, with the daily maximum approximately SEK 702 for 2012.[52] Certain collective agreements contain provisions including supplements that the employer will pay up to a certain amount as to any income lost due to the sick leave.

Parental Leave

One of the more significant rights to employment leave for both parents and employers is the right to take parental leave to care for children as set out in the Parental Leave Act (*föräldraledighetslag* 1995:584).[53] Fifty million days of parental leave were taken in 2011 in Sweden with seventy-six percent of the

---

51 An English translation of the Annual Leave Act is available at the website of the Government Offices at sweden.gov.se.

52 The formula for determining the daily sick leave compensation is the employee's income up to the ceiling of 7.5 times the price base amount (SEK 44,000 – 2012), multiplied by 0.97 and then multiplied by 0.80, with the sum divided by 365. There is also a minimum wage that the employee has to make in order to be eligible, 24 % of the price base amount each month, in other words, SEK 11 000 per month in 2012.

53 An English translation of the Parental Leave Act is available at the website of the Government Offices at sweden.gov.se.

parental leave days taken by women.[54] This system of parental leave and the parental leave cash benefit is based mainly on the Parental Leave Act and the Social Insurance Code.

Insured parents have the right to leave in connection with the birth and care of a child in accordance with the provisions in Chapters 10–13 of the Social Insurance Code. Pregnant women are entitled to leave and a pregnancy cash benefit under the provisions in Chapter 10 of the Social Insurance Code. Parental leave, for which both parents are eligible, is for 480 days at the longest for both parents combined. The parental leave cash benefit can be paid until the child has reached the age of eight or at a later date when the child has completed the first year of school. A parent may refrain from exercising the right to parental leave to the benefit of the other parent with the exception of 60 days for each child, referred to as the "Pappa months," in an effort to encourage fathers to spend more time with their children. If the parent does not take all of these days, the other parent is not entitled to compensation for the days except at the lowest level. The parents are allowed to take up to thirty days at the same time during the first year of a child's life.

The amount of the parental leave cash benefit is regulated in Chapter Eleven of the Social Insurance Code. Different compensation categories are used to calculate the monetary amount of the parental leave cash benefit, the primary ones being the income based benefit and the lowest level benefit. Parents are eligible for compensation for 390 of the 480 days at the income based benefit level. Parental leave compensation for each such day is calculated by the sick leave base income (there is a ceiling of 10 times the statutory price base amount) multiplied by 0.97 and then multiplied again by 0.80 and divided by 365 days. This entails that the maximum amount of the parental leave cash benefit in 2012 was SEK 935 per day. This amount was purposefully raised in 2008 to be higher than the sick leave compensation in order to encourage the parent with the higher income to take more parental leave. There is also now an equality bonus that is paid out when the parents

---

54 This statistic is available at the website of the Swedish Social Insurance Agency (*Försäkringskassan*) at http://www.forsakringskassan.se/omfk/statistik_och_analys/ barn_och_familj/foraldrapenning.

take equal parental leave in the amount of SEK 50 per parent per day up to a ceiling of SEK 13,500.

The remaining 90 parental leave days, guaranteed days, are paid only at the lowest level of SEK 180 per day. This is also a minimum rate of benefit at which the entire leave can be taken when a parent is not eligible to receive any higher amount. There are further rules as to qualification periods as to certain compensation levels, but the basic system is that as set out above. Collective or individual agreements may include provisions further supplementing income lost during parental leave.

16.4.4 DISCRIMINATION LEGISLATION

As discussed in Chapter Two, the Instrument of Government provides certain protections against discriminatory laws and acts by the state, as well as the protections in Article 19 of the rights as granted under the European Convention.

With respect to unlawful discrimination in employment, the Discrimination Act[55] forbids unlawful discrimination on the basis of sex, transgender identity or expression, ethnicity, religion or other belief, disability, sexual orientation or age. A new aspect to this law is that it provides broader protection than with simply employment, covering in addition, education, labor market policy, starting a business and professional recognition, membership in organizations such as labor unions, housing, providing goods and services, social benefits, social insurance, military service and public employment.

---

55 An English translation of the Discrimination Act is available at the website of the Equality Ombudsman at do.se.

The 2008 Discrimination Act replaces seven different statutes[56] that had previously covered different grounds of discrimination in different settings. Two new additional grounds were included in the 2008 Discrimination Act, age and transgender identity or expression, so now the grounds covered are these two plus sex, ethnicity, religion or other belief, disability and sexual orientation.

The Discrimination Act prohibits unlawful discrimination, defined as direct and indirect discrimination, harassment, sexual harassment and instructions to discriminate in its Section 4:

1   *Direct discrimination*: Where a person is disadvantaged by being treated less favorably than another is treated, has been treated or would have been treated in a comparable situation, if this disadvantage is associated with sex, transgender identity or expression, ethnicity, religion or other belief, disability, sexual orientation or age.

2   *Indirect discrimination*: Where a person is disadvantaged by the application of a provision, criterion or procedure that appears neutral but that may put individuals of a certain sex, transgender identity or expression, ethnicity, religion or other belief, disability, sexual orientation or age at a particular disadvantage, unless the provision, criterion or procedure has a legitimate purpose and the means that are used are appropriate and necessary to achieve that purpose.

---

56 These seven statutes were:
· The 1991 Equal Treatment Act concerning unlawful discrimination on grounds of sex;
· The 1999 Measures to Counteract Ethnic Discrimination in Working Life Act;
· The 1999 Prohibition of Discrimination in Working Life of People with Disability Act;
· The 1999 Act Prohibiting Discrimination in Working Life based on Sexual Orientation;
· The 2003 Act Prohibiting Discrimination with respect to Goods and Services;
· The 2006 Act Prohibiting Discrimination with respect to primary school children; and
· The 1992 Act on Higher Education containing prohibitions as to discriminating against students.
For the history of the previous acts and the Labor Court's discrimination jurisprudence, *see* Carlson (2007) at 122.

3   *Harassment*: Conduct that violates a person's dignity and that is
    associated with one of the grounds of discrimination sex, transgender
    identity or expression, ethnicity, religion or other belief, disability,
    sexual orientation or age.
4   *Sexual harassment*: Conduct of a sexual nature that violates a person's
    dignity.
5   *Instructions to discriminate*: Orders or instructions to discriminate
    against an individual in a manner referred to in points 1–4 to a person
    in a subordinate or dependent position relative to the person giving
    the orders or instructions or to an individual who is to perform a
    commission for that person.

These definitions reflect the requirements as set out under EU law and as
set out in the previous legislation. The act came into effect 1 January 2009.

Two other laws set out areas of unlawful discrimination in employment.
The Act Prohibiting Discrimination on the Basis of Part-Time and
Fixed-Time Work (*lag 2002:293 om förbud mot diskriminering av deltids-
arbetande arbetstagare och arbetstagare med tidsbegränsad anställning*)[57] was
legislated under Union law requirements and mandates that employers not
discriminate against part-time and fixed-term workers based on the fact that
they are not full-time employees. There are also provisions in the Parental
Leave Act mandating that employers not discriminate against employees for
taking parental leave. This latter issue has been problematic for both women
and men taking longer periods of parental leave.

---

57 An English translation of the Act Prohibiting Discrimination on the Basis of
    Part-Time and Fixed-Time Work is available at the website of the Government Offices
    at sweden.gov.se.

CHAPTER 17

Land Leases

Land leases (*arrenderätt*) and the lease of premises (*hyresrätt*) are the two main categories of leases set out in chapters eight through thirteen of the Land Code (*jordabalk* 1970:994).[1] Land leases, including general land leases, agricultural land leases, residential land leases and commercial land leases, are the subjects of this chapter. The lease of premises, including residential and non-residential leases, governed by chapter twelve in the Land Code is addressed in the next chapter.

Leases present a legal institution in which the Swedish legislator has successively incorporated social protections for certain types of lessees, particularly agricultural and residential. The purchase of real estate historically entailed that any third-party user rights, such as those of lessees, were extinguished by the transaction (*köp bryter legostämma*). The 1907 act concerning user rights continued to maintain this fundamental principle, but included certain explicit exceptions to protect lessees. The first basically was a codification of custom, in that user rights followed with the property if the seller specifically included them in a provision in the sale agreement. User rights could also survive a transfer of ownership through a sale if registered

---

1   An English translation of the Land Code, as well as of other real property legislation is available at the website of the Department of Real Estate and Construction Management, at the School of Architect and Built Environment at the Swedish Royal Institute of Technology ("KTH"), www.kth.se/en/abe/inst/fob. A complete listing of all the statutes in English as well as an English/Swedish, Swedish/English glossary concerning real estate terms can be found there under Swedish Land and Cadastral Legislation, www.kth.se/abe/om_skolan/organisation/inst/fob/avd/ fastighetsvetenskap/publikationer/slcl/swedish-land-and-cadastral-legislation-1.33609. A printed version of these English translations is also available in Hans Mattson & Tommy Österberg, ed., Roger Tanner, transl., SWEDISH LAND AND CADASTRAL LEGISLATION (3rd ed. Jure 2007).

       441

in the land register. Last, lessees were given heightened protection in that they had the right to remain on the property despite any transfer of ownership if the lease was in writing and the lessee had taken possession of the leasehold prior to the conveyance. The 1970 Land Code strengthened these protections by also prescribing that the rights of lessees would survive a transfer in the event the buyer was in bad faith as to the existence of the right.

Other social protections afforded lessees generally under the Land Code ("LC") include regulations concerning a duty of maintenance by the lessor, maintaining certain quality standards with respect to premises, the allocation of risks between the lessee and lessor, certain duties of new owners with respect to existing lessees, the transferability of leases, the purchase of any investments made by tenants, as well as protections against unilateral rent increases. Another social protection granted lessees was the creation of tribunals, the Regional Tenancies Tribunals (*arrendenämnden*) and the Regional Rent Tribunals (*hyresnämnden*), to facilitate dispute resolution and decrease costs for tenants making claims with respect to conflicts arising in leasing relationships.

Each of the four statutory land leases created in the Land Code, general, agricultural, residential and commercial, reflects a conscious balancing of interests between the lessor and lessee within that category of lease. Agricultural land leases acquired a certain degree of statutory "social" protection (*social arrendelagstiftning*) already in the 1920's. Leases for an indefinite term were to be for a statutory minimum of five years with five-year extensions. The lease could be freely terminated by the lessee but only terminated for certain causes by the lessor. The lessee was also given a restricted right to convey the lease and a right of first refusal with respect to purchasing the leasehold. Additional social protections were later afforded to residential land leases in the 1960's. Lessees in general land leases and commercial land leases have little or no protections, the assumption being that the parties to such leases have equal bargaining power or not as great a need for protection.

17.1 The General Rules

The broad framework for all user rights, not just leases of land or premises, but also easements and other user rights, is set out in the seventh chapter of the Land Code. Chapter eight creates a sub-framework with respect to land leases, so that the provisions in chapter eight, applicable to agricultural, residential and commercial land leases, must be read parallel with their respective lease chapter as well as chapter seven. Site leaseholds are exempted from many of these regulations as the lessee in such a long-term lease is to be equated with an owner for many purposes, thus in less need of protection.

The provisions contained in the eighth chapter are general, so that any specific statutory regulation in chapters nine through thirteen is controlling. The mandatory nature of the social protections provided in the legislation is made clear in LC 8:2, which states that any agreement in conflict with the regulations in chapters eight through eleven is void if it is to the disadvantage of the lessee or any other party having such rights unless otherwise prescribed by statute.

17.1.1 REQUIREMENT OF A WRITING

Agreements as to land leases for agricultural, residential or commercial purposes are to be in writing and all applicable terms and conditions are to be included in the agreement. Any changes or supplements not in writing as a general rule are void. Where a lessee has assumed possession of the leasehold in the absence of a written agreement for a reason not due to the lessee, the lessee has the right to compensation for any damages arising due to the absence of a writing. Notice of termination is to be given in writing unless a written acknowledgment of notice of termination is given.

17.1.2 RIGHTS OF SPOUSES

Spouses have certain protections under these chapters. Where a general, agricultural or residential land lease has been granted for the lifetime of a certain person, the spouse of that person has the right to enter as lessee during her respective lifetime, if the marriage was entered into prior to the lease agreement being executed. If the surviving spouse thereafter enters into a new marriage, the lessor has the right to terminate the lease agreement.

17.1.3 PAYMENT AND REDUCTIONS IN LEASING FEES

Leasing fees are to be paid annually three months prior to the expiration of each leasing year, unless otherwise agreed. The lessee is entitled to a reduction of leasing fees in certain cases, such as where the lessor has provided inaccurate information, for example, as to the extent of the leasehold property. The lessee then has a right to a reasonable reduction in the leasing fees, compensation for damages and in some cases, may terminate the agreement. The lessee also has similar rights where the leasehold property has been decreased or diminished due to flood, landslide or other similar occurrence, and the lessee has not contributed to causing the damage.

17.1.4 RIGHTS OF THE LESSOR

The lessor has the right to inspect the leasehold. If the leasehold is to be vacated, the lessee must allow it to be viewed at suitable times. The lessor is to notify the lessee in good time as to any dates of inspection or viewings of the leasehold. In the event the security as provided by the lessee for the performance of the lease deteriorates, the lessee is obligated upon request of the lessor to provide additional satisfactory security. If the lessee fails to do this within three months, the lessor has the right to terminate the lease as well as a right to damages. The lessee generally may not grant a user right in the leasehold or part thereof without the lessor's consent.

17.1.5 FORFEITURE OF THE LEASE

The lease is forfeited and the lessor has the right to terminate it according to LC 8:23 in five situations, if the lessee:

1   Is more than one month late in paying the leasing fee;
2   Neglects to maintain the leasehold or that required with respect to an agricultural lease under LC 9:35 and fails to take corrective action after being notified of such failure;
3   Uses the premises for purposes other than those intended when the lease was executed, or in the event a certain crop rotation was set out in the agreement or provisions regarding maintenance, and the lessee

deviates from that agreed upon and fails to take corrective action after being notified of such;

4   Conveys the lease or substitutes another as lessee or assigns the lease in violation of the provisions in the Land Code; or

5   Fails to perform a contractual obligation exceeding the lessee's obligations as set out in Land Code, and it must be seen of material importance for the lessor that the obligation be performed.

The lease is not forfeited, however, if the lessee simply fails to perform a minor obligation. If the lease is terminated due to forfeiture, the lessor has a right to damages. Where the lease is forfeited due to a failure to pay the fees, neglect or improper use, but corrective action is taken before the lessor asserts the right to terminate the agreement, the lessee cannot be divested of the leasehold on that basis. The same is true if the lessor fails to terminate the agreement within six months of gaining knowledge of an unlawful conveyance of the lease or failure to perform a contractual obligation.

If the lessee is being evicted for a failure to pay the leasing fee, the lessee may not be evicted if the leasing fee is paid at the latest the twelfth day from the date of the notice of termination. A decision as to eviction may not be executed until fourteen days after a notice of termination has been given.

17.1.6 RIGHT OF FIRST REFUSAL

One of the strongest social protections for lessees can be found in the Leasehold Properties (Acquisition by the Lessee) Act (*lag 1985:658 om arrendatorers rätt att förvärva arrendestället*). According to this act, a lessee in an agricultural land lease with a residence, or in a residential land lease, has the right to purchase the leasehold under certain conditions. The lessee must give notice of the interest in purchasing the leasehold to the land registration authority, which in its turn is to notify both the property unit owner and the lessee that the notification has been registered in the Land Register Section of the Real Property Register. Such notification is valid for ten years.

Once the notification is registered, the property unit owner has to give the lessee the right of first refusal with respect to purchasing the property in most situations before transferring the leasehold to a third party. Such a right need not, however, be granted under several circumstance, including where the lessee does not have the right to renew the lease, or if taking into account the relationship between the property unit owner and the third-party purchaser, or the terms and conditions of the sale generally, forcing such would be unfair. The issue of whether a right of first refusal must be offered is to be decided by a Regional Tenancies Tribunal upon the request of the property unit owner. The offer of sale including a proposed purchase agreement is to be submitted by the property unit owner to the Tribunal, which then is to serve it on the lessee.

17.1.7 BUYOUT OF IMPROVEMENTS

Another protection given to lessees is the right to a buyout of any improvements made by the lessee. If the lessee has erected buildings on the leasehold or generally paid costs exceeding the lessee's obligations, an offer for the lessor to purchase the buildings or improvements is to be given by the lessee. If the lessor fails to accept this buyout offer within one month, the lessee may remove the property or assign it to a subsequent lessee. If the lessee removes the property, the lessee is to restore the leasehold to a serviceable state.

If such property is not removed or assigned within three months from the leasehold being vacated or a buyout offer finally rejected, the lessor becomes the owner of such property without any obligation to pay for it. If materials have been taken from the lessor's property unit and incorporated into the building or improvement, they may not be removed by the lessee or subsequent lessees before the lessor has been compensated for the materials. The parties are free to contract otherwise with respect to these rights and obligations. If the vacating lessee leaves other property in the leasehold and fails to remove it within three months after being so requested, the lessor becomes owner of the property without any obligation to pay for it.

These are the provisions generally applicable to land leases. Specific chapters set out provisions specific to three of the different types of land leases, agricultural, residential and commercial.

17.2 General Land Leases

A general lease of land (*lägenhetsarrende*) is a default category, entailing any lease of land that cannot be seen as granted for agricultural, residential or commercial purposes as stated in LC 8:1. The regulations in chapter eight are applicable, but there are no further statutory provisions. An example of such a general lease of land can be seen as where an amateur soccer team pays to use a practice field for only a few months during the year. Such a use is neither agricultural, commercial nor residential as defined by the Land Code.

17.3 Agricultural Land Leases

The regulations regarding agricultural land leases as found in chapter nine differ in certain respects from those governing other types of land leases, mainly because of the specific nature of farming, as well as its perceived key importance to the Swedish economy. A lessee can often have an enormous investment in an agricultural lease in the form of crops, buildings or machinery, an investment that cannot be reaped until a certain point of time. For example, corn must be planted in the spring and harvested in late summer. A notice of termination effective in August could then be a financial catastrophe for the lessee and an unjust enrichment for the lessor.

Two types of agricultural leases can be granted, one concerning the use of land for agricultural purposes including a residence (*gårdsarrende*), and one which is simply a grant of a use of land for agricultural purposes (*sidoarrende*). The former type of agricultural land lease is afforded even greater protections than the latter, as both the lessee's residence and livelihood are connected to the same land lease.

17.3.1 DURATION OF THE LEASE AND LEASING FEE

An agricultural land lease is to be for a defined period and if not defined, the lease is to be for five years. If the agricultural lease is combined with a residence, the lease period is to be at least five years despite any agreements to the contrary. A Regional Tenancies Tribunal (*Arrendenämnden*) must approve any shorter periods as agreed upon. If the grantor has a right limited to only a defined period, the lease may be limited to that period. The state may grant a lease for the lifetime of the lessee.

The leasing fee is to be defined in a monetary amount, in contrast for example, to a percentage of any crops. If an agreement is made in violation of this, the amount of the leasing fee is to be that determined as reasonable taking into consideration the intent of the parties and other circumstances existing at the time of the execution of the lease. Conflicts regarding such are also to be taken to a Regional Tenancies Tribunal.

17.3.2 RENEWAL, MODIFICATION OR TERMINATION OF THE LEASE

The lease is deemed renewed for a period comparable to the lease period, however, at the longest for five years, unless a valid notice of termination has been given by either party. Where no modification of the lease is requested, the same terms and conditions are then applicable to the renewed period.

When a modification of a lease has been requested, and the parties are not in agreement as to such, the party requesting the modification is to refer the matter to a Regional Tenancies Tribunal within two months before the expiry of the current lease period. If the issue is still not settled upon at the expiration of the current lease period, the lessee has the right to remain in the leasehold until the dispute is decided. The terms and conditions for the previous lease period are then applicable until a decision is issued.

Even if the lessor has given notice of termination of the lease, the lessee has the right to a renewal of the lease (*direkt besittningsskydd*), unless the lessor can show cause as to why the lease should be terminated. The lessor must be able to show that:

1   The lease has been forfeited or the security provided by the lessee has deteriorated and the lessee has not provided additional security;
2   The lessee has neglected duties to such a degree that the agreement reasonably should not be renewed;
3   The lessor, her spouse or children most likely will use the leasehold and it is not unfair to the lessee that the lease be terminated;

4   The leasehold is most likely needed for a more appropriate
    parceling of agricultural units and it is not particularly unfair
    to the lessee that the leasing relationship be terminated;
5   The leasehold will most likely be used in accordance with
    a detailed plan; or
6   The leasehold will be used for purposes other than agricultural and it
    is not unfair to the lessee that the lease relationship be terminated.

If the lessee abandons the leasehold, leaving it unworked or neglected, the lessor may immediately repossess it. The lessee has the right to a renewal of the lease if the lessor's interests can be met by the lessee removing from only a part of the leasehold. In the event the lessor has terminated the lease and a dispute arises, the lessor is to refer the matter to a Regional Tenancies Tribunal no later than two months after the date the termination was to take place.

Leasing fees in a fair amount are to be paid upon the renewal of the lease. In the event the lessor and lessee cannot agree as to that amount, the fees are to be comparable to the value of the lease taking into account the value of any yields, the content of the lease and the circumstances in general.

17.3.3 LESSEE'S RIGHT TO DAMAGES

Another significant social protection under this legislation is the right of the lessee to damages in cases of termination of a lease. If the renewal of a lease including a residence is not granted due to a detailed plan or non-agricultural use, and the land is to be used for purposes for which it can be assumed that a considerably higher profit will arise, or can be met through expropriation, the lessor is to pay the lessee damages. These damages are to be in an amount comparable to the average leasing fees of one year during the most recent leasing period. If the lessee's losses are higher than this amount, the lessor is to compensate the lessee to a reasonable extent for any losses, however at the highest by an amount comparable to three years of leasing fees. The damages can be reduced or nullified if specific reasons exist for finding that such liability is unjust to the lessor.

17.3.4 MAINTENANCE, LEASEHOLD IMPROVEMENTS
AND INVESTMENTS

The lessee is to care for and maintain the leasehold. If the condition of the leasehold deteriorates due to the lessee's failure to do this, the lessor has a right to compensation in any settlement. If the lessee, upon assuming possession of the leasehold, has remedied a defect without a right to compensation at the time when the work is completed, the lessee has the right to compensation during a settlement. This is not applicable to those parts of the leasehold for which the lessee according to agreement has no duty to maintain.

Where the leasehold includes a residence for the lessee or her employees, the lessor is to insure that the residence is in such condition as prescribed by any health regulations and determined by an inspector. Should deficiencies be found, the inspector is to prescribe those measures that must be taken and calculate their costs, as well as set a date by which the measures are to be taken. In the event the lessor fails to take such measures in due time, the lessee may take the measures instead and has the right to compensation from the lessor at the determined amount. If the lessee prefers to terminate the agreement, she may do so if the defect is more than insignificant. The lessee also has the right to a reduction in the leasing fees for the period during which the defect existed and compensation for damages.

An additional social protection under the act has been the reallocation of certain costs. If a government authority decides that the leasehold cannot be used in the intended manner without an existing building being renovated or new buildings put in place, the lessor is to perform such work if necessary for a suitable agricultural use of the leasehold. If the improvements can be deemed a part of the lessee's duty to maintain, however, the lessor has no such duty.

The lessor also has a duty to build or replace a facility where a building, drainage or other facility has been damaged or worn not due to any negligence or intent by the lessee. The facility must no longer be able to serve its purpose and be necessary for suitably planned agricultural activity on the leasehold. If the lessor does not have the obligation to make such repairs, the lessee is to do so. If the lessee did not cause the harm, she has the right to compensation from the lessor for the work performed. Where the lessee has replaced a building and is not entitled to compensation, the lessee has the right to compensation under any settlement for any deficiencies existing in the previous building where the new building is suitable for the use and has been approved by the lessor. Both with respect to orders by government authorities to remedy defects and the general duty of a lessor to remedy defective facilities, if the lessor fails to take the measures required within a reasonable time, the lessee may instead make the improvements. Disputes concerning such matters are to be taken to a Regional Tenancies Tribunal at the request of either party.

If the lessor, in accordance with the lease agreement, finances an investment in a leasehold entirely or partially, and the value of the leasehold has increased due to the investment, the lessee is obligated to accept a reasonable increase in the leasing fees. Such an obligation also exists where the lessor has performed work, paid certain compensation or bought-out an investment.

17.3.5 SETTLEMENT AND INSPECTION

When the lessee is to vacate the leasehold, or if lease is to be renewed after more than nine years, the lessor and lessee are to agree upon a settlement. The settlement is to be based upon inspections conducted both at the beginning and at the end of the settlement period. The inspections are to be conducted by at least two persons familiar with local agricultural conditions and authorized by the county board, appointed jointly by the lessor and lessee.[2]

Everything belonging to the leasehold is to be examined in the inspection, including buildings, gardens, fields and meadows, pastures, enclosures, ditches, roads, bridges, wells and conduits. Certain areas of the leasehold may be exempted from the inspection if the lessor and lessee agree as to the extent the defects are to be taken into account and the inspectors note

---

2   There is a specific regulation relating to inspectors, Ordinance on Inspectors in Agricultural Land Lease Matters (*förordning 2009:28 om synemän vid jordbruks-arrende*). Under this regulation, the County Administrative Board is to appoint inspectors for three-year periods. The inspectors are to have legal capacity and an understanding of leasing and agricultural conditions in the county. Statements as to suitability as inspector are to be obtained by the Board from authorities and organizations having knowledge of the person's suitability.

the agreement. In the event compensation for work performed or damages cannot be agreed upon, the inspectors are to determine the amount of compensation.

17.3.6 ASSIGNMENT OF THE LEASE AND BUYOUT OF INVESTMENTS

The lessee may not generally assign the lease without the consent of the lessor. The lessee may assign the lease, if nothing otherwise has been contracted and where the lease period is for ten years or more, to a party with whom the lessor can reasonably be satisfied. However, the lessee is to first offer the leasehold back to the lessor with a settlement and reasonable compensation for the value of the lease. The lessor must accept such an offer within one month.

A lessee who has made an investment outside the duties of maintenance may assign the lease if the lessee has given a buyout offer in writing to the lessor to buyout the investment and the lessor has not accepted the buyout offer within three months. Under certain circumstances, if the lessee has made such an investment and the lease has terminated, the lessor must buyout the investment. The buyout amount generally is to be comparable to the increase in value of the leasehold due to the investment.

17.4 Residential Land Leases

The balance of interests with respect to residential land leases differs from those as seen above with agricultural land leases, resulting in fewer statutory provisions, as the investments made by the lessee are of a less complicated nature. A residential lease according to LC 10:1 is a lease of land for a purpose other than agricultural and the lessee has the right to build or retain a residence, with the purpose of the lease evidently not other than to provide a residence for the lessee and her family. The provisions in the tenth chapter are also applicable to leases granted to cooperatives for the purpose of subletting premises to its members. This is an exception from the main rule giving such protection only to individuals.

Residential leases have a fixed duration of at least five years, or can be for the life of the lessee. If the lease term is not defined, the lease is for five years. A lease for a shorter period is valid only if approved by a Regional Tenancies Tribunal.

The lessee has the right to a renewal of the lease unless the lessor can show cause, demonstrating that:

1   The lease is forfeited or the security provided by the lessee has deteriorated and additional security has not been submitted by the lessee;
2   The lessee has otherwise neglected obligations to such an extent that the lease ought not reasonably be renewed;
3   Buildings are constructed on the leasehold without the necessary building permits or deviating from the detailed plan or therewith comparable decision of an authority with respect to the use of the land;
4   Buildings on the leasehold are not consistent with the detailed plan or area regulations and the lessor is going to use the leasehold in accordance with the plan or regulations;
5   The leasehold is to be used for residences of a type other than the lease or for agriculture, industry or some other commercial activity, and that the lessor's interest in being able to dispose over the property considerably outweighs the lessee's interest in the renewed lease; or
6   The lessor has justified reasons for terminating the lease.

If the lessor's interest can be met by the lessee withdrawing from a part of the leasehold, and the lease can be suitably renewed with respect to the remainder, the lessee has the right to such a renewal. The same system exists here as with respect to agricultural land leases concerning modifications, renewals or terminations of the lease, with such disputes being brought to and decided by a Regional Tenancies Tribunal. There is also the same system of buyouts of improvements, rights of first refusals, and the right to assign the tenancy in certain cases if the lessor should be reasonable satisfied with the proposed lessee, again with the Regional Tenancies Tribunals deciding any such disputes.

17.5 Commercial Land Leases

Commercial land leases are the category of specified leases in which the least amount of social protections are afforded to the lessee, the understanding being that in a commercial land lease, the parties have equal bargaining positions. As a result, commercial land leases have the least amount of statutory regulation. This is evident from the fact that the parties are entirely free to contract away the provisions found in the eleventh chapter and that the lessee does not have a right to a renewal of the lease (*direkt besittningsskydd*), but in the case of the lessor's termination, only a right to damages (*indirekt besittningsskydd*).

A commercial land lease is defined in LC 11:1 as where land is leased for a purpose other than agricultural or residential and the lessee has the right to erect or retain buildings not insignificant for commercial operations. If the lease is for the lessee's lifetime, or for a fixed term of less than one year, it is not deemed a commercial land lease, but then falls into the category of a general land lease.

Commercial land leases are to be for a fixed-term, and where such is not defined, for a period of five years. If nothing has otherwise been agreed, the lease is to include a term entailing that if notice of termination is not given in due time, the lease is to be deemed to be renewed for a comparable lease period, however, at the most for five years. Notice of termination is to be given six months prior to the expiry of the lease period where nothing otherwise has been contracted. The lessee may assign the lease to a party with whom the lessor can be satisfied unless otherwise agreed.

In the event the lessor has given notice of termination of the lease and refuses to renew it, or a renewal is not made as the lessor requires unreasonable fees or other terms which violate good market practices with respect to leases, or otherwise is unreasonable, the lessor is to compensate the lessee for the lessee's losses based on the termination. This is the case unless the lessor proves that:

1   The lessee has neglected obligations to such an extent that it cannot reasonably be required that the lessor renew the lease;
2   The leasehold is to be used for purposes other than that intended by the lease and that the lessor's interest in being able to dispose over the property for such purposes considerably outweighs the lessee's interest in the renewed lease; or
3   The lessor otherwise has justified reason to terminate the lease.

The same applies if the lessee has terminated the lease and requested a renewal of the lease upon modified terms. Any losses suffered by the lessee in connection with buildings erected or other improvements to the leasehold are to be taken into account with the determination of compensation only if such measures were taken in accordance with the lease.

A leasing fee requested by the lessor for a renewal of the lease is to be considered unreasonable if it exceeds the leasing fee for a comparable leasehold for a comparable lease period as would be charged on the open market disregarding any unreasonable deviations. Only if specific reasons exist can the increase in the value of the leasehold due to measures taken by the lessee be taken into consideration.

If the lessor wishes to terminate the lease, she is to give notice of such as well as inform the lessee as to the terms required for renewing the lease or the reasons for not renewing the lease. Information is to also be included that the lessee, if desiring compensation under LC 11:5, must submit the matter to a Regional Tenancies Tribunal for mediation. Where the lessor fails to do this, the notice is invalid. If the lessee fails to submit the matter to the tribunal in the correct time, the right to compensation is forfeited. The lessor may not require higher fees or terms other than those stated in the notice for the period or renewal prior to the matter being decided. If such is paid, the lessee has the right to compensation.

Where the lessee has terminated the lease and requested a renewal upon modified terms, she must submit the matter to the tribunal for mediation within two months, stating the modified terms requested. If the lessee fails to do this, or withdraws the matter from the tribunal, the notice of termination is void. If the lessee has failed to include the modified terms, the tribunal is to order her to do so within a certain period upon penalty of dismissal.

17.6 Site Leaseholds

Site leaseholds (*tomträtt*)[3] are a legal institution created to allow the state or municipalities to exploit land privately while still retaining ownership and having the right to revenues from the property that can be successively increased. There were 98 000 site leaseholds in Sweden in 2001. In 2012, there are approximately 60,000 single family homes built on site leaseholds.

---

3 Similar types of leases are crown leases, long-term leases and perpetual leases.

Site leaseholds differ from the other types of land leases described above in a number of significant aspects, the most important being that a lessee in a site leasehold is treated as the owner in many, if not for all, practical purposes in most situations. A lessee in a site leasehold is to be the comparable of an owner of a property unit when it comes to disposing over the property (except for the right to sell the actual land), such as with respect to obtaining mortgage deeds and granting user rights.

Site leaseholds are defined in LC 13:1 as granting use in a property unit for an indefinite period of time for a certain purpose in exchange for an annual payment.[4] The minimum period is twenty years. Most site leaseholds are granted for residential purposes, but many are granted for industrial and commercial uses. A site leasehold can only be granted in a property unit owned by the state or a municipality or otherwise in the public domain. The Government can consent to a site leasehold being granted in property owned by a foundation. A site leasehold cannot be granted in a portion of a property unit or several property units jointly.

17.6.1   FORM REQUIREMENTS

Any agreement as to a site leasehold must be in writing and specifically state that the grant is a site leasehold. Amendments or supplements not in writing are not valid. The purpose of the site leasehold is to be stated in the agreement as well as the amount to be paid until otherwise agreed. The agreement is also to include more detailed information as to the use and development of the property unit and the provisions applicable to the site leasehold in general. If any detailed plan or other regulations exist at the time of the grant, they are deemed to be included unless something to the contrary has been agreed.

The granting of a site leasehold is to include the transfer to the lessee of all buildings and other property belonging at the time of the grant to the property unit in accordance with the law. Taking possession of the site or its condition may not be made conditional. Neither may any restrictions be

---

4   A state inquiry was initiated in 2011 with respect to certain site leasehold and land lease issues (dir. 2011:60). The investigation is scheduled to be completed by 2014. Issues to be investigated include whether the site leaseholder should be allowed to purchase the land and simpler rules with respect to the fees to be paid.

placed on the lessee's right to assign the site leasehold or grant security or user rights in it.

17.6.2 FEES AND MODIFICATIONS OF FEES

The fees with respect to a site leasehold are to be determined in a fixed amount for a certain period of time and paid annually. If a longer period is not agreed upon, the period is to be ten years, commencing first on the date of the grant or a later date as stated in the agreement. Any agreement as to changing the amount of the payment for the next period may not be made later than one year prior to the expiry of the current period.

17.6.3 TERMINATION OF A SITE LEASEHOLD

A site leasehold agreement may not be terminated by the lessee. It can only be terminated at the expiry of certain periods of time upon notice by the site-owner. Unless longer periods have been agreed upon, the first period is sixty years, commencing on the date of the grant or a later date as per the agreement, and each subsequent period is forty years from the expiry of the previous period.

If the site leasehold has been granted for a purpose materially other than residential development, shorter time periods can be agreed upon, but not less than twenty years. Termination may only occur if it is important that the property unit be used for development of another type or another manner than that previously.

If the site leasehold is terminated, the site-owner has the obligation to buyout any buildings and other property belonging to the site leasehold. The compensation is to be comparable to the value of the property at the termination of the site leasehold under the assumption that it would exist for the same purpose and in general with unchanged conditions regarding the use and development of the property unit. If unnecessary expenses have been paid with respect to the site leasehold after the notice of termination, the increase in value arising thereto is not to be taken in consideration when determining the buyout amount. Where the site leasehold was granted for other than residential development, the parties may agree that the site-owner need not buyout the property.

After a grant of a site leasehold, any amended agreement by the parties is valid only after its registration in the Land Register Section has been approved. This includes when the site-owner and lessee agree to the expansion or restriction of the site leasehold, a change of its purpose or governing regulations, requirements for the leasehold generally, voluntary modification of the annual fees, termination of the site leasehold, modification of notice of termination period or a buyout of improvements. Lawsuits concerning reassessment or modification of the payment amount, objections to termination or determination of a buyout amount are to be brought to a land and environment court (*mark- och miljödomstol*).

Chapter twenty-one of the Land Code governs the registration of site leaseholds. In many ways, the lessee in a site leasehold is to have the same status as that of an owner of a property unit. A party receiving a site leasehold interest in a property is to register that interest within three months of its assignation. The land registration authority can order a party to register such an interest subject to penalty of fines.

17.7 Lease Disputes

The alternatives to litigation encouraged as means for resolving legal issues as set up in the Land Code include giving land surveyors authority to decide certain legal issues as seen in Chapter Eleven of the Land Code, as well as the establishment of specific land and environment courts. In addition, certain lease disputes are not brought to the general courts, but rather to the Regional Tenancies Tribunals (*arrendenämnden*) or to the Regional Rent Tribunals (*hyresnämnden*). The Regional Tenancies Tribunals have jurisdiction with respect to land leases, and the Regional Rent Tribunals with respect to residential and non-residential leases of premises. The tribunals are housed in the same buildings and share personnel with the general courts. The Act on Regional Tenancies and Rent Tribunals (*lag 1973:188 om arrendenämnder och hyresnämnder*) governs the tribunals. An issue that cannot be taken to a tribunal can be brought to one of the country's five land and environment courts (*mark- och miljödomstol*). Decisions by these courts can be appealed to the Land and Environment Court of Appeal (*Mark- och miljööverdomstolen*).

About one thousand matters are brought to the Regional Tenancies Tribunals each year. A Regional Tenancies Tribunal is to consist of three members, a chair who is legally trained, and two interest members, one an expert in lessor issues and the other an expert in lessee issues. Certain decisions by the tribunals originally could not be appealed, but this aspect of the Swedish legal procedural system is gradually changing. This is mostly due to criticism by the European Court of Human Rights as to the lack of an appeal procedure and a hearing by an objective court under Article 6 of the European Convention.[5]

Several central principles in general Swedish procedural law, that all evidence and arguments be presented orally (*muntlighetsprincipen*), that all evidence upon which the court bases its judgment must be presented at trial (*omedelbarhetsprincipen*), and that all evidence is to be presented in one trial (*koncentrationsprincipen*), have been modified somewhat by the rules applicable to hearings before these tribunals. In addition, the general allocation of trial fees and costs, the English rule that the losing party is to pay the prevailing party's trial costs and fees, has been purposefully abandoned so that lessees can more easily contest issues without being financially penalized for doing so in the form of high trial costs and fees.

Each county is to have a Regional Tenancies Tribunal and the tasks of the tribunals are to include mediating land lease disputes and adjudicating issues as to renewals of agricultural or residential land leases, determining the terms and conditions of such renewals and compensation as well as other issues referred to the tribunal by the Land Code. The tribunal can also act as an arbitration tribunal in a land lease dispute if decided upon by the parties in the lease agreement, or mediate certain issues between the parties.

A lessor or lessee wishing to assert a claim based on the leasing relationship must file such a lawsuit within two years from the date the lessee vacated the premises. With respect to an agricultural land lease, if any inspection as to the leasehold is contested prior to the expiration of this two-year period, this claim can be asserted within two years after the date the objection is finally decided. If one of the parties has filed the lawsuit in due time, the

---

5 *See*, for example, *Langborger v. Sweden*, European Court of Human Rights, judgment dated 22 June 1989, App. No. 11179/84. Sweden was found to be in violation of Article 6(1) as the Swedish Housing and Tenancy Court (*bostadsdomstolen*), with a judging panel appointed by interest organizations, was found to not fulfill the requirements under the European Convention for an objective tribunal.

other party is entitled to a set-off claim regardless of whether their own suit is time-barred.

Certain decisions by a Regional Tenancies Tribunal can be appealed to a court of appeal. Any leasing dispute that is not taken up by the tribunal is to be decided by the land and environment court in which jurisdiction the property unit is situated. Decisions by these courts can be appealed to the Land and Environment Court of Appeal (*Mark- och miljööverdomstolen*).

CHAPTER 18

Landlord Tenant Law

The landlord tenant relationship (*hyresrätt*) is one of the areas providing the greatest statutory protection to lessees beginning already in the 1930's. The Swedish population had grown dramatically at the end of the nineteenth century with increased urbanization, leading to housing shortages and poor residential conditions and abuses. At the same time, the shift from an agricultural-based economy to an industrial one severed the stronger ties of agricultural households, replacing them with the relatively much weaker ties between property owners and tenants. The Swedish welfare state (*folkhemmet*) was being put into place at this time with the objective of eradicating class differences. One goal was that not more than 20 % of a family's disposable income was to be spent on housing. Municipalities began to build rental units to meet housing needs.

The housing shortage continued after World War II and rent controls and other rationing legislation were passed, setting policy standards that would be prevalent for the decades to come. The government supported construction through subsidies, mostly to municipalities, further cementing the role of municipal housing. The shortage of housing still existing in the 1960's led to the legislation setting out the "Million Homes Program" (*miljonprogrammet*) with the goal of building 100,000 new residential units annually during the period of 1965–1975. The "Wallpaper Reform" (*tapetreformen*) was adopted in 1975 to create greater tenant influence as to living conditions. Tenants were given the right to perform minor refurbishments in apartments if done in a professional manner. Many of the social protections as seen with land leases above in Chapter Seventeen, as well as structures with respect to negotiations and dispute resolution, are also found with rental tenancies.

The approximately 4.6 million residences in Sweden can be divided into three main categories, privately owned single-family homes, housing cooperatives and rentals. In 2010, approximately one-third of the households lived in single-family homes, approximately one-fourth lived in housing cooperatives and forty percent lived in rental apartments.[1] Over three million people live in 1.5 million rental units in Sweden, of which approximately forty-five percent are owned by private organizations and fifty-five percent are owned by non-profit municipal housing corporations.[2] Municipalities have the responsibility under the Housing Supply Act (*lag 2000:1383 om kommunernas bostadsförsörjningsansvar*) to provide for the housing needs of their residents. About 90 % of all housing rents are established through negotiations between landlord and tenant organizations as further discussed below.

Chapter twelve governing landlord tenant law constitutes almost one-fourth of the entire Land Code. In contrast to land leases, the agreements falling within chapter twelve concern the lease of a building or part thereof in exchange for payment as defined in LC 12:1. Land can be included in such a lease, or rental agreement as referred to below, and thus governed by the provisions in chapter twelve, but only when rented together with premises, and where the land is used for insignificant gardening or purpose other than agricultural. The mandatory nature of the protections given in chapter twelve is emphasized by the provision that contractual terms contrary to the

---

1   These statistics were taken from Statistics Sweden (scb.se) and the website of the organization representing tenants in Sweden, the Swedish Union of Tenants, *Hyresgäst-föreningen,* at hyresgastforeningen.se. The Swedish Union of Tenants, founded in 1923, is a good illustration of the collective approach taken in Swedish society. This organization is an umbrella organization on the national level with approximately one-half of a million members. There are ten regional offices under the national office, and under the regional offices, there is a total of 200 associations at the municipal level, and 3 000 local tenant associations covering about 45 % of the apartment buildings in Sweden. Rent negotiations take place at the local and mid-levels.

2   These statistics were taken from the Swedish Association of Municipal Housing, SABO. This organization represents public housing companies in Sweden with approximately 300 affiliated companies managing 830 000 dwelling units. This is 20 % of the total housing in Sweden and about one-third of all dwelling units in multi-story houses. Altogether 1.4 million people live in SABO homes. For more information on this organization, *see* its website at sabo.se. The comparable umbrella organization on the private side is the Swedish Property Federation, *Fastighetsägarna Sverige,* with twenty thousand members owning eighty thousand properties and seven hundred thousand apartments. Information in English about this private organization is available at its website at fastighetsagarna.se.

regulations in chapter twelve are generally invalid as against the tenant or any party having the right of a tenant.

A major distinction exists in chapter twelve between residential (*bostad*) and non-residential (*lokal*) units, with the statutory social protections for the latter much lower. A residential unit is defined as a unit in which a grant of rights is made to use the premises entirely or partially as a residence. A non-residential unit consists of premises used for purposes other than residential, such as commercial or recreational.

As seen from the discussion of the regulations below, the protections for residential tenants include the right to a renewal of the lease unless the landlord can show cause (*direkt besittningsskydd*), the right to rent determined at an amount reflecting the utility value (*bruksvärde*) of the apartment as opposed to its market value, the right to certain information as well as the right to a certain standard with respect to the apartment.

18.1 Residential and Non-Residential Leases

As a whole, chapter twelve is organized chronologically with respect to the landlord tenant relationship, beginning with the rental agreement and ending with the resolution of disputes between landlords and tenants.

18.1.1 THE RENTAL AGREEMENT

A rental agreement concerning the lease of premises is to be in writing at the request of either the landlord or tenant. There is no strict form requirement, as in this context a form requirement is perceived of as being detrimental, rather than beneficial, to tenants. A rental tenancy will not be invalid for the failure to follow form, particularly as landlords as a group have better access to legal resources than tenants and can be assumed to be more familiar (or more able to hire assistance) with the law.

The rent for a residential unit is to be in an amount as stated in the rental agreement, or where the rental agreement contains a central negotiation clause, according to the Rent Negotiation Act (*hyresförhandlingslag* 1978: 304), discussed further below in section 18.3.1. The rent under Section 12:19 LC can exclude certain costs relating to heating, hot water, electricity or water and sewage, however, only under certain conditions can these be treated separately. The rent for a non-residential unit is also to be in an amount as determined in the rental agreement to the extent it does not encompass compensation for costs relating to heating, hot water, electricity or water and sewage. However, a provision in the agreement may state that the rent is to be based on the non-residential tenant's revenues or as decided in a written agreement between the landlord, or the landlord and an organization of property unit owners in which the landlord is a member, and on the other side between an organization of tenants. If the agreement is for a fixed term of at least three years, the non-residential rent may be based on a different ground of calculation than that stated above, such as index-based.

The landlord is also obligated to provide information to the tenant as to the landlord's name and the address at which the landlord can be reached in Sweden. If the landlord is a legal person, comparable information is to be provided as to the representative of the legal person. This information is to be in writing and posted visibly in the building.

18.1.2 DURATION OF THE TENANCY AND NOTICE OF TERMINATION

The main rule is that a residential rental agreement is to be for an undefined term, until further notice. A rental agreement can be for a fixed term and such an agreement is to be terminated at the expiry of the rental period, if nothing to the contrary has been agreed. If the tenancy has been for more than nine consecutive months, notice of termination must be given to terminate the agreement regardless of whether it is a permanent or fixed-term tenancy.

A rental agreement for a definite period is renewed until further notice where no timely notice of termination has been given, or where the tenant, despite the fact that the agreement was terminated without notice being given, continues to use the premises one month after the expiration of the rental period without the landlord requesting her to remove.

If notice of termination is to be given with respect to a rental agreement and a notice of termination period has not been agreed upon, notice can be given at the latest:

1   One day in advance if the rental period is no longer than two weeks;
2   One week in advance if the rental period is longer than two weeks but less than three months;

3   Three months in advance if the rental period is longer than three months and it is a residential unit;
4   Three months in advance if the rental period is longer than three months but less than nine months and it is a non-residential unit; or
5   Nine months in advance if the rental period is longer than nine months and it is a non-residential unit.

A residential tenant may always give a three-month notice of termination valid at the end of the month closest to three months from the notice.

Any notice of termination is to be in writing where the tenancy has been longer than three consecutive months as of the date of notice of termination. A notice of termination can generally be given orally if the tenant is giving notice and the landlord has provided a written confirmation of the notice. If the landlord is giving notice of termination for a residential unit that must be in writing, the landlord ought to also state in the notice the reason for the notice. Filing a complaint with a court petitioning that the tenancy be terminated, or that the tenant be evicted, acts as a notice of termination when service has been duly processed. The same is true with respect to an application for eviction under the Act on Payment Orders and Enforcement Assistance (*lag 1990:746 om betalningsföreläggande och handräckning*).

18.1.3 CONDITION OF THE PREMISES UPON POSSESSION

Upon the date of the tenant's possession of the premises, the landlord is to provide premises that are in a condition that is completely usable for their intended purpose in accordance with the general understanding in the geographic area. If the premises concern a recreational use or a non-residential unit, an agreement can be entered into that the premises can be in a worse condition.

In the event the premises deteriorate prior to the date of possession to the extent that that they no longer can be used for their intended purpose, the rental agreement is voidable under LC 12:10. The tenant has the right to compensation where the landlord has caused the damage or does not notify the tenant of it without delay. If a government authority declares the premises unfit for their intended use prior to the date of possession, the rental agreement is voidable even if the government decision is not yet final.

The tenant has a right to compensation if the basis for the decision is due to neglect by the landlord or where the landlord has failed to notify the tenant without delay as to the decision.

If the premises can still be used for their intended purposes, but the damage is not remedied prior to the date of possession, or if the premises in general are not in the condition that the tenant has the right to expect, the tenant may remedy the deficiency at the landlord's expense. This is the case where if the landlord has failed to remedy the defect as soon as possible after being requested to do so. In the event the deficiency cannot be remedied without delay, or if the landlord fails to remedy it as soon as possible after being so requested, the tenant can terminate the rental agreement. Termination may only occur, however, where the deficiency is of material significance. After the deficiency has been remedied by the landlord, the agreement may not be terminated.

The tenant has the right to a reasonable decrease in the rent for the period during which the premises are in a deficient condition. The tenant has a right to compensation for damages where the landlord fails to show that the deficiency did not depend upon the landlord's neglect. If the rental agreement concerns a residential unit, the landlord can be ordered upon the tenant's application to remedy the defect by a remedial injunction issued by a Regional Rent Tribunal. The tenant has a right to a reasonable deduction in rental fees also where a government authority has issued a decision prior to the date of possession that the tenant must refrain from using a part of the premises or in another manner suffer a restriction in the right of use. If this decision results in a considerable restriction, the tenant may terminate the agreement.

The tenant again has a right to a reasonable deduction where the rental agreement concerned premises not ready when the agreement was executed and the premises still are not ready on the date of possession. The tenant also has the right to terminate the agreement prior to the contracted date of possession if it becomes obvious that the premises will not be able to be used for their intended purpose. The tenant also has the right to compensation unless the landlord can prove that the delay did not depend upon the landlord's neglect.

If the previous tenant has not vacated the premises by the date of possession, the new tenant has the right to a rent reduction for the period during which the tenant could not use the premises or part thereof. If the

466

previous tenant is not removed immediately after the landlord being notified, the tenant has the right to terminate the agreement and the right to compensation for any loss unless the landlord can prove that the impediment did not depend upon the landlord's neglect.

18.1.4 CONDITION OF THE PREMISES DURING THE RENTAL PERIOD

The landlord is to maintain the premises during the rental period in a condition that is fully usable for their intended purpose in accordance with the general understanding in the area. If the premises are entirely or partially used for a residence, the landlord is to wallpaper, paint and perform other customary repairs in the residential part at reasonable intervals based on wear, age and use. Where the rental agreement confers a right to use spaces intended for the common use of tenants, the landlord generally is to keep such spaces in the same condition.

The landlord can be ordered through a remedial injunction to remedy the condition of the premises generally where the premises are damaged during the rental period not due to the tenant. This can be the case where the landlord neglects the duty to maintain the premises or where an impediment as to using the premises arises not due to the tenant. A Regional Rent Tribunal may upon a residential tenant's petition, order the landlord to remedy the defect based on penalty of fine.

A residential unit is to be deemed to have the minimum acceptable standard if it is equipped with that necessary within the premises for:

1   Continuous heating, hot and cold water and sewer drainage;
2   Electricity for normal household consumption;
3   Personal hygiene facilities comprising a toilet, wash basin as well as bathtub or shower; and
4   Food preparation facilities comprising a stove (cooker), sink, refrigerator, storage and counterspace.

The property unit itself should also have access to both storage and laundry facilities. The building cannot have significant deficiencies in areas such as structural integrity, fire safety or sanitary conditions in order to be deemed to have the lowest acceptable standard. If the residential unit does not meet this minimal acceptable standard during the tenancy, a Regional Rent Tribunal, upon the tenant's petition, may issue an improvement order requiring the landlord to take those measures necessary for the premises to reach such a standard based on penalty of fine.

18.1.5 TENANT'S CONSENT TO IMPROVEMENTS AND MODIFICATIONS

A landlord wishing to carry out improvements in the rental unit is to notify any concerned residential tenants of this in writing. The consent of the residential tenant or a Regional Rent Tribunal is necessary for a property unit owner to carry out certain measures for improvements. These measures include those to the property unit having a significant effect on a residential unit's utility value and consequently rent; or entailing a significant change to a residential unit or a communal part of the property unit.

If the affected residential tenant does not consent to the measure, the landlord may apply to a Regional Rent Tribunal for permission to perform the measure at the earliest two months after notification has been given to the tenants. The reason for this appeal process with respect to such improvement measures likely to lead to a higher utility value is that they could potentially have a greater impact on the tenant than just physical disturbances in that they could lead to a higher rent.

18.1.6 THE USE AND CARE OF THE PREMISES BY THE TENANT

A residential tenant may not use the premises for any purpose other than that intended by the rental agreement. However, a landlord may not cite insignificant deviations of use by a residential tenant as reasons for forfeiture or non-renewal. A non-residential tenant may not use the premises for any other purposes unless consent has been given by the landlord. Such consent can be conditional, and is to be given where the tenant has been in possession of the premises for more than two years and has a significant reason for changing the use and the landlord has no justified reason for opposing this.

The tenant is to take good care of the premises and its fixtures during the rental period. The tenant is obligated to compensate the landlord for any damages arising due to the actions or neglect of:

- The tenant;
- Any party belonging to the tenant's household;
- Any guests or other parties invited onto the premises; or
- Any party performing work for the tenant in the premises.

The tenant is liable for damages caused by fire only to the extent she has failed to observe due care or supervision.

The tenant has a duty to immediately notify the landlord as to damages, defects or infestations that have arisen and must be remedied immediately in order to avoid serious consequences. In the event the tenant and household members are away when the damage, defect or infestation arises, and the landlord has access to the premises in their absence, it is sufficient that the tenant notify the landlord immediately upon return. Information concerning other types of damages, defects or infestations has to be provided by the tenant to the landlord without unreasonable delay. If the tenant fails to do this, the tenant can be liable for any damages caused by this neglect. If the tenant has subleased the unit without the necessary consent or permission, the tenant is liable for damages caused by the failure of a sub-lessee to give such notice. Agreements can be reached as to tenant liability for non-residential units that is greater than that stated above.

Residential tenants are entitled to paint, wallpaper or take similar measures at their own cost, a consequence of the wallpaper reform. If the utility value of the premises thereby decreases, the landlord has the right to be compensated for any damages. An example would be where a tenant uses aluminum foil for wallpaper or paints all the walls and ceilings black. A Regional Rent Tribunal is to decide such issues. Where the rental agreement concerns a single-family home not rented commercially, or premises let by a co-op owner, this right is applicable only if nothing to the contrary has been agreed.

The tenant is to insure in her use of the premises that any neighbors are not subjected to disturbances that can be harmful to health or otherwise negatively affect the living environment to such a degree that they ought not to be tolerated. The tenant is to observe all that is required in her use of the premises to keep them in a sound, orderly and good condition. If a tenant knows or has reason to believe that an object is infected with vermin, the tenant is not to take the object onto the premises. The tenant is also to exert adequate supervision over those parties for whom she is responsible as stated above.

In the event of disturbances by a residential tenant, the landlord can immediately give notice to the tenant to cease such activity as well as notify the appropriate municipal social welfare committee (*socialnämnden*). The latter is not necessary, however, where the landlord immediately terminates the rental agreement due to the fact that the disturbances are particularly serious taking into consideration their nature and extent.

18.1.7 THE LANDLORD'S RIGHT TO ENTER OR REPOSSESS THE PREMISES

The landlord has the right to immediately enter the premises in order to supervise or carry out improvements that cannot be delayed without risk of harm. When the premises are free to be let to a new tenant, the current tenant is obligated to allow the premises to be shown at suitable times.

The landlord has the right to carry out improvements of a less immediate nature not causing too much inconvenience after a one-month notice. Such work cannot be performed in the last month of the tenancy relationship without the tenant's consent. If the landlord wishes to perform other work on the premises, the tenant may within one week of receiving such notice terminate the rental agreement. Such work may not be commenced without the tenant's consent prior to the termination of the agreement. These provisions are not applicable to work that the landlord has agreed to do for the tenant or has been ordered to do by a tribunal.

Where such work is to be done, the landlord is to insure that the disturbances to the tenant are kept at a minimum. Harm caused to the tenant by the work is to be compensated by the landlord, even where the harm is not due to the landlord's neglect. The tenant is obligated to tolerate such limitations in rights that are caused by measures necessary due to infestation even if not in the tenant's own premises. If the tenant fails to provide the landlord with access to the premises where the landlord has such a right, the Enforcement

Authority (*Kronofogden*)[3] may provide assistance in gaining physical access in accordance with the Act on Payment Orders and Enforcement Assistance.

If the tenant abandons the premises, the landlord has the right to repossess them. If property is left in the premises after the tenant leaves or is evicted, and the tenant does not remove the property within three months of being so requested or after six months from leaving or being evicted, the property becomes that of the landlord without any obligation to pay compensation to the former tenant.

18.1.8 ASSIGNMENT AND SUBLEASING OF THE TENANCY

A tenant may not generally assign the tenancy without the consent of the landlord. If the landlord unreasonably refuses consent, or does not give a decision within three weeks after such a request, the tenant may terminate the rental agreement under LC 12:32. Section 12:32 has been used by commercial tenants to break leases prematurely. A non-residential tenant can request that the landlord give consent to a lease assignment. If the landlord fails to respond within three weeks, or denies the request without reasonable cause, the tenant then can terminate the lease. The burden of proof is on the landlord to have reasonable cause. In addition, the landlord does not have any right to request additional time to carry out any type of investigation. This has been referred to as "vacation notice" (*semesteruppsägning*) as it sometimes is given, for example, at the beginning of July right before most people in Sweden go on vacation. Residential tenants do not have the same need to use this clause to break a lease as they have at the most a three-month termination notice.

A tenant not intending to use her residential unit may assign the tenancy to a close relative permanently living with her if a Regional Rent Tribunal gives consent to such assignment. Such consent is to be given if the landlord can reasonably be satisfied with the change. The permission may be conditional. The same is true if an estate of a decedent wishes to make such an

---

3   For information in English on the Enforcement Authority, *see* its website at kronofogden.se.

assignment. In the typical case, the landlord must have cause for refusing the assignment. A tenant may also assign a residential tenancy in exchange for another residence if a Regional Rent Tribunal consents. Such consent, which may be conditional, is to be granted if the tenant has considerable reason for the exchange and it can occur without any tangible inconvenience to the landlord or any other reasons speak against the exchange.

A tenant may not generally sublease premises without the consent of the landlord. Under LC 12:40, the tenant may sublease the premises in their entirety despite the landlord refusing consent if a Regional Rent Tribunal approves it. Consent is to be given if the tenant due to age, health, temporary work or studies in another area, specific family conditions or comparable circumstances such as long-term stays abroad, has considerable reasons for the subleasing; and the landlord does not have justified reason for refusing consent. Consent as given by a Regional Rent Tribunal is to be limited to a fixed period and can be conditional. A tenant is not allowed to have third parties living in the premises if this is determined to be detrimental to the landlord.

18.1.9 FORFEITURE OF THE TENANCY

The tenant is deemed to have forfeited the right to rent the unit under LC 12:42 where:

1   A residential tenant is more than one week late in paying rent and no decision by a Regional Rent Tribunal is involved;
2   A non-residential tenant is more than two working days late in paying rent;
3   A tenant assigns the tenancy without the necessary consent or permission or otherwise places another party in her stead and does not, after being so requested, take corrective measures or otherwise apply for permission;
4   The premises are used for purposes other than that agreed upon, or by parties other than those authorized to use the premises;
5   The tenant or sublessee through negligence causes an infestation of the premises or fails to inform the landlord of this, contributing to the spread of the infestation in the premises;

6   The premises in another manner are neglected or the tenant or sublessee neglects to ensure against disturbances to neighbors in the use of the premises or fails to supervise as required and corrective measures are not taken without delay after such a request;[4]

7   The landlord is refused access to the premises and the tenant does not provide a valid reason for the refusal;

8   The tenant neglects a contractual obligation exceeding that mandated in chapter twelve of the Land Code, and which performance must be deemed to be of material significance to the landlord; or

9   The premises wholly or partially are used for such criminal operations or similar activities that are criminal or in which criminal actions are present to a more than insignificant degree or used for temporary sexual relationships for compensation.[5]

The tenancy is not forfeited if the misconduct by the tenant as defined above is of minor significance. Where the rental agreement has been terminated due to forfeiture, the landlord has the right to damages.

With certain of these grounds, the tenant cannot be divested of the premises for the conduct where corrective action is taken prior to the landlord giving notice of termination. This is not applicable, however, with respect to serious disturbances. The tenant may not be divested of the premises where the landlord has failed to give a notice of termination within two months

---

4   A termination of the rental agreement with respect to a residential unit for disturbing neighbors in violation of Section 12:25 may only be given after notification to the appropriate municipal social welfare committee as prescribed in that section. However, if it is a question of a particularly serious disturbance, the rental agreement may be terminated even if no request for correction has been made. Such termination of a rental agreement with respect to a residential unit may be made even without notification first to the social welfare committee. However, a copy of the notice of termination is to be provided to the committee. These provisions are not applicable if the party causing the serious disturbance is a sublessee with the consent of the landlord or permission of a Regional Tenancies Tribunal.

5   Under Swedish law, it is legal to sell sexual services, but illegal for customers to purchase them. It is also illegal for a third party to profit from the sale of sexual services, including by leasing premises that are used to provide such sexual services. Thus landlords have a strong incentive under Swedish law to evict persons known to be selling sexual services as they may otherwise face criminal prosecution for accepting rents.

of receiving knowledge of an infestation, a failure to perform a contractual obligation or criminal activity. The same is true where the landlord failed to request corrective action within two months of receiving knowledge of an unauthorized assignment.

Where the forfeiture is due to a failure to pay rent on time and the landlord has terminated the tenancy, a residential tenant may not be removed from the premises if the rent is paid generally within three weeks. This has to be three weeks from the date that the residential tenant has been served notice that by paying the rent in the prescribed manner, the tenant will recover the tenancy. At the same time, a notice of termination must be sent to the appropriate municipal social welfare committee. If a defaulting non-residential tenant pays within two weeks of being served notice as to paying the rent in the prescribed manner, the tenant will recover the tenancy. A decision regarding an eviction cannot be issued until two days after the expiry of these periods to allow the tenant to comply with the terms.

A residential tenant cannot be removed from the premises if the municipal social welfare committee gives notice[6] within the three-week period that it will assume responsibility for payment. A tenant can also not be removed for a failure to pay where the tenant has been prevented from paying late rent within the three week period due to illness or similar unforeseen circumstances and the rent is paid as soon as possible, however at the latest prior to a lawsuit concerning eviction being decided by the first instance.

When an agreement has been terminated due to reasons such as damage to the unit, decision of a public authority as to unfitness, the unit not being ready, a prior tenant's failure to vacate the premises, damage, default, impediment or public decision, infestation or prior better right, the agreement ceases to be valid immediately according to LC 12:6. The same is true with respect to forfeiture by the tenant for failure to pay rent unless the rent has been paid.

18.1.10   RENEWAL OF THE TENANCY

A fairly automatic right to renew a residential tenancy is one of the social protections woven into chapter twelve, constituting a mandatory right that

---

6   The Government or authority as designated by the Government is to adopt the notification form for use under this section.

in the majority of cases cannot be contracted away. An explicit agreement between a landlord and tenant that a rental agreement does not include a right of renewal is valid generally only if approved by a Regional Rent Tribunal. Any agreement as to no right of renewal is valid against a spouse or cohabitee residing in the residential unit but not listed as tenant only if consented to by that spouse or cohabitee.

The tenant has a right to a renewal of the rental agreement where the landlord has given notice of termination of the rental agreement, or where the tenant has continued to use the premises with respect to a fixed term agreement for more than one month after its expiration. However, under the following exceptions this automatic right can be negated:

With respect to the actions by the tenant:
- The tenancy is forfeited for the reasons as set out above in Section 18.1.9 without the landlord having already given notice that the agreement is to be terminated prematurely; or
- The tenant in another case has neglected her duties to such a high degree that the rental agreement cannot reasonably be renewed.

With respect to the physical building:
- The building is to be demolished, undergo extensive alterations where it is not evident that the tenant can remain in the premises without considerable inconvenience, or that the premises no longer are to be used as a residential unit; and
- It is not unfair to the tenant that the tenancy ceases.

With respect to the landlord:
- The rental agreement concerns premises in a single or multi-family home not commercially rented and the landlord has such an interest in disposing over the premises that the tenant reasonably ought to move; or
- The rental agreement concerns a cooperative apartment let by a party who is the co-op owner and the premises are still held as such and the co-op owner has such an interest in disposing over the premises that the tenant reasonably ought to move.

With respect to tenancies based on employment:

- The tenancy is dependent upon employment with the state or a municipality combined with a mandatory residence or agricultural employment or other position, and it is of such a type that it is necessary for the employer to dispose over the premises to let them to another employee in that employee's stead, as well as that the employment has been terminated; or
- The tenancy depends on employment other than that above which has been terminated and it is not unfair to the tenant that the tenancy is also terminated, as well as where the tenancy has been for more than three years, the landlord has particular reasons for dissolving the tenancy.

Last, there is a catch-all exception of other cases where it would not be in violation of good landlord tenant practices or unfair to the tenant that the tenancy be terminated. If the interest of the landlord can be met by the tenant removing from a part of the premises, and the rental agreement can be suitably renewed with respect to the remaining part of the premises, the tenant has the right to such a renewal. In the event a residential tenant has removed from the premises due to a significant alteration, the tenant is to be offered the possibility of moving back to similar premises after the alteration.

Where the landlord has given notice of termination of the rental agreement and there is a dispute as to a renewal of the rental agreement, the notice is without effect unless the landlord at least one month after the termination of the tenancy submits the dispute to a Regional Rent Tribunal, or the tenant in any event has removed from the premises at the expiry of the tenancy. If the issue as to renewal has not yet been decided at the expiration of the rental period, the tenant has the right to remain in the premises until it is finally decided. This is not true, however, where a Regional Rent Tribunal has issued a decision in accordance with the Act on Regional Tenancies and Rent Tribunals (*lag 1973:188 om arrendenämnder och hyresnämnder*) that an eviction order be enforced even if not yet final. The previous terms and conditions in the rental agreement are applicable for the period in which the tenant remains in the premises until the issue is finally decided.

18.1.11 MODIFICATIONS OF RESIDENTIAL RENTAL AGREEMENTS

Where either a residential tenant or landlord wishes to change the terms and conditions of the rental agreement for the tenancy, that party is to notify the other in writing. Modifications can be made orally. If the parties are unable to come to an agreement as to modifications, the party requesting the modification has the right to apply to a Regional Rent Tribunal for a modification of the terms or conditions. Such an application can be made at the earliest one month after the notification has been given to the other party. If specific reason exists, the Regional Rent Tribunal can also assess other terms and conditions that have a connection with the term or condition cited in the application to the Regional Rent Tribunal. A decision as to modification of a rental term or condition is deemed a contract on the terms and conditions for a renewed lease. Non-residential tenants do not have the same degree of protection as discussed in the next section. Instead, they are entitled simply to damages for a landlord's refusal to renew the lease or for changing terms of the lease unfavorably to the tenant.

In the event a landlord wishes a written notification of a rent increase to be deemed a contract for a renewed tenancy, that notice is to include information as to the landlord's address, the amount of the rent increase in Swedish crowns if a rent increase is being requested, and the entire rental amount as well as the day when the new increased rent is to begin. In addition, the landlord must notify the tenant that she will be obligated to pay the higher rent if she does not inform the landlord that she contests the increase by a certain date, at the earliest two months after the notification is given and that a Regional Rent Tribunal can assess the fairness of the requested increase, and what the tenant needs to do for such an assessment to take place.

If the notification contains all the required information and the tenant does not contest the increase within the prescribed time, the tenant is deemed to have entered into a contract with the landlord to pay the rent increase requested. The increased rent commences after the last day on which the tenant can object to the rent increase.

Where a rent increase with respect to a residential unit is contested between the landlord and tenant, a Regional Rent Tribunal is to determine the rent at a fair level. An amount is not considered fair if it is markedly higher than rent for premises that with respect to utility value (*bruksvärde*) are similar. The utility value of a property is distinct from its market value. The utility value is determined by taking into account a number of factors, for example, the size, number of rooms, the degree of modernity, layout and condition of the premises. Other factors considered are soundproofing, access to elevators, laundry and storage facilities, building facilities and administration, as well as access to garages or parking places. More general factors can also be taken into account, such as the general condition of the building, the residential environment and access to public transportation. The utility value is to be assessed objectively and not be based on that which an individual tenant considers important, but on what is good for tenants generally. The utility value is not measured monetarily, but rather a measure of how the premises and building function for tenants. Improvements made by the landlord or tenant may only be taken into consideration with respect to the utility value under limited circumstances.

In order to determine a fair rent based on utility value, the Regional Rent Tribunal primarily looks at the utility value for apartments as agreed upon according to the Rental Negotiations Act. If no such premises can be found, the Regional Rent Tribunal can look at the utility value of similar apartments located in another area with comparable rental conditions in an general similar circumstances on the rental market as stated in 12:55 LC. The rent in the comparison object then becomes an indicator of rent in that market. The greater the number of premises used for comparison, the more certain the rent level determined is deemed. Deviating high rents are typically removed from any comparison. The utility value has functioned as a type of rent control, entailing that apartments in highly sought residential areas can have lower rents consistent with the utility value of similar apartments in less highly sought areas. The result of this system is that landlords are not free to set rents at market terms.

This system is not without controversy. The strong protection in favor of a tenant continuing a tenancy coupled with rent set at the utility value has been seen by some as a deterrent with respect to new construction of rental properties. A regulation was recently passed to stimulate new construction by allowing new rental properties to have rent set at market rates for a period of ten years. Some municipal housing associations are also beginning to deviate from the pure utility value and allowing aspects such as geographical popularity to be assessed.

If the dispute between the landlord and tenant concerns a term or condition other than a rent increase, the term or condition being requested by either the landlord or tenant is applicable to the degree it is fair taking into account the content of the rental agreement, the circumstances existing at the time the contract arose as well as later.

18.1.12 NON-RESIDENTIAL AGREEMENTS

In the event the landlord has given notice of termination of a non-residential tenancy and refuses to renew it, or where a renewal is not effected as the tenant does not accept the rental terms and conditions required by the landlord for the renewal, the tenant has the right to compensation, but not a right to an automatic renewal of the rental agreement. There is no right to compensation, however, if:

1 The tenant has neglected her obligations under the rental agreement to such a high degree that it is not reasonable to force the landlord to renew the tenancy;
2 The building is to be demolished or undergo such significant renovation that the tenant obviously cannot remain in the premises without marked inconvenience and the landlord has offered different designated premises that should be acceptable to the tenant or that the rental agreement contains a term that the tenancy is to cease due to renovation and the renovation is to commence within five years from the date of the term;
3 The landlord in other situations has reasonable cause to terminate the tenancy; or
4 The terms and conditions of the tenancy the landlord has required to renew it are fair and consistent with good practice in landlord tenant relations.

Another distinction between residential and non-residential tenants exists with respect to how rent levels are decided. Rent for non-residential premises is not seen as fair if it exceeds the rent that the premises would have on the open market, in other words, the market value rent. This market value rent is first to be decided based on a comparison with rent for other similar non-residential premises in the geographic area. Only if specific reason exists can increases in the value of the premises as brought about by the tenant be considered.

In the event the landlord wishes to terminate a non-residential rental agreement, the landlord must notify the tenant as to the terms and conditions she requires in order to renew the tenancy, or the reason for the refusal as to a renewal. The notice is also to inform the tenant that if she does not wish to vacate the premises without compensation, she has two months from the date of notice to submit the matter to the Regional Rent Tribunal for mediation. If the landlord fails to include this information, the notice is not valid.

If the landlord has done this and the tenant refuses to vacate the premises without compensation, the tenant must submit the matter to a Regional Rent Tribunal for mediation within the stated period of time. If the tenant fails to do this, she forfeits the right to compensation unless within the same period of time, the matter is submitted to the tribunal. The landlord cannot demand higher rent or change any term or condition of the tenancy prior to the conclusion of the mediation. In the event the landlord does this anyway, the tenant always has the right to compensation.

The landlord is to pay compensation in an amount comparable to one year's rent for the premises in accordance with the terminated rental agreement to any tenant having the right to compensation for the landlord's refusal to renew the tenancy or the landlord's demand for higher rent or other condition unfavorable to the tenant. In the event the non-residential tenant has suffered a loss not compensated for by this amount, the landlord is to compensate for the loss to a reasonable degree. If the loss is connected to the tenant paying for modifications of the premises, the loss is to be considered only if the landlord has consented to the modification or if the tenant entered into the rental agreement under the condition that the tenant would perform the modifications.

18.1.13 MISCELLANEOUS PROVISIONS

The last part of chapter twelve in the Land Code can be seen best as an assortment of various provisions with respect to both residential and non-residential tenancies not addressed elsewhere. However, these are not necessarily of minor importance, as criminal sanctions are included in this part.

Statute of Limitations

A landlord or tenant wishing to make a claim based on a tenancy is to file suit thereof within two years from when the tenant vacated the premises. Any claim thereafter is barred unless otherwise agreed. If one party has presented a timely claim, the other party is not barred from making a set-off claim even if the right to file a complaint is time barred.

Criminal Offenses

It is a criminal offense for a party to intentionally demand specific remuneration for the actual conveyance of a residential tenancy or for the conveyance of the right to rent such premises. Such a party can be sentenced under LC 12:65 to fines or imprisonment of at the most six months, however, minor violations are not to be sentenced by imprisonment. Such terms are invalid and the party receiving any remuneration is to repay it.

If the offense is serious, the sentence can be imprisonment up to two years. As to the assessment of the seriousness of the offense, consideration is to be taken as to whether it constituted a part of operations that are conducted professionally or to a greater extent or whether the accused has in a significant manner abused her position as owner or administrator of a building.

No party can receive, enter into an agreement or request remuneration from a party seeking residential premises for purposes other than recreation as prescribed by LC 12:65a. However, such remuneration can be charged for professional brokering of premises according to the regulations of the Government or authority designated by it. Any party intentionally violating this rule can be sentenced to fines or imprisonment of up to six months. If the offense is serious, imprisonment can be up to two years. Any unlawful remuneration is to be repaid. Specific regulations are applicable as to fees for waiting lists regarding municipal apartments.

Arbitration Agreements

An agreement between a landlord and tenant entailing that any future dispute based on the tenancy is to be decided through arbitration with no right to appeal is without effect with respect to certain issues. Disputes concerning the tenant's rights or obligations to possess and retain the premises, modifications of terms and conditions and/or as decided by a Regional Rent Tribunal, as well as the repayment of rent or payment of compensation, cannot be decided through arbitration. As to the appointment and number of arbitrators, as well as the proceedings, the Arbitration Act (*lag 1999:116 om skiljeförfarande*)[7] is applicable and the arbitration agreement is valid in all other respects. The parties are free to appoint a Regional Rent Tribunal as the arbitration panel and to determine the date for the issuance of the arbitration award.

18.2 Cooperative Rentals

A fairly recently legislated variation with respect to residential living is cooperative rentals (*kooperativ hyresrätt*), governed by the Cooperative Rental Rights Act (*lag 2002:93 om kooperativ hyresrätt*). Cooperative rentals are a hybrid between housing cooperatives and residential rentals. This legal institution was created in 2002 to facilitate the new construction of rental properties and expand tenant influence. It allows a housing unit to be based on a concept, such as housing for the elderly, golf enthusiasts or environmental sustainability. A co-op tenant rents a cooperative apartment on terms similar to a residential tenant under chapter twelve of the Land Code with certain key differences. Again, only certain of the provisions of the 2002 act are included below.

A co-op tenant rents a cooperative apartment from a cooperative rental association instead of a municipal or private landlord. A cooperative rental is defined as the conveyance of residential premises by a cooperative rental association to a co-op tenant who is a member of the cooperative as a resident. A cooperative rental association is a legal person having the objective of renting out apartments to its members. The association can either lease a building from its owner, usually a municipality, or own the building outright. A cooperative rental association can be formed in an existing rental building if two-thirds of the tenants in the building support such a decision. If the building is converted to a cooperative rental building, all existing tenants

---

7   A translation in English (and seven other languages) of this act can be found at the website of the Arbitration Institute of the Stockholm Chamber of Commerce at sccinstitute.com under the headings of library and then legislation.

in the building become co-op tenants and members in the association. However, the rental agreements of those persons not wanting to convert to a cooperative will completely fall within the provisions of chapter twelve of the Land Code.

Cooperative rental associations have legal requirements similar to those of housing cooperatives. A cooperative rental association is a legal person, is to be registered, have at least three members, bylaws and at least one auditor. The bylaws are to include information as to how rent levels are to be calculated for the cooperative apartments and the basis for setting aside funds for the maintenance of the buildings the association owns. Many of the regulations found in the Act on Commercial Cooperatives (*lag 1987:667 om ekonomiska föreningar*) are also applicable to cooperative rental associations.

Each member in the cooperative rental association is to provide a member contribution to the association that in the majority of cases is only a nominal amount. In addition, the co-op tenant may have to pay a fee for the conveyance of the apartment to the cooperative. This latter fee can vary significantly, from a nominal amount up to several thousand Swedish crowns per square meter.[8] The objective with the conveyance fee is to allow members to finance construction if such is necessary. In certain geographic areas that financial institutions consider to be a risk, this has been argued to be one of the few ways to finance new construction. If a member leaves the association, the membership and conveyance fees are to be returned to the member.[9] This arrangement creates a security for the co-op tenant, in that the conveyance fee in its entirety is to be returned, entailing an investment with a lower risk of loss. However, it should be kept in mind that no profit accrues to the co-op tenant, in contrast with a co-op owner, who bears the risk for losses but also has the opportunity for gains.

The provisions as found in chapter twelve of the Land Code are applicable to co-op tenants with certain exceptions as set out in the 2002 Act. Co-op

---

8 Information in Swedish is available at the website of the organization representing municipal housing units, SABO (sabo.se) and in English at the website of the organization representing cooperative rentals, SKB (skb.se).

9 The penal prohibition against the sale of residential apartments in Section 12:65 of the Land Code is applicable to cooperative rental apartments. Thus a co-op tenant can never realize any increase in the value of the apartment.

tenants have a fairly automatic right to a renewal of a lease, and the right to exchange residential premises is granted co-op tenants under certain conditions.

Many of the exceptions from chapter twelve as set out in the act are to allow members in the association a greater freedom as to influence with respect to their residential living terms. The parties are free to contract as to the condition of the premises upon possession and members are free to determine through the bylaws the degree of member responsibility for administration. A co-op tenant cannot be held responsible for repairs of sewer, heating, gas, electrical or water lines where the association has supplied the apartment with such and they serve several apartments. In the same vein, a provision in the association's bylaws stating that the co-op tenant is to bear the costs of repairs due to fire or water damage or infestation is only applicable to damage that has arisen due to the negligence of the co-op tenant, or the negligence of a party over whom the co-op tenant is to exert supervision to the extent the co-op tenant has failed to observe due care.

The provisions in the Land Code with respect to remedial injunctions and tenant influence are not applicable to co-op tenants. Neither are the provisions as to rent based on utility value applicable to co-op tenants. The rent is to be that as decided by the members of the association in the bylaws. This entails that rent levels can be determined outside the negotiation procedure mandated for residential rentals in the Rent Negotiation Act (*hyresförhandlingslag* 1978:304) and chapter twelve of the Land Code. An individual co-op tenant cannot request a Regional Rent Tribunal to assess the fairness of the rent.

A co-op tenant may not use the premises for purposes other than those intended. The association has a right to compensation where any measure taken by a co-op tenant in the apartment is not professionally performed or in another manner is unsatisfactory. A representative of the association has the right to enter the premises when necessary for inspection or to perform work for which the association is responsible. When the apartment is to be rented, the co-op tenant is to allow it to be shown at suitable times. The association is also to ensure that the co-op tenant is not affected by any inconvenience greater than that necessary.

A co-op tenant forfeits the tenancy if the apartment is used for purposes other than those intended, or has persons living in the apartment other than those so authorized in violation of the Land Code, and does not take corrective action after being requested to do so. The tenancy can also be forfeited for the tenant's refusing access by a representative of the association to the apartment without a valid excuse after being requested to do so. A co-op tenancy can also be forfeited if the co-op tenant fails to perform an obligation as set out in the bylaws exceeding those obligations under the act that is of particular importance to the association, or where the tenant has acquired the tenancy in a manner in violation of chapter twelve and has not applied for membership.

Another significant difference between a housing cooperative and a cooperative rental association is that with a housing cooperative, the member's share in the cooperative is tied to the right to use an apartment. This entitles the member to sell the right to use an apartment (but not ownership to the apartment itself) conditional upon membership acceptance. With membership in a cooperative rental association, there is no fixed relationship between a member's share in the association and the right to use an apartment. This means that the right to use a certain apartment cannot be sold. A waiting list as to membership can then be created, in contrast to the situation with housing cooperatives. The objective with this setup is to create a legal institution in which speculative investments become less attractive and less prone to drive market prices up or down. A rental unit can be converted to cooperative rentals at the request of the tenants under the same conditions as for cooperative apartments.

18.3 Dispute Resolution

Parallels can be drawn between labor law and landlord tenant law with the alternative dispute resolution mechanisms that have been put into place including central rent negotiations. The motivation has been to try to equalize the bargaining positions of the parties, the landlords and tenants through large central organizations. The Regional Rent Tribunals are to provide dispute resolutions mechanisms that are quick and inexpensive.

18.3.1   RENT NEGOTIATIONS WITH RESPECT TO RESIDENTIAL PREMISES

The collectivism that characterizes many aspects of the Swedish legal system is seen in full force with respect to rent negotiations for residential premises. According to the Rent Negotiation Act, negotiations as to rent levels can be conducted between a landlord and the interest organization of which it is a member, on one side, and a tenant organization on the other. A landlord as covered by the act is a landlord leasing residential premises other than those that are for recreational purposes or those having no more than two units. The act is also not applicable to cooperative rentals.

Negotiations are to be conducted in accordance with a negotiation agreement between the parties, or a decision by a Regional Rent Tribunal. Such a negotiation agreement is to encompass all the residential premises in the building, and is to be in writing and dated. Specific premises can be excluded through a signed written agreement between the landlord and tenant entered into after the tenancy has been in place for three months.

After a negotiation agreement has been entered into between the parties, the parties can include a negotiation clause (*förhandlingsklausul*) in the rental agreement by which the tenant agrees to rent levels as decided by the parties in accordance with the negotiation agreement.[10] Any dispute as to the adoption or removal of such a clause in a rental agreement is to be brought to a Regional Rent Tribunal. Where the tenant has submitted an opinion, the Tribunal is to decide in accordance with the tenant's view unless specific reasons against this exist. If the tenant fails to submit an opinion, the Tribunal is to decide consistent with the landlord's view, as stated in Section 2 of the act.

Once a negotiation agreement is in place, the landlord on her own initiative is to negotiate with the tenant organization with respect to the following issues:

---

10   Unless otherwise stated in a decision by the Regional Rent Tribunal. The Tribunal can also decide that a negotiation agreement is not to be applicable with respect to a certain building.

1   A rent increase for an apartment;
2   Provisions concerning rent for a new tenant if the requested rent exceeds the previous tenant's rent;
3   Changes in the base for calculations of rent levels as set out in chapter twelve of the Land Code; and
4   Changes in the terms and conditions of tenant use of common areas.

A negotiation agreement can also entail that the parties are to negotiate on issues regarding:

1   The terms and conditions of the lease;
2   The condition of the apartment and building;
3   The common areas and facilities in the building; and
4   Other residential conditions affecting all the tenants.

The parties can agree that such issues are exempted specifically in the negotiation agreement. The failure by the landlord to request negotiations for such issues can result in liability for damages.

The parties can also agree that the tenant organization can request negotiations as to terms and conditions affecting individual tenants where that tenant has given the organization a written power of attorney to represent her. A negotiation agreement cannot limit tenant rights with respect to requesting an assessment of rent by a Regional Rent Tribunal. Once a negotiation agreement is in place, it is applicable to any new landlord taking over the premises. If the previous landlord has failed to inform the new landlord as to the existence of a negotiation agreement, the former landlord is to compensate the new one for any damages caused by the neglect to inform.

In the event that either the landlord or tenant organization refuses to enter into a negotiation agreement, the party requesting the agreement can have the matter tried by the Regional Rent Tribunal. The tribunal is to determine whether the right to have such an agreement exists, taking into consideration the qualifications of the organization, the number of apartments the agreement is to encompass, and the circumstances in general. If the Regional Rent Tribunal finds such a right to exist, it is to determine the terms and conditions of the negotiation agreement.

A negotiation agreement can be terminated by notice in writing served on the other party three months in advance where the agreement is until further notice, or three months in advance of any termination date contained in the agreement. Disputes arising under this act in general are to be tried by a Regional Rent Tribunal and can be appealed to the Svea Court of Appeal as the court of last resort. The Act on Litigation of Certain Rental Tenancy Cases before the Svea Court of Appeal (*lag 1994:831 om rättegången i vissa hyresmål i Svea hovrätt*) is then applicable.

18.3.2 REGIONAL RENT TRIBUNALS

About 30 000 matters are brought to the eight Regional Rent Tribunals (*hyresnämnden*) annually.[11] The Regional Rent Tribunals have the task of mediating landlord tenant disputes or in some cases, acting as an arbitration panel. A tribunal is to consist of three members, a chair who is legally trained, and two interest members, one an expert in building administration (the landlord's side) and the other an expert in tenancy relationships (the tenant's side).

The Regional Rent Tribunal is to decide certain tenancy issues as well as certain issues arising for co-op owners and co-op tenants, including:

- Renewals of rental agreements after a tenant has received a notice of termination with a notice period according to the rental agreement;
- Determinations of rent and other tenancy conditions;
- Transfers of a tenancy to a cohabitee;
- Exchanges of apartments;
- Subletting of tenancies and cooperative apartments;
- Approvals of waivers of a right to a renewal of the tenancy;
- Landlord liability with respect to repairs of residential premises;
- Tenant liability with respect to paying damages in the case of improperly performed repairs by a tenant;
- Memberships in housing cooperatives;

---

11 For more information in Swedish, see the website of the Regional Rent Tribunals at hyresnämnden.se.

- Conversions of a rental unit to a housing cooperative or cooperative rental apartments; and
- Permission for, or prohibitions against, improvement work involving a rent increase.

Certain decisions by the Regional Rent Tribunal can be appealed within three weeks to the Svea Court of Appeal.

BIBLIOGRAPHY

Books

Catherine Barnard, EC Employment Law (3rd ed. Oxford 2006)

Michael Bogdan, ed., Swedish Legal System (Norstedts Juridik 2010)

Iain Cameron, An Introduction to the European Convention on Human Rights (5th ed. Iustus 2006)

Iain Cameron, An Introduction to the European Convention on Human Rights (6th ed. Iustus 2011)

Laura Carlson, An Introduction to Swedish Real Property Law (Jure 2008)

Laura Carlson, Searching for Equality, Sex Discrimination, Parental Leave and the Swedish Model with comparisons to EU, UK and US law (Iustus 2007)

Roger Congleton, Improving Democracy through Constitutional Reform – Some Swedish Lessons (Springer 2003)

Ronnie Eklund, Tore Sigeman and Laura Carlson, Swedish Labor and Employment Law: Cases and Materials (Iustus Förlag 2008)

Reinhold Fahlbeck and Bernard Johann Mulder, Labour And Employment Law In Sweden (Lund 2009)

Jonny Flodin, Security in Real Property – An Introduction to the Swedish System (Jure 2007)

Sören Häggroth et al., Swedish Local Government – Traditions and Reforms (The Swedish Institute 1993)

Göran Lind, Common Law Marriage: A Legal Institution for Cohabitation (Oxford 2008)

Gabriella Sjögren Lindquist and Eskil Wadensjö, NATIONAL SOCIAL INSURANCE: NOT THE WHOLE PICTURE, SUPPLEMENTARY COMPENSATION IN CASE OF INCOME LOSS (ESS 2006:5)

Gabriella Sjögren Lindquist and Eskil Wadensjö, THE SWEDISH WELFARE STATE: THE ROLE OF SUPPLEMENTARY COMPENSATIONS (SOFI 2006)

Eva Liedholm Johnson, MINERAL RIGHTS – LEGAL SYSTEMS GOVERNING EXPLORATION AND EXPLOITATION REPORT 4:112 (Section of Real Estate Planning and Land Law, Royal Institute of Technology. Stockholm 2010)

Max Lyles, A CALL FOR SCIENTIFIC PURITY: AXEL HÄGERSTRÖM'S CRITIQUE OF LEGAL SCIENCE (Stockholm 2006)

Hans Mattson & Tommy Österberg, ed., Roger Tanner, transl., SWEDISH LAND AND CADASTRAL LEGISLATION (3rd ed. June 2006)

Patricia Mindus, A REAL MIND: THE LIFE AND WORK OF AXEL HÄGERSTRÖM (Springer 2009)

Olle Mårsäter, FOLKRÄTTSLIGT SKYDD AV RÄTTEN TILL DOMSTOLSPRÖVNING (Uppsala 2005)

Síofra O'Leary, EMPLOYMENT LAW AT THE EUROPEAN COURT OF JUSTICE (Hart Publishing 2002)

Vicki Paskalia, FREE MOVEMENT, SOCIAL SECURITY AND GENDER IN THE EU (Hart Publishing 2007)

Jenny Paulsson, 3-D PROPERTY RIGHTS – AN ANALYSIS OF KEY FACTORS BASED ON INTERNATIONAL EXPERIENCE, Report 4:99 (Section of Real Estate Planning and Land Law, Royal Institute of Technology, Stockholm 2007)

Annina Persson, Sweden – Commercial and Economic Law in the series, Roger Blanpain, ed., INTERNATIONAL ENCYCLOPAEDIA OF LAWS (Kluwer International 2003)

Marcus Radetzki, PRAKTISK SKADESTÅNDSBEDÖMNING (Studentlitteratur 2010)

Gabriella Sebardt, REDUNDANCY AND THE SWEDISH MODEL (Iustus 2005)

Maria Steinberg, SKYDDSOMBUD I ALLAS INTRESSE (Stockholm 2004)

Hugo Tiberg, et al., SWEDISH LAW – A SURVEY (Juristförlaget 1994)

Articles

Ulf Bernitz, *The European Constitutional Project and the Swedish Constitution* in Scandinavian Studies In Law – Constitutional Law, Vol. 52 (Stockholm 2007)

Margareta Brattström, *Spouses' Pension Rights and Financial Settlement in Cases of Divorce* in Scandinavian Studies In Law – What Is Scandinavian Law? Vol. 50 (Stockholm 2007)

Åsa Gunnarsson, *Myten om vad den könsneutrala skatterätten kan göra för jämställdheten,* 2000 Skattenytt

Joakim Nergelius, *Constitutional Law* in Michael Bogdan, Swedish Legal System (Norstedts Juridik 2010)

Elizabeth Palm, *Human Rights in Sweden* in Hugo Tiberg, et al., Swedish Law – A Survey (Juristförlaget 1994)

Alf Ross, *Tû-Tû,* 70 Harv.L.Rev. 812 (1957)

Jo Shaw, *Gender Mainstreaming and the EU Constitution,* EUSA Review, Vol. 15, No. 3 (2002)

Göran Skogh, *Law and Economics in Sweden* in Encyclopedia of Law and Economics (Edward Elgar Publishing 2000)

Hans-Heinrich Vogel, *Sources of Swedish Law* in Michael Bogdan, ed., Swedish Legal System (Norstedts Juridik 2010)

Konrad Zweigert and Hein Kötz, An Introduction to Comparative Law (3rd ed. 1998)

Ulf Öberg, *Tre lösa trådar: mer om förarbeten, statens processföring vid EG-domstolen och det gemenskapsrättsliga uppenbarhetsrekvisit,* SvJT 4/2003

INDEX

Directives

Regulations